THE HENRY WOOD PROMS

THE
HENRY WOOD
PROMS

David Cox

BRITISH BROADCASTING CORPORATION

Published by the
British Broadcasting Corporation
35 Marylebone High Street
London W1M 4AA

ISBN 0 563 17697 0
First published 1980
© British Broadcasting Corporation 1980

Printed in England
by Jolly & Barber Ltd, Rugby

Contents

	Introduction	7
1	The Background	9
2	The Beginning	22
3	The Music 1895–1899	33
4	Progress and Difficulties	42
5	The Music 1900–1904	47
6	From Sea-Songs to Schoenberg	51
7	The Music 1905–1913	58
8	War and Survival	64
9	The Music 1914–1918	69
10	The Proms flourish	72
11	The Music 1919–1926	75
12	The BBC becomes involved	82
13	The Music 1927–1937	100
14	Into war again – with and without the BBC	109
15	Promenade Jubilee – and the End of an Era	127
16	The Music 1938–1944	134
17	A New Era begins	139
18	The Music 1945–1947	151
19	A Plain of Achievement	155
20	The Music 1948–1959	167
21	Wider still and wider	182
22	The Music 1960–1973	204
23	Interlude: The Prommers	227
24	The International Festival continues, 1974–1979	233
	Appendices	
A	'Novelties' at the Proms 1895–1979	256
B	Orchestras and Conductors 1895–1979	309
C	Some typical programmes and repertoires	316
D	Ticket prices 1895–1979	378
	Bibliography	380
	Index	381
	Acknowledgements	390

Introduction

The story of the Proms; the music of the Proms. They can't really be separated. The shape which this book has taken, however, seemed to come about quite naturally. I divided up the eighty-four years into convenient stretches: with each stretch, I first told the story in general terms, and then went back and looked more closely at the music performed. But this is not very hard-and-fast, because the general chapters contain a good deal about the music, and the music chapters contain a good deal of story; and in the last chapter they combine. The double-track method will, I hope, achieve a reasonable overall impression by a kind of stereo effect – except that you can't read two chapters simultaneously. The Appendices will help to fill out the picture; but it has been impossible, in a single volume, to deal adequately with the vast number of solo artists who have appeared at the Proms.

My thanks are due to the staff of the BBC Written Archives Centre, Caversham, for much help, and to the BBC Concerts Management department – Christopher Samuelson in particular – for explaining certain things and making available collections of press-cuttings and a complete set of Prom programmes from 1895 to the present day; also to Felix Aprahamian and my ex-BBC colleagues Eric Warr and Lionel Salter, all of whom read the book in typescript and made many valuable suggestions.

D.C.

Bell Cottage
Magpie Bottom
Shoreham
Kent

January 1980

As Peter the Great is said to have opened a window to Europe, so it can be said that Sir Henry Wood opened a window to music for the public in England.

The Russian-born conductor, Anatole Fistoulari

1
The Background

Saturday, 10 August 1895, at 8 p.m.: Queen's Hall, near Oxford Circus, in upper Regent Street, adjacent to the Nash church of All Souls, Langham Place. The occasion was the opening of a new London season of Promenade concerts organised by Robert Newman, the enterprising manager of Queen's Hall. For this venture the Queen's Hall Orchestra had been formed, and Robert Newman had appointed as its permanent conductor the 26-year-old Henry Wood, whose experience had so far been in the theatre rather than the concert hall.

The singer Agnes Nicholls (who was later to marry the conductor Sir Hamilton Harty) was among the large audience for that first concert. Looking back on it in 1951 she wrote:

> When the great night arrived, I started off from our home in Camden Road – my mother and I and our two friends. Those were the days of the two-horse buses, and to Oxford Circus we went. We went early, having heard that a row of seats ran round the back of the Promenade, and I was anxious to get one for my mother . . . Just before 8 o'clock I saw Henry Wood take up his position behind the curtain at the end of the platform – watch in hand. Punctually, on the stroke of eight, he walked quickly to the rostrum, buttonhole and all, and began the National Anthem . . . A few moments for the audience to settle down, then the *Rienzi* Overture, and the first concert of the new Promenades had begun.

It was the beginning of a remarkable enterprise, which has continued year after year up to the present and is still as flourishing as it has ever been. That first concert was also the re-establishment of a tradition reaching back through various nineteenth-century prototypes to its origin in the pleasure garden and the dance hall.

'Promenade' – the name originated in France: *se promener*, to go for a walk; *promenade*, a walk, or a place for walking. The name to describe

Thomas Rowlandson's impression of a concert at Vauxhall Pleasure Gardens in 1785 (see p. 12).

A Henry Wood Promenade Concert at Queen's Hall in 1895. A drawing by Thomas Downey.

concerts seems to have been used for the first time in England in 1838, when London's Lyceum Theatre announced 'Promenade Concerts *à la Musard*'. Philippe Musard, a French musician (of whom more later), had introduced Parisian audiences to concerts along the lines of those heard in London's pleasure gardens (Vauxhall, Marylebone, Ranelagh). Then, as now, the character of the concerts was quite definite: the audience – at least a large part of it – could move about (that is, if people were not jammed together like sardines), see and hear the performance from different and contrasting angles, close or distant, in a more relaxed atmosphere than that of formal concerts, and at a popular price. The music was predominantly or exclusively light-hearted, easy to enjoy. As audiences became established, they could be led to enjoy some more 'serious' items – items different from those borrowed from ballroom and the opera stage, the everlasting waltzes, quadrilles, cornet solos, and so on, which were the normal Promenade ingredients. Many people find they can enjoy music (at all levels of appreciation) standing up as well as sitting down. An audience on its feet can certainly achieve full concentration, frequently remaining still and silent for very long periods.

Today, during every Prom season, a fountain is a traditional feature of the concerts, situated in the arena at the Royal Albert Hall, just as it always was at Queen's Hall. Ornamental, and suggesting cooling streams in summer, the fountain is also symbolically a link with the *al fresco* forerunners of the Proms: music among the beauties of nature heard by promenading audiences at London's pleasure gardens – in particular Vauxhall and Ranelagh.

Go back to the mid-eighteenth century – to the Spring Gardens of Vauxhall on the South Bank of the Thames. They had been a favourite resort of the fashionable world of London on summer evenings from the time of Samuel Pepys and John Evelyn. The lawns, the vistas delighted the eye:

> Methought, when first I entered,
>   Such splendours round me shone,
> Into a world I ventured,
>   Where rose another sun.

So runs an anonymous poem; and the literature of the period has many references to the beauty and elegance of the place. Under the enterprising Jonathan Tyers, who obtained a lease of the Gardens from 1728, entertainments of every kind were provided – including fireworks, masquerades, acrobatics, cascades; there were dark walks favoured by lovers; there were other more dubious amorous activities; and arbours where happy feasters made merry; there was dancing, and much drinking. And amongst all this entertainment, an important activity was music – some of it very light-hearted, but also concerts which included some of the best compositions of the time. Dr Thomas Arne was appointed composer of the Gardens in 1745. His theatre music was renowned, including 'Rule, Britannia' (from the masque *Alfred*). Many of his songs achieved enormous popularity at Vauxhall.

Music performances took place in a pagoda-like building, situated in a central part of the Gardens; a covered section of it housed the musicians, including an orchestra. In a drawing by Thomas Rowlandson, we see the singer Mrs Weischell giving a performance accompanied by an orchestra of strings, wind, and timpani, from the musicians' gallery, with a promenading audience below which includes the Prince of Wales and various members of the aristocracy – while in one of the supper-boxes below Dr Johnson, James Boswell, Mrs Thrale and Oliver Goldsmith are enjoying a meal. Similarly, the music-making at the shorter-lived Ranelagh Gardens (1742–1803) attracted much attention. There the performers and audiences were all under cover, sheltered from the whims of our English climate. The infant prodigy Mozart appeared there, sensationally; Dr Burney is reported to have played on the organ that was installed in 1746; and Haydn was a visitor.

These pleasure gardens were performing in their time a function for which the Henry Wood Proms have always been renowned – to make available, not only to the affluent, a wide range of the best music, presented by leading musicians. In the eighteenth century the composers would have included Handel, J. C. Bach, Shield, Mozart, Boyce, Hook, Arne, Stanley. Perhaps the most spectacular event that took place at the Vauxhall Gardens was the rehearsal for Handel's *Music for the Royal Fireworks* (written to celebrate the peace of Aix-la-Chapelle). This was on the morning of 21 April 1749 and attracted the largest crowd ever assembled there. It also caused a London traffic-jam of positively prophetic proportions.

Vauxhall had become a national institution – one which continued until 1859. In the early nineteenth century it was still at the height of its popularity, enjoying the patronage of royalty and the aristocracy – a place where 'people of quality' and ordinary folk could mix easily and pleasantly. The French Revolution and the wars with Napoleon were over. England was now in the midst of the Industrial Revolution and enjoying a century of prosperity. The official composer to the Gardens was Sir Henry Bishop (known to us mainly for his 'Home, sweet home', and for the sprightly 'Lo, here the gentle lark', with virtuoso flute obbligato). The concerts were still going strong and keeping abreast of the times in their choice of music. An overture by Weber or Rossini might have been included, a new and brilliant concerto, or a symphony by Beethoven (one or more movements). Many of the charming songs by Bishop, written for performance at the Gardens, would have been heard, and special 'grand finale' items which were a tradition at Vauxhall. For example, the prolific Bishop wrote a work called *The Halt of the Caravan* to round off the concert season of 1830. Like a foretaste of Albert W. Kétèlbey, it portrayed a band of oriental merchants pausing on their journey, and the music was a Turkish March (a form used light-heartedly by Mozart and Beethoven, among many others), scored for chorus and a large orchestra which included much percussion.

Concerts along these lines were developed in Paris in the early 1830s by the ambitious French violinist, Philippe Musard (1793–1859). Unprepossessing in appearance, he was nevertheless a competent and successful conductor whose informal promenade concerts, tricked out with lighting effects, fireworks and champagne, made an important contribution to the desperate gaiety of the French capital, alongside the excitements of the Strausses and Offenbach. In 1838 the series of 'Promenade Concerts *à la Musard*' began in London at the Lyceum Theatre (then the English Opera House) and two years later Musard himself was in England conducting them. The poet Thomas Hood described him as solemn and grim, marshal-like. With an orchestra of not less than sixty, Musard was presenting successful programmes which were a mixture of overtures, waltzes, popular instrumental solos and quadrilles. The quadrilles would be of his own composing, in several sections of different tempi, and based (as was the custom of the time) on popular themes of the moment.

Musard's success led to a positive spate of musical promenading in London and in the provinces. From 1839 we find the Crown and Anchor Tavern in the Strand giving a series of 'Grand Instrumental Promenade Concerts *à la Valentino*'. (Henri Valentino, a conductor at the Opéra, was a Paris rival of Musard, but with more serious musical aims.) These concerts were performed by the band of the Theatre Royal, Drury Lane, and the music consisted of 'the most admired selections from the Classic and Modern Schools'. Admission was one shilling, as it had been for the Musard concerts. The hall of the Tavern was said to be large enough to accommodate an audience of 2500.

In 1840 a new series began at the Drury Lane Theatre, managed and directed by Edward Eliason, the orchestra's leader and a well-known soloist. These were the famous *Concerts d'été*, with an orchestra of nearly a hundred players and a chorus. Now a figure of importance in the history of promenade concerts makes his first appearance – Louis Antoine Jullien

Jullien's Concert Orchestra with four military bands at Covent Garden Theatre.

A Jullien Promenade Concert at Drury Lane Theatre.

(1812–60), a versatile French conductor and composer of dance music – first as assistant to Eliason, then later conducting a complementary series of *Concerts d'hiver*. His combination of genuine musicality and blatant showmanship proved irresistible to audiences: the glamour, the theatrical effects, the ostentatious donning of white kid gloves brought in on a silver salver, the use of a jewelled baton for music by Beethoven. In its worst sense, the era of the 'personality' conductor had arrived. Grove's Dictionary describes his appearance on the platform: 'coat thrown widely open, white waistcoat, elaborately embroidered shirt-front, wrist bands of extravagant length turned back over his cuffs, a wealth of black hair, and a black moustache' – and going through a display of circus antics before finally sinking exhausted into a gorgeous velvet chair.

By 1842 Jullien was reigning supreme, with ever-more-grandiose schemes to increase his public impact. His orchestra was sometimes merged with bands of the Royal Artillery, or Coldstream Guards, or drummers from the French Garde Nationale. A picture from the *Illustrated London News* of 6 January 1855 shows a Jullien concert at Covent Garden: the Allied Armies Quadrille, celebrating the victory of Alma, with processions of boys carrying Tricolors and Union Jacks. Other pictures show him facing the audience, not the orchestra, while conducting – a prevalent practice of the time, known as 'the French style of conducting'. It was adopted also by Jules Rivière, who came to London as a protégé of Jullien in 1857. Rivière started Proms at Covent Garden in 1871, and these proved immensely popular; but later he left London and became active as a conductor in the North of England. In December 1899 the *Musical Times* recorded his 'farewell to London' concert, pointing out that his reputation 'was chiefly built up by his great ability as a conductor of light music – and this was well deserved, as was shown by the vivacious and finished renderings given at his farewell concert . . .' The programme included the Graceful Dance from Sullivan's *Henry VIII* music, Litolff's *Robespierre* Overture, a Spanish Suite by Lacombe, and the *Rose Mousse* waltz by A. Bosc. Earlier, Henry Wood's impressions of Rivière had been less positive; in his autobiography he wrote:

> . . . I sustained the shock of my life. As I took my seat I saw an elderly gentleman seated in a gilded armchair *facing* the audience. He was elegantly dressed in a velvet jacket on the lapel of which reposed a huge spray of orchids more fitted for a woman's corsage. He held a bejewelled ivory baton in his hand from which dangled a massive blue tassel. This he wound round his wrist. He bowed ceremoniously to the audience and tapped loudly on his golden music-stand. Still seated, he began the overture to *Mignon*. After two

bars a hoarse voice from the side of the orchestra said, '*Six* beats in a bar, please!'

Another French conductor associated with Covent Garden was 'Hervé' (1825–92), well known in his time as a composer of light operas. His real name was Florimond Ronger. In 1870 we find him writing a work for the promenade concerts – an 'Heroic' Symphony entitled *The Ashantee War* (Sir Garnet Wolseley was sent on a campaign to the Gold Coast in that year). The degree of descriptiveness is indicated by the titles of the different sections: 'State of things at Cape Coast Castle – Efforts of the Governor to maintain peace and good relations with the Africans – Impossibility of obtaining from the Ashantees the respect and fulfilment of treaties – The Fantees, themselves victims of their treachery and cruelty, appeal to England for help and protection . . .'

Towards the end of the Jullien régime the composer Michael Balfe (of *The Bohemian Girl* fame) gave promenade concerts in London, at Her Majesty's Theatre; so did Jullien's son, Louis; but they failed to make much impression. After Jullien's tragic decline and death (in a lunatic asylum) in 1860, the English conductor Alfred Mellon (1820–67) succeeded him at Covent Garden, and though he remained there for several seasons his success was only moderate. In England, the real conductors were considered to be something that came from abroad – an attitude which can still be found today. It was something which in his time Henry Wood had to contend with and overcome.

We may believe that Jullien, despite all his pretentious nonsense, had a genuine desire to widen the scope of his audiences' musical appreciation – to present serious items as well as mere superficial ear-tickling. Perhaps the following programme may be said to be representative of his wish to infiltrate some better music, albeit small doses, into the Covent Garden concerts.

17 November 1845

Part 1

OVERTURE – *La Barcarolle*	*Auber*
QUADRILLE from *Ernani*	*Verdi*
CORNET SOLO – *Cujus animam*	*Rossini*
POLKA – *The Imperial*	*Jullien*
SYMPHONY IN A, the *Allegretto*	*Beethoven*
OBOE SOLO – *Jenny Jones*	*Barret*
THE ORIGINAL *Napolitaine*	*Jullien*

Part 2

SELECTION – from *Beatrice di Tenda*	–	–	–	–	–	*Bellini*
VALSE – *à deux temps* –	–	–	–	–	–	*Jullien*
FLUTE SOLO	–	–	–	–	–	
THE ORIGINAL *Polonaise* (first time)	–	–	–	–	–	*Jullien*
THE POST-HORN GALOP	–	–	–	–	–	*Koenig*

For more notable results, however, we have to look to the Promenade seasons from 1874 to 1877 at Covent Garden, conducted by Luigi Arditi (1822–1903), who is remembered now as composer of that charming waltz-song 'Il Bacio'. The *Musical Times* of September 1876, discussing the series, expresses satisfaction that the direction of the concerts is 'entrusted to so eminent an artist as Signor Arditi, and that the programmes rarely include such sensational pieces of clap-trap as those which had their origin in the days of M. Jullien, and have been continued down to very recent times'. The report goes on to complain about the refreshments – an important aspect of the concerts from the point of view of the (then) lessees of Covent Garden – the firm of Messrs Gatti, the restaurateurs. Although refreshments were served and partaken of 'behind the orchestra', the effect was still too audible, visible and distracting to the listening audience.

Wood is rather disparaging about Arditi. He tells how his knowledge of English was very limited, and 'almost every day at band rehearsal he would tap and stop, look towards a particular section of the orchestra and cry in a piping falsetto: "Play nice, play nice" . . .' And whenever the music was complicated he would noisily tap out every first beat of the bar on the top of a piano . . . But there can be no doubt that Arditi achieved a great deal in his Covent Garden concerts. A London report in an Italian musical periodical (*Gazzetta musicale di Milano*, 2 January 1876) assesses these as follows:

> What is remarkable about the concerts is that, in spite of their extremely popular character, the evenings with the greatest attendance are those on which serious music is played, be it old or new. Remarkable, too, is the silence, the respect with which a large audience listens to classical works – an audience which has come primarily to stroll about and have a good time rather than to benefit from good music. All this says much for the musical future of England, and moreover justifies the faith of those large institutions established both for education and for producing national artists and composers.

(The reference here is to the Royal Academy of Music, the National Training School of Music – which became the Royal College of Music, Trinity College of Music, and perhaps some institutions outside London.)

In the same report we read that under the inspiring artistic direction of Arditi the concerts gained enormously in popularity. Music of all kinds was included, from the purely classical to the most bizarre. Selections from operas had become much in vogue – pot-pourris of *Lohengrin*, *Aida*, *Les Huguenots*, *Il Trovatore*. (This type of ingredient was featured also for a good many years by Henry Wood.) And all the very best artists, vocal and instrumental, were included. In October of that year, the same periodical reported that at Covent Garden Arditi was giving promenade concerts devoted to one master per programme – a Rossini evening, a Beethoven evening; likewise Verdi, Gounod, Handel . . . 'The Wagner evening drew the largest crowd, the novelty being the funeral march from *Siegfried*.' The character of these 'Proms' of 1876 is not unlike that of some of the Vauxhall concerts of Arne's day and the Henry Wood concerts which were to come more than twenty years later.

Before the opening of Queen's Hall in 1893 the musical tastes of London's cultivated minority were looked after through concerts given by the Philharmonic Society and the Royal Choral Society, the Richter Concerts, all at a high price. There was also a London Symphony series, directed by George Henschel, which started in 1886 but petered out after a few years. From July to October the fashionable world absented itself from London, and during this time (the period of the year when the Henry Wood Proms were to flourish) there was little good music to be heard, even for ready money. There was a public hungry for something more adventurous than the stolid oratorios which were a staple diet in the Victorian era. The potential Prom audience was ready for life and colour from many different countries – ready to discover Tchaikovsky, Rimsky-Korsakov, Wagner, Liszt, Berlioz, Beethoven – and later, Handel and Bach.

For nearly half a century before the Wood Proms started in 1895, there had, however, been many successful enterprises aimed at giving people in London and other parts of the country opportunities of hearing good music at popular prices. 'Concerts for the People' became something of a slogan. For example, in 1852 the Mayor of Bath was 'offering to the working classes of the city a series of cheap concerts in the noble banqueting room of the Guildhall'. And the following year the 'mayor, gentry and clergy' of Canterbury were giving people 'an opportunity of hearing good music at a cheap rate'. And not only orchestral music: the 'Popular Concerts' on Saturday and Monday at London's St James's Hall provided, amongst much else, a wide range of chamber music for forty years (1858–98). The People's Concert Society was active and highly successful, and the 'South Place' concerts of chamber music 'at popular prices', organised with missionary zeal, have been an important feature of London musical life since 1887. The Philharmonic Society, always very much the professional musicians' society, which normally provided excellent but expensively-priced orchestral concerts, became more accommodating – as the *Musical Times* of April 1869 reported:

> [it] yielded to the popular demand for music at a reasonable price, and moved from its aristocratic headquarters in Hanover Square to the People's Music Hall [St James's Hall] in Regent Street, a step which we are glad to find has been attended with complete success, the subscription for the present season being far in advance of that of last year.

If Henry Wood had a comparable predecessor as a populariser of orchestral music, however, it was undoubtedly August Manns (1825–1907), the German-born bandmaster and conductor who made England his home from the age of twenty-nine. His name is associated principally with the famous Saturday Concerts at London's Crystal Palace – that enormous Victorian conservatory-like structure which housed the great London Exhibition of 1851. He began conducting these concerts in 1855, and continued until 1901. The developments in concert-giving at the Crystal Palace were largely due to the enterprise of George Grove (of subsequent Dictionary fame): Grove had been appointed Secretary to the Crystal Palace Company. To begin with, the music was provided by a good military band, with which August Manns was first connected. Before long, however, through Manns' efforts and the co-operation of Grove and the directors, the band became a full symphony orchestra, the string section consisting of sixteen first and fourteen second violins, eleven violas, ten cellos and ten double basses. The Crystal Palace Orchestra and the Hallé Orchestra of Manchester were to be the only 'permanent' symphony orchestras in England until the Queen's Hall Orchestra (with Henry Wood) was founded in 1895.

With the Saturday Concerts, and the daily and special performances, Manns in his time directed around 20,000 programmes at the Crystal Palace, besides many other activities, including a promenade season at Drury Lane in 1859, and various Handel festivals. Like Wood, he coped with a constantly arduous schedule of music-making by abundant energy and immense practicality. *The Times* in 1857 was able to write that this German conductor 'makes the orchestra express all the modifications of feeling that an imaginative soloist would give voice to on a single instrument'.

But the most remarkable thing about these Crystal Palace concerts was the discovery, the vision, the enterprise displayed by Manns and Grove in the range and choice of the music performed. The form the programmes took was usually an overture, a symphony, a concerto or lighter orchestral piece, some songs, and another overture. Besides well-known classics, music by Schumann and Brahms was included, for example, at a time when these composers were not at all familiar concert names; Schubert symphonies made their appearance; Mendelssohn's 'Reformation' Symphony was first heard there and his *Wedding of Camacho* overture; Smetana, Liszt, Wagner, manuscript works of Schubert and Mendelssohn . . . And, very important, the works of British composers were performed extensively – Sullivan, Benedict, Parry, Stanford, Cowen, Mackenzie, and many no longer remembered. The influence on the course of British music was considerable.

One important aspect of orchestral concerts, now taken for granted, but which in fact only developed during the second half of the nineteenth century, is the role of the conductor, as a personality and interpreter, imposing his will and his ideas on the body of orchestral players – as a pianist controls the mechanism of his instrument. No longer, as in the eighteenth century, was it sufficient for music to be discreetly directed from the keyboard. No longer could the 'leader' of the orchestra (the principal first violin) take charge and co-ordinate, as for a period was the custom. At first, few finer points were indicated by the conductor: the artistry depended on the individual players; the conductor indicated tempo and the general lines of the performance. The custom of wearing white gloves and grasping a heavy baton did not make for subtlety of interpretation – even if, as we read of a German conductor, he occasionally changed to black gloves (for example, to conduct the funeral march of the *Eroica*). Some conductors felt it was discourteous to turn one's back to the audience, and consequently a large part of the orchestra could not see his indications. When Spohr, in 1820, was invited to take part in a Philharmonic concert in London at which one of his symphonies was to be played, he was expected to direct from the piano, but in fact took a baton from his pocket, stood in front of the orchestra, and conducted as he had been accustomed to do in Germany. But only very gradually and during the second half of the nineteenth century was the custom established of using a light baton and indicating interpretation with delicacy and finer points. Doubtless the change was necessary when music became a complex *personal* expression, as in Beethoven, Berlioz, or Wagner, and a detailed and meaningful co-ordination was looked for by the players. Berlioz was famous as one of the greatest *chefs d'orchestre* of his time (the equivalent of 'conductor' for us), not only for his own music, but also for his clear and impassioned directing of Beethoven symphonies.

The orchestra came to expect a stimulus, a real inspiration, from the man with the stick. Today, the audience and the orchestra demand a great deal from the conductor as a matter of course. He is expected to have nothing less than a complete understanding of every bar of the music and a clear sense of how a composer's ideas are to be realised in performance; and he is expected to have a personality large enough and vital enough to convey his understanding of the music in a decisive, authoritative way. Orchestra and audience must both feel that this is happening. The conductor is paid a lot of money to be leader, inspirer, composer's interpreter, in a clear and purposeful way. To carry this out really satisfactorily needs a rare combination of inwardness and exteriorisation, plus a stick technique, a rehearsal technique of mutual understanding, personality, authority – and with it all, a strongly practical streak. Also, he is *presenting* the music to the public, and a certain amount of ceremony and panache may not be out of keeping. But here one is on dangerous ground. If the presentation degenerates into mere showmanship and applause-hogging, the conductor will lose the goodwill and respect of the orchestra and he will become ridiculous to the more intelligent part of his audience.

Against this kind of background, we can judge the achievement of Henry Wood. Besides a relaxed, informal atmosphere, characteristic of promenade concerts in general, there was always with the Henry Wood Proms a mutual understanding of a special sort between conductor, orchestra and audience. As the orchestra was from the start a permanent one, the principal players became known to the audience and received their due appreciation; there was a stable relationship between conductor and orchestra. From the start, the audience responded to Wood with respect, trust, enthusiasm, and a sense of adventure. For fifty years it was as though they were exploring together a wide range of established music and, by degrees, all the new and unfamiliar musical paths as well.

2
The Beginning

When Henry Wood's Proms began in 1895, England was between Queen Victoria's two jubilees. The first jubilee, in 1887, had been a time of general rejoicing by all classes – thankfulness for a long reign in which there had been increased prosperity and noticeably improved social conditions (though with many persistent dark sides). The Navy gave security. There had been eighty years without any great war or serious national threat, for an island with 'an Empire on which the sun never set'. There was Jingoism and surface puritanism, and an overall feeling of stability.

London was a smaller place – with the suburbs it only extended to about a six-mile radius. Important people had residences in Portland Place and Park Lane. All transport, including buses and trams, was horsedrawn. It was the period of the frock coat and high stiff collar for men; and for women narrow waists, and skirts reaching down to the ground. Writers, poets, musicians, actors adopted their own freer styles of dress.

And in this London, at the northern end of Regent Street, opposite the Langham Hotel, an important character in the story of the Proms had been established in 1893 – the Queen's Hall. It at once became the focus of many different aspects of British musical life, including choral and festival activities, Wagner Concerts, Philharmonic Society concerts – and, of course, the 'Proms'. For nearly fifty years it continued to be London's most important concert hall, until its destruction by enemy action in 1941.

Queen's Hall was the result of a decision made in 1887 to build a concert hall on the Crown land next to St George's Hall in Regent Street – and it was to be called either Victoria Hall or Queen's Hall. The Victoria Concert Hall Company (Limited) invited the assistance of the public in the building of it, and the construction work began in 1891, financed by private enterprise. The hall was mainly designed by the architect T. E. Knightley. It had a corner site of 21,000 square feet; next to it stood All Souls' Church, Langham Place (built by John Nash earlier in the century). The front of the hall was constructed of Portland stone, in a French Renaissance style seen through Victorian eyes, and at first-floor level there was an open-air balcony. Busts of great composers adorned the front of the building. There were seventeen entrances, on three sides, and the main hall, with the grand circle at ground level, had seating capacity for 2492 people. Inside, there were two balconies, the lower one containing the Royal Box in the centre. The platform was large enough to accommodate a large orchestra and choir. Ornamental panels on each side of the stage displayed portraits of composers. Above this, a fine Hill organ had been installed. There was an arched ceiling with an elaborate design painted by Carpegat of the Paris Opéra. E. M. Forster in *Howard's End* refers to 'the attenuated Cupids who encircle the ceiling of Queen's Hall, inclining each to each with rapid gesture, and clad in sallow pantaloons, on which the October sunlight struck'. Nobody seemed to think much of the interior decoration – the grey and terracotta colour scheme about which Knightley had been so definite (he insisted that the main colour be that of a London mouse's belly). On that background, seats, carpets and lampshades were Venetian red. Gas and electricity were used for lighting. Acoustically, the hall had been carefully tested and had proved very satisfactory. In addition, the second, small hall of the building could seat 500 for recitals, and had many other uses.

On 2 December 1893, Queen's Hall had been officially opened with a choral and orchestral concert conducted by Frederick Cowen (who was to be knighted in 1911, the same year as Henry Wood). The principal work in the programme was Mendelssohn's Symphony No. 2 (*Hymn of Praise*), and the organist was Henry Wood, then twenty-four years old.

Robert Newman (1858–1926) became at the age of thirty-five the first lessee and manager of Queen's Hall. He came from a well-to-do family and had not had to decide quickly on a definite career. He had been a stockjobber, but left the City after two years. This was the age of oratorio, and he was next attracted to singing, studying for a time in Italy. There followed some experience, none too successful, as a concert agent, and in managing some promenade concerts with Cowen at Covent Garden. But his true gifts were realised only when he took over Queen's Hall. He was described as 'a bulky, commanding figure with a heavy black moustache and a stern expression, very like Kitchener'. A sternness and brusqueness of manner tended to conceal a kind and generous nature. But the important thing about him was the splendid way in which he explored the challenge of having under his control what was potentially the most important centre of music-making in London. Energy, persistence, enthusiasm, vision, enterprise, practicality, a sense of involvement, a first-hand knowledge of music as well as musicians –

Queen's Hall (1893–1941).

The opening ceremony at Queen's Hall, 25 November 1893.

all these attributes combined to produce extremely positive results. He could quickly sense what he wanted, and directly and fearlessly set about achieving it. Wood described him in his autobiography as 'always brisk and busy, but the moment he discussed music his blue eyes – they were *very* blue – lighted up as with fire, and the soft inner kindness of the man showed him to be a deep lover of music'.

Newman was eleven years older than Wood. Both had been students at London's Royal Academy of Music. Newman knew something of Wood's work as organist and accompanist, and he had seen him several times as conductor of opera, but not in the concert hall. He was convinced that, given the right orchestra, this man would become a great conductor. In the England of 1895 this was a daring notion. Wood had had the traditional English grounding in organ and church music, and in his late teens held various organist posts in London. He also had aspirations as a composer. But by the age of twenty his conducting career had begun: a four-month tour with the Arthur Rousbey Opera Company, quickly followed by work with Sullivan and D'Oyly Carte, opera at Crystal Palace, *Carmen* with the Carl Rosa, and an English version of *La Cenerentola*.

All this led to his conducting what looked like an important season of opera at the Olympic Theatre (in the Aldwych area of the Strand) arranged by Serge Lago, an impresario from St Petersburg. The first production was Tchaikovsky's *Eugene Onegin*, and it was Wood's first real encounter with Russian music – the beginning of an enthusiasm which was later to be strongly reflected in his Queen's Hall programmes. Wood's first – and last – taste of conducting grand opera ended abruptly after a few weeks, when Lago disappeared, leaving everybody high and dry. Many different kinds of engagement followed, and he showed a great flair as a teacher of singing, particularly in the operatic repertoire.

In 1894 Wood moved, with his mother (who had been his first teacher and nurtured his early talents) and with his father as secretary, to a new home – No. 1, Langham Place. And there, a few doors away, was the recently-built Queen's Hall. 'Little did I realise', wrote Wood later, 'the significance of its nearness!'

The significance became clear very soon, as he tells in his autobiography. It began with a message from Newman and a visit to Queen's Hall. As they looked down into the arena, Newman asked: 'What do you think of the idea of having Promenade concerts here?' And Wood replied: 'Well, with your knowledge of concerts, and given the right orchestra and artists, it should be a grand success.' And so Newman, the original architect of the Queen's Hall Proms, told Wood of his plan: 'I am going to run nightly concerts and train the public by easy stages. Popular at first, gradually raising the standard until I have *created* a public for classical and modern music.'

In the years before 1895 the quality of the music performed at London promenade concerts had declined since the days of Arditi. Bernard Shaw writes of the depressing state of Covent Garden concerts in the 1880s. 'It was Wood who dragged British orchestral music alive out of that abyss.' His opportunity came in February 1895, when Newman called on him and, without beating about the bush, said: 'I have decided to run those Prom-enade concerts I told you about last year. I want you to be the conductor of a permanent Queen's Hall Orchestra. We'll run a ten weeks' season.' 'I can still feel the thrill of that moment', said Wood (writing in 1938). 'An orchestra . . . in Queen's Hall . . . *My* orchestra.'

It was not all plain sailing. Newman believed that the time was ripe for an English conductor and that the public would give its support. At the same time he wanted Wood to put up some capital – two or three thousand pounds (in those days a considerable sum) – and Wood was not able to do so. The money eventually came from a well-to-do friend of one of Wood's singing pupils, Dr George Cathcart, an ear and throat specialist. He speci-fied two conditions: that *low pitch* be established at the concerts, and that Newman should engage Wood as his *only* conductor. The second condition was apparently to ensure that Wagner programmes could be conducted by Wood, whose flair for Wagner was admired by Cathcart. To many people at the time the idea of an English Wagnerian conductor was an absurdity. The German conductor Felix Mottl (1856–1911) was famous especially as an interpreter of Wagner and had very recently come to England, to Queen's Hall, and given the first of a number of programmes of that composer's music, leading (in 1898) to celebrated performances of *The Ring* at Covent Garden.

The other condition, the establishing of low pitch, was a troublesome question, very difficult to resolve. In England, between about 1845 and 1895, the pitch of keyboard and wind instruments had gradually risen by approximately a semitone – and by a whole tone since the time of Handel. Handel's tuning fork (which still exists) gives the pitch of the note A at 422·5 vibrations per second, and by 1895 this had become 452·5 (known as 'Philharmonic Pitch'). The French, in 1859, had adopted by decree a pitch between these two extremes approximating to that known by Beethoven – 435, called *diapason normal* – and this had become favoured in Europe generally, but not in England. It was Dr Cathcart's view, as a throat specialist, that England's constant performance of works at a pitch higher than originally intended was ruining English voices. Hence his stipulation regarding the promenade concerts. Newman in fact liked the high pitch, but was prepared to go along with the Doctor's wishes; and so, in the printed programmes of the 1895 promenade concerts a notice appeared:

> At these concerts, French Pitch (Diapason Normal) will exclusively be used. Mr Newman is glad to say that it will also be adopted in future by the Philharmonic Society, the Bach Choir, Mottl and Nikisch concerts, and also the concerts under his direction: i.e. The Queen's Hall Choir, and the Sunday Afternoon Orchestral Concerts which begin on October 6th.

The change of pitch meant that the generous Cathcart had to buy new wind instruments and at first lend them to the orchestral players, who had initially no faith in the low pitch – though at the end of the first season, Wood tells us, they were in fact buying their instruments from Dr Cathcart, and the battle had been won.

Wood was now Music Director of the Promenade Concerts. He selected his permanent orchestra largely from among the young players in London orchestras. The leader for the first season was Fry Parker, to be followed, for many seasons, by Arthur Payne. The accompanist for that first season was the song-writer H. Lane Wilson.

If Dr Cathcart had not given the necessary financial support, no doubt Newman would have found it somewhere else, because he was determined to start these concerts. Wood clearly states, however, that Dr Cathcart 'was directly responsible for the inception of the Promenade concerts in August 1895' – and it was the beginning of a life-long friendship between the two men.

The fountain in the arena at the Proms was Cathcart's idea, persisting to the present. It was partly to break up the standing audience a little, but also for the psychological effect of cooling the air on summer evenings, and to help maintain the appropriate degree of humidity in the atmosphere. About five feet in diameter, it was an attractive sight from the start with its flowers, ornamental rocks, and soon its famous goldfish. Sir Thomas Beecham's fantasy was that fascinating young females were constantly falling into the fountain and being rescued by chivalrous swains. The *al fresco* effect also extended to the platform, which was always decorated with palms, ornamental shrubs and, later, flowers as well.

And so, at eight o'clock on that Saturday, 10 August 1895, at Queen's Hall, the first season of Henry Wood Promenade Concerts began – a season lasting eight weeks (to 5 October). The printed programmes consisted of one large folder ($12'' \times 9\frac{1}{2}''$), with advertisements for cigars, whisky, tailoring, and so on; also with programme notes of a generally good standard by Edgar E. Jacques, who continued to write them for several years. The prices of admission were within everybody's reach: Promenade or balcony, one shilling; Season tickets (transferable) one guinea; Grand Circle seats (numbered and reserved) 2/6d, half-a-crown. Refreshments were obtainable at every concert, on the Promenade floor itself – often adding unwanted percussion effects to the music – 'Beethoven to an accompaniment of popping corks'. Besides drinks, there were ices, flowers, and cigars (smoking was permitted, except in part of the Grand Circle).

Looking back in 1938, Wood wrote:

> I can see the packed house now and hear the welcome I received. Many such welcomes have been mine since then; but the first will always remain green in my memory – not only because it so encouraged me at the time, or even because it was the first, but because I doubt whether more than twenty people in that crowded audience had ever seen me raise a baton . . .

The permanent Queen's Hall Orchestra, eighty-strong, had been hand-picked by Wood. At the first concert five singers and three instrumental soloists were engaged. There were twenty-four items (see p. 33), the most substantial being Wagner's *Rienzi* Overture and Liszt's Hungarian Rhapsody No. 2; the rest was all popular light music, of the kind one had come to associate with promenade concerts. There was the inevitable cornet solo, which was to be a regular feature for the next five years. Wood did not want it; but Newman was aware of its drawing power. The programmes of the season as a whole were designed by Wood with close scrutiny from Newman, who was constantly assessing the audience appeal of each item. Starting as 'popular orchestral concerts for the people', the Proms later became indistinguishable in content from symphony concerts proper. But in those early days Wood was trying to keep the different Queen's Hall series for which he was responsible – the Proms, the Saturday Symphony Concerts, and the Sunday Afternoon Concerts – 'as distinct in character as possible'.

How was it possible for one person to undertake so much? And in addition there were his activities with choral societies up and down the country and with festivals of different sorts; and (very important to him) his work as a singing teacher. Exceptional ability, unlimited energy, self-discipline, immense practicality, all combined to make a life that was committed wholeheartedly to the service of music. He had a total of only nine hours of rehearsal for six Prom concerts a week. This meant a rigid economy; a precisely-timed rehearsal schedule, meticulously adhered to;

selfless care over interpretation, and the scrupulous marking-up of orchestral parts with bowings and breath-marks, phrasing, dynamics, and so on — which became Wood's normal practice. Of that first season he wrote:

> Out of each evening's eighteen or twenty pieces, at least five were with piano. On Beethoven nights the pianist often played a sonata rather than a concerto; thus I could avoid a concerto rehearsal. In this way I managed to squeeze everything in, especially as popular items of Wagner, Tchaikovsky, Grieg, Schubert and Mendelssohn could be repeated as often as three or four times a season. But the hours of intensive work were not in vain, for I had the satisfaction of knowing at the end of the season that I had become established as a conductor in England.

For the second season — after some financial uncertainty — the orchestra was increased to ninety players 'in consequence of the generous support given by the public and press to the season of Promenade Concerts' (as Newman put it). At first Wood's insistence on punctuality at rehearsals, the constant demands he made on all the players, the battle against slackness of any kind, often made him temporarily unpopular. But an orchestra soon senses integrity, purpose, professionalism and musicianship and comes to respect and value these qualities. He went in for none of the tricks and 'temperamental' displays of the virtuoso conductor, although with his generous beard and unruly mane of black hair he was a striking figure, presenting music in a colourful, dramatic way. His later nickname 'Timber' was more than a play on words; it suggested those qualities of solid reliability and strength of purpose which were evident in all that he did. He never 'wasted' time at rehearsals with lengthy lectures to the orchestra about interpretation; his feelings for the music were unmistakably and often vividly conveyed through his conducting technique rather than through words. There was a penetrating nasal quality in Wood's voice, with an accent peculiar to himself, and at rehearsal he liked to confine his remarks to short, staccato, telling phrases: 'Rhythm in the fingers!' for strings; 'More life, more vitality! Vermilion, not yellow!' and so on — phrases often becoming exaggerated and sarcastic, which the orchestra learned to accept with humour, knowing that they were made against a background of sympathy and understanding of the players' problems. And he never conducted from memory.

> A conductor may know his scores off by heart [he wrote], but his orchestra prefers him to have the copy before him . . . If a soloist's memory fails him it is obvious to everyone; if a conductor's memory fails him the orchestra goes on playing and his plight may remain unnoticed.

In the middle of the first season of Proms, Wood was confronted with 'the deputy system' – a common nightmare of conductors at the time. He arrived at a morning rehearsal to find seventy or eighty unfamiliar faces in the orchestra. It was not until 1904 that something definite was done to prevent this kind of thing happening (see p. 54). Another bone of contention was tuning. Wood never trusted the 'oboe A', which he said often proved to be 'any old A'. He supervised the tuning of every instrument in his orchestra, checking it every night with a tuning-fork (on a resonant box) giving the *diapason normal*. Another example of his leaving nothing to chance.

In the 1896 season (and for several after) Newman showed his business flair in quite a different way – by showing 'animated pictures' (the fore-runners of cinema films) on a screen in the small hall during the interval and after the concert, at an extra charge of six pence. 'Mr David Devant's Animated Photographs' included such things as 'A Wedding Procession' (on a night when Mendelssohn's Wedding March was being played), 'Up the River', 'Ladies Drilling', 'Arrival of the Paris Express', 'The Serpentine Sun Dance in brilliant colours' . . . While the audience enjoyed the pictures, the members of the orchestra repaired to 'The George', which became known as 'The Glue Pot', the licensed premises in Great Portland Street, within two minutes' walk from Queen's Hall. Walking there today, along Great Portland Street, one can still read the sign 'Queen's Hall' at what was once a back entrance to the building.

An eyewitness of the early years reported that comparatively few women were to be seen in the Promenade arena, not many adolescents at that time, and a fair number of foreigners (carrying scores). And applause was not as 'indiscriminate' as it later became.

In the early part of 1896 Wood was mainly concerned with rehearsing Stanford's opera *Shamus O'Brien*, and in the midst of this his mother died suddenly of bronchitis – a loss which caused him an agony of distress. To overcome this as best he could, he absorbed himself in the preparation of *Shamus*, which eventually proved highly successful, running for over a hundred nights from March to July, at London's Opéra Comique, which stood just off the Strand, roughly where we now find the Aldwych Theatre. The Promenade season began on 29 August. Percy Pitt became organist and accompanist of the Proms, and remained so for six seasons. Later, as Musical Director of the BBC, he had an important influence on the course of the Proms by persuading Wood to continue – but of that more later.

The dual purpose of the Proms was being achieved: the creation of a public for classical and modern music; and the building-up of an orchestra which would not have to depend largely on musicians from other countries,

Robert Newman, manager of Queen's Hall, who founded the Proms and appointed Henry Wood as their conductor.

but would carefully train British players to achieve a really high standard. Also, it was the policy from the start – largely dictated by financial considerations – to engage promising young soloists, rather than celebrities, for these concerts. After the first season, Wood insisted that every unknown artist must attend an audition; it was not sufficient to rely on the word of influential people. There were some disasters in performance – on two occasions through soloists not having been heard at auditions; there was also a pianist who had to kick the sustaining pedal noisily in a vain attempt to keep time; and a blonde singer who went so persistently wrong that in the end Wood had to leave the rostrum and accompany her on the piano. But the policy of using the Proms as a platform for a wide range of new performing talent, as well as a wide range of new music, was a fruitful one and has persisted over the years.

By 1898 Wagner was proving an immensely popular composer in London, and his music was an essential and very substantial ingredient in every Promenade season. Monday becoming established as Wagner Night. Wood's flair for Wagner has already been mentioned. 'Whether I was popularising him,' wrote Wood, 'or whether he was doing a like office for me was difficult to decide – but his name and mine were being linked together at the end of 1898.' That year Wood and the Queen's Hall Orchestra gave a royal command concert at Windsor Castle, and Queen Victoria herself chose the programme, which contained several items by Wagner. The Queen was tremendously enthusiastic, saying that she knew Richard Wagner quite well and especially enjoyed *Parsifal*. Wood was disconcerted at being expected to wear white kid gloves for the occasion (shades of Jullien!), but he and the orchestra returned to London immensely satisfied.

3

The Music 1895-1899

The programme of the opening concert was unpromising – recalling for the most part the blatant trivialities of early promenade concerts. It is worth giving in full, if only to show how quickly the programmes changed for the better once they had started. Wood began with the concept of a new venture, which *had* to be popular, and at first this meant a variety of singers and instrumental soloists and light orchestral items. The following is what was heard on Saturday, 10 August 1895 at the Queen's Hall – the first concert of a series which was gradually to develop into a series of Proms of symphonic stature.

OVERTURE: Rienzi – – – – – – – –	*Wagner*
SONG: Prologue (I Pagliacci) – – – – – –	*Leoncavallo*
(*a*) HABANERA – – – – – – – –	*Chabrier*
(*b*) POLONAISE IN A – – – – – – –	*Chopin*
SONG: Swiss Song – – – – – – – –	*Eckert*
FLUTE SOLOS (*a*) Idylle (*b*) Valse } from Suite – – –	*Benjamin Godard*
SONG: "Since thou hast come" – – – – –	*Kenningham*
CHROMATIC CONCERT VALSES from the opera Eulenspiegel	
(first performance in England) – – – – –	*Cyrill Kistler*
SONG: "My heart, at thy sweet voice" – – – –	*Saint-Saëns*
GAVOTTE from Mignon – – – – – –	*Ambroise Thomas*
SONG: Vulcan's Song from *Philemon and Baucis* – – – –	*Gounod*
HUNGARIAN RHAPSODY (No. 2) – – – – – –	*Liszt*

INTERVAL

GRAND SELECTION from Carmen – – – – – –	*Bizet*
SONG: Largo al factotum – – – – – – –	*Rossini*
OVERTURE: Mignon – – – – – –	*Ambroise Thomas*

SOLO CORNET: Serenade – – – – – – –	*Schubert*
SONG: "My mother bids me bind my hair" – – – –	*Haydn*
SOLO BASSOON: "Lucy Long"	
SONG: "Dear Heart" – – – – – – –	*Tito Mattei*
THE UHLAN'S CALL – – – – – – –	*Eilenberg*
SONG: "Loch Lomond"	
SONG: "A Soldier's Song" – – – – – –	*Mascheroni*
VALSE: Amoretten-Tänze – – – – – –	*Gung'l*
GRAND MARCH: Les Enfants de la Garde – – – –	*Schloesser*
(first performance)	

Only a few days later, however, the tone had changed completely, for a 'classical' evening. Part 1 of the first Wednesday concert (14 August) included Beethoven's Overture *King Stephen*, both movements of Schubert's 'Unfinished' Symphony, the Prize Song from Wagner's *Die Meistersinger* and an aria from *Tannhäuser*, Weber's *Freischütz* Overture, a recitative and aria from Gounod's *La Reine de Saba*, and Liszt's Hungarian Rhapsody No. 4. Part 2 contained an opera fantasia, which became a favourite and established ingredient, well-known ballads, and light instrumental pieces. As Bernard Shaw remarked, it was like having two different concerts in one evening – and the pattern was by no means new. Apart from Saturday, the usual form became a thoughful Part 1 and a light-hearted, relaxed Part 2. The 'novelties' of the season – that is, works new to British audiences – included Massenet's Meditation from *Thaïs* and his overture *Phèdre*, the Prelude to Act I of Richard Strauss's *Guntram*, Wagner's *Rienzi* Overture, and also some Russian works – Rimsky-Korsakov's *May Night* Overture and Tchaikovsky's *Marche solennelle*. British composers were not treated well in those early years of the 'Proms': in general, audiences felt no prejudice against contemporary music as such, in the way that they do today; the prejudice was quite simply that British music was inferior to music from abroad. During that first season, Wood introduced the *Carnival Scenes* of G. H. Clutsam (a composer best known probably for his song 'I know of two bright eyes'); a recitation with orchestra, *Eugène Aram*, by A. C. Mackenzie, and also his *Benedictus* (originally a violin and piano piece which Wood liked very much); a Suite in four movements by Percy Pitt, who was to be much associated with the Proms as accompanist and programme-note writer for several years; and Stanford's *Suite of Dances* (later frequently repeated). *The Battle of the Flowers* by T. H. Frewin, one of Wood's first violins, was a novelty of the first season. Frewin provided novelties for the next three seasons also. 'I have always been pleased,' wrote Wood, 'to produce works by members of my orchestra. Although not always of first-rate quality in the composition sense, they have always been interesting, and written in a practical manner. In 43 years I have introduced many such compositions.'

A concert in which Part 1 was devoted to Sullivan and Part 2 included *The Lost Chord* (played as a cornet solo) attracted a full house. Before long the 1895 season was establishing the practice of devoting Part 1 to a single composer for some of the concerts each week: Wagner in particular; also Gounod, Beethoven, and Mendelssohn (including his 'Italian' Symphony, Violin Concerto, *Ruy Blas* and *Athalie* Overtures, music from *A Midsummer Night's Dream* . . .). Schubert's 'Great' C major Symphony was heard complete. In contrast another concert harked back to Jullien and featured his *British Army Quadrille* and *Drum Polka*. The same concert ended with the Soldiers' Chorus from Gounod's *Faust*. One of the most regularly recurring works was the *Marche heroïque* by Saint-Saëns. Schubert's *Erl King* made a deep impression.

The *Musical Times* of October 1895 spoke of 'the excellence of the programmes offered by Mr Robert Newman with the co-operation of a high-class orchestra, and Mr Henry J. Wood as a conductor of marked intelligence . . .' It was in every way a highly promising inaugural season.

In 1896 Wagner Night on Monday and Beethoven Night on Friday were firmly established, and remained so. Instead of the obligatory cornet solos, there were frequent appearances by a cornet *quartet*, the Park Sisters, performing, for example, the *Tannhäuser* March and *The Lost Chord*, but also decidedly unexpected items such as Fauré's *Les Berceaux*. Mondays sometimes became Wagner and Liszt instead of purely Wagner. Liszt's symphonic poems were featured – including *Orpheus*, *Tasso*, *Les Préludes*. Two Wednesday nights were devoted to Schubert in Part 1, with the 'Great' C major Symphony, and the Phantasie in F minor, Op. 103, orchestrated by Mottl. A Schumann night included the *Manfred* Overture, the Piano Concerto, songs, and the D minor Symphony. A Sullivan Night was again a success. Gounod was similarly honoured, and his concert included the whole of Act III of *Faust*. One concert contained a song, 'The King and the Miller', by Henry Wood himself; and the Grand Fantasias on well-known operas were a regular and immensely popular ingredient of the lighter second part of concerts. Novelties of the season were wide-ranging and included Glazunov's *Scènes de ballet*, Rimsky-Korsakov's *Capriccio espagnol* and *Scheherazade*, and Tchaikovsky's *Nutcracker* Suite. The last night included an orchestral version of 'A New Minuet in A' by Paderewski. Saturday night Proms continued that winter (1896–7) until April. On 14

November the première took place of Dvořák's tone poem *The Water-goblin*.

The concert of 23 September 1896 was called 'Musical Development during the reign of H.M. the Queen', and the printed programme set the scene by referring to the musical gifts of Queen Victoria and Prince Albert – gifts, it was emphasised, acknowledged by no less an authority than Mendelssohn himself. The programme continued:

> It was natural that the Art so lovingly cultivated by the royal pair should receive their encouragement, and that the example thus set should be followed by their children. To this influence, so worthily exerted, is due in a great measure the enormous development and popularity of music in England at the present day. Society, following the Court, regards music with favour and its exponents flourish accordingly; while the impetus given to musical education by the foundation of the Royal College – made possible by the efforts of the Prince of Wales – is evident in all directions.
>
> The Royal Academy of Music was founded in 1822 and granted a Royal Charter in 1830, but when Queen Victoria ascended the throne Exeter Hall was the only building available for concerts on a large scale. Things musical have changed since then, and it is peculiarly appropriate that the longest reign in British history should be commemorated in this hall named after our great Queen, and itself one of the latest and most conspicuous signs of that change.

For that occasion a choir of 400 voices, augmented by boys from the London School of Choristers, was assembled by Newman to take part in Mendelssohn's *Hymn of Praise* (Symphony No. 2). Mackenzie's popular *Britannia* Overture and Percy Pitt's *Coronation March* were also performed at this concert.

By 1897 a number of works were becoming very popular at the Proms and were constantly being repeated. These included Rossini's *William Tell* Overture, Mendelssohn's Violin Concerto, Wagner's *Rienzi* Overture, the *Siegfried Idyll*, the *Ride of the Valkyries*, Schubert's 'Unfinished', German's *Henry VIII* Dances, Beethoven's Fifth Symphony, and (one of the most popular) Tchaikovsky's *Nutcracker* Suite.

A notice in the 1897 programmes reads: 'These concerts are advertised to commence at 8 o'clock and terminate at 11 o'clock, but the persistent demands for encores sometimes necessitates the omission of certain items in order to finish within reasonable time.' Now enthusiasm was shown for programmes of a more consistently distinctive kind, with works such as Mendelssohn's Violin Concerto, Liszt's *Orpheus*, Tchaikovsky's Fourth and Sixth Symphonies, and Schubert's 'Unfinished'.

Lessee and Manager - ROBERT NEWMAN.

Promenade Concerts

SEASON, 1896.

(Under the Direction of Mr. ROBERT NEWMAN.)

EVERY EVENING AT 8 O'CLOCK.
DOORS OPEN AT 7.30.

Programme for Saturday, September 19th, 1896.

Miss EVANGELINE FLORENCE. Mr. HERBERT GROVER.
Mr. CHARLES SANTLEY *(His first appearance at these Concerts.)*

PERCY FROSTICK - - Solo Violin.
(Pupil of Herr August Wilhelmj.)
Mr. ALBERT FRANSELLA - Solo Flute.
Mr. HOWARD REYNOLDS - Solo Cornet.
The PARK SISTERS - - Cornet Quartet.

FULL ORCHESTRA
Principal Violin - Mr. ARTHUR W. PAYNE.

ACCOMPANIST - - Mr. PERCY PITT.

Conductor - Mr. HENRY J. WOOD.

MR. DAVID DEVANT'S ANIMATED PICTURES in the Small Hall during the interval. Admission 6d. extra.

PROMENADE - - ONE SHILLING.

BALCONY, 2/- GRAND CIRCLE, Numbered and Reserved, 3/- FRONT ROW, 5/-
SEASON TICKETS, Transferable, ONE GUINEA.

Tickets for all Concerts and Theatres may be obtained at ROBERT NEWMAN'S BOX OFFICE.

TELEPHONE, 3521B.
TELEGRAMS, "CHORD, LONDON."

QUEEN'S HALL,
LANGLAM PLACE, W.

Erard New Model Concert Grand with Piano Resonator attached.

PRICE TWOPENCE.

A typical early title-page of the printed programme of a Promenade Concert (1896) – the front of a single large folder (12 × 9½ inches), which was the standard format from 1895 to 1926.

Wagner's music was always very well represented in these early Prom seasons – and yet Wood tells us that in these early days Wagner failed to fill the Promenade, though every reserved seat was always sold. The difficulty could be overcome by adding a Beethoven symphony to a Monday Wagner-night programme. In these early days, too, the cornet solo and opera fantasia were still regular Part 2 features. The final concert was 'Mr Robert Newman's Benefit' – Saturday 16 October. One would expect the end of the season to be relaxed and frivolous; but no: Part 2 even contained Grieg's *Peer Gynt* Suite No. 1, Beethoven's *Leonora No. 3*, and Rossini's *William Tell* Overture.

The featuring of composers was very strong throughout the 1898 season: Monday was Wagner, or Wagner and Liszt; Tuesday was Sullivan/Gounod, or Schubert/Mendelssohn, or Grieg/Massenet, or Weber/Dvořák; Wednesday was predominantly Tchaikovsky Night (occasionally varying to Tchaikovsky and Brahms, or Tchaikovsky and Berlioz); Thursday became a Popular Night; Friday continued as Beethoven Night (combined twice with Mozart, once with Gluck, once with Schumann). Twice in the season Tuesday became a 'Plebiscite Night' – a curious titling: a serious but popular first part (including, for example, Mendelssohn's Violin Concerto, Grieg's *Peer Gynt* music and Tchaikovsky's *Pathétique*), and a customary Part 2 (for example, including a Grand Fantasia on *Il Trovatore* and Mendelssohn's Wedding March). British music was more adequately represented that season: there was a 'British Composers' Night' (see p. 39). Elgar was described in the programme notes as 'one of the most promising of the younger generation of English composers' (he was 41 – a late starter). Among 'novelties' of the season were Strauss's *Festmarsch*, Coleridge-Taylor's Four Characteristic Waltzes, a successful *Valse brillante* by the 23-year-old violinist W. H. Reed, and some new Edward German pieces. The season also included some out-of-the-way Massenet – the ballet music from *Hérodiade* and *Scènes hongroises*, and Vincent d'Indy's orchestral version of Anton Rubinstein's popular Melody in F (W. H. Squire, leader of Wood's cellos, was soloist). There was also an orchestration by Raff of Bach's D minor Chaconne.

On 31 August 1898, Arthur Sullivan, who was going to conduct a Tchaikovsky symphony at the Leeds Festival, came to a Tchaikovsky Night at the Proms and heard *Casse-Noisette*, the *Pathétique* Symphony and *Caprice Italien*, conducted by Wood. Writing to Wood afterwards, he said:

. . . I say quite sincerely that I have never heard a finer performance in England than that of the Tchaikovsky Symphony last Wednesday. It was a perfect delight to listen to such accent, phrasing, delicacy and pace, and I congratulate both the gifted conductor, and the splendid orchestra. And what a lovely work it is! I could see that you and the band, too, revelled in bringing out its beauties . . .

The programmes given below are representative ones of this 1898 season – the fourth year of the Henry Wood Promenade Concerts (even to the New Vocal Waltz in Part 2 – conducted by the composer and 'plugged' at all six concerts that week!).

Monday, October 10th
WAGNER AND LISZT NIGHT

OVERTURE AND VENUSBERG MUSIC (*Tannhäuser*) – – – –	*Wagner*
PRELUDE AND LIEBESTOD – (*Tristan and Isolde*) – – –	*Wagner*
OVERTURE – – – "Die Meistersinger" – – –	*Wagner*
HUNGARIAN FANTASIA for Pianoforte and Orchestra – – –	*Liszt*
GOOD FRIDAY MUSIC from *Parsifal* – – – – – –	*Wagner*
RIDE OF THE VALKYRIES – – – – – – –	*Wagner*
TRAUERMARSCH from *Götterdämmerung* – – – – –	*Wagner*
POLONAISE IN E – – – – – – –	*Liszt*
FANTASIA – – –"Reminiscences of England" – – –	*Godfrey*
NEW VOCAL WALTZ – – "Love Me" – – –	*J. M. Coward*
(*Conducted by the Composer*)	
SCHILLER MARCH – – – – – – – –	*Meyerbeer*

Tuesday, October 11th
BRITISH COMPOSERS' NIGHT

OVERTURE – – "Land of the Mountain and Flood"	– *Hamish McCunn*
FOUR OLD ENGLISH DANCES – – – – –	– *F. H. Cowen*
PRELUDE TO ACT III. – "The Troubadour" –	– *A. C. Mackenzie*
OVERTURE – – – "Taming of the Shrew" –	– *Percy Pitt*
THREE DANCES from *Henry VIII* – – – –	– *Edward German*
OVERTURE – – – "Shamus O'Brien" –	– *Villiers Stanford*
THREE BAVARIAN DANCES, Op. 27 – – – –	– *Edward Elgar*
(*First performance in London*)	
OVERTURE – – – – "Di Ballo" – – –	– *Sullivan*
FANTASIA – – – – "Faust" – – –	– *Gounod*
NEW VOCAL WALTZ – – "Love Me" – – –	– *J. M. Coward*
IMPERIAL MARCH – – – – – – –	– *Sullivan*

Wednesday, October 12th
TSCHAIKOWSKY NIGHT

SUITE – – – – "Casse-Noisette" – –	*Tschaikowsky*
PIANOFORTE CONCERTO in D minor – – – – –	*Rubinstein*
SYMPHONIE PATHÉTIQUE, No. 6, in B minor – – –	*Tschaikowsky*
FANTAISIE after Dante's "Francesca da Rimini" – – –	*Tschaikowsky*
FANTASIA – – – – "Carmen" – – – –	*Bizet*
NEW VOCAL WALTZ – – "Love Me" – – –	*J. M. Coward*
TRIUMPHAL MARCH from *Alfred* – – – – – –	*Prout*

Thursday, October 13th
POPULAR NIGHT

SUITE – – – "Scènes Hongroises" – – –	*Massenet*
(*First performance in London*)	
ACADEMIC FESTIVAL OVERTURE – – – – – –	*Brahms*
OVERTURE – – – – "Bellona" – – –	*T. H. Frewin*
(*First time of performance*)	
PRELUDE TO ACT III (*Lohengrin*) – – – – –	*Wagner*
CONCERTSTÜCK for four Horns and Orchestra – – –	*Heinrich Hübler*
OVERTURE – – – – "Leonora No. 3" – – –	*Beethoven*
VALSE – – – "Amoretten Tänze" – – –	*Gung'l*
FANTASIA – – – "Cavalleria Rusticana" – – –	*Mascagni*
NEW VOCAL WALTZ – – "Love Me" – – –	*J. M. Coward*
GAVOTTE – – – "À la Mode Ancienne" – –	*George Elvey*

The programmes also contained songs with piano – songs of many different varieties. In one of the early Prom ballads, Mrs Vander Veer-Green sang this dialogue, set to music by Braga. The title is 'The Angels' Serenade'.

> *Child*   What lovely tones awaken me,
> Swelling upon the breeze,
> As it sweeps through the open balcony
> On to the distant trees?
> *Mother*   I hear no tones of melody;
> Calm is the summer air;
> Only the gentle zephyrs . . .
> *Child*   Hush! They are not earthly music!
> O mother dear! I must away! . . .

The eight-week season of 1899 opened with a Saturday concert in which a twelve-year-old French cellist, Paul Bazelaire, was soloist in the A minor Cello Concerto of Saint-Saëns. He made a striking impression and Newman engaged him several times during the season. In later years he became a well-known professor at the Paris Conservatoire and edited a large amount of cello music.

Wood's marriage to Princess Olga Ouroussoff the previous year had made him even more aware of the world of Russian music. The new music of this season included Balakirev's *Overture on Russian Themes* and his Symphony in C, the *Caucasian Sketches* of Ippolitov-Ivanov, four Tchaikovsky works (one being the Symphony No 3), a Scherzo by Cui, three Glazunov works, and pieces by Glinka, Liadov and Wolkov (*Cossack Dance*). Russian composers, in fact, were far better represented than English ones during this season. Elsewhere Wood was performing works like Elgar's oratorio *Lux Christi*, but British music at the Proms was lightweight: three pieces by Percy Pitt, Sullivan's masque music from *The Merchant of Venice*, an Overture *Touchstone* by W. H. Reed, whose earlier *Valse brillante* had been a great success. On the other hand there was a wide choice of novelties from other countries, ranging from symphonic poems by Dvořák to Five Flemish Dances by Blockx and the première of a work by an Anglo-Brazilian composer, Amy Horrocks – an orchestral ballade *The Romaunt of the Page*.

This was a season in which the programmes tended to be more general in character: except for the Wagner and Beethoven nights, each programme was a mixture of composers, well varied and far-reaching. The cornet solo was no longer a regular part of the programmes: this ended with the final retirement of its main exponent, Howard Reynolds. In compensation, on the lighter side, the Meister Glee Singers (a male quartet) were immensely popular.

4

Progress and Difficulties

Wood, despite his enormous enterprise, always maintained that the public knows – and must be given – what it wants. For himself, he would have had festivals devoted entirely to new works – works which would represent the ideas and feeling of the time. But he knew the public far too well to carry this out; rather he would have two classical works, for example, with a modern work in between. In those early years of the Proms it was easier than it is now to attract audiences with 'novelties', partly because orchestral concerts were not numerous, as they are today, and partly because there was less gap, in general, between what composers were writing and what audiences could readily appreciate. Part of Wood's great practicality was a constant give-and-take feeling between audiences and himself in the various enterprises with which he was connected.

A difficult situation arose in 1901 with the Queen's Hall Orchestra, which for some years had been under the personal control of Newman, and was in fact called 'Mr Robert Newman's Queen's Hall Orchestra'. Newman had extended his activities to theatrical enterprises and some of these had gone wrong, landing him seriously in debt. He was no longer able to carry financial responsibility for the orchestra. There were various offers of help, but of a kind that might have involved undesirable conditions of acceptance – if, for example, a publisher had assumed full responsibility. The solution came through one of Wood's musical connections. In 1900 Leonora von Stosch, a favourite pupil of Ysaÿe, had played the *Introduction and Rondo Capriccioso* of Saint-Saëns at the opening night of the Proms, and this had led to a lasting friendship with Wood. Her husband was Sir Edgar Speyer, Bt, a wealthy German-born banker, a Privy Councillor, and a highly cultured enthusiast of music. Speyer offered his backing, heading a private and influential syndicate to organise the financial side of the orchestra. This arrangement was to continue in a beneficial fruitful way until 1915. Wood found in Speyer an understanding and generous friend, always ready to agree (for instance) to extra rehearsals when necessary and to the engagement of the right artists, thus maintaining the standard of the concerts. Speyer was keen, too, to invite important foreign composers to come to Queen's Hall for the symphony concerts and to conduct their own works – Debussy, Strauss, Grieg, and many others.

The financial crisis could have meant the end of the Queen's Hall Orchestra and of the Proms – or at best their continuance in a different and less satisfactory form. In fact, the standard, the character, the progressive spirit of these concerts remained unchanged. The adventurous spirit was indeed enhanced by the involvement of Speyer and his wife. Newman continued as manager; the lessees of the Queen's Hall were now the publishers, Chappell and Co., but they had no say in the choice of music. (Later, when Chappell's had financial control of the orchestra and the concerts, it was a little different, but never seriously affected the overall quality of the programmes.)

In 1901 Sibelius appeared in person for the first time at the Proms, when Wood, who was one of his earliest champions in England, performed his *King Christian II* Suite. During that season, also, Wood was one of the pianists in the Vivaldi-Bach Concerto in A minor for four keyboards and strings, which became a favourite item for future Bach nights. And Mrs Henry Wood (Olga) made her début at the Proms, singing Elisabeth's Prayer from *Tannhäuser* 'most beautifully'.

From 26 December 1901 to 1 February 1902 an additional winter season of Proms was put on, similar in pattern to the summer ones. But, as with more recent attempts of this kind, they did not prove successful enough to become a regular venture. The summer season of 1901 had included a concert devoted entirely to works by living British composers. It had not been very successful, and in the winter Prom season, British composers were very poorly represented.

The day after the end of those winter Proms (Sunday 2 February) King Edward VII and Queen Alexandra were present at one of Wood's Sunday Afternoon Concerts at Queen's Hall. Queen Victoria had always been an active supporter of the art of music, and it was encouraging that in the new reign the King was showing interest so soon. 'This was indeed a proud day for Newman, the orchestra, and myself', wrote Wood in his memoirs.

During the 1902 Prom season Wood's health broke down – and small wonder, when one considers the Herculean volume of work which, as always, he was carrying: besides Proms there were the series of Saturday Symphony Concerts and of Sunday Afternoon Concerts at Queen's Hall; also various festivals and much activity with four or five choral societies in provincial cities, the Nottingham Symphony Orchestra (which he founded), and much teaching. At the end of the previous year Wood reckoned that he had conducted 150 concerts (plus all the rehearsals involved) and given 500 lessons. He had also recently teamed up with his wife for a series of 'Mr and Mrs Henry Wood's Vocal Recitals' in London and the provinces. Dr Cathcart now insisted on his having a complete change of scene and occupation for three weeks – a cruise to Morocco. It meant being away from the Prom concerts from 13 October to 8 November, and Arthur Payne, the leader of the Queen's Hall Orchestra, conducted in Wood's absence. And while Wood was away on his 'rest cure' he received the distressing news that his father had suddenly been taken ill and died.

In 1899 Henri Verbrugghen, a young Belgian pupil of Hubay and Ysaÿe, had played Dvořák's Violin Concerto with Wood, and had made a very favourable impression on him. When Arthur Payne resigned in 1902, to take up a musical directorship in Llandudno, Verbruggen was appointed leader of the Queen's Hall Orchestra for the Promenade concerts, and this arrangement continued until 1905, when he began a successful career as conductor in Scotland, Australia and the USA. The singer Frederic Austin, best known for his long-popular performing arrangement of *The Beggar's Opera*, made the first of many Prom appearances in 1902, in music by Tchaikovsky.

At this time Wood was becoming the staunch champion of British composers – an important aspect of his reputation – but with caution. In the Sunday Afternoon series his policy at each was to sandwich one work by a British composer between the finest classical items. A less regular but significant strand of British music ran through the Prom season of 1903: Cyril Scott, Holbrooke, Rutland Boughton, Elgar, W. H. Reed, Bantock, Bainton . . . It was also the season when the First Symphony of Sibelius was heard in England, on 13 October, and eight days later the First Symphony of Mahler, which according to Wood was 'the first note of his music to be played in England'. There was also Bruckner's Seventh Symphony on 15 October – the 'first and last' performance at the Proms as far as Wood was concerned. Only comparatively recently has Bruckner been accepted by audiences in England.

Early in 1904 Wood, his wife and Dr Cathcart spent a month in America – after Wood had with much difficulty obtained leave of absence from Robert Newman. The concerts at New York's Carnegie Hall were an enormous success, with applause lasting longer than Wood had ever known, and the hospitality was of course overwhelming. The result was an invitation to visit the States for three months each year – a tempting offer, financially and musically, which Wood considered very seriously. But his main allegiance was to Newman and the Queen's Hall Orchestra, and in the end he was glad that he had not accepted that American offer.

An aspect of the Proms normally taken for granted, but nevertheless important, is the writing of programme notes – the printed presentation of the programmes. In 1895, when the Proms started, a tradition had already been established, notably by Sir George Grove. It was Grove who for forty years (1856–96) supplied 'analytical and historical' notes on every kind of orchestral work then current (with help for some of the modern works) for August Manns's Saturday orchestral concerts at the Crystal Palace. These notes were clear, thoughtful, extremely knowledgeable, and written in a distinctive, very readable style. They demonstrate the qualities of the best programme notes of any period – communicating useful information and enthusiasm to the audience. For several years Henry Wood's programme-note writer was Edgar E. Jacques, who coped single-handed with this formidable task of providing written material for about sixty-five concerts over a period of eleven weeks. Many of the works, of course, were repeated both during the same season and in future seasons, but there were always many novelties which had to be considered and written about for the first time. Jacques did a solid professional job, clear, informative without being too technical, sometimes rather naïve in generalisations ('This Concerto is called the "Emperor" for the same reason as the organ is called the "King" of instruments. Both have "Divine right" to their titles.')

This arrangement worked smoothly enough until 1902, when Wood found that Jacques was becoming slack over the preparation of his analytical notes, and Newman had to pay Percy Pitt a weekly salary to keep an eye on things. Soon 'old man Jacques' was dropped and the overall task went to Percy Pitt and the journalist Alfred Kalisch, who between them maintained a good standard until in 1908 Mrs Rosa Newmarch (1857–1940) became 'official programme annotator to the Queen's Hall Orchestra' – continuing single-handed (with a little help over certain works) until 1920, and then for another twenty years in collaboration with Eric Blom and others. Rosa Newmarch was able to bring a real distinction to this task in both content and style. English by birth, she became an expert in Russian music and art in general, which brought her close in spirit to Henry Wood. She was an accomplished linguist and wrote biographies of Tchaikovsky, Borodin and Liszt, a study of Russian opera, and did many translations; she also edited the series of books *The Living Masters of Music*, herself contributing a volume on Henry Wood. Rosa Newmarch's programme notes were eventually collected and published in book form, in six volumes.

For most music-lovers the Proms are a widening of experience. Even

today, when an infinite variety of music is available on radio and disc,
actually to be present at the performance of the finest music, old and new, is
a different and more deeply satisfying experience. Its value in the early years
of the century is conveyed by Thomas Burke:

> My own first Promenade was experienced in 1901. I had seen a poster
> announcing Promenade Concerts at the Queen's Hall; Smoking Permitted;
> Admission One Shilling. I wasn't sure what a Promenade Concert was; the
> word probably brought an image of a seaside promenade and its band; but I
> soon discovered what a Promenade Concert wasn't. It wasn't a concert at
> which, except in the interval, you could do any promenading. The Prom-
> enade floor was a jam, mainly of young men and women, most of the young
> men wearing straw hats . . . We were young, and the majority was, I imagine,
> in my own condition; that is, keenly responsive to music, but knowing little
> about it.

The situation is basically similar today. The main difference is probably that
in the early years there was a wider range of light music in the concerts. But
the policy of presenting the established classics together with the best of
what is new from all countries has remained unchanged.

1904 was the last year that the Grand Operatic Fantasy was a regular
ingredient of Part 2 of the programme. From then on, Part 1 was equal to a
symphonic concert in all respects, with a vocal or instrumental soloist for
certain items; and Part 2, considerably shorter and less substantial, contained serious orchestral items, but of a more popular kind, and songs.

5
The Music 1900-1904

Today it is easy to forget that in 1900 orchestral concerts were not easy to come by. They were normally expensive and few in number. The Proms, by providing ten or eleven weeks of concerts for one guinea (the price of a promming season ticket) were making available to all a richness, an adventurous scope of musical experience within a relaxed social context in a way that has continued to have a tremendous appeal right up to the present, despite the developments of gramophone and radio, and despite the proliferation of concerts of all sorts.

In the first week of the 1900 Prom season there was a 'Thanksgiving Concert to celebrate the Victory of the Imperial Troops' in South Africa, and the main works performed were the same as those heard in 1896 at the concert called 'Musical Development during the reign of H.M. the Queen' – the Overture *Britannia* by Mackenzie, the Coronation March of Percy Pitt, and Mendelssohn's *Hymn of Praise* (Symphony No. 2). The similarity of programme led Wood mistakenly to say in his autobiography that this 1900 concert was the first *choral* concert at the Proms, but in fact the first was the one in 1896.

As had by now become established, Monday nights were Wagner Nights and Fridays were substantially Beethoven, but frequently Beethoven and Mozart combined. Otherwise, the focusing on composers was irregular: Tchaikovsky was well featured as usual; one of the Brahms Nights included the Second Symphony and the Double Concerto (with soloists from the orchestra); and Thursdays and Saturdays were general and 'popular' nights, one of them including the first English performance of Rachmaninov's First Piano Concerto. British composers had fairly good representation: premières of Josef Holbrooke's Variations on *Three Blind Mice*, and of George Fox's *The Boy and the Butterfly* (a descriptive piece for flute, bassoon and orchestra), and of Landon Ronald's 'Suite de ballet' (a work which elicited a reprimand from Wood for the careless way it was scored!).

Two famous artists, in the early stages of their careers, made their appearance at the 1901 Proms: Mark Hambourg, playing Liszt's E flat Piano Concerto, and Backhaus, playing Mendelssohn's G minor Concerto. Also Marie Roze, previously of the Carl Rosa Opera Company and once 'the idol of the British Public', made an appearance; she had previously done much for Wood in his early years and he had conducted her 'farewell' operatic tour in 1893.

It was an enterprising season for novelties: these included Glazunov's *The Seasons*, MacDowell's *Indian Suite*, Saint-Saëns's *Africa*, Sibelius's *King Christian II* (in the presence of the composer), Tchaikovsky's *Swan Lake*, and Weingartner's Second Symphony. (This last work was included through the composer's long-standing friendship with Wood: Wood in fact preferred Weingartner's arrangement of Weber's *Invitation to the Dance* to Berlioz's). But the most resounding first performance was of Elgar's *Pomp and Circumstance* March No. 1 in D. 'The people simply rose and yelled', wrote Wood. It had to be given a double encore – something unique for the Proms – before the audience would allow the concert to continue. Arnold Bax was present on this occasion and he later recalled that Sir Henry Wood and the orchestra could scarcely be seen because one of the most stupendous of London fogs had entered the Queen's Hall unbidden. 'These lively and chivalric marches', he added, 'represented, at the time, a new manifestation of the British national spirit, corresponding in some ways to that of Kipling's verse.' It is a spirit that dies hard . . . The occasion was a Prom on 22 October 1901 – a programme chosen from works by living British composers: Cowen, Stanford, Coleridge-Taylor, Mackenzie, German, McCunn. The most substantial work was Parry's *Symphonic Variations*. It was the first British night of this sort at the Proms.

The winter season that year had some unusual first performances in England: the Piano Concerto, Op. 28, by Ludwig Schytte; a symphonic poem *Alastor* by Ernest Blake – an allegory of states of mind, from joyous youth to solitude and death; and the Second Symphony of Hans Huber, each movement inspired by a picture (like Mussorgsky's famous work).

The following may be taken as a typical mixed programme of that year. (Jessie Goldsack was to be an important person later in Wood's life.)

Thursday, October 24th

1. OVERTURE	–	–	"Le Cheval de Bronze"	–	–	–	*Auber*
2. DRAMATIC PRELUDE	–	–	"Oreithyia"	–	–	*Reginald Steggall*	
			(First time of performance)				
3. OVERTURE	–	–	– "Semiramide"	–	–	–	*Rossini*

4. PIANOFORTE CONCERTO in E flat   –   –   –   –   –   –   *Liszt*

5. PRELUDE –   –   –   – "Lohengrin"   –   –   –   *Wagner*

6. DANCE OF NYMPHS AND SATYRS, "Amor and Psyche"   –   *George Schumann*
                           (*First performance in England*)

7. OVERTURE   –   –   – "William Tell"   –   –   –   *Rossini*

8. GRAND FANTASIA   –   – "Gondoliers"   –   –   –   *Sullivan*

9. MARCHE HÉROIQUE   –   –   –   –   –   –   *Saint-Saëns*

Miss Jessie Goldsack
Mr. Charles Knowles
Mr. Mark Hambourg - Solo Pianoforte
Mr. Albert Fransella - Solo Flute

The featuring of composers was again evident in the 1902 season: Saturday was good popular, Monday Wagner, Tuesday Schubert and Brahms, Thursday general (popular) and Friday Beethoven. Among the novelties was César Franck's *Symphonic Variations* (ever-popular in England since), and, especially attractive to Wood, dances from the opera *Der Wald* by Ethel Smyth, an opera which had been produced in Berlin and London (Covent Garden) – indeed an achievement for an English composer at that period. Brahms's First Symphony made a deep impression, as did also Tchaikovsky's Piano Concerto No. 3 in E flat. It is pleasant to find Fauré's *Pelléas et Mélisande* Suite included in one of the popular concerts.

The 1903 season included the première of Cyril Scott's First Symphony, in A minor, in an otherwise 'popular' night, and Josef Holbrooke was the pianist in his own *Concerto Dramatique* in F minor, which Wood found 'deeply interesting'. Another success was the première of Rutland Boughton's symphonic poem *Into the Everlasting* (based on Walt Whitman). There was also the première of a tone poem *Pompilia* by Edgar Bainton, a composer whom Wood esteemed highly. It was indeed a rich season: Elgar's *Enigma* Variations, and a featuring of several of the symphonic poems of Strauss, now so familiar but then quite new-sounding. The production of *Ein Heldenleben* at a symphony concert the previous year (with the composer conducting) had been the beginning of a lasting friendship between Wood and Strauss. Wood admired him greatly as composer and as conductor.

Strauss had high praise for Wood and his achievements, as he expressed in a letter after a performance of his *Sinfonia Domestica* at Queen's Hall in 1905:

> . . . I cannot leave London without an expression of admiration for the splendid Orchestra which Henry Wood's master hand has created in such a short time. He can be proud indeed of this little colony of artists, who

represent both discipline and quality of the highest order. After the thirty performances of the *Sinfonia Domestica* which I have conducted this winter, and of which only very few indeed can compare to the masterly rendering of the new and, in that sense, youthful Queen's Hall Orchestra, I can well appreciate what an amount of hard work, expert knowledge and sympathetic comprehension of my intentions have been expended on this performance through the energy and self-effacing labours of Mr Wood. Performances such as these mark days of rejoicing in a composer's life . . .

The outstanding 'first in England' at the tenth season of Proms, 1904, was undoubtedly the *Prélude à l' Après-midi d' un faune* of Debussy. It riveted the attention of the promenaders and Wood received many letters asking for a repeat. It became a very popular piece at the Proms almost immediately, and remains so to this day. Wood speaks appreciatively of 'the beauty of the harmonies, the exquisitely beautiful orchestration, the atmosphere so fresh and original'. It was the prelude to many works by Debussy which Wood was to perform at the Proms – including the rarely-heard *Martyrdom of St. Sebastian*. As a whole, however, 1904 was a rather routine season musically. A highlight for many would have been Coleridge-Taylor's 'Onaway, awake, beloved'. The young Percy Grainger made his début, playing Tchaikovsky, but Wood was not particularly struck by this performance and preferred his playing of Grieg, for whose music Grainger felt a special sympathy. Egon Petri, a pupil of Busoni, also made his first appearance, playing Liszt with immense fire and panache; so did the 29-year-old many-sided Donald Francis Tovey, then known primarily as a pianist. For this Prom appearance he played Book 1 of Brahms's *Paganini* Variations. Following an ovation, he was permitted to play 'a short piece' as encore – and he gave them the whole of Book 2! After which a large part of the concert had to be cancelled.

York Bowen was a composer much admired by Wood, and at various times Wood introduced all his piano concertos at the Proms, with the composer as soloist. In the previous season, his symphonic poem *The Lament of Tasso* had had a considerable success. In 1904 Prom audiences heard his *Concert Overture* and his E flat Piano Concerto.

6

From Sea-Songs to Schoenberg

1905 was the year of the *Fantasia on British Sea Songs* – the famous medley put together by Wood as 'a real popular climax' (as he described it) to a matinée Prom on 21 October. Newman, as Wood often remarked, always had a shrewd eye to the main chance, and he would not have missed the chance of a concert to celebrate the Nelson Centenary – one hundred years since the battle of Trafalgar. The result was a whole-hogging 'sea-business' programme which included works such as Mackenzie's *Britannia* and Wagner's *Flying Dutchman* Overtures, Tchaikovsky's *1812* and songs like 'Heart of Oak', 'Rocked in the cradle of the deep', and so on. The *Fantasia* was specially advertised and was repeated at the Prom the same evening – and virtually unceasingly ever since, particularly on the Last Night (though Wood by no means restricted performance to the Last Night of a season). After research, Wood was able to present the correct naval calls in their proper order, and he cleverly scored the sea songs so as to spotlight a wide range of soloists. The climax was 'Rule Britannia', Dr Thomas Arne's patriotic song (from the masque *Alfred*) which has so often been sung with genuine feeling in the course of Britain's island history. The feeling reverberates still, however inappropriate the words in their literal meaning may be to us today.

Here is the form of the *Fantasia on British Sea Songs*, as set out in the 1905 programme:

I. Bugle Calls:
  (a) Admiral's Salute
  (b) Action
  (c) General Assembly
  (d) Landing Party
  (e) Prepare to Ram
  (f) Quick, Double, Extend
      and Close

II. The Anchor's Weighed
    Solo Trumpet
    Solo Trombone
III. The Saucy Arethusa
    Solo Euphonium
IV. Tom Bowling
    Solo Violoncello

V. Jack's the Lad (Hornpipe)
    Solo Violin
    Solo Flute
    Solo Piccolo
VI. Farewell and Adieu, Ye Spanish
    Ladies
    Quartet of Solo Trombones
    Clarinet cadenza, leading to

VII. Home, Sweet Home
    Solo Oboe
    Solo Harps
VIII. See, the Conquering Hero
    Comes
    Solo Horn
    Three Flutes
IX. Rule, Britannia!
    Organ and Full Orchestra

It was an expression of a time when we prided ourselves on being a seafaring people; when we were dependent on the Navy for the safety of our people, at the centre of 'an Empire on which the sun never set'. The full character and diversity of that Empire had been brought home to Londoners when representatives of the distant lands came to pay homage to Queen Victoria during her two Jubilees. With the new century a tremendous revolution in all things was beginning. The age of the railway, horse traffic and bicycles was soon to give way in importance to that of the motor car, the submarine, the aeroplane – not only quickening the pace of life, but also destroying the benefit of an insular position which England had so long enjoyed, safely guarded by her Navy. Coupled with all this were immense improvements in social services, and education-for-all was becoming general. (This educative spirit had been a vital part of the Henry Wood Proms right from the start.)

But the seafaring tradition certainly dies hard. Henry Wood played the *Fantasia on British Sea-Songs* for more than forty Prom seasons, and it has persisted ever since. Once Wood thought he would leave it out – but the protests were so great that he never did so again. The same thing happened much more recently: William Glock decided we had had enough of the *Fantasia* and omitted it one season, causing headlines in the newspapers and such protests that it had to be reinstated as a planned encore. Wood described the enjoyment which it brought to the hundreds of young Promenaders of his day:

> They stamp their feet in time to the hornpipe – that is, until I whip up the orchestra in a fierce *accelerando* which leaves behind all those whose stamping technique is not of the very first quality. I like to win by two bars, if possible; but sometimes have to be content with a bar and a half. It is good fun, and I enjoy it as much as they. When it comes to the singing of *Rule, Britannia!* we reach a climax that only Britons can reach, and I realise I can be nowhere in the world but in my native England.

Such, then as now, is what Wood called the epitome of the Proms; such is the ritual of the Last Night, behind which genuine feelings are being expressed – feelings of love for one's native country, concern for her well-being and safety, reflected even today through the vital but outdated images of 'Land of Hope and Glory' and 'Rule, Britannia!' And even on the last gala night of a season, as on other nights, audiences, young and old, will (almost without exception) listen intently while the serious music is in progress. In 1938, Wood wrote: 'And how they have listened all these forty-odd years! How still they have stood! How they have loved their Bach, their Beethoven, their Brahms, and their Wagner! More than I ever hoped they would in my wildest dreams.'

It is natural for tension to be released occasionally, especially at the end of a season. Applause and vocal exclamations greet members of the orchestra as they appear on the platform. The opening of the lid of the piano has a special little ritual of its own, with accompanying noises ('*Heave!*'). So does the orchestral tuning, with a helpful(?) 'A' from all and sundry. (At other times it has been a mocking A flat.) There are also various forms of chanting and responses – to say nothing of the costumes, often suggesting carnival in Rio rather than music in England – and those dangerous whistles and toy trumpets 'which unguarded children blow'. Banners, slogans, balloons (which pop) are much in evidence. The leader of the orchestra may get as much applause as the conductor. There is an atmosphere in which anything might happen, culminating now (but not in Wood's time) in an obligatory speech by the conductor.

One of Wood's main problems in the early days was that of maintaining a high standard of performance despite the 'deputy' system which was rampant among orchestral players. The rate of pay was appallingly low, even making all allowances for the changes in the value of the pound. In 1897, the rank and file of the orchestra received only 45 shillings a week for six Promenade concerts with three rehearsals, a guinea for one Symphony concert and rehearsal, and half-a-guinea for a Sunday afternoon or evening concert without rehearsal. Wood was later proud of having managed to get these basic rates improved, by dint of constant pressure on Newman. Thirty-five years later, however, they were still only £7 or £8 a week. (The BBC, when it came into the field with its own orchestra in 1930, was to improve on this considerably.) Standard of performance depends very much on having the same group of musicians who rehearse and play together on a regular basis, but it was not always possible for Wood to achieve this continuity with players who had several irons in the fire. If a player were offered a more attractive engagement, he would simply send a

deputy: and during a busy Prom season when every minute of rehearsal time
was important, the situation for Wood was intolerable. Of the very first
Prom season Wood wrote:

> I realised something more like a nightmare on the morning of September 30. I
> found an orchestra with seventy or eighty unknown faces in it. *Even my leader
> was missing*. Arthur Payne, the deputy-leader, told me of a certain musical
> festival. My regular players were all there. Moreover, they would be absent
> for a *week*. I had to put up with this sort of thing for years. It was hardly fair on
> a young conductor to have to rehearse a week's concerts in three mornings
> (nine hours all told) with new and often inexperienced players. I made up my
> mind there and then to fight what is a bad principle, but little did I think how
> many years it would take me to bring about a reform.

In 1904 Wood took a definite stand, backed up by Newman. At a
rehearsal Newman, 'a man of few words' who knew what he wanted,
announced: 'Gentlemen, in future there will be *no* deputies! Good morning!' And he strode off. The immediate result was that forty members of the
orchestra resigned *en bloc* and formed the nucleus of the London Symphony
Orchestra, who gave their first concert in June of that year, with Richter as
their principal conductor. The Queen's Hall Orchestra had little difficulty
finding replacements, and so, as Wood said, there were now two permanent
orchestras of first-rate quality instead of one. There was an Orchestral
Association in those days which tried, not very successfully, to protect the
interests of orchestral players. The Musicians' Union was formed much
later.

1908 was a specially busy year for Wood. The Sheffield Festival clashed
with part of the Prom season, as it had done previously. So while Wood was
in Sheffield with the Queen's Hall Orchestra, Newman engaged an ad-hoc
body, the New Symphony Orchestra, and brought over Edouard Colonne
from Paris to conduct them. (In 1896 Newman had engaged Colonne with
his *own* orchestra to give concerts at Queen's Hall, which included French
music new to England.) In February 1908, Debussy was accorded a warm
welcome at Queen's Hall – the popularity of *L'Après-midi* and *La Mer* being
by then well established. Wood himself had been sent to Paris by Speyer to
persuade the great French composer to come to London. Debussy was not
the most competent of conductors: at one of the concerts the Queen's Hall
Orchestra saw him through *Sirènes* in a remarkable way. The composer had
wrongly indicated something, and then showed he wanted to stop and
restart. The orchestra, however, refused to be stopped, disregarded
Debussy's signs and carried on to the end of the piece. They knew what was

wanted: the piece had been thoroughly rehearsed by Wood beforehand.

The following year was a tragic one for Wood. The final concert of the Prom season, 23 October, proved to be the last occasion his wife Olga sang in public, for she died two months later. At that last concert she had been in great pain: her contribution had included two songs by Stanford, to poems by Edmund Holmes, 'I think that we were children' and 'O flames of passion', which the composer had orchestrated specially for her. The second of these ended radiantly with words that consequently came to have a particular significance for Wood: 'In love's white flame, in love's transcendent light!'

At the time of this bitter personal loss, Wood needed and received the full sympathy and help of the friends with whom he worked most closely – the Speyers, Dr Cathcart, Robert Newman – and especially Siegfried Schwabacher (a very close friend who had at one time made a fortune as a diamond merchant in South Africa). 'To Schwabacher', wrote Wood, 'I owe my ultimate recovery . . . for he helped me to regain my normal stride . . . He was ever my great and privileged friend.' Schwabacher helped Wood in both his musical and his private life – and as far as possible in his financial affairs. The loss of Olga was for Wood the loss of the embodiment of an artistic ideal, personally enhanced by a sophistication stemming from her aristocratic upbringing – a sophistication which Wood (perhaps happily) lacked. At all events, Wood found consolation in the usual amazingly full schedule of work – a way of life into which he could enter with complete commitment.

In 1911 Wood was knighted by the recently-crowned King George V, 'setting the seal' upon his work, demonstrating for him the readiness of the Royal Family to give positive recognition to the art of music. Reporting the opening night of the 1911 Prom season, the *Musical Times* found more than the usual exuberance:

> Of course there was an enormous audience . . . The game of 'spotting' Messrs Catterall, Renard, Fransella, and other leading members of the orchestra as they arrive on the platform, and showing acquaintance by vigorous applause, is largely cultivated, it appears. The conductor receives an ovation. In the eyes of a Promenade audience this was his first public appearance since his knighthood, and the event was signalled with an extra lively demonstration of esteem and affection.

1911 was also the year of an event not mentioned in his personal reminiscences: his marriage to his 21-year-old secretary, Muriel Ellen Greatrex, which proved to be disastrous and ended in separation (see p. 92). This same year, one of Wood's other activities had a public showing. Like

Winston Churchill, he had a talent for painting, which (along with carpentry) he exercised as a recreation. 'An Exhibition of 50 sketches in oil by Sir Henry Wood' was held for a fortnight in the Piccadilly Arcade Gallery, and the Queen's Hall Orchestra Endowment Fund – which was to help members of the orchestra when they retired – benefited by £200 from the exhibition. (The proceeds of the last night of each Prom season usually went towards this cause.) It was a year when Wood 'filled practically every moment' with, this time, a total of 140 concerts (and their rehearsals), festivals at Norwich and Sheffield, four concerts at the Empire Festival in the Crystal Palace, the London Music Festival, and forty chorus rehearsals in the provinces; also, as usual, a great deal of teaching. Not many conductors could achieve a self-discipline and self-organisation to make such a work-load possible.

The 1912 and 1913 seasons were two of Wood's richest and most satisfying. What a galaxy of great names were appearing in person in England round about that time. Conducting their works or hearing Wood conduct them were Richard Strauss, Debussy, Reger, Scriabin, Schoenberg, Rachmaninov. And Casals taught Wood something about how to accompany a hypersensitive soloist. Before a Casals performance, Wood explained the intensely light orchestral accompaniment that this artist wanted. 'I beg you, strings, to try to play on one hair of your bow; perhaps two – sometimes three – but never more.'

An important experience of the 1912 Prom season was the first English performance of Schoenberg's *Five Orchestral Pieces*. Despite a fair amount of hissing at the end, most people doubtless were glad to hear something by 'the most talked-of German composer of the day' (as the programme note of the concert described him) who represented the last word in modernity, whatever individual opinions about the work may have been. Such experiences are a vitally important aspect of the Proms.

On a lighter note, Wood had reason to remember the Prom of 11 October 1912. It was the only occasion in his whole career when he was late for a concert. There was a fog and the taxi bringing Wood to the Queen's Hall had an accident. He was rather badly cut by glass, but otherwise unharmed. His head was bound up when he eventually walked on to the platform at eight-twenty, to be greeted rapturously by the waiting audience.

1913 was the year in which Wood and Newman allowed women players in the Queen's Hall Orchestra, even paying them the same rates and giving them the same status as the men. When the rumour first spread that women were to be admitted to the orchestra, Wood found that he had 137 applications to fill six vacancies. But not yet for the Proms: it was argued by

Newman and some others that women would never stand the strain of nightly concerts for ten weeks at a stretch. The orchestra as a whole took kindly to the idea (previously only a female harpist had been allowed). 'I have never regretted my decision', wrote Wood twenty-five years later.

7

The Music 1905-1913

.It was a far cry in 1905 from the Jullien-like popular concert which opened the first Prom season ten years before. The general impression during the 1905 series is of different kinds of orchestral concerts on a high level of interest. Even the lighter second half of the opening Saturday night began with Grieg's *Peer Gynt* Suite No. 1, rather than a Grand Operatic Fantasia on themes from *Faust*, or something of the sort. Monday was indisputably Wagner Night; Tuesday and Thursday were classical, but popular in feeling; Wednesday – Tchaikovsky Night; Friday – Beethoven Night; and Saturday a popular concert . . . Broadly speaking, that was the shape of a week, with room for flexibility. Occasionally Wood allowed the final item of Part 2 to be conducted by the leader of the orchestra, Henri Verbrugghen.

Novelties that season included the *Helena* Variations of Bantock, the *Suite on Russian Folk-melodies* by Max Bruch, the première of *Four Studies from Victor Hugo* by Cecil Forsyth (one of the viola players of the Queen's Hall Orchestra). The Forsyth work was repeated the following week by request. Of outstanding importance was the first performance in England of Mahler's Symphony No. 4, with Mrs Henry Wood as soloist in the last movement. (The famous Gervase Elwes sang in the same concert.) Another novelty was the *Swan of Tuonela* by Sibelius.

In 1906 Bach became an important ingredient of the Proms, thanks to Wood's enthusiasm: the Brandenburgs and orchestral Suites were becoming established. Arthur Catterall the violinist, who later became famous as leader of the Hallé and then of the BBC Symphony Orchestra, made his first appearance that year as soloist in Joachim's *Hungarian Concerto*. Busoni came to London and heard his *Lustspiel* Overture, and was soloist in his C minor *Konzertstück*. Of younger soloists, the violinist Marie Hall was outstanding; her soloist career, alas, seemed to fade out with marriage. Arensky's *Variations on a theme of Tchaikovsky* made 'quite a hit'. There was the first performance in England of Sibelius's *En Saga* and *Finlandia*. About the latter, Wood remarks: 'What a furore *that* created! It was a revelation to London.' Also first in England that season were Mussorgsky's popular *Gopak* (from the opera *Sorochinsky Fair*), *Baba-Yaga* by Liadov, and a Symphony in E flat by Glière. Two English premières were *A Norfolk Rhapsody* by Vaughan Williams and a Prelude *Sappho* by Bantock.

In 1907 Chopin's Funeral March (from his Second Piano Sonata), in a special orchestral version made by Wood, was played as a tribute on two occasions at the Proms: for Joachim, who died just before the Prom season opened, and for Grieg within a fortnight after that. The season lasted ten weeks (sixty concerts). A report in the final programme of the season noted with satisfaction the large audiences attracted on the nights when British novelties were performed, and the number of composers who were present on these occasions; formerly a British night had not proved so popular. The British novelties that year were wide-ranging: the Delius Piano Concerto played by Theodor Szánto, the dedicatee; two works by Havergal Brian (who still needs his advocates): his Overture *For Valour* and his *English Suite*; the Overture *Princess Maleine* (after Maeterlinck) by Cyril Scott; a Serenade by Quilter; a new Symphony by an Australian professor, Marshall Hall; a Suite, *The Mysterious Rose-Garden*, by Garnet Wolseley Cox (who showed brilliant promise, but died young); the première of Frank Bridge's symphonic poem *Isabella* and of the singer-composer Frederic Austin's *Rhapsody*. Another première was Hamilton Harty's *Comedy Overture*.

A 'curiosity' that season was a concerto by Mozart for three pianos and orchestra (two oboes, two horns and strings), which we know as K242, but was then recently discovered and having its first performance in this country. Mozart wrote it in Salzburg in 1776 for three lady pianists. In 1907, at Queen's Hall, the pianists were York Bowen, Frederick Kiddle (the resident accompanist of the Proms) and Henry Wood. Some of the Haydn works which Wood produced at various times were also appearing for the first time in England. The leader of the orchestra, Henri Verbrugghen, was soloist in another novelty that season – Sibelius's Violin Concerto. His *Karelia* Overture, d'Indy's *Symphonie Montagnarde*, and Ravel's *Introduction and Allegro* also had their 'first in England' performance.

By now the performance of Beethoven symphonies and piano concertos in chronological order had become established. The 1908 season was enhanced by Rosa Newmarch's lucid and scholarly programme notes (see p. 45). Two British premières – important at the time – were a Symphony in E flat by Balfour Gardiner and York Bowen's Piano Concerto No. 3, in G minor, with the composer as soloist. Dukas's *L'Apprenti sorcier* was played several times, and the Meditation from Massenet's *Thaïs* became popular.

Applauding a promising young singer at Queen's Hall during a Prom directed by Henry Wood in 1908.

A pianist who was to become a great favourite with promenaders made her first appearance in 1908 – Myra Hess, playing Liszt's E flat Concerto. She later became associated particularly with Schumann, Brahms and Bach. Wood tells us that the dark-haired eighteen-year-old of 1908 was already a great artist.

The opening concert of the 1909 Prom season included Wood's *Fantasia on British Sea-Songs*. He also produced Fantasias on Welsh and Scottish melodies, and another Prom favourite, Walford Davies's *Solemn Melody* (written for the tercentenary of Milton's birth), had its first concert performance on 8 September. The season also saw the première of Walford Davies's *Songs of Nature*. The list of novelties for 1909 includes a Concerto in A minor by Paderewski, a Fantasy for piano and orchestra by Anton Rubinstein, and 'first time in England' Ravel's *Rapsodie espagnole*. Mahler's now-famous *Adagietto* for harp and strings was first heard in England on 31 August, in a programme that included a new Violin Concerto by Hamilton Harty. Saint-Saëns, a favourite composer at the Proms, was represented by his Third Symphony, two tone-poems, and ballet music from *Henry VIII*. There were two performances of Elgar's great A flat Symphony. Percy Grainger played the Grieg Concerto and Liszt's *Hungarian Fantasy*. The French oboist of the Queen's Hall Orchestra, Henri de Busscher, who had been appointed to the Orchestra after Wood and Speyer had gone on an audition trip to Paris, played a Handel Concerto with great success.

There was some variation in the planning of the 1910 Proms. Fewer symphonies were given than in some of the previous seasons (but the nine Beethoven were there, in chronological order), and Wood and Newman tried to discover whether the public really preferred a lighter musical diet on three nights a week. The Monday Wagner Nights held their ground and the classical programmes on Fridays frequently filled the hall to overflowing. The novelties included pieces by Bax and Vaughan Williams, and Mussorgsky's *Song of the Flea*, arranged by Wood, which was a 'tremendous success' and continued to be so.

In 1911, out of seventy-eight soloists, thirty made their first appearances. Opportunities were also given for members of the orchestra to act as soloists. The Tuesday and Thursday programmes were lighter than in previous years, and on Wednesdays a symphony was invariably given – Mozart, Schubert, Brahms, Dvořák, Tchaikovsky. Beethoven was reserved for Friday, the 'sold out' classical night, and Wagner remained firmly established on Monday.

Novelties of 1911 included two Georges Enesco works – a Suite and the Rumanian Rhapsody No. 1. Debussy's *Children's Corner* Suite in its orchestral form and Ravel's *Pavane pour une Infante défunte*, described by Wood as 'this little gem', made their appearance. Something of a sensation was caused by the waltz from *Der Rosenkavalier*, an opera not yet produced in England. The *Miniature Suite* of Eric Coates, who was then a member of the orchestra, had its première, and Debussy's *L'Après-midi*, already heard many times at the Proms, was played this season on the last night, after Chopin's First Piano Concerto.

The outstanding 'first time in England' of 1912 was undoubtedly Schoenberg's *Five Orchestral Pieces* on 3 September, a celebrated occasion on which Henry Wood was hissed – or rather the music was hissed. 'This', said Wood, 'I think goes to refute the popular idea that the Promenaders accord acclamation to every work played, no matter what.' (Nothing daunted, Wood repeated the work in January 1914 with Schoenberg himself conducting, and it attracted a large and appreciative audience.) Perhaps the programme-note presentation of the work in 1912 had predisposed the audience to hostility. It included the following: 'Schoenberg's Five Pieces for orchestra – at least as they appear on paper – lead to the conclusion that they are merely experiments in dissonance; protests against all preconceived notions of music and harmony . . .'

Novelties that season included Ravel's *Mother Goose* Suite, Enesco's Rumanian Rhapsody No. 2, and pieces by Roger Quilter, Poldowski, Edgar Bainton and Benjamin Dale. It was a good season for English music, with Elgar's new Coronation March (written for the Coronation of King George V and Queen Mary the previous year) as well as four songs with orchestra, and the first concert performance of his *Crown of India* Suite. An important première was Frank Bridge's suite *The Sea*, with its four movements entitled 'Sea-scape', 'Sea-foam', 'Moonlight' and 'Storm'; the work became a great favourite of Wood's and he played it with success in France, Germany, Italy, Holland, South Africa and the USA. Grainger's *Mock Morris* and *Molly on the Shore* were also heard in 1912, and the leader of the Queen's Hall Orchestra was soloist in the first performance of Coleridge-Taylor's Violin Concerto; it was very shortly after the composer's death.

The last season before the war was one of the most successful. An official notice in the programme states: 'Fortunately the Promenade audience has now been educated to such sound and liberal tastes that it is possible to organise programmes of a very high order and to include a good many novelties, provided the experimental note is not over-emphasised.' (Does that last phrase refer to the Schoenberg experience of the previous season?) It is indeed true that the programmes this season had all the appearance of symphony concerts, without having to resort to the frivolities associated with Promenade concerts in the past. Eighty-four soloists (fifty-three singers and thirty-one instrumentalists) were engaged, many still beginners and of native origin – 'a very desirable plan' – but many, too, were well-known and experienced artists. The season included several new works. A Suite by Dohnányi was warmly received and repeated by request; and Stravinsky's *Firebird* Suite made a strong impression. 'The orchestration is very full and fantastic,' wrote Rosa Newmarch in her programme note for the Stravinsky work, 'and the music is not of the kind which lends itself to verbal analysis.' There were premières of Havergal Brian's Overture *Dr Merryheart* (a portrait of a genial astronomer), of the young Eugene Goossens's *Variations on a Chinese theme*, and of an *Idyll* by Eric Coates – which was played, curiously, after a performance of the closing scene of Strauss's *Salome*. There were two Grainger novelties – *Shepherd's Hey* and the *Irish tune from County Derry* – and the first concert performance of Vaughan Williams's incidental music for *The Wasps* (first heard at Cambridge five years previously). From the modern French school, the novelties were Debussy's *Ibéria* (impressions of Spanish life), Ravel's *Valses nobles et sentimentales* and Fauré's *Ballade* for piano and orchestra. In all, it was a rich and varied season.

8

War and Survival

As soon as war was declared, on 4 August 1914, the first question facing Newman, Wood and Speyer was whether the Promenade concerts should take place at all. Newman was emphatic: 'Why not? The war can't last three months and the public will need its music and, incidentally, our orchestra its salaries.'

The Proms opened on 15 August. Not without difficulties, however. Sir Edgar Speyer and his wife were both German by birth, and although he had done so much not only for music but for the arts in general in Britain, and had severed his business connections with Germany, he did not escape insults in the press and in public. It was estimated that in all he had personally contributed about £30,000 for British music, often having had as much as a £4000 loss to meet at the end of a Prom season. In certain quarters, however, this cut no ice, and in May 1915 Speyer wrote to the Prime Minister, Asquith:

> For the last nine months I have kept silent and treated with disdain the charges of disloyalty and suggestions of treachery made against me in the Press and elsewhere. But I can keep silent no longer, for those charges and suggestions have now been repeated by public men who have not scrupled to use their position to inflame the overstrained feelings of the people. I consider it due to my honour as a loyal British subject, and my personal dignity as a man, to retire from all my public positions. I therefore ask you to accept my resignation as a Privy Councillor and to revoke my baronetcy.

The Prime Minister, acting for the King, refused his request. Nevertheless, public feeling being what it was, a disillusioned Speyer departed to the USA – and the Queen's Hall Orchestra lost its generous and liberal-minded backer.

There was trouble at the start of that Prom season about the Wagner Night on the first Monday. Debased patriotic feelings were rife, and

Newman was receiving many hysterical letters demanding that all German music be banned from programmes. The then managing director of Chappell and Co., William Boosey, also wished to get rid of Speyer and programmes that were 'aggressively German'. Many people in authority behaved in a very unenlightened way, and even the Royal Philharmonic Society seems to have cast off its customary world-wide approach between 1914 and 1918. The immediate result was that the advertised Wagner Night concert on Monday 17 August had to be replaced by a programme of Russian, French and British composers, beginning with the National Anthem and ending with *La Marseillaise*.

An admirably firm stand against this nonsense was taken by both Wood and Newman. In the Monday programme a notice appeared:

> Sir Henry Wood begs the kind indulgence of those members of his audience who may be disappointed at the non-performance of the customary Monday Evening Wagner programme, the postponement of which has been rendered necessary by a variety of circumstances. He confidently hopes for a continuance of their valued support.

On Friday of the same week the programme contained this notice, beautifully clear and direct in its attitude:

> The Directors of the Queen's Hall Orchestra think that some explanation of the change of programme on Monday evening, August 17, is due to their Subscribers and to all those who have so loyally supported the Promenade Concerts in the past. The substitution of a mixed programme in place of a wholly Wagnerian one was not dictated by any narrow-minded intolerant policy, but was the result of outside pressure brought to bear upon them at the eleventh hour by the Lessees of the Queen's Hall.
>
> With regard to the future, the Directors hope – with the broadminded co-operation of their audience – to carry through as nearly as possible the original scheme of the Concerts as set forth in their Prospectus.
>
> They take this opportunity of emphatically contradicting the statements that German music will be boycotted during the present season. The greatest examples of Music and Art are world possessions and unassailable even by the prejudices and passions of the hour.
>
> For the Directors of the Queen's Hall Orchestra,
>
> ROBERT NEWMAN,
>
> Manager.

The very next Monday the planned Wagner programme was given, and German music was not boycotted during the four years of war. To even up the balance, Newman arranged for a bronze bust of King George V to be placed under the rostrum at Queen's Hall in a conspicuous position; and flags of the Allies were displayed on the great organ. The national anthems of the Allies, gradually more and more of them, were specially scored by Wood and played before every concert in 1914 and 1915 – resulting, for him, in 'untold boredom'.

When Speyer left the country, Chappell's became responsible for running the Queen's Hall Orchestra. William Boosey failed to come to an agreement with Speyer over the orchestra's title, and the eventual solution was for it to be called the New Queen's Hall Orchestra, Robert Newman continuing to be manager. It was a difficult time financially: the attendances were variable, still on average well worth while, but more money was being lost on the concerts than in previous years, and this expense had to be carried now by Chappell's. It was mitigated to some extent by the publicity possible for their pianos, grand and upright, and by the inclusion in the Prom programmes of songs and ballads published by them. Matinée Proms were tried, but with little success. It was remarkable that somehow the Proms continued at all, despite Zeppelin raids, despite the departure of many instrumentalists into the services and the strong feeling of resentment which many people felt because some remained to make music. The raids, though in no way comparable to those of the second world war, could nevertheless be worrying and prevent Prom audiences from being released from the hall until the 'Raiders past' signal was given. A Prommer at Queen's Hall in 1915 has told of a concert at which there was a crash, a cracking sound, and a shower of plaster from the roof, causing a rush towards the walls and even an anxious Henry Wood, continuing to conduct but glancing upwards. For an encore, a soloist gave them 'We won't go home till morning', amid much laughter and applause. Refreshments were laid on; there was dancing; and home till morning they did not go: the 'Raiders past' was not till 1 a.m.

> The dignity and control displayed by the audience, night after night, during the war years, was amazing, [wrote Wood] and although I had my back to the people I was always conscious of what was happening. I could not actually hear the air-raid warnings, but I knew that the Promenaders were gradually receding towards the walls of the Grand Circle, which was, of course, the natural instinct to 'take cover' . . . Every member of the orchestra behaved with exemplary calm.

At the end of the 1914 season, a note appeared in the programme of the final concert:

. . . With the anxious attention of all sections of society riveted day by day upon the war news, it was not to be expected that the Season of 1914 should be as successful as its predecessors in drawing crowded audiences. The attendance has been necessarily somewhat fitful; cheering or depressing intelligence from the front being apparently accountable for the state of the house. During the later weeks of the Season the Concerts have been better attended. This has encouraged the Directors to persevere in their courageous policy of keeping the Concerts going to the end of the Season.

Despite everything, the 1915 season (the 21st – the coming-of-age of the Promenade Concerts) was successful; so much so that at the close of it Newman arranged three extra matinées, bringing the season's concerts to sixty-six. Attendances at concerts were markedly better than in the previous season. During those uncertain war years, Wood's policy of engaging women to play in his orchestra really had a chance to prove its effectiveness: many were engaged on a temporary basis only, 'but their fortitude and loyal work', said Wood, 'were something I shall ever remember with gratitude and pride'. (A different attitude, indeed, from that of Sir Thomas Beecham, who is reported to have said of women in orchestras: 'If they are well-favoured they distract the other players; if they are ill-favoured they distract me.' There are several versions.)

It was during the war, also, that Wood had an important personal decision to make: he was wooed by the Boston Symphony Orchestra – the orchestra he had admired so much when he heard it very early in his career. A tempting offer was made in 1918, which he considered very carefully.

The question I had to answer was whether I could carry out the season's conducting at Boston each year, and, at the same time, keep faith with the man who had helped me build up my career – Robert Newman – and Chappell's – to say nothing of my loyal public.

When the news of Wood's possible departure leaked out and appeared in the press, there was a deluge of letters from the 'loyal public', beseeching him not to leave England. Newman also had many letters, some from members of the armed forces. It was a serious threat to a firmly established tradition, to something which had become an essential part of England's musical life – the Symphony Concerts, the Sunday Concerts, the Proms. If Wood were away for six months of each year, how could these be planned, rehearsed, carried out? And what about his provincial festivals and concerts? Definitely he could not be spared! Artistically Wood would have liked to extend himself in this way; the conditions, too, and the financial side were excellent; but finally he gave up the idea, swayed by the wishes of so many people and by the fact that he had so many musical associations in England. There was relief all round.

Had Wood accepted the American offer, it is conceivable that Thomas Beecham might have taken over the Proms. During the war – in the summer of 1915 – Beecham and Landon Ronald, between them, ran a rival series of Promenade concerts in the Albert Hall. So high-class were the programmes that the *Musical Times* described the series as 'one of the most admirable ever given in London'. But the audiences were small, and the scheme had to be discontinued. For music-lovers 'The Proms' meant Queen's Hall and Sir Henry Wood, in war or peace.

9

The Music 1914-1918

It was difficult, of course, to have soloists from other countries during the war years; and similarly with music – the orchestral scores and parts of new foreign works were not always forthcoming. In 1914, however, 105 soloists were engaged (against 84 in 1913) and they were almost entirely of British nationality. Among the singers were such famous names as Norman Allin, Gervase Elwes, and a 'first appearance' of Plunket Greene (singing Stanford's *Songs of the Fleet*). New violinists included Abert Sammons, who, Wood felt, should have acquired an international reputation with his pure tone and impeccable technique – but he was English, and somewhat retiring by nature; and so one of the finest violinists of this century received only a fraction of the recognition that was his due. Two pianists making their first appearances that year and winning instant acclaim were Benno Moiseiwitsch and the 'really wonderful' 11-year-old boy, Solomon, whose grasp of Beethoven's Second Piano Concerto was considered far from childish, and whose tackling of Tchaikovsky's B flat minor was sensational. Wood tells us that this child 'appealed tremendously to the audience with his winning, soulful eyes, his little silk shirt and short knickers'. The piano seemed too large for him, but the music was never beyond his reach. And a few nights after Solomon's début at the Proms, Moiseiwitsch appeared, playing a new work by Ernest Schelling. He brought many more new works (in addition to the standard concerto repertoire) to Prom audiences in the years that followed. From 1914 onwards, he settled permanently in England, becoming a naturalised British subject in 1937.

Two premières of 1914 which Wood considered outstanding were Eugene Goossens's symphonic poem *Perseus* (conducted by the composer) and *Conversations* for piano and orchestra by Walford Davies, with the composer playing the piano part. A Suite by Béla Bartók, whose music was virtually unknown in England, caused some of the orchestra to rebel. They were calmed down by Wood explaining his policy of interpreting *all* schools of music, much of which he did not care for himself – but he was of the opinion that Bartók's music would one day take an important place. To emphasise this conviction, he included Bartók's *Deux Images* later in the season. Frank Bridge conducted his *Dance Rhapsody* and Balfour Gardiner the première of his tone-poem *In Maytime*; while Cyril Scott was represented by *Britain's War-March* (dedicated by permission to HRH The Prince of Wales).

The largest audiences in 1914 were for the Friday classical evenings which now firmly featured 'the three "B"s'. After that first uncertain week, Mondays were Wagner Nights.

The sixty-one concerts of the twenty-first season, 1915, were all, as usual, conducted by Sir Henry Wood except one, on 9 October, when the guest conductor was Mr Thomas Beecham. During this same week Prom audiences heard Moiseiwitsch, Solomon, Albert Sammons, and the many-sided Hamilton Harty, conducting his tone-poem *With the Wild Geese*. A richness, indeed! Another pianist who was to become celebrated, the Australian William Murdoch, made his Prom début that season in Liszt's *Totentanz*. He became at once one of the regular Prom artists.

Wood was constantly re-scoring music: sometimes it was to accord with the orchestral forces available, and sometimes to achieve the maximum effectiveness as he saw it. If he transcribed an organ work of Bach, he believed in forgetting the organ altogether – and he criticised Stokowski for failing to do this. Wood himself was often criticised for inappropriateness of style and for lack of taste in his transcriptions, but in each case he achieved what he set out to achieve – a convincing and effective result in modern orchestral terms, whether one likes it or not. In 1915 his orchestral version of Mussorgsky's *Pictures from an Exhibition* was so successful that it was repeated on the last night. The following year Wood arranged for another version, by a Russian composer Toushmalov, to be performed – a version which (like Stokowski's) boringly leaves out some of the movements for no apparent reason. After the appearance of the famous Ravel version, Wood modestly withdrew his own.

In the 1915 season there were some Russian Nights. Rachmaninov's *The Island of the Dead* (another example of music inspired by painting) was one of the novelties, and a suite of *Fantastic Miniatures* by 'a rising composer' (now sunk beyond trace) Bagrinovsky. There was a 'first in England' of Debussy's *Printemps* and *Le Martyre de S. Sébastien*. The latter, divorced from any dramatic context, made little impact. British novelties included an *African Suite* by Hubert Bath, Bridge's touching *Lament*, the overture *The Boatswain's Mate* by Dr Ethel Smyth, Cowen's *Fantasy of Life and Love* –

the last three works conducted by their composers. Elgar directed a performance of his *Polonia*, and met with a hearty reception.

Between 1916 and the end of the war, the interest and variety of the Prom programmes continued, following the same patterns as before, but novelties were less frequent. In 1916 Prokofiev was only twenty-five, and better known as a pianist than as a composer; his *Scherzo humoristique*, featuring four bassoons, was given its première at a Prom, and later repeated quite often. Rimsky-Korsakov's *Scheherazade* had several performances, making its way to popularity rather slowly; his glittering *Coq d'Or* Suite made more definite impact. Wood was the first to introduce to England the orchestral music of Joaquín Turina – then a representative of the (French-educated) new musical movement in Spain: his *Procesión del Rocío* (Procession of the Virgin of the Dew) made a strong impression, which was confirmed by his *Danzas fantásticas*. Chabrier's *España* became popular about this time, and some pieces by Albéniz, notably *Catalonia*.

A moving novelty in 1917 was George Butterworth's *A Shropshire Lad*, the beautifully-written pastoral by a composer of immense promise, killed in action the previous year at the age of only twenty-one. John Ireland was represented by the première of *The Forgotten Rite*, a work which deserves not to be forgotten. Walford Davies's *Solemn Melody* continued as a Prom favourite, and on the last night there was a *Fantasia on Scottish Melodies* arranged by Wood.

Novelties of 1918 included the Suite *Adventures in a Perambulator*, now the best-known work of the American composer John Alden Carpenter, who died in 1951; and Malipiero's *Impressioni dal Vero* (Impressions from Nature) Part 1 – Part 2 followed later – an example of the 'advanced school of Italian composers'. Wood showed considerable interest in Scriabin, and felt that this problematic composer had really 'found himself' in his Third Symphony, *The Divine Poem*. It made a vivid impression that season.

Among the performers, Moiseiwitsch, Myra Hess, York Bowen, Irene Scharrer, William Murdoch, of the pianists, and Norman Allin, George Baker, Gervase Elwes, of the singers, were firmly established as Prom favourites – besides many other names not so well remembered. Chappell and Company, lessees of Queen's Hall and financial backers of the Proms, were advertising regularly in the programmes of the Proms, drawing attention to the Chappell Ballad Concerts at Queen's Hall and the 'New Songs of the Season' which they published. Also, when Moiseiwitsch, for example, played a concerto, 'Chappell Concert Grand Pianoforte' appeared below the pianist's name. These things were part of the conditions under which Chappell's had agreed to finance the concerts.

10

The Proms flourish

The first post-war season of 1919 opened in a newly decorated Queen's Hall. A bluish green, not very well liked, now became the principal colour, and was to remain until 1937. The improvements and decorations to the Small and the Large Hall were carried out for the Silver Jubilee of the Proms: they included various alterations to the artists' and orchestra's rooms, improvements to the platform and conductor's rostrum, and more efficient sanitary arrangements.

The 1919 season of the Proms was the beginning of a period in which these concerts blossomed with renewed vigour, as if the enforced prunings of wartime had had a specially invigorating effect. A new leader of the orchestra, Charles Woodhouse, was appointed in 1920, so capable in every way that Wood could hand over the baton to him at rehearsal and judge the quality of the orchestra's performance from the body of the hall. When Wood wished to interrupt he would ring a small handbell – a practice which caused frayed nerves and which seems to have been generally unpopular. The standard of playing was improving through a sectional rehearsal system: strings (3 rehearsals), woodwind (2), brass and percussion together (2), followed by full rehearsals.

The highest honour the Royal Philharmonic Society can bestow – the Gold Medal of the Society – was awarded to Sir Henry Wood in 1921 for his outstanding services to music. (Previous recipients included such names as Gounod, Joachim, Brahms, Paderewski, Ysaÿe, Casals.) And in the 1921 season of Proms, a sprightly 26-year-old composer called Malcolm Sargent came on to the rostrum and conducted, with dashing assurance, *An Impression on a Windy Day*. It was not the only composition of his to be played at the Proms (his *Nocturne* and *Scherzo* appeared in 1922); but he was soon to acquire a high reputation as an orchestral, choral and operatic conductor, rather than as a composer.

In the 30th season, 1924, the Proms were given the seal of Royal approval:

King George V and Queen Mary experienced a Prom as it had existed for many years past, with (as a report of the time states) 'its frank enjoyment of every item in the programme, its fraternal affection for Sir Henry J. Wood, and its powers of applause unrivalled by any other assemblage, with the exception possibly of a Cup Tie gathering'. The event was recorded in the King's diary: 'At 8.0 we went to the Promenade at Queen's Hall, such a good orchestra conducted by Sir Henry Wood. House very full, they gave us a great reception and sang the National Anthem at the end.' The King had asked for Elgar's Overture *Cockaigne*, 'O Star of eve' from *Tannhäuser*, and Wood's *Fantasia on British Sea-Songs*. There was no royal box at Queen's Hall (it had been taken away a long time before, because uneconomically it was taking up too much room in the Grand Circle); so, instead, a whole block of seats to the left of the platform was reserved for the Royal party. Elgar, Master of the King's Musick, conducted the Overture himself; and later in the programme another distinguished composer, Frank Bridge, conducted his Suite *The Sea*. Wood also included a suite which had always been one of his favourites   from André Wormser's 'charming' *L'Enfant prodigue*, a play (with music) which he had seen several times and enjoyed as far back as 1891. It was considered 'wiser and safer' on this occasion to play only two movements of the Beethoven Violin Concerto. The soloist was a well-established Prom personality, Jelly d'Aranyi, after whose first appearance in 1920 Wood had written: 'What a personality and what a born violinist! The Promenade audience was completely carried away by her fire and dash.'

The King congratulated Wood (together with Elgar and Bridge) during the interval, and sent for Wood again at the end of the concert to tell him how much he had enjoyed the Sea-Songs. His Majesty found *Rule, Britannia* 'a jolly fine tune' and better than *The Red Flag*. The full programme was:

Wednesday, October 15th, at 8
GOD SAVE THE KING

OVERTURE –	–	– Cockaigne (In London Town)	–	–	*Elgar*
	(Conducted by the Composer)				
SUITE –	–	– L'Enfant Prodigue	–	–	– *Wormser*
SONGS with Orchestra	(*a*) Lament of Isis	–	–	–	*Bantock*
	(*b*) Invocation to the Nile	–	–	–	
VIOLIN CONCERTO in D (Adagio and Rondo)		–	–	–	– *Beethoven*
ARIA –	–	– O star of eve (*Tannhäuser*) –	–	–	*Wagner*
SUITE –	–	– – The Sea –	–	–	*Frank Bridge*
	(Conducted by the Composer)				

ENTR'ACTE AND VALSE (*Coppélia*)   –   –   –   –   –   –   *Delibes*
FANTASIA ON BRITISH SEA-SONGS   –   –   –   *Arr. by Sir Henry J. Wood*

GOD SAVE THE KING
Miss Leila Megane
Mr. Eric Marshall
Solo Violin - Mlle. Jelly d'Aranyi

Now the Proms were a 'national institution'. Wood was fifty-five, knighted, established, but in no sense in a rut, respected by all for his self-less commitment to his art, his undiminished energy always stretching him to the full – and beyond. As though his immense work-load were not enough, he took on, from 1923, weekly rehearsals with the students' orchestra of the Royal Academy of Music, and became so attached to this work that he continued with it for the rest of his life, often at considerable personal sacrifice, only missing these rehearsals when absolutely compelled to do so. The achievements of this students' orchestra were often for him a source of pride and considerable satisfaction, and he never regarded it as a chore. He later made the Academy a gift of his library of 2800 orchestral scores and 1920 sets of parts, all with his own careful and practical markings; also a financial endowment to help students.

The sudden death of Robert Newman, towards the end of 1926, at the age of sixty-nine, cast a dark shadow over Queen's Hall and immediately raised questions about the future of the Proms. Wood in his memoirs wrote of his closeness to the man who had originally conceived the idea of the Proms, and with whom he had worked for thirty-two seasons realising this vision, through the many years before government subsidies had been heard of: 'Our friendship had been built and maintained on an artistic and business basis, even though neither of our private lives seemed ever to enter it. We never argued and we never fell out . . .' Wood's arrangement of Chopin's Funeral March was played in his memory at the Queen's Hall concert on 6 November 1926, just as previously it had been played as an *in memoriam* tribute to Joachim, Grieg, Sarasate.

W. W. Thompson, who was later to become the BBC's Concert Manager, had been Newman's assistant since 1916 as the result of a chance reply to a newspaper advertisement. He was sixteen then and it was a time when top hats and tail coats were still worn at daytime concerts by the manager and his chief assistants. Having studied with Dr Stanley Marchant, Thompson had musical as well as business qualifications. It was he who now, ten years later, stepped into Newman's shoes and took over the management of the Queen's Hall Orchestra with (in Wood's words) 'assurance, tact, and ability'.

11

The Music 1919-1926

There were some unusual novelties in the 1919 season. For example, the *Sinfonia sacra* by the French organist and composer Widor, whom Wood considered to be a musician of outstanding talents. Dr Stanley Marchant played the solo organ part. And Casella's ballet music *Le Couvent sur l'eau*, one of several twentieth-century Italian works which Wood introduced to England. This was followed by Casella's stark *Pagine di Guerra* (War Pages) in 1920. (At a Sunday afternoon concert Casella was pianist in Franck's *Symphonic Variations*, which he played, according to Wood, 'so brilliantly that I wonder he has not visited us again'.) There was the 'first in England' of Mussorgsky's *Nursery Songs*, arranged by Wood, and a novelty by the somewhat Teutonic French composer Florent Schmitt – his *Rêves* (Op. 65). English composers made a good showing: the première of a *Scherzo* for orchestra by Bax, of Quilter's *Children's Overture*, and of Coates's Suite *Summer Days*, conducted by the composer. Holst conducted one of his most imaginative works, the *Japanese Suite*. Lord Berners – composer, writer, diplomat and (like Wood) painter – was represented by the première of his satirical *Fantaisie espagnole*, and in the same programme were Spanish dances by Granados, one of the composers whose music was being satirised by Berners.

In 1920 the Wagner evenings followed a new pattern: instead of miscellaneous items they consisted of substantial selections from particular music-dramas using the best available singers – and this proved an unqualified success with the public. Beethoven on Fridays and the popular Saturday nights drew large houses. Pianists included Myra Hess, Harriet Cohen, Leonard Borwick, Harold Samuel, Lamond and Francesco Ticciati ('a talented pupil of Busoni'), and there were distinguished string soloists, too – Jelly d'Aranyi, Isolde Menges, May and Beatrice Harrison.

Eighteen novelties were produced that season, eight of them premières. Of the ten by British composers the most important was Arnold Bax's

Symphonic Variations for piano and orchestra in which the soloist (making the first of numerous appearances at Proms) was Harriet Cohen. 'Her devotion to the music of Bax', wrote Wood, 'has been a noble gesture, and her continued and persistent interest in his splendid piano works is deserving of all praise.' There was another success for Eugene Goossens – the première of his symphonic poem *The Eternal Rhythm* (the rhythm of nature and its effect on the free mind). Another première, also conducted by the composer, was Herbert Howells's *Merry Eye* (and his famous *Procession* was to follow in 1922). Landon Ronald's Suite from an exotic theatre production, *The Garden of Allah*, was well received. Eric Fogg, later on the staff of the BBC and the composer of a famous bassoon concerto, was then seventeen; his ballet suite *The Golden Butterfly* was bold and adventurous – and well received. York Bowen and Armstrong Gibbs conducted works of their own that season, as did the Scottish composer William Wallace (no connection with the composer of *Maritana*) – his symphonic poem *François Villon*, which is considered his most representative work.

Among foreign novelties that season, Fauré's delightful *Fantaisie* for piano and orchestra and his *Masques et Bergamasques* had their 'first in England': so, too, did piano concertos by Prokofiev (No. 1) and Selim Palmgren (No. 2, 'The River').

Despite terrible summer weather, the overall attendance in the 1921 season was extremely good, with some falling off on Tuesdays and Thursdays, the evenings on which novelties most often appeared. On Wednesdays symphonies by Dvořák, Tchaikovsky, Brahms, Scriabin, Mozart and Borodin were successfully presented. Wagner on Mondays, Bach and Beethoven on Fridays always drew good houses, and the popular Saturday nights were always crowded. The death of an important Prom singer, Gervase Elwes, was deeply felt.

It was a good season for British composers. Many important works (not necessarily new) were brought before a large and receptive public. There were two performances of Elgar's great symphonic poem *Falstaff*, both conducted by the composer. Frank Bridge again conducted his suite *The Sea*, and Holst three movements of *The Planets*. Dr Malcolm Sargent, as already noted, conducted his *Impression on a Windy Day*, insisting in the programme note that the piece was not to be thought of as merely descriptive. In the same programme Wood conducted Scriabin's *Poème de l'Extase* and Spivakovsky was the soloist in Tchaikovsky's B flat minor Piano Concerto. Brailowsky and Pouishnoff were among the other pianists appearing that season. Albert Sammons played Delius's Violin Concerto.

The British novelty which aroused most interest was the 30-year-old

Arthur Bliss's *Mêlée Fantasque*, because it showed outstanding promise. A work by Bernard van Dieren, *Introito*, provoked conflicting criticism, and the late George Butterworth's two *Folk-song Idylls* became inevitably part of the English orchestral repertoire. Other British composers represented that season were Ethel Smyth, Desirée MacEwan, Dorothy Howell, Bantock, Cyril Scott, Edric Cundell and Eric Coates. Foreign novelties included a Suite by the Italian composer Santoliquido, and a 'very difficult' modern work by Béla Bartók – his *Rhapsody* for piano and orchestra. There was a Piano Concertino by John Alden Carpenter, and Järnefelt's Suite *The Promised Land*.

Saint-Saëns's music had always appeared frequently at the Proms, and in 1921 his Fantasia *Africa* was performed, with Harold Craxton as solo pianist. There was also an effective *Poema gregoriano* for piano and orchestra by the young Italian pianist Francesco Ticciati, who took part.

The Proms had never known such packed houses as during the ten-week season of 1922. It seemed that, after the uncertainties of the war, the public were now in a more settled state and could enjoy the musical benefits which the Proms offered. London's expanding musical culture was not just for the privileged few, but drew all classes of society. This public was becoming increasingly discriminating in its appreciation both of the artists and of the music offered. They would not accept benevolently, for example, the (complete) *Petrushka* ballet music of Stravinsky, which appeared that season ('a work of indisputable and daring originality', as the programme described it), or *Juventus* by Victor de Sabata, representing the youngest generation of Italian composers, or the highly dissonant Suite No. 2 of Milhaud. There was some hissing of all these works.

Foreign novelties also included Roussel's *Pour une Fête de Printemps*, a version of some instrumental music of Monteverdi, and Ernest Bloch's *Schelomo*. There were also a large number of English novelties, usually conducted by the composers themselves: Bridge's Christmas Dance, *Sir Roger de Coverley*, and *Joyous Youth* by Eric Coates were among them, but most have sunk into oblivion. On the other hand, many successful works of past seasons were given a fresh hearing, including Bax's *November Woods*, Holst's ballet music from *The Perfect Fool*, and Elgar's full-bodied orchestration of Bach's Fantasia and Fugue in C minor.

Maggie Teyte impressed with her interpretation of Tatiana's Letter Song from *Eugene Onegin*. (She had changed the spelling of her name from Tate, because the French made it sound like 'Tart'!) That outstanding violinist Marie Hall had achieved a sensational success with Tchaikovsky's Violin Concerto at Queen's Hall under Wood in 1903 at the age of nineteen, and since her marriage in 1911 had made comparatively few public appearances. Now in 1922 she appeared again at a Prom, playing successfully this same work. Walford Davies was pianist in his own *Memorial Suite* (written for an RAF memorial service).

The opening night of the 1923 season included the 'Grande Fantaisie Zoölogique', *The Carnival of the Animals*, by Saint-Saëns – the first performance in England of a work which was to become an overwhelmingly popular favourite. The composer, who despised this composition, had forbidden performances of it in his lifetime (he died in 1921). There were, in all, twenty-two novelties this year, the most interesting being Holst's Fugal Overture and Fugal Concerto, the Violin Concerto in D by the Hungarian composer and pianist Ernö Dohnányi (or Ernst von Dohnányi, as he preferred to be called), with Isolde Menges as soloist, the symphonic poem *Sortilegi* (Witchcraft) by Riccardo Pick-Mangiagalli, of the young Italian school, and one Russian work, *Alastor*, by Miaskovsky. Arthur Bliss's Concerto for tenor solo, piano, strings and percussion was heard: later the composer withdrew it, and it reappeared in 1933 as a Concerto for two pianos and orchestra.

Beatrice Harrison played the Elgar Cello Concerto that season – a work which became very much associated with her. Henry Wood made a characteristic orchestration of Handel's Organ Concerto in G minor, and the soloist was Frederick B. Kiddle, the permanent and utterly reliable organist and piano accompanist of the Proms from 1902 to 1927. Members of the orchestra continued to appear regularly as soloists, including the leader, Charles Woodhouse, and Léon Goossens, now recognised as a great oboist. In 1923 Wood had reason to admonish Léon Goossens in a letter, for being 'so intensely humorous during concerts and rehearsals'. He went on:

> No one appreciates more than I do the buoyancy of your spirits, which I hope you may long keep, but there is a time and a place for everything, and it is certainly not either the band rehearsal or when you are under the eyes of several thousand members of an audience. Probably you do not realise that every little note scribbled, every message passed round, and every little joke is noticed by a number of the audience and found very distracting by some . . .

To which, very reasonably, Goossens replied: 'I am tremendously sorry for the worry and trouble I have caused you and only wish I had been pulled up before.' In this straightforward, pleasant manner could differences be ironed out.

Two important Prom singers made their first appearance at this time, Isobel (Bella) Baillie and Astra Desmond. Wood's immediate impression of

Isobel Baillie was of 'a young and pretty girl with masses of golden hair and a voice equally golden' – and always note-perfect whatever she was singing. The charming Astra Desmond also 'looked as well as she sang' and was immediately successful in Erda's Warning (from *Das Rheingold*). There was a first appearance, too, for José Iturbi, the pianist who became a Hollywood film-star. And the Halifax Madrigal Society sang Bach's motet *Singet dem Herrn*, and madrigals and part-songs, for the first time at a Prom.

For a change, the 1924 season contained no novelties, but became more like a consolidation of past successes, including Sargent's *Impression on a Windy Day*, Eric Fogg's Suite *The Golden Butterfly*, and *The Sea* by Bridge – each conducted by its composer. The dominating event was the visit by the King and Queen on 15 October. Mostly the concerts followed the same pattern as before, but Tuesday evenings, formerly devoted to miscellaneous programmes, were transformed into 'early classical' nights, featuring two short symphonies, often Mozart and Haydn – which drew better audiences. Friday programmes were exploring (amongst much else) the concertos of Bach for one, two, three and four keyboards, using of course pianos, not harpsichords. The violin concertos of Bach were also proving popular – especially, as one would expect, the Double Concerto in D minor. Wood was never presenting Bach in a dry, mechanical way, but always with vitality and a full, warm expressive range.

1925 followed the traditional pattern, but organ solos became a prominent ingredient in the Saturday programmes, with such well-known artists as Edward C. Bairstow, G. D. Cunningham and Harold Darke. Among singers, Steuart Wilson and Keith Falkner made their débuts, as did the harpist Marie Goossens – yet another member of that talented family – and the pianists Walter Gieseking and the 18-year-old Clifford Curzon, playing Schubert very poetically from the start. The part-song ingredient, started two years before, was established on a weekly basis on Thursday evenings by The English Singers, introducing Prommers to the vast national treasure of madrigals, motets, balletts, and to the folk-song arrangements of contemporary composers (Holst, Vaughan Williams, and others). In similar vein, there was a group of string pieces by Orlando Gibbons, commemorating the tercentenary of that composer's death. English novelties by George Dyson, Ethel Smyth, and Susan Spain-Dunk were produced, and there were some unusual ones from abroad, including Ibert's *Ballad of Reading Gaol*, an orchestral piece based on Oscar Wilde. Wilde was also the inspiration for the Austrian composer Franz Schreker's ballet music, *Birthday of the Infanta*, scored for an exceptionally large orchestra. The most striking new works were undoubtedly Honegger's *Pacific 231* (impressions of an American railway engine) and Bartók's highly original *Dance Suite*. Holst's *The Planets* were no longer new; this season five of them were heard (Venus, Mercury, Saturn, Uranus and Jupiter, in that order) as well as his *St Paul's* Suite. Harriet Cohen was the soloist in Falla's nine-year-old *Nights in the Gardens of Spain*.

So to the last season of the Proms under the management of Robert Newman. Attendances generally in 1926 were high. When, exceptionally, there were poor houses, it was difficult to find the reason. Wagner and the classics remained the strongest attraction, and a new development in taste was shown in the programmes where Bach and Handel predominated – on alternate Wednesdays – which never failed to attract large, enthusiastic audiences.

The fine Australian singer Florence Austral, who had made a strong impression on the last night of 1924, appeared again in 1926, and Joseph Hislop and Peter Dawson were not new to Prom audiences. A young Russian pianist, Nicholas Orloff, made an impressive first appearance at the Proms in the *Emperor* Concerto, while Clifford Curzon was heard in a new French work, Germaine Tailleferre's *Ballade* for piano and orchestra. The array of fine pianists also included Myra Hess, Moiseiwitsch, Irene Scharrer and Harriet Cohen. For the Brahms Violin Concerto Jelly d'Aranyi was soloist, while Egon Petri played Mozart; and in a Mozart horn concerto Aubrey Brain, from the orchestra, displayed the capabilities and the poetry of his instrument in the now legendary family style. With Brain, Hislop and Curzon together in the same programme, the concert of 22 September 1926 must have been a memorable one.

Wednesday, September 22nd, at 8

OVERTURE – – – Leonora No. 2 – – – –	*Beethoven*
ARIA – – – Cangio d'aspetto (*Admeto*) – – –	*Handel*
BALLADE for Pianoforte and Orchestra – – –	*Germaine Tailleferre*
ARIA – – – O Paradiso (*L'Africana*) – – –	*Meyerbeer*
HORN CONCERTO No. 4, in E flat (K.495) – – – – –	*Mozart*
SYMPHONY No. 1, in B flat – – – – – –	*Schumann*
THREE DANCES (Nusch-Nuschi) – – – – –	*Hindemith*
SLAVONIC DANCE No. 1, in C (1st Series) – – – – –	*Dvořák*

Miss Marjorie Burt

Mr. Joseph Hislop

Solo Pianoforte - Mr. Clifford Curzon

Solo Horn - Mr. Aubrey Brain

The season included new works by Malipiero (Italy), Vincent d'Indy

(France), the Concerto for Orchestra, Op. 38, by Hindemith (Germany), the *Ruralia hungarica* by Dohnányi (Hungary). Honegger's *Pacific 231* had proved such a fascinating curiosity the previous year that it was repeated at the opening concert of the 1926 season. English composers were well represented, and many conducted new works of their own: a Viola Concerto by Gordon Jacob, the overture *The Wreckers* by Dame Ethel Smyth, another overture by a female composer, *The Kentish Downs* by Susan Spain-Dunk, Arthur Bliss's Introduction and Allegro for full orchestra (not for strings only, like Elgar's), Frederic Austin's Suite of incidental music for Karel Čapek's *Insect Play*, the overture to Rutland Boughton's *The Queen of Cornwall* (a choral drama on the Tristan-and-Isolde theme), and Vaughan Williams's *Pastoral* Symphony (in a programme which also included Falla's *El Amor Brujo*). Years later Wood wrote that he had presented almost every orchestral work of Vaughan Williams at the Proms, and invariably the composer had been at the rehearsals, always ready with helpful suggestions. The Fourth Symphony, in Wood's opinion, had 'beaten these striving-for-originality moderns at their own game, but with a far stronger *musical* result'. But Vaughan Williams is reported to have said, 'If this is modern music, I don't like it!'

The ominous absence of Newman during this Prom season called for some explanation, and the following note appeared in the programme of the last night:

> The familiar presence of Mr Robert Newman, the popular founder and manager of the Promenade Concerts, has been greatly missed at Queen's Hall during the last few weeks. In all the thirty-two years since the first inauguration of the 'Proms' Mr Newman has never before been absent for a single evening. His assiduous attention to business and to the service of the musical public are too well known to need comment. In answer to many kind enquiries we regret to say that Mr Newman is still too seriously indisposed to be here this evening, but he will no doubt have the thoughts and the sympathy of his many friends present among the audience of the Promenade Concerts.

12

The BBC becomes involved

At Queen's Hall, on the wall of the Second Circle behind the seat which Newman usually occupied at concerts, a small brass tablet was placed. (It did not survive the great fire of 1941 which destroyed the building.)

In Memory of
ROBERT NEWMAN
b. 1858 – d. 1926
Founder of the Promenade Concerts
Queen's Hall
And for thirty-two years
Manager of the Concerts
of the Queen's Hall Orchestra

Before he died, Newman had confided to Percy Scholes (then music critic for the BBC and for *The Observer*) his belief that the future of the Proms lay with the BBC and his wish for an arrangement with Chappell's whereby a part of the expenses could be borne by the BBC in return for being allowed to broadcast part of each concert. William Boosey, then managing director of Chappell's, had been fighting a losing battle against the broadcasting of music, believing that it spelled the end of concert-giving, and a private meeting arranged at Scholes's flat between Newman and John Reith, the Director of the BBC, had produced no immediate results.

Orchestras, like opera, have always needed patronage. State subsidies for music are a recent thing in England. The Proms had been lucky to find the necessary backing – from Dr Cathcart, from a swings-and-roundabouts arrangement by Newman at Queen's Hall, from Sir Edgar Speyer, and finally from a commercial backer, Chappell and Co. For Chappell's it was a worthwhile scheme in a business sense, because they had a platform for their own publications in the lighter Part 2 of each programme, and Chappell pianos were mainly used at the concerts. At the same time, such considerations did not restrict the scope of the concerts, and there was always a lot of musical interest in the shorter second half of the programmes as well as in the first.

William Boosey's anti-BBC attitude had been clearly expressed in a letter which he had written to *The Daily Telegraph* on 19 May 1923.

> No one in the entertainment world is so foolish as to imagine that broadcasting can be opposed or wiped out. It has obviously come to stay. The objection of the entertainment world is against broadcasting under its present conditions. The first thing that the public should appreciate, and which they do not yet appreciate, is that the Broadcasting Company is a big commercial concern exploited by very able business men. In other words, the Broadcasting Company is a competitor of the entertainment industry, paying no entertainment tax, but being absolutely subsidized by the Government. It is in the extraordinary position that it has obtained from the Post Office a monopoly for trading, and the curious thing is that the bulk of its trading is bound at the present moment to be at the expense of other people's property. The very form of its licence, as drafted by the late Postmaster-General, who is now a director of the Marconi Wireless, states in so many words that although broadcasting must pay a subsidy to various Press agencies for cables, etc., it may use theatrical entertainments and concert matter without payment. This amazing licence, of course, cannot override the Copyright Act of 1911, which protects authors' and composers' rights, but for what it is worth it is part of this licence handed to this big trading company.

It was generally known that the Proms were being run at a loss, and with the cost of everything rising since the war, the loss became larger each year. Orchestral musicians, who had previously put up with low fees, were now banding themselves together to form the Musicians' Union and demanding better terms of service. Early in 1927 rumours were rife that the Proms were in peril. The death of Newman seemed to have clinched matters. Finally, on 7 March 1927 it was publicly announced that Chappell's would no longer be able to support the Promenade and Symphony Concerts at Queen's Hall. The *Musical Times* commented that 'everybody raised shocked eyebrows', but the right attitude should have been gratitude to the firm who had subsidised the Proms at a considerable loss each season – and the crisis might indeed have proved a blessing in disguise if it could have led to a sorting-out of the general muddled state of concert finance in England. Public feeling was strong that Sir Henry Wood and his Orchestra must not be lost to London. *The Times* observed that other countries, too, had admired the Henry Wood Proms and had sought to imitate this enterprise.

Wood issued a statement to the press:

> I am, of course, the greatest admirer of what Messrs Chappell have done. The
> scheme has not been a financial success so far as they are concerned. They
> have seen us through, and all we musicians, orchestral players and artists, are
> very grateful to them. They have carried on for years and must have lost
> something like £60,000 in the interests of the musical public of London and
> of England. But they do not see the commercial value of running the Queen's
> Hall Orchestra any longer.
>
> I think I am right in saying we have done more to encourage British artists
> than any other organisation. We employ young people and encourage young
> artists, and the 'Promenades' have such world-wide fame that it would be a
> very serious thing for our reputation on the Continent if they ceased. It would
> indeed give them an opportunity to call us unmusical.
>
> It would be a disgrace to this country if the 'Promenades' were to go. But
> we have done so much that I am sure that we are going to do a great deal
> more. The education that has been given to the public is going to tell, and the
> help given by broadcasting and by very fine gramophone records is, I am
> sure, going to bear very great fruit in the future.

A drawing in *Punch*, by the famous artist Sir Bernard Partridge (see
illustration opposite) expressed pungently what was generally felt.

1927 was the year in which the young British Broadcasting Company
became a Corporation under Royal Charter, with the mandate '*to inform,
educate, and entertain*'. The BBC's Director, John Reith, went further: the
aims of broadcasting were to promote 'the highest interests of the community and of the nation at large'. And the BBC was not then short of money
to do things within the terms of its Charter. Already, with a former Proms
personality, Percy Pitt, as music director since 1923, the BBC had considerable experience in the organising of concerts and other kinds of music
programmes, and it welcomed the opportunity to take over an already
famous and musically (if not financially) very successful series. Negotiations
with Chappell's were started, but proved complex and difficult. William
Boosey's attitude seemed to be that if his terms were not accepted there
could be no Proms. The BBC, however, was able to indicate that it could
perfectly well put on Proms itself, using a different hall (the Central Hall,
Westminster, for example). At last they reached agreement, in terms rather
favourable to Chappell's, both for the taking over of Proms and the renting
of the Queen's Hall for a series of winter Symphony Concerts. A new
contract for the orchestra was negotiated with the Musicians' Union, and
the enterprise became in the process far more costly than before. But the

FOR THE HONOUR OF LONDON

SHADE OF BEETHOVEN (Father of Modern Symphonic Music) to Sir
Henry Wood: 'This is indeed tragic, but I cannot believe that this rich
city, once so generous to me, will fail to find us a permanent home.'

broadcasting side was a major justification, providing good 'live' orchestral music every evening for a season, and establishing from the start what has been an important side of the BBC music policy: namely, some element of promotion in broadcasting – not merely a *reflection* of what is happening in the musical world.

So, in May 1927, the BBC issued the following press notice:

SAVING THE PROMENADES

The BBC announces that ever since the possible suspension of the Queen's Hall Promenades was announced, the Corporation has been anxious to do whatever was in its power, consistent with its wider obligations, to bring about an arrangement not only with regard to the Promenades, but also on the larger issue of the Queen's Hall.

Negotiations have been in progress for several months. A number of proposals have been considered and abandoned. Ultimately, however, agreement has been reached between the BBC and Messrs Chappell.

A six weeks series of Promenade Concerts at the Queen's Hall, *starting on Saturday, August 13*, is to be given by the BBC, under the conductorship of Sir Henry Wood. The BBC is also to give twelve special Symphony Concerts at the Queen's Hall during next season. Moreover, the microphone is no longer banned from the Queen's Hall for other occasions.

The news had come as a surprise to the manager, W. W. Thompson, as he explained:

William Boosey of Chappell's telephoned to ask if I thought sufficient time was available to put on a series in August as usual. It took my breath away but without stopping to think of the difficulties I said immediately 'Yes' . . . Within an hour the wheels were again in motion and all was set for the third phase of Prom history.

When the British Broadcasting Company became a Corporation in 1927, it freed itself from connections with radio manufacturers and achieved a new independence. During the four years of its existence it had already developed an impressive musical output. In 1927 music formed about two-thirds of all programmes (this is stated in the BBC annual report for that year as presented to Parliament). Listeners who wrote to the BBC were about equally divided between wanting classical music and wanting dance music. A Wireless Military Band had been formed; also a permanent orchestra in Wales, to give regular concerts there. The Corporation contrived to co-operate with such bodies as the Hallé Concert Society and the British National Opera Company. Besides symphony concerts in the studios, many were given in public and broadcast. In the early part of the year there was a series at the Albert Hall with 150 players and eminent conductors, British and foreign, and including such works as the Berlioz *Requiem* and Honegger's *King David*. Later, there was a series at Queen's Hall and at the People's Palace (in the Mile End Road, now part of Queen Mary College) featuring some new works from the Carnegie Collection of British music. And, most successful, there was the six-week series of Promenade Concerts which the BBC had just taken over. Light music and dance music were also given their fair share. There were weekly chamber music programmes, including an international series, and twenty-nine special performances of opera from the studios, in addition to relays from Covent Garden and provincial theatres. Cantatas, oratorios and other sacred works were presented too: fifteen works by British composers were performed for the first time. There were special programmes, such as a concert of Elgar's music on his seventieth birthday, and programmes for Empire Day and Dominion Day. A total of 886,000 copies of the libretti of studio operas were issued during the year. And 'music appreciation' talks by Sir Walford Davies and Percy Scholes became popular.

Such, in brief outline, is an impression of the range of musical achievement of the BBC in 1927. The policy had remained consistent. As far as the Proms were concerned, the general shape and character of the programmes remained unaltered: the BBC was prepared to trust the judgement of the man who had a profound knowledge of what the public wanted and what it could be made to want. Continuity was therefore achieved in the takeover.

There were some improvements. First, the programme was printed as a booklet – still with admirable notes by Mrs Rosa Newmarch (now assisted by Eric Blom). Some people, however, preferred the large single folder which had been the format from the very first season in 1895 – a folder where everything could be seen clearly and at a glance. But that never returned.

More important, the 'platitunes', as they were sometimes called, in Part 2 – the sentimental ballads about Mother of Mine, the cottage by the waterfall, June, and so on – were dropped, and replaced by songs of quality. For example, on the first night of the Proms under BBC control, the songs in Part 2 (with piano accompaniment) were by Schubert, Roger Quilter and Parry; and they increased in range and adventurousness throughout the thirties – French, German, Italian, Scandinavian, Russian – extending even to Medtner. Wood was fortunate to have Berkeley Mason as his organist and accompanist from 1928 onwards, right into the war years – a job which was often taken for granted but required very good musicianship together with a lot of tact and understanding. Berkeley Mason's predecessor, Frederick Kiddle, had been another distinguished organist and piano accompanist.

Everybody seemed very pleased with the coming-together of the Proms and broadcasting. Including Sir Henry Wood. A microphone was now hanging over his head at Queen's Hall, to transmit the first part of every concert into millions of homes. His feelings were expressed in a public statement:

> With the wholehearted support of the wonderful medium of broadcasting, I feel that I am at last on the threshold of realising my life-long ambition of truly democratising the message of music, and making its beneficent effect universal . . . I am quite convinced that not only in music, but generally, the medium of broadcasting, as utilised and developed in this country, is one of the few elements ordinarily associated with the progress of civilisation which I can heartily endorse.

The orchestra was the same one as before, with Charles Woodhouse as leader, but its name had to be changed. Its original title, 'The Queen's Hall Orchestra', was owned by Speyer, who refused to release it when Chappell's took over. (He passed it on to Wood.) The solution then was to call it 'The New Queen's Hall Orchestra'. Now Chappell's refused to let the BBC have *that* title, and a way out was found in 'Sir Henry Wood and his Symphony Orchestra' – which lasted for three seasons until it was merged with the London Wireless Orchestra as the nucleus of 'The BBC Symphony Orchestra' in 1930.

The take-over by the BBC had, amongst other things, one very happy result for Wood: instead of three rehearsals (of three hours each) for six concerts, he was allowed twice as much – *daily* rehearsals – and, after a time, preliminary rehearsals on four days before the first concert. He was allowed *extra* players when the score demanded it: too often in the past he had had to edit a work to avoid having a bass clarinet, for example, or a second harp, which the composer specially asked for. And he was now, as he put it, 'free from the everlasting programme-*versus*-box-office problem for the first time in thirty-two years'.

The BBC retained W. W. ('Tommy') Thompson as manager. He had had to decide whether to stay with Chappell's or with the Proms and become a BBC official. At a loss of salary he chose the latter, and did not regret it, for he was soon appointed BBC Concerts Manager, which meant being responsible for the Proms and all other BBC-originated public orchestral concerts as well. Trained in the Newman school, astute on the business side, knowing how to handle orchestral musicians and their problems, and with a wide experience of coping with temperamental and often grasping soloists (British and foreign), he was exactly the right person for the job. Wood was glad to have this link with past and present. Above all, it came as an immense sense of relief to feel that his life work had been saved, and that he was working with people who were helpful, understanding, and always prepared to discuss programmes and other matters in a positive way. (The atmosphere did not remain like that always, however.)

Rosa Newmarch, writing in the programme of the opening concerts of 1927, remarks:

Sir Henry's capacity for fresh enterprise seems to grow with the years. Those who work with him realise that he is more interested in his art than in himself; therefore he is never bored. This enviable and joyous keenness for every branch and phase of music is the secret of his perpetual flow of vigour and enthusiasm. He is essentially a sower – a broadcaster.

The spirit of broadcasting – the democratic appeal – was felt to be in complete accord with the spirit of the Proms, which were always intended for a general audience. The writer Ernest Newman expressed the view that 'more and more each year the musical destinies of the country will be bound up with the activities of the BBC'.

People were wondering whether the Promenade Concerts would win new listeners for the BBC. Many who had the wireless scarcely bothered to listen – so much of the broadcast material was trivial and commonplace. But the BBC offered two alternative programmes – one of a general, thoughtful kind; the other light and entertaining. The BBC had the necessary funds to finance good music; and they could *popularise* good music. The trash in the Prom programmes had been eliminated. Edwin Evans (a future regular programme-note writer for the Proms), writing in *Time and Tide* on 2 September 1927, had this to say:

So far the predictions of the pessimists that our promenaders, instead of rallying once more to the old flag, would settle in their armchairs and turn on the loudspeaker, have proved the very reverse of correct.

And in fact the broadcasting of these concerts did not diminish their attendance-figures in the least, any more than it does now. The extra publicity seemed to increase the interest considerably, and in 1927 the 2/– Promenade was fuller than usual.

There was a general feeling that the Proms were presenting a very comprehensive survey of the masterworks of the past, with imaginative excursions into recent and present musical developments. The 3000-odd

who came to Queen's Hall on a good night were now only a fraction of the
total listening audience – in the provinces, as far afield as Scotland, and even
across the Channel.

And what of the standard of performance? Blemishes which might go by
unnoticed in the atmosphere of a concert hall became more obvious in the
detached listening conditions of a broadcast. What was Wood achieving?
Perhaps *The Times* of 20 August 1927 gave a fair summing-up, with which
few would disagree:

> The performances may not always be entirely satisfactory to the connoisseur,
> but they are invariably workmanlike, and the actual playing is far better this
> year. To demand of a single conductor an absolute standard of perfection in
> all styles of music would be to ask the impossible. Let us be grateful for what
> we are given – a plain, unvarnished reading of the scores, which enables us,
> each according to his bent, to estimate a composer's relative worth and his
> place in history, to surrender to the enchantment of imaginations stronger
> than our own, or just to take an hour's pleasure in the sensuous beauty of
> musical sound.

Another critic, Filson Young, writing earlier, described Wood as 'a great
master of savage rhythm and of extreme nuances, but not of those subtler
dynamic variations . . . he can always produce an effect, but he is not so
good at interpreting a condition or a mood'. Was it not, in fact, because he
had to give *so many* performances each week of such a wide range of works,
as safely and satisfactorily as possible, with always very limited rehearsal?
He asserted categorically that no work with which he was connected was
ever performed in public unrehearsed. But one of the Prom violinists, Daisy
Kennedy (wife of John Drinkwater), had caused something of a sensation on
one occasion, when her memory failed her in the Brahms Concerto and she
publicly announced that this had happened because she had not had a
rehearsal. If this was true, it was certainly an exceptional case.

An assurance on the general standard of performance was given by Sir
Adrian Boult in a broadcast talk on 13 February 1938.

> . . . Every minute of the Promenade rehearsal is planned beforehand, and
> everybody knows exactly when everything is to be rehearsed. In particular I
> find myself marvelling at the way Sir Henry manages to insinuate a new or
> difficult work into the rehearsal scheme some days before its performance, so
> that it gets the benefit of several rehearsals, with the result that even the worst
> performance of the Promenade season can still be called a fine one, and the
> average is something far finer than that.

For its second season, 1928, the BBC tried to save the expense of hiring Henry Wood's orchestra by asking him whether he would carry out the Proms with the BBC's own London Wireless Orchestra – an extremely versatile and flexible body which could give a symphony concert one day, accompany a musical comedy or a revue the next, take part in an opera or oratorio the following evening, and so on. Correspondence in the BBC archives shows that Wood was not at all happy about this suggestion, and he even accuses his former Prom colleague, the then BBC Director of Music, Percy Pitt, of unreasonable and unfair treatment. Whatever might happen, however, Wood wanted to keep Charles Woodhouse as leader of the orchestra. In the event, the BBC eventually gave way and allowed Wood to continue with his own orchestra – which he did, for two more seasons. Then, in 1930, an advance guard of ninety players of the newly-forming BBC Symphony Orchestra, led by Charles Woodhouse, was used for the Prom season – before making its official début with 114 players, under the leadership of Arthur Catterall, in the first of the BBC Symphony Concerts at Queen's Hall on 22 October. This large body of players, which had absorbed both the old Queen's Hall Orchestra and the London Wireless Orchestra, was formed as a permanent full-time symphony orchestra, with continuity and entity established on a 'no deputy' basis. It was the aim of the BBC that its Symphony Orchestra should set a standard for English orchestral playing and should bear comparison with the finest orchestras in the world. The best players obtainable were secured for the principal positions, and the rank and file, too, were very carefully chosen. They would play under the most eminent conductors.[1]

When playing for the Proms, this orchestra was led, until 1934, by Charles Woodhouse. He had been leader at the Proms for fifteen seasons, when he had to resign through ill-health, and Wood (in consultation with the BBC orchestral manager of the time, R. C. Pratt) further demonstrated his championing of the cause of women players by appointing Marie Wilson as leader for the Proms. For years she had shared the first desk with the leader, and Wood knew that she could be trusted with this highly responsible job – although there were some who still maintained that a woman could not 'stay the course' of a Prom season. She proved her powers, as Wood relates, 'and finally banished any fear of women not being able to hold their own with men in symphony orchestras'.

The physical and mental strain on the ninety-strong BBC Symphony Orchestra was of course immense: they would play, as was customary, every

---

[1] See Nicholas Kenyon's study, *The BBC Symphony Orchestra* (BBC Publications, 1980).

weekday evening, six days a week, for eight weeks throughout the Prom season, and with daily rehearsals as well. It must be unparalleled in orchestral history. And how much greater the strain on Henry Wood, whose custom it was to conduct every item of every concert (except the few instances where composers conducted their own works). The strain did not show: performances sounded authentic, committed, enthusiastic.

Some of the orchestral players did, in fact, find a Prom season a terrible test of endurance and prepared for it with 'keep fit' exercises. Reginald Pound, in his biography of Wood, tells us that Wood's own regimen was very strict at that time of year, sacrificing lunches with friends such as Quilter or Bantock and instead taking piano rehearsals – never allowing his liking for food and wine to become his master. In the ordinary way, through most of his life, he would rarely be in bed before 1 a.m.; then up at 6.30 for a cold bath and an hour of score-reading before breakfast.

For rehearsing and conducting the Proms, Wood received £2300 from the BBC in the early thirties (the standard rate of income tax was 5 shillings in the pound). With his various other activities – additional concerts, festivals and engagements outside London, gramophone recordings, royalties from arrangements, his work at the Royal Academy of Music, and his private teaching – his income totalled about £7000 a year. His bank manager reported that 'to him, money means nothing'. He was certainly not extravagant in his tastes, and there was often money to spare, for investment.

But all was far from well in his personal life. He desperately needed a wife who would look after him in a selfless way, so that he could concentrate on his music without the usual mundane distractions. How else could he get through the tremendous programme which he set himself? Olga, with her aristocratic background, her culture and her successful career, had still been able to look after the material things. With Muriel, his second wife, however, there seemed to be no such satisfactory arrangements, and little understanding or sympathy. The consequences of the incompatibility became evident in the mid-1930s, though Wood always kept his private life very much to himself – partly, at that time, through consideration for his two daughters. But it is ironic that Wood, who in his memoirs was later to criticise audiences at symphony concerts for not troubling to wear evening dress, should become for a time very noticeably slack in his appearance and in his personal hygiene, besides becoming less sprightly, less good-humoured – causing members of his orchestra to enquire 'What's the matter with Old Timber?' He also became less precise in his timetable of rehearsing, at times with disastrous results (slammed by the critics); and he could be querulous, which was uncharacteristic, often losing patience with the

BBC and its sometimes high-handed manner of working. From this phase he was eventually rescued by a former pupil.

The story of how Jessie Linton (*née* Jessie Goldsack) renewed her friendship with Wood, after the death of her husband in 1933, is told in Reginald Pound's biography. After a physical collapse – a slight heart-attack – Wood confessed to her his desperate need of help. She began by acting as his music manager and agent, and soon discovered that outside the field of music he was pathetically incapable of fending for himself. In brief, she took over – abandoning her hopes of returning to the concert platform. She later took the name of Lady Jessie Wood by deed poll because Wood's wife would not divorce him. Reports that he had left his wife Muriel in dire financial circumstances were malicious and completely unfounded.

Order was joyfully restored in his life, and in September 1935 he was writing to his friend Tosta de Bennich, the Swedish pianist, as follows:

> Yes, the Proms are going and have been going superbly, and personally I never felt so happy and contented and enjoyed my work more . . . Of course you know that Mrs Linton, as my secretary and business manager, is doing wonders for me – and everybody in the BBC and in the provinces works so splendidly with her that my business has almost doubled. No more rows, no more bad tempers, and I am not 'sent to Coventry' for three days or a week. If you only knew the 'joy of living' which I am experiencing for the first time for some years . . .'

Rosa Newmarch rejoiced that Wood was looking 'ten years younger and so well "turned out"'.

No doubt anybody faced with the daunting task of devising an eight- or ten-week series of Promenade Concerts would be thinking about it, off and on, throughout the year. So it was with Wood. In collaboration with the BBC Music Department he held auditions in Queen's Hall. He and the other members of a small panel of assessors each wrote a report on every candidate heard. Many of these still exist in the BBC archives and make fascinating reading. A now very distinguished knighted tenor, for instance, was once written off by Wood in one sentence at a Prom audition: 'A noisy bleaty yellow voice, of no distinction and certainly no charm.' The final list of items for a season was hammered out at his home, over a period of several days, with representatives of the BBC – Edward Clark and Julian Herbage of the Music Department, and Wood's old friend 'Tommy' Thompson. On these occasions it was necessary to know timing, orchestration, and amount of rehearsal time needed for each of the items, besides considering very carefully the audience-appeal of everything.

Edward Clark, who played an important part in the shaping of the programmes of the Proms at this period, held the position of 'principal programme builder' in the BBC's Music Department, under the musical directorship of Sir Percy Pitt, from 1927 to 1936 (when he retired to join the British section of the International Society for Contemporary Music, later becoming its chairman). In his early days he had for a time studied with Schoenberg; and he acquired an international reputation as a conductor, particularly for his knowledge, understanding and advocacy of a remarkable range of contemporary music. He married Elisabeth Lutyens, who with Humphrey Searle was one of the few British composers of that time to be attracted to a 12-note idiom, which in the first half of the twentieth century seemed a very un-English practice! In the Prom discussions with Wood, Herbage and Thompson, Clark was a strong influence, particularly when it came to 'novelties' – of England and of other countries. And yet, strangely enough, Wood made no reference to him in his autobiography. (Clark's work as a bold champion of new music was a powerful inspiration for a later programme-builder of the BBC, William Glock.)

By providing more rehearsal time than had previously been possible, the BBC was enabling Wood to perform new works far more easily – though the actual number of novelties did not increase. The Proms did a great deal to encourage and establish the renaissance of creative work in England by providing a popular platform and immense listening audience for the music of composers such as Ireland, Bax, Vaughan Williams, Tippett, Walton, Rubbra, and later Britten and a host of younger composers.

In 1936 Paul Beard, who had already appeared as a Prom soloist, became leader of the BBC Symphony Orchestra – a position which he held until he retired in 1962. He had previously been leader of the City of Birmingham Orchestra under their conductor Adrian Boult (who became the BBC's Director of Music and later its principal conductor). Then, for four years from its foundation by Beecham in 1932, Beard had led the London Philharmonic Orchestra. The principal violin of an orchestra, called 'leader' in England and 'concert master' in the United States, has the responsibility of acting as a liaison between conductor and orchestra, and of maintaining discipline and working towards a high performance standard – an important job when the world's most distinguished conductors and artists are constantly appearing with the orchestra. Paul Beard took over from Marie Wilson the leadership at the Proms from the 1937 season onwards.

The well-known viola-player Harry Danks joined the BBC Symphony Orchestra in June 1937 and played for several seasons of Proms, besides many BBC studio concerts. He has recalled those days.

The BBC Symphony Orchestra, led by Paul Beard, at a Prom rehearsal with Sir Henry Wood in 1937.

Sir Henry Wood rehearsing En Saga *by Sibelius (c. 1938).*

Wood's day was always planned to the minute. This included his rehearsals. I well remember a Prom rehearsal at Queen's Hall at which the Russian operatic soprano Oda Slobodskaya was expected. As we came to the last chord of a piece, Sir Henry glanced towards the stage door and a look of annoyance flashed across his face. Seeing nobody there, he took his famous enormous turnip watch from his waistcoat pocket, and, in a voice that could drown an orchestra when they were tuning up, shouted: 'Mays, where is Miss Slobodskaya? I told her to be here at 11.29; it's now 11.30. This is not good enough, you know.' This was said in all seriousness . . . On another occasion, Mays [the concert assistant] came on to the platform during a rehearsal to inform Sir Henry that a soloist had telephoned to say he had been detained and would be five minutes late. Wood looked shocked, and exclaimed: 'Five minutes late! My God, five minutes means an Aria to me.'

Harry Danks also remembers the meticulous care with which all the string parts were marked by Wood in blue pencil beforehand, so as not to waste a minute at rehearsal. And his constant concern about tuning.

There was a period when Sir Henry insisted that every violinist in the orchestra went to the conductor's room just before going on to the platform for the evening concert. There he received an 'A' from a huge tuning-fork mounted on a box and struck with a mallet. Sir Henry was inclined to exclaim to most of the players 'Sharp!' and insist on a slightly lowered pitch. This routine became tiresome to the players, and it was really unnecessary. So a plan was devised. It meant a lot of quick moving. As one player left the room, the violin was passed to the player who was about to enter – and so on. Thus the same violin was tuned several times – with Sir Henry's observation 'Sharp!' After about the sixth violin farce, however, he quietly remarked: 'I think I've seen that violin before.' Everyone, including Sir Henry himself, enjoyed the joke; and soon after that the tuning system was changed.

'The new colour scheme at Queen's Hall is quite nice and the new ventilation excellent. We have had very trying weather to open with and no faints in the Promenade . . .' Wood was writing to a friend in August 1937, and the 'new look' of the hall had been the subject of a fulsome notice before the season began.

The BBC is glad to announce that when the audience assembles for the opening night of the 'Proms' on August 7, they will find a newly decorated and transfigured Queen's Hall. Not only will there be a new and harmonious colour scheme, but the seating throughout will have been entirely renovated, the lighting will have been greatly improved, and last, but not least, an

Some of the audience at a Prom in 1938, the year of Wood's 'half-century conducting'.

entirely new and up-to-date ventilation plant will have been installed. A practical and very comfortable type of seat has been adopted and will be installed in every part of the house, including the section behind the orchestra. The ceiling and walls will be repainted in clear tones; and the lighting will be softer and better distributed. The Hall will in fact have been brought thoroughly up-to-date, especially as regards ventilation, and it is hoped that these important alterations and reforms will combine to increase very greatly the comfort of concert-goers and enhance the amenities of London's favourite concert hall.

The year of Henry Wood's sixty-ninth birthday, 1938, was the year of his Golden Jubilee as a professional conductor. On 1 January 1888 he had (for a fee) conducted a concert of the All Saints' Choral and Orchestral Society, Clapton, and the main work in the programme was the cantata *May Day* by Sir G. A. Macfarren – performed in memory of the composer, who had died the previous year. (A good many works by Macfarren were later to be presented by Wood at the Proms.) The many celebrations and tributes during 1938 culminated in a special concert at the Royal Albert Hall in which the BBC Symphony Orchestra and Chorus, the London Symphony and the London Philharmonic Orchestras all gave their services, together with the Royal Choral Society, the Philharmonic Choir and the BBC Choral Society. Vaughan Williams wrote his *Serenade to Music* specially for the occasion, and it involved the sixteen singers who had been most closely associated with Wood for the Proms and other concerts at Queen's Hall: Isobel Baillie, Stiles-Allen, Elsie Suddaby, Eva Turner, Margaret Balfour, Muriel Brunskill, Astra Desmond, Mary Jarred, Parry Jones, Heddle Nash, Frank Titterton, Walter Widdop, Norman Allin, Robert Easton, Roy Henderson and Harold Williams. Wood had hoped that the concert could be on St Cecilia's Day; but there had been an offer by Rachmaninov, a great friend of Wood, to take part in the concert and play his own popular C minor Concerto; in order to fit in with his commitments the date had to be 5 October. It was in every way a splendid occasion – the only disappointment being that Rachmaninov steadfastly refused to allow his part of the concert to be broadcast. This was a matter of principle with him, an inflexible rule – apparently the result of some unfortunate experience in America when one of his records had been played over the air and the broadcasting company had pretended that it was a 'live' broadcast. So the BBC, considerably put out, was obliged to omit the Rachmaninov concerto from its broadcast of the Henry Wood Golden Jubilee Concert.

The proceeds of this concert, and various other donations, were devoted by Wood to a fund which he set up for the endowment, in perpetuity, of nine beds in six London hospitals specially for the use of orchestral musicians. On the first night of the Proms that year, Wood had broadcast a five-minute appeal on the national wavelength during the interval. It was his first spoken broadcast, apart from a very brief appearance on television. The benefit amounted to about £9000 in all.

Three days before this concert Wood was writing to his Swedish friend Tosta de Bennich:

> The Proms this year have been terrific. Sold out night after night. The BBC Symphony Orchestra played like angels all through the season. And they gave me a cheque for one hundred guineas for my Fund – real good of them. I don't feel the slightest fatigue, in fact I cannot believe that I have directed 49 consecutive concerts. Not bad for 69. All seats are sold for the Jubilee concert on the 5th at the Albert Hall . . .

The Proms of 1938 had indeed been a tremendous success, and attendances had set up a new record. Every night the promenaders demonstrated their loyalty, respect and affection for Wood as never before. It had become a tradition at the end of a concert, after Wood had been recalled again and again, that he would reappear first in his overcoat, next with his scarf over his shoulders, then with gloves and hat. But the audiences this season would not accept any of these good-humoured gestures as final.

In 1938, also, the experiment was tried of broadcasting frequently from the Proms on the television wavelength (sound only) between 8 and 9 p.m. This idea followed from the Toscanini concerts with the BBC Symphony Orchestra of the year before which had been transmitted in the same way. For many listeners this was a success, because the quality of the television sound could be excellent. It was just another aspect of a season which represented a climax in the history of the Proms.

13

The Music 1927-1937

When, in 1927, the Proms were in danger of being abandoned, many attributed the financial difficulties of these concerts to broadcasting, the habit of listening to concerts in an armchair at home supposedly making people reluctant to go out to the concert hall. This argument was soon proved to be false, but in taking over the Proms the BBC had to make its position clear. An article 'The BBC and the Proms', printed at the time in the concert programmes, stated:

> The two-and-a-half million people who pay their ten shillings wireless licence fee do so in the hope that the money will be spent on the provision of the best available programmes distributed as efficiently as possible. In allocating its resources the BBC is guided by this prior responsibility. There are about 65,000 programme-hours to fill in a year. Entertainment in itself is a many-sided enterprise. A nice balance must be maintained between the various ingredients. Music naturally predominates; but within music itself many distinctive tastes must be faithfully served, if efficiency is to be maintained. Disproportionate effort or expenditure on any one programme ingredient would seriously affect the whole service, and earn the dissatisfaction of the listening public. When, therefore, the BBC thought of intervening to save the Promenade Concerts, it was not enough to prove that these represented a great and deserving musical enterprise, highly appreciated by large numbers of people in London. The basic test to which this and similar proposals are submitted is their 'programme value' . . . The BBC decided that the proposal to take over the Promenade Concerts did pass its basic test at least for an experiment. And so it came about that broadcasting, which was blamed for the threatened collapse of the 'Proms', actually made them possible in 1927. The six weeks' season then given, with Sir Henry Wood conducting a strengthened orchestra, playing a somewhat wider range of music than in previous years, more than justified the estimates upon which BBC participation had been approved.

When the BBC took over, the general form and character of the Proms remained as they had been before. The complete repertoire for the first year is listed in Appendix C (pp. 328 ff.). Saturday was a mixed popular programme; Monday was Wagner; Tuesday featured Haydn and Mozart, Wednesday Brahms or Bach, Thursday was a mixture, with some unusual items, and Friday was Beethoven Night. British novelties included Walton's *Portsmouth Point* Overture, Alwyn's *Five Preludes* for Orchestra, the première of Frank Bridge's *Impression* ('There is a willow grows aslant a brook'), the tone-poem *Elaine* by Susan Spain-Dunk, and Hely-Hutchinson's *Variations* for Orchestra. Most of these were conducted by their composers. Foreign novelties included Hindemith's Piano Concerto No. 1 and Marcel Dupré's *Cortège et Litanie* for organ and orchestra.

The unqualified success of the first BBC season of Proms, and the recognition by the BBC of its exceptional programme value, led to an extended season of eight weeks in 1928. Thanks to pioneering work by Wood, Bach (on alternate Wednesdays) was proving an immensely strong attraction, drawing some of the best attendances of the season, and the audience for Brahms nights was steadily increasing. When Myra Hess was playing Bach Concertos, the floor of the hall could have been filled again with those who had to be turned away. There were still songs with piano in Part 2, which as a whole was short and light in character. Bax's First Symphony, powerfully romantic, was a great success, and was repeated in the following and a number of subsequent seasons. Vaughan Williams made a deep impression with his *Pastoral* Symphony, which he conducted, and Arthur Bliss conducted the last movement of his *Colour* Symphony. Two very important novelties were Sibelius's *Tapiola* and the exciting *Háry János* Suite by Zoltán Kodály. To conduct the latter the composer came over specially from Hungary. It was tremendously successful – repeated the following season – and rapidly became a popular favourite.

While drawing attention to unusual items, it must be borne in mind that one of the greatest benefits of the Proms, now as then, is the presentation of the 'classics' for an enormous number of people who are not familiar with the musical masterpieces of the past. These are often a special kind of Prom audience, attracted by the informal atmosphere and made up largely of people who would never attend orchestral concerts in the ordinary way.

A striking aspect of the 1929 season was that the Thursday concert each week was devoted to British composers – indeed an important innovation. Otherwise the same kind of pattern as before, but with Tchaikovsky intruding on Tuesday's Haydn and Mozart. The most important British première was Walton's Viola Concerto on 3 October, conducted by the composer and with Hindemith playing the solo part. What a concert that must have been! In the same programme were two other novelties – the première of three orchestral pieces by Bax (*Overture, Elegy, Rondo*), and Herbert Howells conducting his song-group *In green ways*. Other British novelties included the *Music for Orchestra* by Constant Lambert, a Suite by Lennox Berkeley, *A Carol Symphony* by Hely-Hutchinson (a work which enjoyed considerable popularity and is still heard sometimes today) – all these conducted by their composers. Peter Warlock conducted his *Capriol* Suite; Julian Herbage edited a piano concerto by Arne for Angus Morrison to play; and *The Triumph of Neptune* by Lord Berners made its first concert appearance. (A revival in 1975 on a last night was so successful that one wondered why such a witty and brilliant work was so rarely heard.) There were two Honegger novelties – *Rugby* and the Concertino for piano and orchestra. The Elgar Violin Concerto played by Albert Sammons was becoming a regular Prom feature.

At the concert of 5 October 1929 one of the items was Bach's Toccata and Fugue in D minor for organ, 'orchestrated by Paul Klenovsky'. 'Klenovsky' was none other than Henry Wood himself; he had long had it in mind to make a transcription of this work – and he wanted it to be different from Stokowski's, which he felt was too organ-conscious. Wood was quite frank about his purpose in this and other transcriptions – he wanted to forget the organ and the orchestra of Bach's time and present the music vividly in terms of rich, modern orchestral colours. For this he was sometimes taken to task for lack of taste. He realised that if he put his own name to the scoring, the criticism would again begin; so he had this little joke, using the name of one of Glazunov's promising pupils who had died young – Paul Klenovsky. The programme note of the concert went so far as to say that 'in the opinion of his teacher, A. Glazunov, he was one of the great masters of orchestration among the younger Russian school, and his early death was a distinct loss to the musical world'. When the secret came out, at the time the transcription was to be published, a rumpus ensued, giving rise to a *Times* Fourth Leader and a Strube cartoon in the *Daily Express*. The joke, a dubious one, was against English concert audiences who blindly prefer foreign names. The success of the transcription, and the controversy aroused by the leg-pull, gave Wood 'enormous satisfaction'. It might also have landed him in court.

In Gordon Jacob's treatise on orchestration, Wood's version of this Bach work is given in a list headed 'Masterly Transcriptions'. Toscanini used it 'with enormous success', and Stokowski, in the film *Fantasia*, used it in preference to his *own* transcription. It became a regular feature of the Proms for a long time.

1930 was a particularly interesting year for new works. Among foreign composers there were novelties from Villa-Lobos, Janáček and Krenek; and Marcel Dupré was soloist in his Symphony for Organ and Orchestra. Honegger's fine Cello Concerto was heard, with Maurice Maréchal as soloist; also, Kodály's impressionistic *Summer Evening* made its first English appearance. There were British premières, notably John Ireland's Piano Concerto — a Prom favourite for many years to come — with Helen Perkin, the young pianist who inspired it; and Léon Goossens (now very famous on both sides of the Atlantic) was soloist in his brother Eugene's Oboe Concerto. There was the première of 23-year-old Elizabeth Maconchy's suite *The Land*, and novelties also by Bridge, Ethel Smyth and Grainger. Walton's Viola Concerto was performed again that year with Bernard Shore as soloist; the following year, too, it was to be included, with Lionel Tertis for whom it was originally written (he thought at first that it was unplayable, and the première had been taken over by Hindemith). In this rich 1930 season Bliss, Holst, Bridge, Walton, Lambert, Alan Bush, Smyth and Vaughan Williams conducted works of their own. Performers included Myra Hess (Brahms No. 1), Lamond, Gladys Ripley, Elsie Suddaby. The Harrison sisters, May and Beatrice, were soloists in Delius's Concerto for Violin and Cello.

Among the eight British Composers Concerts of 1931, several were devoted to a single composer — Delius, Vaughan Williams, Elgar (twice). Cyril Scott was soloist in his own Piano Concerto, and Francis Poulenc came from Paris to play in the first English performance of his *Aubade (concerto chorégraphique)* for piano and orchestra. Eric Fogg wrote a Concerto for the famous bassoonist Archie Camden, soon to be a member of the BBC Symphony Orchestra; it continued to have quite a success. There was an opportunity to hear the latest composition of Elgar, Master of the King's Musick — the *Nursery Suite*, dedicated to a royal group of the time, Their Royal Highnesses the Duchess of York and the Princesses Elizabeth and Margaret Rose. It was in fact a good season for British composers. Other novelties included Lord Berners' *Luna Park* (a fantastic ballet in one act) and the 22-year-old Ivor Walsworth's *Rhapsodic Dance*. Constant Lambert again conducted his *Rio Grande* (with Angus Morrison, to whom it is dedicated, as soloist), and Vaughan Williams his *Flos Campi*, with Bernard Shore as the solo viola. Berg's Six Songs with Orchestra (1907) and Webern's Op. 1 *Passacaglia* were also featured, and the haunting beauty of Satie's *Gymnopédies*, in Debussy's orchestration.

In 1932 Monday, as usual, was Wagner Night, but it was something of an innovation to include whole scenes from *The Ring*. Wednesdays alternated between Brahms and Bach, and Friday (as expected) was Beethoven. Tuesdays and Thursdays throughout the season were divided between Tchaikovsky, Haydn and Mozart, and British composers – and there was one evening each of Schumann, Schubert and Mendelssohn. Frank Bridge conducted his *Sonnet by Rupert Brooke*, originally composed for Gervase Elwes. Holst, who had recently returned from a successful tour of America where much of his music had been well received, conducted *The Planets*. Novelties were fewer than usual, but included the 'first in England' of Ravel's Piano Concerto for the Left Hand, in which the soloist was the one-armed Austrian pianist Paul Wittgenstein, for whom it was written. Arthur Catterall was soloist in Beethoven's unfinished *Konzertstück*, which the Catalan violinist Joan Manén had rescued and completed in appropriate style. Delius, at his home in Grez-sur-Loing, France, heard a performance of his *Song of the High Hills* and sent a telegram – 'Thanks, dear Wood, for your lovely interpretation . . . thanks to orchestra, chorus and soli for a beautiful performance.'

In the Christmas holiday period of that year, an extra fortnight of Proms was considered to have justified itself. The concerts followed the familiar pattern, and some of the most popular Prom artists took part – Solomon, Harold Williams, Elsie Suddaby, and others. Although short, the season included two novelties – Hindemith's characteristic *Philharmonic Concerto*, and Dame Ethel Smyth's fantastic and delicate *Fête galante*, which she conducted herself. A similar series of 'Christmas Proms' was held in each of the following two years.

The programmes of 1933 followed the well-established patterns. An outstanding novelty was Liszt's great *Faust* Symphony, which – apart from Beethoven's Ninth – was the longest work so far presented to a Prom audience. Elgar conducted his Second Symphony – a long work, too, for a largely standing audience, and Dr Vaughan Williams conducted his *Pastoral* Symphony. There was a good crop of artists from abroad: Poulenc and Jacques Février played Poulenc's Concerto for Two Pianos, Marcelle Meyer played Ravel's G Major Concerto, Josef Szigeti the Brahms and Beethoven concertos, and Samuel Dushkin the new Violin Concerto which Stravinsky had written for him.

In 1934 Henry Wood was conducting his fortieth season of Proms, and it was perhaps the most successful season so far. Besides the usual Wagner, Bach, Brahms and Beethoven, there were concerts devoted to Tchaikovsky, Delius, Richard Strauss, Sibelius, Liszt and Vaughan Williams. This year saw the first Prom appearance of the famous operatic soprano Eva Turner. British music had a wide representation, and there were some unusual novelties, including the première of Ernst Toch's Symphony for Piano and Orchestra, in which the composer was soloist; *Circus Day* by the American Deems Taylor; Kodály's *Dances of Galanta*; and the latest work of Arnold Bax, *The tale the pine-trees knew*. Three fragments from the opera *Wozzeck* by Alban Berg made a strong impression. The work had not yet had a stage production in England, but the BBC had earlier in the year given a complete concert version.

1934 was a tragic year for British music, for it saw the loss of three of its greatest figures – Elgar, Delius, and Holst. Music by each was played in a spirit of memorial at the Proms that season. The Delius memorial concert (23 August) was particularly impressive – the whole of Part 1 devoted to Delius works, including the Piano Concerto (with Clifford Curzon as soloist).

The writer Felix Aprahamian remembers a Prom on 25 August 1934 when there was a vociferous protest because Wood had cut an orchestral 'Da Capo' in a Handel aria – 'Sound an alarm' from *Judas Maccabaeus* – which Frank Titterton was singing. 'First you mutilate Wagner,' shouted a prom-enader (the reference was to Wood's 'bleeding chunks of Wagner'), 'now you hack Handel!' . . . Felix Aprahamian also remembers a performance of Elgar's *Falstaff* about this time. The audience on this occasion was a very sparse one, and in the interval Wood walked among the promenaders trying to find out why Elgar's brilliant symphonic study was not the inevitable 'draw' that he felt it should be.

Some breaks with tradition occurred in 1935, though the normal fare continued as usual. There was a concert devoted to the music of Debussy and Ravel (the first time these two had shared a Prom). For only the second time in Prom history, a Schubert evening was given; and a whole pro-gramme was for the first time devoted to Saint-Saëns in honour of the centenary of his birth. It included his Third Symphony, which has an important part for organ. Unusual also was a concert devoted to the music of Liszt. Previously, Liszt had usually been mixed in with Wagner.

Many composers conducted their own music. Novelties included Shostakovich's First Symphony, a concerto for saxophone and strings by the Swedish composer Lars-Erik Larsson, and – a curiosity by a member of 'Les Six' – a Concerto for two pianos, mixed chorus, saxophones and orchestra, by Germaine Tailleferre. Saturday evenings now included a larger share of serious music than before – works such as Sibelius's Seventh Symphony, Elgar's *Enigma* Variations, movements from Holst's *The Plan-ets*. Distinguished soloists from abroad included Elisabeth Schumann, Elena Gerhardt, and the cellist Piatigorsky. From home, the Grinke Trio were heard in Beethoven's Triple Concerto; Albert Sammons was making the Delius Violin Concerto very much his own (as he made the Elgar). The Russian operatic soprano Oda Slobodskaya, who made England her home, was at the height of her powers. Also, among singers, Heddle Nash and Parry Jones were frequently appearing.

From the beginning of the BBC régime in 1927, it had become the custom to broadcast the first half of every concert – with rare exceptions. In 1936, however, the BBC's Controller of Programmes made a public announcement regarding the Proms in a national broadcast:

This year we are adopting a new principle and are endeavouring to use the Promenade concerts in such a way as to produce better balanced programmes, with music more evenly distributed throughout the evening.

Now I know that some people are disappointed that we are not going to broadcast every first half, but I would like to explain what lies behind our decision. If any of you who are listening to me this evening had to build programmes for broadcasting, you would, I think, whatever your own personal inclinations, feel as we do, that all categories of listeners must be considered (and by all categories I mean not only those who like music and those who do not, but also those who can only listen early and those who can only listen late). If you are faced, as we are at this time of year, with the fact that for forty-nine consecutive nights, excluding Sundays, there were concerts of serious music available from 8.00 to 10.30 p.m. (with a short break of fifteen minutes for the interval), I am sure you would be a little perplexed at the problem of programme-building presented. You could not help feeling that despite the fact that many people can listen to good music every night of their lives, a block of music occurring at the same time every evening for forty-nine evenings in succession was not in the interests of listeners as a whole. Our usual plan is to spread concerts about the programmes, and this summer, in addition to the Promenades, you will find concerts of good music sometimes in the early evening, sometimes in the middle of the evening, and sometimes in the late evening. The old arrangement of broadcasting the first half of every Promenade Concert – lasting from a hour and a half to an hour and forty minutes – inevitably meant that the good music became concentrated, that alternatives were restricted and that the general spread-over of music in the programmes was not possible during those eight weeks of the Promenade Concert season.

So this year we are making the Promenades fit more into the general scheme of programme planning. Up to date we have already arranged our programmes for every night of the Promenade Concert Season, and as a result of the new policy, the general shape of the programmes and the variety in them – and by variety I don't just mean light entertainment – is far better than was possible before during this particular period. We have taken one full first half of a Promenade Concert almost every week, and each night there is an excerpt – maybe a complete symphony, maybe several works – covering from forty minutes to an hour and a half.

A disappointment to some; a better balance for others. Previously, by broadcasting each time the whole of the first half of a concert, the character of a programme was clearly established. The BBC's freedom of choice often meant, for the radio listener, a less definite 'programme' impression. Later, with the advent of a third radio network in 1946, it was possible for the BBC to broadcast the Proms in their entirety – at one period divided between the networks; at another, exclusively on the Third, which became largely devoted to music.

During the 1936 summer season of Proms fifty-three works by British composers were performed. Walton, then aged thirty-four, was given a programme to himself for the first time. Granville Bantock conducted the première of his comedy overture *The Frogs* (after Aristophanes). Other first performances in England included Muriel Brunskill singing *The Ferryman's Bride* by Sibelius; Sigurd Rascher as the soloist in Jacques Ibert's *Concertino da Camera* for saxophone and orchestra; Casella's transcription of the Bach D minor *Chaconne*, which outdid Wood in lavish orchestration; and the 29-year-old Elizabeth Maconchy's Concerto for Piano and Chamber Orchestra, with Harriet Cohen as soloist. The symphonic poem *François Villon* by the Scottish composer William Wallace was revived: it had proved successful at the Proms many years before. On a lighter note, there was a good reception for the three Scottish Dances by Ian Whyte, conductor of the BBC Scottish Orchestra (founded the previous year), and these and many other Scottish dances of Whyte became popular, mostly through broadcasting.

A striking feature of the 1937 season was the inclusion of all seven symphonies of Sibelius, in addition to two evenings entirely devoted to that composer. This experiment was a success. There was also a Richard Strauss concert and one devoted to a meaningful combination of Debussy and Stravinsky. Beethoven concerts, as expected, were always filled to capacity; so, too, were the Bach evenings. The concerts devoted to Elgar and Vaughan Williams also drew encouragingly large houses. Kodály again conducted his *Háry János* Suite, by then established as a Prom favourite, and several English composers conducted their own works – Vaughan Williams his

Fourth Symphony (interpreted by some, including Boult, as a prophecy of the world conflict that was shortly to come), Bliss.his *Colour Symphony*, Maurice Johnstone his *Welsh Rhapsody*. (Johnstone was later to become the BBC's Head of Music Programmes, a position which, under a slightly different title, Bliss held from 1942 to 1944.) Walton conducted *Crown Imperial*, the march he had just written for the Coronation of King George VI and Queen Elizabeth. In that Coronation year, too, one of the novelties of the season was Bax's *London Pageant*. There was the première of a *Fantasia* for violin and orchestra by the 36-year-old Edmund Rubbra, with Frederick Grinke as soloist. Novelties from abroad included the Harp Concerto by Germaine Tailleferre (whose works had been heard several times at the Proms), the soloist being Sidonie Goossens (one more member of the brilliant musical family of Belgian descent). A violin concerto by the prolific and much-discussed Italian composer Gian-Francesco Malipiero made a first English appearance with Antonio Brosa as soloist.

By the end of 1937 the Proms had achieved forty-three seasons – under one conductor – presenting the great works of the past, often to people who were experiencing them for the first time; and presenting also much that was new and adventurous. The Proms were unique.

14

Into War again
with and without the BBC

After the 1938 Proms and the Jubilee celebrations which followed in October, one might have expected Henry Wood to 'call it a day' – to regard this, his sixty-ninth year, as a triumphant finale to a remarkably rich and fulfilling career, and to 'take things easy' from now on. But he was not made that way. Like Queen Victoria he had two Jubilees to celebrate, and in 1938 he was already writing of the Jubilee of the Proms, which would be taking place six year later. Who could tell, in those uncertain times, what would happen in the meantime? 'But rest assured,' asserted Wood, 'I shall be there if I am on this side, perhaps with my carnation and my baton – but perhaps only with my carnation – to partake in the rejoicings that will be heard in Queen's Hall on that August night in 1944 . . .'

One could rest anything but assured at that time. As the Prom audience of 27 September 1938 heard broadcast in the auditorium of Queen's Hall, the Prime Minister, Neville Chamberlain, was saying:

> . . . Armed conflict between nations is a nightmare to me; but if I were convinced that any nation had made up its mind to dominate the world by fear of its force, I should feel that it must be resisted . . . As long as war has not begun there is always hope that it may be prevented, and you know that I am going to work for peace to the last moment.

The British Fleet was mobilised. There followed the Munich agreement, and the 'phoney' peace in our time continued for another year.

So the 1939 season of Proms was planned: forty-nine concerts along the normal lines. They began on Saturday, 12 August, excellently supported as usual. Nobody, as yet, seemed to believe that war would actually become a reality; somehow it would be avoided and everything would go on as before. Then, on Friday, 1 September, Hitler invaded Poland, and the Beethoven concert that evening was brought to an abrupt end after the *Pastoral* Symphony. Wood returned to the platform and in a controlled voice stated:

Owing to the special arrangements for broadcasting which are now in force, the BBC very much regrets that the Symphony Orchestra will no longer be available for these concerts in London. I am therefore very sorry to say that from tonight the Promenade Concerts will close down until further notice. I must thank you, my dear friends, for your loyal support, and I hope we shall soon meet again.

After that, backstage and on the way home, he remained very silent, in a sort of childlike incomprehension, angry and resentful that the BBC had treated him unreasonably, as he thought, by pulling down the shutters unnecessarily – whereas in the 1914 war he and Robert Newman had been able to carry on as before, despite danger of air raids. The BBC, fully aware of the completely different scale of danger this time, and fearing that Broadcasting House (in very close proximity to Queen's Hall) would be an important target for the enemy, put into operation at once an emergency plan prepared some time before. Three days after Britain declared war on Germany, the BBC's Music Department had left London and set up a small number of units manageably 'organised' at their wartime base in Bristol. The musical resources there included the BBC Symphony Orchestra (reduced to seventy players, but later to be augmented to ninety), the Theatre Orchestra, the 'Salon Orchestra' (consisting of fifteen musicians), and professional choral groups. Less single-minded than Wood, the BBC at first could see no possibility of sponsoring the Proms in wartime; and this soon became a bitter wrangle.

For a few months the whole range of broadcast programmes had to be accommodated on one channel. In February 1940, however, the Forces Network was set up, and it was possible for it to be used for presenting much of the lighter music and popular classics. Thus, time allotted in the Home Service could be used mainly (but not exclusively) for 'serious' music. With the unavailability of most foreign artists, and many British musicians called into the services, it was a difficult time; but a great deal was accomplished by the BBC in providing a remarkably wide range of music-making in all the different categories, supplemented by gramophone programmes (which had from the start of broadcasting been an important ingredient). With regard to the Proms, it had become, in the pre-war years, the policy to plan them carefully in conjunction with the Wednesday Symphony Concerts and Sunday Orchestral Concerts. Now, in wartime, it was difficult to make orchestral plans on this scale: concerts became shorter – it might be one symphony by itself or an orchestral half-hour of short works. At the same time the BBC continued its policy of engaging the greatest possible number of British musicians and broadcasting a great deal of music by British composers. Many London concerts were relayed, but the general focus of broadcasting was regional.

During the last months of 1939, Wood did some travelling about the country, in difficult and often exhausting circumstances, conducting concerts in Manchester, Bristol and elsewhere. He was naturally very concerned and depressed about the uncertain state of the Proms. The BBC files of the period show that Sir Henry and Lady Wood wanted to start a three-week winter season of Proms at Queen's Hall in January 1940 with the London Symphony Orchestra, if the BBC Symphony Orchestra was not available. Wood asked the BBC for a guarantee against financial loss, but the BBC said they could only co-operate indirectly through paying a fee for concerts which were broadcast. The idea was dropped.

In January 1940 the police agreed that Queen's Hall was suitable for public entertainment (although it was without an adequate air-raid shelter) and that it could stay open until 11 p.m. Proms in the summer became a possibility. In December 1939, and again in the following month, Chappell's, as lessors of Queen's Hall, had asked the BBC to decide whether they wished to sponsor a season of Proms in the summer – if not, they would have to make other arrangements for the letting of the hall. Much as the BBC may have wished to carry on with the Proms in some form or other, it was very difficult for them to give a clear answer six months in advance, during an illusory period of calm and completely uncertain about how hostilities would develop. There were wartime limitations on the Home Service; the BBC Symphony Orchestra was based in Bristol. A Prom season in Bristol was considered, but the BBC could not claim the exclusive use of the title 'Promenade Concert' (if anybody could, it would surely be Henry Wood). And other organisations were known to be interested in sponsoring the Proms in London.

Wood was pressing the BBC for a reply to letters he had written asking them to say one way or the other whether they were prepared to sponsor the 1940 Proms. The Music Department urged Wood 'to leave the matter in our hands and trust us implicitly'. This was unfair and somewhat monolithic in attitude. Anybody who has worked in the BBC knows all too well the inevitable committee meetings, the slow and tortuous routes towards decisions, and the unpredictability. In this case there were sharp differences of attitude – between the Controller of Programmes, B. E. (later Sir Basil) Nicolls, on the one hand, whose concern was primarily with the overall plan of the broadcast programmes, and, on the other hand, the Music Department, headed by Sir Adrian Boult, who were far more concerned with the value of the Proms as such and what was owed musically to Henry Wood.

The points made by Nicolls may be summarised as follows:

1. It would have to be clearly established that the London County Council would permit standing in the promenade area of Queen's Hall: otherwise the takings would be seriously diminished.
2. The Proms, normally run at a loss, might well find a richer backer prepared to stand the loss.
3. Was it desirable at all that there should be a Prom season in wartime?
4. Was a Prom season necessary in terms of broadcast programme requirements? 'To satisfy them, two or three short relays a week are quite sufficient under the present single-programme system, and there is no particular reason why equivalent concerts should not be provided in the studio.'
5. There were three possible schemes for an 8-week Prom season in London: (a) with the BBC Symphony Orchestra; (b) shared between the BBC Symphony Orchestra and London Symphony or London Philharmonic Orchestra; (c) with the outside orchestra for the whole season.
6. Defence: if the BBC Symphony Orchestra were to undertake the concerts, the whole orchestra would have to be allowed to take refuge in Broadcasting House if it desired to do so.
7. The season could be shortened. A four-week season would be quite sufficient to keep the tradition going and to satisfy public demand.
8. An outside body might run the Proms. But the BBC would then lose control of programme content, and Chappell's would feel no obligation to offer the BBC the option of booking Queen's Hall for the following Prom season: the connection would be severed.

The conclusion which Nicolls reached was:

From many points of view the best solution of the problem to my mind would be to co-operate in a season run by an outside body, with safeguards for our permanent interests and rights. This would save us a lot of money and would ensure the continuity of the tradition both in the Hall and on the microphone . . . The decision may be rather a difficult one for us to come to, as it involves handing over our child temporarily to an outside nurse, but that is only wartime evacuation in another form.

The BBC's Music Department disagreed with a good deal in Nicolls's arguments. The statement that the Proms were normally run at a loss was misleading: in 1938 a profit of £4800 was shown. This did not reckon the cost of the staff orchestra, but at least as many broadcast hours were obtained from it as if it had been playing in the studio. Regarding Nicolls's point about equivalent concerts being easily provided in the studio, it was felt that if there were no Prom season there would be a serious dearth for several months of 'the stimulus and publicity of public concerts in our music schedule'. It might be possible to start with a four-week season and extend to six weeks if the advance bookings a month before the opening date were sufficiently encouraging.

The main concern of the Music Department was expressed as follows:

> For forty-five years the Promenade Concerts, under Sir Henry Wood, have been the leading series of popular orchestral concerts in London. The Proms effectively cater for an audience far wider in taste than any other series of concerts in the world. Since broadcasting took them over, thirteen years ago, they have become more than ever a national institution, and by careful building up and the adoption of a far-sighted programme policy they had by 1939 reached a degree of popularity never previously achieved. That they are the best of concert propositions from the Box Office angle is proved by the fact that outside enterprises are prepared to take the risk of financing them in spite of the uncertainty of the present times. . . . There is the greatest danger, if the BBC hands over any part of the control of the Proms, of the interested party merely exploiting for its own ends the commercial value of the goodwill of these concerts.

It was felt that if there were to be co-operation, the first person to approach should be Sir Henry Wood. And the co-operation should bring together the BBC, Sir Henry Wood and Chappell's.

In February, the BBC was told by Chappell's that 'other interests' were prepared to take over the concerts. William Walton, on behalf of the Association of British Musicians, informed the BBC that they were able to put on a Prom season. The BBC made known to Chappell's its willingness to co-operate, but was told that the projects had fallen through. They then approached Chappell's with a view to running a shortened series, but asked to be permitted to cancel the concerts without obligation nearer the time if the state of the war compelled them to do so. That provision was refused.

During all this uncertainty it was impossible for the BBC to tell Henry Wood anything definite. The situation was explained to him (but no mention was made of a *shortened* season) and he gave the BBC until 3 April as far as his own availability was concerned. It was not until the end of March that the BBC decided to hold a four-week Prom season from 10 August to 7 September. They asked Chappell's on 28 March whether the Hall was available for that period. But it was too late: the Hall had been otherwise booked.

In *The Times* of 5 April an announcement appeared which stated:

> The BBC has decided not to continue to be responsible for the Promenade Concerts . . . Sir Henry Wood said he was grieved that the BBC could not see their way to continue the concerts. They had been hesitating about the matter since last December but had now reached a decision.

The announcement further stated that the lessors of the Queen's Hall had made arrangements with Sir Henry Wood to give a Prom season under the aegis of the Royal Philharmonic Society, and that it would be his last.

This announcement provoked a letter to *The Times* from Sir Adrian Boult (on behalf of the BBC) regretting that Wood had given the impression that the Corporation had voluntarily decided to abandon its association with the Proms. In fact, it had been 'forced reluctantly to abandon the idea' through the unavailability of Queen's Hall – a statement which was refuted in a letter to *The Daily Telegraph* from Louis Dreyfus, Chairman of Chappell's, which explained how the BBC had had from December to 1 March to make up their minds, after which Chappell's could wait no longer and had to take immediate steps to carry on their business. Further letters to the press from Henry Wood complained about the BBC's protracted indecision, lack of consideration, and casual manner of conducting its business. He felt that the 'official explanation' by the BBC was 'couched in terms so ambiguous as to convey a reflection upon my integrity and loyalty to the Corporation'. A strong denial that anything of the sort was intended by the BBC was printed in *Radio Times* and issued to the press.

Wood made his views on the matter very clear in a letter dated 13 April 1940 to R. J. F. Howgill of the BBC's administration department:

> The outstanding reflection of these many months awaiting the Corporation's decision – for I wrote you on 10 January regarding the summer Promenade Concerts – is the amazingly casual way in which the Corporation has regarded my vocation, and had I not endeavoured to bring about some definite decision, I might have found myself relieved of my long association with these famous concerts.
>
> It has all caused me untold sorrow and grave anxiety in the cause of music, the more so, as I was hopeful of introducing my colleagues to the Promenade audience this year under the Corporation's management with a view to the time which would come for me to announce my retirement from the strenuous six days a week – of which suggestion your music department is well aware – but which is not now a workable proposition under a new management with courage born of a determination that *the Proms must go on*, but whose wishes in the matter I have now to consider.
>
> The announcement of my retirement from these concerts is the direct

outcome of the retirement of the Corporation from the management, for the reason stated in the preceding paragraph.

In an internal memorandum, Nicolls referred to 'the deceptive and hostile attitude of Chappell's'. But were they in fact not simply carrying on their business as best they could in a difficult and indecisive situation? It was hardly fair for the BBC to state that it was prevented from making arrangements for a Prom season because Chappell's, 'four months before the opening date of the season and without warning or prior consultation with the BBC, entered into another arrangement with Sir Henry Wood and the Royal Philharmonic Society'. On the other hand, Chappell's seemed to be demanding an unreasonably high fee of £150 for each broadcast from the 1940 Proms, when for this privilege it was normally £75; and the BBC had understandably found this unacceptable. In the BBC files there is evidence that Boult was very unhappy about the whole matter.

At all events, the result was a temporary divorce from the BBC, and the beginning of a new collaboration fraught with difficulties. The seasons of 1940 and 1941 must have made Wood long to return to BBC management, dilatory or otherwise. He now had as chief sponsor Keith Douglas, honorary secretary of the Royal Philharmonic Society and honorary organiser of the hospital concerts of the Incorporated Society of Musicians – a clever but somewhat unreliable individual with inherited wealth which he was prepared to spend on music, the art that really interested him. With Keith Douglas was Owen Mase, previously of the BBC's Music Department (and still for Wood a link with the BBC); he had been organiser of the London Festival of 1939, which had included famous Toscanini concerts. And there was help from the impresario John Tillett. Douglas disclosed that he was acting through the Royal Philharmonic Society to avoid entertainment tax. He also decided to print the Society's Royal coat-of-arms on the Prom programmes.

For Wood the main thing was that the *Proms must go on*, and he was grateful to Douglas and Mase for making this possible. He was tired of arguments over his concerts. Such was now his attitude; but he was in for much exasperation. The new management was very slow-moving and inexperienced. They thought larger audiences would be attracted if they advertised the season as 'Sir Henry Wood's forty-sixth and Final Season' – giving the impression that it was a last chance to experience the Proms conducted by Wood. And they wanted to engage artists and the orchestra (the London Symphony Orchestra) at reduced rates, which was contrary to things that Wood had fought for in the past. The prospectus was late appearing, because the management was clearing with the LCC and the police the question of whether a promenading audience (1600 people bunched together) would be allowed. The pussy-footing, numerous obstacles and lack of action were driving Wood to despair, at one point to such a degree that he threatened to withdraw from the whole business – only to be told that if he didn't conduct, Keith Douglas would!

'Gradually', wrote Lady Jessie Wood, 'the buoyant step returned, however. The Proms would go on after all, and Henry refused to allow air-raid warnings or blackout to assail his determination to keep the flag flying.' In March, April and May he conducted concerts in London, and in many parts of the country, regardless of wartime difficulties.

The 1940 Prom season opened precisely at 8 pm on 10 August. Audiences, large and enthusiastic, now consisted of those who had had to remain in the capital from choice or necessity. The raids on London soon began in earnest, each day from about 8 pm and continuing till 4 or 5 o'clock the next morning. There was the very real danger of a direct hit. A warning sign in the hall showed *Air-raid alert* or *All clear*, while concerts went on, uninterrupted.

During the Proms, Wood made the Langham Hotel, Portland Place, his headquarters, in readiness for morning rehearsals with the orchestra. Thus he remained perpetually in the danger area, but so single-minded was he, so identified with the music he was making, that the historic events taking place in the world about him could largely be ignored. If there was still an air-raid alert at the end of the concert, any of the audience that wished could remain for improvised entertainment – as in the first world war. (Underground stations were closed during alerts.) To pass the dangerous time, Basil Cameron, who was to be Wood's first associate conductor, would organise a music quiz for the two thousand or so who remained in the arena and the stalls. Gerald Moore would accompany from memory any song that was asked for. There was community singing. Members of the orchestra put on humorous items – in one case, for example, it was a take-off of Beecham 'to the T'. And sometimes entertainment talent was revealed in members of the audience.

But as the raids intensified it was considered too dangerous to continue the series, and everything had to stop after the concert of Saturday 7 September. The 46th season of Proms had run for only four of its eight weeks. Fatefully, that final concert on 7 September was in fact the last Prom to be given at Queen's Hall. It was also an entirely characteristic Prom – a lively judicious mixture of nineteenth- and twentieth-century music, which included a première:

VARIATIONS on *Three Blind Mice* –	–	–	–	–	*Holbrooke*
BELL SONG (*Lakmé*) –	–	–	–	–	*Delibes*
Joan Tribe					
PIANO CONCERTO No. 2, in C minor	–	–	–		*Rachmaninov*
Moiseiwitsch					
SYMPHONIC POEM, *En Saga* –	–	–	–	–	*Sibelius*
ARIA, 'E LUCEVAN LE STELLE' (*Tosca*)	–	–	–	–	*Puccini*
Frank Titterton					
THREE PIECES FOR ORCHESTRA	–	–	–	–	*Elisabeth Lutyens*
(*first performance*)					
THREE SLAVONIC DANCES –	–	–	–	–	*Dvořák*
THE LONDON PAGEANT –	–	–	–	–	*Bax*
OVERTURE, *Ruy Blas* –	–	–	–	–	*Mendelssohn*

Queen's Hall was seriously damaged by blast in December 1940, and again in April 1941; but both times hasty repairs were possible. On Saturday 10 May, the Royal Choral Society, with the LPO, gave a performance of Elgar's *Dream of Gerontius*, conducted by Malcolm Sargent. It was the very last concert to be given in Queen's Hall. That night (in the official words of the Ministry of Information):

came the Luftwaffe's final fling before its journey to – or towards – Moscow. For five moonlit hours, over three hundred bombers dropped great numbers of incendiaries and high explosives, causing a serious fire situation, setting a new record for casualty figures (1436 killed and 1792 injured) and doing great damage to public buildings. The House of Commons Chamber was destroyed. Westminster Abbey was hit; so were the British Museum, the Law Courts, the War Office, the Mint, the Mansion House, and the Tower. Five of the Halls of the City Companies were destroyed and many famous churches damaged.

And Queen's Hall was set on fire. Firemen tackled the blaze, at first hopefully, but lack of water, through damaged mains, prevented them from saving the building. The next morning the interior of the building was completely gutted and only an outer shell remained. At 10 am members of the LPO arrived to rehearse for a concert that afternoon – a concert which had to be transferred to the Duke's Hall of the Royal Academy of Music, half a mile away.

Amongst the rubble at Queen's Hall, the bronze bust of Henry Wood, by Donald Gilbert, remained undamaged in its niche. This had originally been unveiled by Sir Walford Davies at a ceremony in Queen's Hall during Wood's Jubilee celebrations of 1938. Eventually it found a home, appro-

Queen's Hall gutted by enemy action, May 1941.

priately, in London's Royal Academy of Music. But for each Prom season, with Lady Jessie Wood's approval, it is transported to the Albert Hall, where it presides, gazing fixedly from a plinth on the platform just below the organ console. Ceremonially it is crowned with a laurel wreath by two privileged Promenaders during the festivities of the last night.

Before the destruction of Queen's Hall, Wood had had discussions with the BBC about the future of the Proms. A lunch with Sir Adrian Boult and two other members of the music department (Julian Herbage and W. W. Thompson) had come to nothing, however. They had shown little enthusiasm for bringing the Proms back under the BBC wing in wartime England: the BBC Symphony Orchestra could not easily spend that amount of time in London, and there were many difficulties over artists. When Queen's Hall was no more, the way was clearer. As Lady Jessie Wood has written, the German bomb wiped out (besides much else) the history of difficult relations, as already described, between Chappell's and the BBC. The decision to hold the 1941 Proms in the Royal Albert Hall was like a fresh start. Characteristically protracted negotiations began; Wood had an encouraging talk (over lunch at the Hyde Park Hotel) with the BBC's Controller of Programmes (Nicolls) and high-level discussions followed. But it was not until 11 February 1942 that the BBC finally resolved to sponsor the Proms once again. Wood was greatly touched when three members of the Music Department called on him personally at his hotel to break the good news. Had the BBC decided not to take over, there had already been a firm offer of combined sponsorship and management from the impresario Harold Holt. At this stage the BBC could easily have lost the Proms for good.

Meanwhile, however, Wood had to contend with the 1941 season, again sponsored by Keith Douglas 'under the auspices of the Royal Philharmonic Society'. At least Douglas had been extremely prompt in deciding to hold the Proms in the Albert Hall – another royal building associated with Queen Victoria, twice the size of Queen's Hall. The Albert Hall was designed in the mid-nineteenth century as a home of the arts and sciences in London and as a memorial to the Prince Consort; it had been officially opened by the Queen in 1871. Here 1250 people could stand in the arena, with 1150 on the floor in the gallery, and there could be 4900 people sitting down. Wood was worried at first about whether the Prommers would be prepared to make the journey to South Kensington. He was also considerably worried and embarrassed by the situation in which Douglas had placed him with regard to the cut in fees which was now being asked for. Douglas was trying to engage distinguished artists such as Solomon, Myra Hess, Moiseiwitsch and Pouishnoff 'on the cheap'. Wood disliked what he felt was amateurish handling of the situation generally.

Another worry was the acoustic of the Albert Hall. As with St Paul's Cathedral, the excessive echo was a problem to be reckoned with. Keith Douglas sprang into action: screens were placed around the orchestra, and the velarium – a large horizontal structure designed to catch things which might drop off the roof – was made lower. The authorities, however, objected: if, for example, a large piece of glass fell it would have acquired so much more momentum that it might penetrate the velarium. So back it went, to its higher position. Douglas next called in a representative of the Government Building Research Station, Hope Bagenal. Besides screens, the orchestra was given a roof of its own, held by chains, and a large hard and flat surface behind the conductor became a resonator. This was a considerable improvement. The effect for broadcasting was good, but for the audience in the hall the results depended very much on where one was sitting. No satisfactory solution was found until 1968, when the inner roof area of the building was covered with large convex plastic discs, known popularly as 'flying saucers', with a view to diffusing the sounds and preventing echoes from forming. Now at last we are able to listen to music satisfactorily in the Albert Hall, but this has only really been possible since 1968. The cost was £8000, shared between the BBC and the Arts Council of Great Britain. In 1941, the Albert Hall provided more elbow-room for promenading, but acoustic conditions were then vastly inferior to the old Queen's Hall. The general appearance of the hall was decidedly dingy and neglected, and on hot summer nights the ventilation seemed (and still seems) very inadequate. Douglas had a clause in his agreement which would have enabled him to close the Proms down if the box-office receipts fell below a certain figure. They did not – but the possibility hung like a sword over Wood's head – as did also the possibility of Douglas being called up for national service. 'I was obliged to avoid "novelties" and other musical satisfactions,' wrote Wood, '. . . for, as everyone knows, to *close down* meant defeat and disaster, from which even my courage and renown might never recover.'

Despite many 'misunderstandings' between Douglas and Wood, the 1941 season of six weeks was undoubtedly a success. The then Director-General of the BBC, F. W. Ogilvie, congratulating Wood on the season of Proms, described what he had done as 'a grand piece of national service, both in itself and as bearing witness in wartime to the things of permanent value and beauty'. During the Prom season Wood, despite his dislike of public speaking ('I speak with my baton'), took part in the BBC radio feature 'The

The opening of the Royal Albert Hall of Arts and Sciences by Queen Victoria in March 1871.

Sir Henry Wood conducting a Prom in the Albert Hall in July 1942.

Story of Queen's Hall, London'. 'I marked my own band parts, travelled all night in order to be punctual to the dot for a rehearsal, and in my day I've done as many as 140 concerts in a year! But what I've been given back is worth more than I've given out.'

Wood was now informally opening negotiations again with the BBC, at the risk of incensing Keith Douglas. Douglas was certainly incensed at not being mentioned in Wood's brief speech on the last night of the season. He had lost money in the 1940 season and, by disputing contracts, hoped to recover something from the profits of 1941. Such was Wood's generosity and dedication to his art that he could lose fees that were due to him, and be constantly irritated and distressed in his dealings with Douglas, but at the same time register his gratitude to Douglas, who had made the 1940 and 1941 seasons possible. The BBC helped, by allowing W. W. Thompson to be Wood's personal manager and take over from him certain irksome discussions of management problems. Somewhat optimistically, Wood felt on firmer ground now with the BBC, and arranged with the Albert Hall's manager, Reginald Askew, to pencil in the weeks that would be needed for the Proms in the next two years. And having settled that, he remarked to Lady Jessie: 'Good! Now all's safe for the 50th anyway [the 50th season of Proms], and I hope for the BBC too.' It was indeed safe, as we have seen – though not without delay and hesitation. According to Lady Jessie, Sir Henry was 'perturbed and ruffled' by the leisurely and seemingly none too keen way in which the BBC received back the gift of the Proms, which he regarded as 'the finest possible musical shop-window, an established wonder and envy the world over'.

At the age of seventy-two, in 1941, Wood finally conceded that he should share the conducting burden with somebody else. This broke completely with tradition. Perhaps if there had not been all the vexation over the Douglas management, he would not have 'capitulated' in this way. However that may be, for the 1941 Proms, Wood and Basil Cameron divided each concert between them – Part 1 was usually Wood and Part 2 Cameron; but sometimes the other way round.

Basil Cameron had first played violin in Wood's Queen's Hall Orchestra in 1908, since when (as he wrote to Wood) 'your great example has been my inspiration and stimulus'. Even in his first conducting appointment – miniature Promenade Concerts with an orchestra of thirty in Torquay – the influence of Wood was apparent when he organised a Wagner Festival to mark the hundredth anniversary of that composer's birth. After war service and some minor conducting jobs in England, he had made a name for himself in America, conducting the San Francisco Orchestra for two seasons and taking over the Seattle Symphony Orchestra after Beecham. He returned to England in 1938 to conduct the Covent Garden opera company when they went on tour. But his re-association with Wood and the Proms was, he considered, the most important thing that happened to him; he became well-liked by audiences over a period of twenty-four years. In a letter to B. E. Nicolls at the BBC, Wood (in 1944) gave his impressions of Cameron:

> He is now undoubtedly established in favour, a fact which gives me much comfort, for he is undoubtedly a practical professional musician with a real grip over the orchestra, and a knowledge of the repertoire and tradition, second to none. I admit he takes a bit of knowing and have come to the conclusion he is a very shy, sensitive man, but his music is right.

The shyness, lack of exhibitionism, down-to-earthness, sincerity, friendliness, together with an ability to give clear, carefully-prepared, sensible performances, made him a personality for whom the Prom audiences could feel respect and affection. He was a friend of Sibelius and his interpretations of that composer's music were considered to have an authentic flavour. (But *The Times* in 1944 thought his Sibelius Seventh at the Proms 'needed a more taut precision'.)

Wood became concerned about the poor response to the work of British composers, as he forcibly expressed in a talk to the 'Proms Circle', a society of enthusiastic Prommers founded in 1933. 'If we put on an Elgar symphony, or Vaughan Williams's *London* Symphony, or a Bax concerto, the box-office suffers.' It was a perennial problem – and still is; but in the 1942 season, now once again under the aegis of the BBC, there was no shortage of British music. After the dearth of novelties in 1941, the list of premières and 'first in England' (see p. 277) is impressive. The opening work of the 8-week season, in fact, was the *Epic March* of John Ireland, specially commissioned by the BBC for this concert. For the first time two orchestras shared the load: the London Philharmonic and the BBC Symphony Orchestra – the latter in rather an unsettled, unreliable state of mind after being hastily shifted back to London. The conducting also was shared, between Wood, Cameron and Boult, the regular conductor of the BBC Symphony Orchestra. For Wood it was a 'glorious season', largely capturing again the pre-war Prom spirit, and with nightly broadcasts again. The audience on the last night was granted the privilege of a speech, conventional, measured, but heartfelt: '. . . I must thank you and tell you what a wonderful audience you are. How you listen! Your attention is so encouraging and exhilarating.'

Sir Adrian Boult, in a letter to Wood at the end of the season, wrote of the happy co-operation. '. . . It has been a great experience for me, and I have learnt much from it, but I keep harking back to 41 years ago when you first began to teach me. I think I should have gone mad if anyone had told me then that I should one day act as your assistant at the Proms! And it has really happened.'

At the same time, Boult was writing to the new Director of Music at the BBC, Arthur Bliss, expressing the hope that the BBC orchestra would never be asked to do more than four weeks at a stretch. They had stood up well to the ordeal of the last season, but the strain was considerable. He commended the work of the orchestra's leader, Paul Beard – in particular, the excellence of his solo playing. And Boult added that, although he had derived much enjoyment from this season, he disliked the Proms.

> I like at least several days to prepare an important performance, and I cannot help feeling that nightly work of this kind is in danger of becoming very superficial. This applies also to the Orchestra, which, as a rule, gets only one single rehearsal for everything it does.

This attitude was entirely consistent with the thoughtful, dedicated approach to his art which Boult has always demonstrated. By 1942 he had extricated himself from the irksomeness of BBC administration, and could devote himself wholeheartedly to the work of the BBC Symphony Orchestra, which he had founded in 1930 – developing the scope and standard of that orchestra in the same way that he had built up the City of Birmingham Orchestra and its activities before joining the BBC.

Between the 1942 and 1943 Proms, Henry Wood's health seriously deteriorated, and he seemed unequal to the strain of the various engagements that he constantly accepted – including *The Dream of Gerontius* on Good Friday and a particularly taxing Easter Sunday orchestral concert. Lady Jessie tells how he started behaving strangely at times, and despite the semblance of the old Wood spirit there was 'a veiled touchiness that was new to him and betokened the weariness of the spirit'. He was determined to open the 49th Prom season – which he did. There was a packed audience of 6000, largely young people, and all went well. Two days later, however, at the Mozart–Brahms concert on the Monday, he had a semi-collapse when conducting Brahms's Second Symphony. 'Damn silly – I've tried to keep upright – can't understand it – had to beat almost below the desk.' He was all anger and frustration.

After that, Wood was ordered to have a month in bed, and Cameron gallantly shouldered that whole month of concerts with the London Philharmonic Orchestra. The press congratulated him on the generally high

Sir Henry Wood arriving at the Albert Hall with Lady Jessie Wood on Sunday 11 July 1943, to attend the Prom as a member of the audience. (It was the first occasion on which a Prom had been held on a Sunday.)

Sir Henry in his box (right) at the Albert Hall, 11 July 1943.

standard he achieved in his onerous task – a task which included the study of many unfamiliar scores at very short notice.

The first *Sunday* Prom took place this season – by necessity, not by design. The Albert Hall was required on 7 July by the Government 'for a meeting in honour of China on the occasion of the Sixth Anniversary of the outbreak of the Sino–Japanese War'. The programme scheduled for that evening was transferred intact to the following Sunday afternoon. Wood managed to persuade his doctors to allow him to attend. Then another quiet week and he was able to return to the rostrum. Lady Jessie reported: 'For the rest of the season he showed all his old serenity and nothing was lost musically. The old fire returned, glowing throughout the remaining concerts.' The BBC wanted a speech from him on the last night; but it was feared that the strain of doing something which he disliked would be too great. Instead, he recorded his speech and it was relayed to the last night audience, and to listeners at home. Returning to the platform, it was as though he had been speaking into a microphone off-stage.

Not many conductors like to have members of the public attending rehearsals as a regular thing – least of all to have hordes of children milling about. In 1943, however, Wood was arranging with the LCC to allow children up to fifteen years of age to be admitted free of charge to Prom rehearsals, the only stipulation being that they be kept as far as conveniently possible from the orchestra, so as to be out of earshot of what the conductor was saying. How this could be ensured, it was difficult to see, but the whole idea was well-meaning and of considerable educational value. Wood was also continuing his work at the Royal Academy of Music, and his teaching of singing. There were regular auditions, too, for the Proms. And in the last part of the year he was again busily involved with concerts in various parts of the country.

The 1943 audiences for the Proms totalled nearly a quarter of a million, with an average attendance of about 4000. The Queen's Hall could not have accommodated such numbers.

15

Promenade Jubilee
and the End of an Era

63 Harley House
Regent's Park, NW1

26th May 1944

The Director General
BBC
Broadcasting House
Portland Place, W.1.

Dear Mr Haley,

It is my desire to perpetuate my life's work for the good of the people and I feel that the BBC is the most suitable organisation to carry on my Promenade Concerts after my retirement. I am, therefore, now writing to say that it is my wish that the BBC should have the exclusive right to use the title, 'The Henry Wood Promenade Concerts', or some similar title involving the use of my name, for any future series of Promenade Concerts which may be presented by the BBC. It is, however, understood that, if at some future time the BBC is not prepared to carry on the annual presentation of the Promenade Concerts, adequate notice will be given of that intention and I or my personal representatives may authorise some other body or person to use the title.

Yours sincerely,

(Sgd) Henry J. Wood

Broadcasting House
London W.1.

30th May, 1944

Sir Henry Wood,
Cromwell Hotel,
Stevenage, Herts.

Dear Sir Henry,

Thank you for your letter of 26th May. I fully understand your desire to perpetuate your life's work in connection with the Promenade Concerts, and I appreciate your choice of the BBC as the most suitable organisation to carry on the Concerts after your retirement. I am sure that the exclusive right to use the title 'The Henry Wood Promenade Concerts', or some similar title involving the use of your name, which you are so generously granting to the BBC, will be the most effectual way of linking your name with the future series of Promenade Concerts which, as you know, it is the intention of the BBC to continue annually as at present. In the event of the BBC abandoning this intention, notice shall be given to you or your personal representatives within three months of the end of the last season.

Yours sincerely,

(Sgd) W. J. Haley

Director-General

63 Harley House
Regent's Park, N.W.1

1st June 1944

W. J. Haley Esq.
Broadcasting House
W.1.

Dear Mr Haley,

Thank you for your letter of 30th May. I am very pleased to have your agreement with regard to the continuation of the Promenade Concerts, and I hope with all my heart that the BBC will never have to give me that three months' advice mentioned in our exchange letters.

Sincerely yours,

(Sgd) Henry J. Wood

On 3 March 1944 Wood was seventy-five years old; on 10 August 1944 the Proms were fifty years old. To celebrate these events jointly, a national Jubilee Fund was launched, under the chairmanship of Lord Horder, 'to mark an epoch in English music and to provide a new and much needed concert hall in Central London to hold 4000 people'.

On the surface Wood was back to his old form, with a heavy list of engagements for the year of his double celebration. Among these was a lunch given by the BBC in his honour on 5 June. The guests included Sir Allan Powell, Chairman of the BBC's Board of Governors, Sir Adrian Boult, and Brendan Bracken, Minister of Information. In reply to speeches, Wood emphasised his wish that the BBC become curator of the Proms and carry on the concerts as long as they thought fit. He hoped, too, he said, that enough money would be subscribed to his Fund to build a London concert hall, acoustically perfect and conveniently situated for everyone.

In another distressing bout of correspondence with the BBC, Wood had been worried that the Corporation were being slow in seeking an automatic option on the Albert Hall each year for the Proms, and he threatened to offer himself to another management if this option were not settled. He was afraid the BBC would place the Proms 'in their archives, merely for future reference, as a relic of the past!!!!!' It was the future of the Proms, not his own future, that he was considering. After 1944, he told the BBC, he would be easing off, but certainly not retiring from the rostrum.

King George VI sent a telegram of congratulations: Wood was 'the Nation's greatest teacher of music'. More luncheons. Arthur Bliss wrote a fanfare in Wood's honour. The Poet Laureate, John Masefield, rose to the occasion – though not, perhaps, with one of his best poetic utterances.

To Sir Henry Wood

> How many thousand times have you upheld
> A batonette between two multitudes,
> Each hushed to ready and receptive moods,
> Waiting your mind's impulsion, that will bring
> Oneness to beat, to breath and stroken string,
> And beauty's presence, holding the house spelled?

Ah, many times to me, as to the race,
You have compelled this ecstasy of law
Lifting the human pattern from its flaw,
In the dry desert giving living dew.
Lord of sweet Music and of Langham Place,
Today, this Nation thanks and praises you.

On 25 March 1944, in the presence of HM The Queen and her two daughters, Elizabeth and Margaret, a special combined Birthday and Jubilee concert (which had been postponed owing to bomb damage) took place in the Albert Hall. Organised by *The Daily Telegraph*, three orchestras – the ones then associated with the Proms – London Symphony, London Philharmonic, and BBC Symphony Orchestra – joined together for the occasion.

Then, on 10 June, the ill-fated Golden Jubilee season of Proms began, starting earlier in the summer than usual. The concerts were timed to begin at 7 and end at 9.15 pm, in order to make the most of the hours of light and enable as many people as possible to return home before blackout time. Cameron and Boult were again the associate conductors. Eighteen novelties were planned.

It was the year of the flying bombs, popularly known as 'doodle-bugs' – one of Hitler's most morale-shaking weapons, with their clear buzzing approach, then the cut-out and ominous silence for a second or two, followed by the explosion. Despite this menace, the hall was packed each evening and enthusiasm knew no bounds. But again, the risk of a bomb amongst such a throng caused the authorities to bring the public concerts to an end, after less than three weeks. This time, however, not completely to an end, because the parts of the concerts which had been earmarked for broadcasts – about twenty of them in the Home Service and ten in the General Forces Programmes – were performed in Bedford, with 'invited' audiences of between 100 and 200 in the Hall of Bedford School (burned down in 1978 by an arsonist) and in the Corn Exchange. Both these halls were acoustically excellent. Bedford was where the BBC Symphony Orchestra was then stationed, and the distance from London, fifty-two miles, was reasonably convenient for soloists.

Thus the season continued, often with satisfying results. Paul Beard, after Wood had conducted a fine performance of Sibelius's *En Saga*, greeted him warmly with 'Thank you, Sir Henry – that is living again – that is what musicians need!' But as Lady Jessie has told, Wood was acting strangely, in rehearsals and in social situations. The climax came with a performance of

Sir Henry Wood and his first two associate conductors, Basil Cameron (right) and Sir Adrian Boult.

The BBC Symphony Orchestra, with its conductor Sir Adrian Boult, in the Corn Exchange, Bedford, c. 1944.

Beethoven's Seventh Symphony – that joyous 'apotheosis of the dance', as Wagner called it. Those who heard this performance describe it as extraordinary – unlike any other he had given. Boult, for example: 'It swept us along with all the torrential energy of that immortal work, and any stranger who was listening at home might well have thought that the performance was in the charge of some brilliant young conductor in his early forties.' Afterwards, though cheerful, Wood looked drawn and tired. He had 'given his all', and the strain had been immense. That night he suffered a frightening rigor similar to that of the previous year. Again he rallied – but this was followed a few days later by a relapse, and complete rest was ordered. He seemed much better by 7 August, and was showing interest in the broadcasts from the Proms.

The actual day of the fiftieth anniversary was 10 August. The concert was given from a Bedford studio of the BBC, and it was to bring the season to an end, somewhat before its time. Wood was too ill even to listen to the radio, too ill to hear Thalben-Ball play a Handel Organ Concerto which Wood had scored not long before. The announcer, Stuart Hibberd, read over the air a message of good wishes which Wood had sent, and Lord Horder made an appeal as chairman of the Jubilee Fund. When Lady Jessie had told him about the concert, Wood seemed content, satisfied that it had been a success. Now, after a long lifetime of unremitting music-making, his energy was slipping away and he could depart in peace. He died just over a week later, on 19 August 1944.

Fate denied him a complete rounding off of his fifty years of Prom conducting; but his career was surely one of the most complete and fulfilled in the history of music. By his utter commitment to music, coupled with inexhaustible energy, he was able to communicate his knowledge and enthusiasm in direct and practical ways: first, an enormous range of music, old and new, brought to millions who might otherwise not have discovered it; second, the teaching of music, the 'how' of music-making; third, the training of orchestral players and the establishing of a *standard* of performance; fourth, the encouragement and opportunities given to composers – an aspect which has altered the course of British musical history. With justice, he is called the father of British orchestral music. An outstanding personal quality was his constant generosity of spirit.

The Jubilee Fund became the Henry Wood Memorial Fund. There were large contributions from the 75th Birthday Concert in 1944 and the Memorial Concert the following year; also from a Sir Henry Wood Birthday Concert in 1946 (all these being sponsored by *The Daily Telegraph*). Originally all the profits from the 1944 Prom season were to go to the Fund: it had been estimated that these would be around £10,000. But the public concerts had ended in less than three weeks, so it was in fact much less. Further correspondence with the BBC: in July 1944 Wood wrote to Nicolls asking whether the BBC could not keep to the figure of £10,000, contributing it to the Fund in acknowledgement of all the help and co-ordination they had had from him. Lady Jessie thought the BBC was legally obliged to do so; but this was not so – and finally the Treasury agreed to a figure of only £1000. The Gramophone Company, the Performing Right Society, The Musicians' Benevolent Fund each contributed £1000. Eventually the Fund closed with a sum of about £77,000. Following a suggestion by Boult, Cameron and Sargent, the government agreed that the money should be used for building a smaller hall within Queen's Hall, when the latter would be rebuilt. It would be called the Henry Wood Rehearsal Hall and would accommodate a full symphony orchestra and a choir of 300. But when? 'How long, O Lord, how long?' Meanwhile, the value of the money declined.

During the long wait, the concert halls on London's South Bank came into existence. Not till 1975 was the Henry Wood project realised – and then it was only a partial realisation. The deconsecrated Holy Trinity Church, Southwark, was converted to become London's first-ever permanent rehearsal hall – primarily for the London Philharmonic and London Symphony Orchestras. Further grants for it had come from the Arts Council of Great Britain, the GLC, the Department of the Environment, and EMI, which brought the total (with the earlier contributions) up to the £450,000 that was needed. Arup Associates (the architects responsible for the converting of the Maltings, Snape) were put in charge of the project, and the Henry Wood Hall in this form was opened on 16 June 1975.

16
The Music 1938-1944

The BBC's twelfth Annual Report, 1938, states quite simply: 'The 44th season of Queen's Hall Promenade Concerts was given under the conductorship of Sir Henry Wood, and the attendance at these concerts constituted a new record.' That was all. No further comment. But it was in every way a special season – not only as a personal success for Wood, in his Jubilee season, with Prommers demonstrating tremendous enthusiasm at every concert and a twenty-minute ovation on the last night; it was also an immensely satisfying series musically. The full repertoire of that year is given in Appendix C (see pp. 332 ff.).

A feature of the season was the inclusion of many well-established works first heard at the Proms – premières and 'first time in England'. Basically, the usual kind of pattern was followed: Monday Wagner; Wednesday Brahms; Friday Beethoven. There was a concert devoted to Rachmaninov – a composer with whom Wood had become very friendly. Benjamin Britten was soloist in the première of his Piano Concerto (later revised), and he conducted his Frank Bridge Variations. Constant Lambert conducted the first concert performance of the Suite from his successful ballet *Horoscope*; also his *Rio Grande*, with the pianist Angus Morrison. The *Pastoral* Symphony of Vaughan Williams was again conducted by the composer.

In 1939 Hitler brought the season to an end after barely three weeks. It was a season of big names – Richard Tauber, Moiseiwitsch, Albert Sammons, Roy Henderson, Solomon, Louis Kentner . . . Of novelties, audiences managed to hear (before the season was interrupted) the first English performance of Sir Arthur Bliss's Piano Concerto, which had had its première at the New York World Fair that same year; and the first English performance of Samuel Barber's *Essay for Orchestra*.

'Sir Henry Wood's Forty-sixth and Final Season': so proclaimed (falsely) the notices of the 1940 season. Again, it was closed down prematurely – after only four of the planned eight weeks – this time through danger from air attacks. Those four weeks were problematic ones, but audiences were large and musically there were rewarding experiences. Wood this time made notes about the concerts. 'LSO nearly perfect in Beethoven's No. 5.' About a concerto by Palmgren played during a Scandinavian Concert, he wrote: 'Cyril Smith played well but the concerto is not interesting.' Beatrice Harrison 'gave the best performance of the Elgar Cello Concerto I ever directed and the LSO accompanied perfectly.' Maurice Cole 'finer than ever in Schumann' (Concerto). Joan Tribe, singing the 'Bell Song' from Delibes's *Lakmé*, 'was a great success with the public – looked well and was well dressed.' And *The Times* reported that Albert Sammons was 'on the top of his form' in the Elgar Violin Concerto.

Among the novelties of 1940 was the première of an *Introduction and Allegro* for two pianos and orchestra by Lennox Berkeley – the solo pianists being the composer and William Glock, in twenty years' time to become an important figure in the shaping of the Proms. Wood described Berkeley's work as 'modern but interesting and good'. Another première was a piece called *Once upon a time* by William H. Harris, organist of St George's Chapel, Windsor, who conducted. According to Wood it was 'a nice clean clever work, a great success'. And Walton conducted both his *Façade* Suites. The final concert before the close-down, the final Prom concert in Queen's Hall, included the *Three Pieces for Orchestra* by Elisabeth Lutyens, in an individual 12-note style for which British audiences were apparently not ready. 'Did not get a hand,' wrote Wood. 'Thank God, only 5 minutes of excessive boredom.'

A frequent visitor to the 1940 Proms was the American Ambassador, Joseph P. Kennedy, father of the future President of the USA. 'The pleasure your concerts gave me', he wrote to Wood, 'was perhaps the most satisfying thing I experienced during this sorry autumn.'

Musically, the 1941 season was safe, unadventurous. There were no novelties and the threat of closure was very real. The conducting was shared between Wood and Cameron. Cheeringly, there were twenty broadcasts from the Proms in 1941, which helped to make that season financially viable under the difficult Douglas management.

Back with the BBC in 1942, Wood had two orchestras and two associate conductors (Cameron and Boult). In contrast to the unadventurousness of 1941, it was possible to present an impressive array of 'novelties'. These included several important British premières: the Violin Concerto of E. J. Moeran, with Arthur Catterall as soloist; the Symphony No. 4 by Edmund Rubbra, conducted by the composer; the Symphony in C by Alan Bush, with its left-wing 'programme' sparking off controversy in the press. And there were other premières – works by Harry Farjeon, W. L. Reed (a young Oxford composer), Alec Rowley, W. H. Harris, Norman Demuth, Leighton Lucas and Mary Anderson Lucas. Walton conducted his *Scapino* Overture, and Alan Rawsthorne conducted his First Piano Concerto, which (like his Second) has enjoyed considerable popularity at the Proms. As already stated, the BBC had commissioned the *Epic March* by John Ireland, which opened the 1942 series. For wartime, it was indeed an enterprising series as a whole.

In 1940 that excellent writer of programme notes, Rosa Newmarch, died. She was a 'treasured friend' of Wood and her name had for a great many years been associated with the Proms. After her death, the onerous task of providing 'analytical notes' for each concert was taken over by Edwin Evans, whose breadth of outlook, clear style and reliability made him an admirable choice. From 1943 onwards, however, several writers shared the task.

Now that the Proms were again under the management of the BBC, it was necessary for them to be planned within the framework of BBC music activities as a whole. To some extent this may have been inhibiting, but it could also be useful in the case of non-repertoire works which had already been rehearsed for other symphony concerts by the same orchestra. Friday was still Beethoven night in 1943; but otherwise the pattern of concerts was more flexible than usual. This was the season in which Wood, after a concert in which he was conducting Brahms's Second Symphony, partially collapsed and had to be away from the Proms for a month. A number of concerts during the season were presented as 'Music of our Allies', with evenings devoted to American, Russian, French, Belgian, Polish, Czech and Norwegian music. It was part of the BBC's aim to provide listeners overseas with an impression of British musical life, which was extremely vigorous during the war. Among other kinds of concerts, the Proms were reflected in the main overseas services. This has continued; the BBC's World Service (previously the General Overseas Service) has each year broadcast numerous relays and recordings from the Proms.

American works, new to England, heard during the 1943 Proms included *A Lincoln Portrait* by Aaron Copland, William Schuman's Symphony No. 3, and Walter Piston's Sinfonietta. The Czech Army Choir and the Polish Army Choir took part in concerts of the music of their countries. ·The Russian 'novelties' included Alexandrov's *Overture on Russian Folk-tunes*, Kabalevsky's Suite from *Colas Breugnon*, and Khachaturian's *Legend*. Florence Hooton was soloist in the première of the Cello Concerto by William Busch (conducted by Boult). Wood returned on 24 July to conduct Part 2 of a concert which included his Bach–Klenovsky Toccata and Fugue.

Wood was made a Companion of Honour in 1944, and the Prom season, the 50th, should have been a climax of jubilation in his seventy-fifth year. But, as already recounted, it was abortive, partly through the flying bombs, partly through Wood's illness. A letter from the then Director-General of the BBC, William Haley, expressed warm admiration for the way in which Wood and Cameron had carried on for so long 'with these robots flying about'. He thanked Wood personally 'for keeping the Jubilee flag flying so gallantly and so successfully amidst so much hazard: it is another notable milestone in your long and distinguished career.' Nineteen premières and first British performances had been arranged for this Jubilee season, but only a few of these were realised. Before the public concerts at the Albert Hall ended there had been two premières: Bantock's *Two Hebridean Sea Poems* and Montague Phillips's *In Praise of my Country*, in both cases conducted by the composer. Eda Kersey was soloist in the Violin Concerto by the American Samuel Barber and Irene Kohler in a Fantasy Concerto for piano and orchestra by Eugene Goossens — both first British performances.

To include artists and works associated with the past Henry Wood Proms was an important aspect of the planning of this season. Moiseiwitsch, Mary Jarred, Eva Turner appeared; Maggie Teyte sang Berlioz; Clifford Curzon was soloist in Delius's Piano Concerto and he joined with Benjamin Britten in the latter's *Scottish Ballad* for two pianos and orchestra (a partnership which later extended to some gramophone recordings of other pieces by Britten).

The broadcast-only concerts (and parts of concerts) from Bedford included a wide range of Prom music, including Louis Kentner playing Liszt's Piano Concerto No. 2, and Myra Hess playing the Grieg Concerto, Beatrice Harrison again in the Elgar Cello Concerto, and Eileen Joyce in Prokofiev No. 3. Boult conducted a special Soviet programme, with the Russian soprano Oda Slobodskaya. There were also two other 'first in England' performances of Soviet works: the Symphony No. 8 by Shostakovich, who was still only thirty-six years old; and the *Ode to Stalin* by Khachaturian. The brilliant Australian-born pianist and composer, Noel Mewton-Wood, was heard this season in Bach's D minor Concerto. (He was twenty-one; eight years later, in tragic circumstances, he committed suicide.) Pouishnoff was heard in Tchaikovsky's B flat minor Concerto – a favourite then as now – and in the same programme Roy Henderson was soloist in Delius's *Sea Drift*. For radio listeners, the 'Bedford Proms' in fact presented much that was worth-while and in the true Henry Wood traditions.

And so it continued – to the Jubilee Concert itself, 10 August, which also became the last night of the series. In *Radio Times* it appeared as follows:

50 YEARS OF PROMS

Programme to celebrate the fiftieth
anniversary of Mr. Henry J. Wood's first
Promenade Concert, at Queen's Hall, on
August 10th, 1895.

BBC Symphony Orchestra, conducted by
Sir Henry Wood and Sir Adrian Boult

George Pizzey (baritone)
George Thalben-Ball (organ)

OVERTURE: RIENZI – – – – – – –	*Wagner*
PRÉLUDE À L'APRÈS-MIDI D'UN FAUNE – – – –	*Debussy*
'LARGO AL FACTOTUM' (*Barber of Seville*) – – – –	*Rossini*
ORGAN CONCERTO No. 4, in F – – – –	*Handel, arr. Wood*
FANFARE FOR SIR HENRY WOOD – – – – – –	*Bliss*

Sir Henry Wood speaks about the Jubilee Fund

THEME AND VARIATIONS (Suite No. 3) – – – –	*Tchaikovsky*
RULE, BRITANNIA!	
GOD SAVE THE KING	

The Overture to *Rienzi* and 'Largo al factotum' were heard in the 1895 opening concert (see p. 33), but otherwise, in overall character and content, it felt very different. A letter was handed to Wood just before the concert, as he lay terribly ill, forbidden by his doctors even to have a radio at his bedside. The message was signed by Sir Adrian Boult and a number of others connected with the concert: 'Here we are, audience, orchestra, announcer, soloists, and conductor, waiting to begin your Jubilee celebration, and very sad that you are not with us. We all send our love and wish you a quick recovery, and many more Proms to come!'

It was like a performance of *Hamlet* without the Prince of Denmark.

17

A New Era begins

Henry Wood had steered the Proms through the troubled waters of the Second World War. As early as 1942 he had delivered them from the uncertainties and perils of private enterprise and brought them again into the relatively calm harbour of the BBC, where he hoped they would be permanently safe. For nearly half a century he had built them up, a musical and social institution with which his name was closely associated, but which now had a life of its own and was bigger than any one person. And it was at the mercy of those who came after.

In Wood's time, the Proms had reflected his own wide-ranging tastes and adventurous outlook. No one could say he was swayed by fashion or motivated by personal gain: success was measured purely by what he managed to achieve musically. This amounted to the planning of an overall picture of what was best and most representative in the orchestral repertoire over two centuries (complemented by certain other kinds of music), with due regard to the work of British composers – and then realising this picture in a series of some fifty-four concerts over a period of eight weeks, making the whole thing available to as wide an audience as possible.

The Proms, as a 'going concern', were passed (after Wood's death) from a single individual to a hierarchical Corporation – from one viewpoint to a collection of viewpoints. One of the problems of planning in the BBC is that the professional departments, including music, which propose and supply the programmes, are subject always to the control, tastes and wishes of the overall planners of the various broadcasting services (Home Service, Light Programme and Third Programme – as they became in 1946). A lot of mutual understanding is needed, and this is not always easily found. A service planner is in a position to accept or reject the professional advice offered to him; and often a person in a powerful position who is not a musician may make musical judgements in terms of his own generalised knowledge and the needs of the broadcasting service as he sees them.

It was no doubt some decision of this sort in 1945 which caused all the 'novelties' of the Prom season to be put in the second (and non-broadcast) part of the programme. It was a season rich in novelties – including Schoenberg's Piano Concerto, Britten's Four Sea Interludes and Passacaglia from *Peter Grimes*, Rawsthorne's *Cortèges*, Hindemith's ballet overture *Cupid and Psyché* – but not one of them was heard by radio listeners, no doubt because the planners wanted 'safe' programmes for the Home Service, at a time when the only alternative service was the General Forces Programme. In 1946 the situation was similar: the highly cultural Third Programme, which made it easy to accommodate unfamiliar and 'difficult' works, did not start until after the Prom season in that year.

Immediately after the war, the BBC's Director of Music was Victor Hely-Hutchinson, the South African-born pianist, conductor, teacher and composer (his best-known work is *A Carol Symphony*). He succeeded Arthur Bliss in 1944, when the latter resigned in order to devote himself to composition. In an internal memorandum to the Controller of Programmes, Hely-Hutchinson makes his position clear. The BBC would run the Proms in accordance with Henry Wood's known wishes. So, in normal BBC fashion, a Committee was formed: it consisted of the Deputy Director of Music (Kenneth Wright); Julian Herbage, who had been closely connected with the programme side of the Proms for a good many years; the Concert Manager (W. W. Thompson), who had been associated with the management of the Proms for a generation; and the two joint chief conductors for the season – Basil Cameron and Adrian Boult. When Constant Lambert's appointment as associate conductor was made public, he too would join the Committee. Lambert (one of the bright lights of the musical world at the time, and a brilliant critic) was already well known to Prom audiences as composer and conductor – notably with his *Rio Grande* and *Horoscope*. The BBC Symphony Orchestra, it was planned, would do four weeks: the London Symphony and the London Philharmonic Orchestras one fortnight each. There was trouble, however, with the LPO over relay fees for broadcasting: they were demanding £150 per concert, when the regular fee for this was £120. In the end the LPO had to withdraw.

Originally it was planned to have a 'Victory' season of winter Proms, but this idea was dropped in preference to making the summer Proms as good as possible – a real continuity of Wood's great work. To quote Hely-Hutchinson: 'The Committee is quite unanimous in feeling that we must regard ourselves in this case as Trustees, for the present season at any rate, of what has become a National Institution.' Others in the BBC, less musically committed, felt that this reverent attitude was unrealistic. The

Constant Lambert (1905–51), who as a composer and 'associate' conductor made a strikingly individual contribution to the Proms.

'terms of reference' of the Proms included the encouragement of new and outstanding talent; but Hely-Hutchinson was writing to about a dozen established composers asking them 'whether they had got any new works which we might include in the series': a dangerous request, which could easily saddle the BBC with several indifferent works rescued from drawers! In cases of disagreement over works or artists, the final court of appeal would be Hely-Hutchinson, as 'musical representative of the BBC which is promoting the season'. There was also the feeling that the series should be 'de-personalised' – meaning, presumably, that the series should not be a showcase for one conductor, or be manipulated to one conductor's advantage. The music must come first, as it did for Wood – and for Cameron and Boult.

The first season after the outbreak of peace was an enormous success, and once more attendance records were broken. It was again possible to admit the audience to the top gallery – which had not been permitted in wartime. Everything, in fact, combined to make it financially the most successful season ever. Boult and Cameron both proved popular figures (Boult marginally more so, according to statistics in the BBC files). Constant Lambert, the associate conductor, who was given four half-concerts with each orchestra and one whole concert with the BBC orchestra, was rather less of a draw, but this was partly because he was given works in which he was considered to specialise but which were not necessarily the best box-office ones (for example, Liszt, Chabrier, Ravel). Hely-Hutchinson reported to his Controller:

> Our own feeling is that Lambert's inclusion was abundantly justified, and that in a year or two, if we persevere with him (as I think we should), he will have won a permanent place in the series. He did make a positive contribution to the season, and materially confirmed his reputation in the musical world.

Hely-Hutchinson's conclusion from the results of this season was that 'the Promenade audience, though broad-minded and welcoming, is essentially a conservative one, and also that it likes its favourite composers in large doses'. Adrian Boult found the programmes 'better than ever'. They were largely the work of Julian Herbage and W. W. Thompson, the former continuing to be chief programme-builder and co-ordinator for the Proms – first from inside the BBC and later in a free-lance capacity – until the planning of these concerts was taken over completely by William Glock at the end of the 1950s.

An important feature of the 1945 season was the performance of all seven Sibelius symphonies. The public response was not entirely wholehearted, but warm enough for the Music Department to feel that this should be a regular event, which for a time it was.

The 1946 season followed the same pattern of orchestras and conductors. Boult was not keen to carry on with the Proms, for reasons already given, but Hely-Hutchinson persuaded him to continue for that year. The Proms might well have suffered if his personality had been suddenly withdrawn. Lambert was given another season, despite objections by Cameron – not objections to Lambert personally, but disagreement with the Music Department about the need to *have* a post of associate conductor. Hely-Hutchinson wanted to establish the post on a secure basis, seeing the work of a younger conductor as being 'the main plank at present in the forward-looking policy of the Proms', and continuing to recommend Lambert for the position. If Cameron had proved too difficult over this, they might have had to drop him (Cameron) from the series, with reluctance. Alternative ideas had been considered in January 1946: to approach Eugene Goossens to take over Cameron's share of the Proms; to try to get Barbirolli and the Hallé Orchestra for that month. In the event, the cast remained the same.

In his preface to the 1946 Prom prospectus, Julian Herbage considered the slowly changing face of the Proms.

> Looking casually through the list of the 300 or so works to be played during the season the same old war-horses rear their heads with consistent regularity. The same old Beethoven nights on Fridays, the mixture of Brahms, Tchaikovsky, Mozart, and Bach as before. Once again the 'classical' repertoire is covered with the usual conscientious thoroughness, and the forty-nine nights provide once more an anthology of the masterpieces of orchestral music . . . Perhaps the most important change this season is that the programmes, taken as a whole, are becoming ever more symphonic in character.

He mentions that not only all the Sibelius symphonies but also all the Vaughan Williams symphonies (five by then) were to be included, and the Wednesday programmes were planned to reflect the important musical developments of the time. The 'novelties' list was shorter than usual, but nearly all the works in it were of major calibre (see p. 278). But while the programmes developed in their own right, the broadcasting of the more unusual aspects of the season remained very incomplete and unsatisfactory.

Not everybody in the BBC was happy about the Proms becoming 'ever more symphonic in character'. In February 1947 Nicolls, now Senior Controller, was reproving the Music Department in an internal memorandum, first by outlining the aims of the Proms as he saw them:

The Interval at the Albert Hall during a Prom, 21 August 1945.

Vaughan Williams conducting the London Symphony Orchestra at a Prom on 31 July 1946.

(1) to provide popular programmes of good music designed to attract new listeners and new concert-goers, and lead them on to an appreciation of the classics of the orchestral repertoire, and (2) to encourage British music, to perform new works, and to bring out new artists . . .

The programmes in recent years, especially in the 1946 season, have become too symphonic and advanced in character. In the 1947 season this tendency should be corrected by (a) introducing a leavening of short popular works, without prejudice to the standard repertoire, especially on Saturday nights and (b) skilfully combining the novelties and difficult works with the more familiar favourites.

For his own, different reasons, Sir Adrian Boult was asking Hely-Hutchinson for

a fundamental overhaul of our attitude to the Proms, which seem to me to have over-reached themselves to a dangerous degree. On paper, we are giving programmes of identical calibre with our Symphony Concerts, at greater length and at half the price. Even the artists are now on the same plane. This is not only an absurd situation, it is dishonest, for the slipshod nature of our performances cannot be understood by most of that young audience, and even our professional critics seem to assume that we have three rehearsals for every concert.

As it happened, in the next summer Proms season (1947) there *were*, thanks to Boult, three rehearsals for each concert. A scheme was adopted which had originally been suggested by Thomas Russell, secretary of the Royal Philharmonic Orchestra, namely that two orchestras should be booked *concurrently*, and that one should play for the concerts on Monday, Wednesday and Friday, while the other played on Tuesday, Thursday and Saturday. Thus each orchestra, with a day between concerts, could have two rehearsals on that day, followed by a morning rehearsal on the day of the concert. The standard of orchestral playing at the Proms reached a high level during that season, but apparently this scheme was considered too costly, because the following year the BBC decided to have alternate full weeks divided between two orchestras, with three days' rehearsal in the week off duty, thus making only two spread-out rehearsals for each concert.

Boult, in 1946, was much concerned about the standards of performance in general by the BBC Symphony Orchestra. Toscanini in 1939 had stated that he had never conducted a finer orchestra, but since then it had been doing too much, with inadequate rehearsal, in order to satisfy the various needs of the broadcasting services, and the standard was dropping. Boult appealed to 'those in charge of Corporation policy' to decide what kind of an orchestra it wished to have. To return to the 1939 Symphony Concert standard, more rehearsal time must be allowed. Eventually this was granted. At this time also, Boult was urging that he be released from the Proms. This was partly because he disliked having to prepare works hastily; but he also stated: 'I am convinced that new blood must come at once into the Proms. And I would urge that a second associate [conductor] be given at any rate one or two appearances in the January experiment, whether I appear in this or not (I hope not).'

The 'January experiment' was the revival in 1947, after eleven years, of the Winter Proms. (These continued till 1952, and were then abandoned again.) The fortnight's season in January 1947 was given by the BBC Symphony Orchestra, and Boult in fact shared the conducting with Cameron. In the prospectus of the 1947 Winter Proms, C. B. Rees gave the justification for this addition to the normal schedule:

> The early days of a New Year are essentially a time for jollification, for music and singing, for getting together in small and large parties. What could be more fitting to this period of renewed hope and expectancy, of beginning again, than a fortnight of fine music? . . . Large numbers of young people are enjoying their school holidays. The youngsters want to 'go places'. Let the concert add its delights to the lure of theatre and cinema. The addition of a fortnight to the year's normal Promenade season is an important contribution to the satisfaction of the ever-growing demand for good music, especially by the younger generation. I cannot imagine anything more appealing, or exciting, to those who are beginning to discover and explore the vast and variegated treasures of music, than to congregate in a warm, comfortable hall on a cold, dark, and perhaps wet, winter night, to hear a great orchestra discourse Beethoven, Mozart, Handel, Wagner.

It was policy that the winter programmes should be confined, for the most part, to the familiar. 'January', wrote Rees, 'is too young for elaborate exercises in the experimental and recondite.' Despite this dubious argument, there was one première (*The Hills* by Patrick Hadley) and rarely heard works by Constant Lambert and Bantock.

For the summer Proms Hely-Hutchinson would have liked a season of ten rather than eight weeks, for the programme to be 'really varied and interesting'; but this was not agreed. To fulfil the scheme of rehearsals described above, three orchestras were engaged, and Hely-Hutchinson wanted to have three chief conductors – Boult, Cameron, and Barbirolli. Barbirolli could not make himself available, so in the end the third conductor was Dr Malcolm Sargent, who had made his first appearance as composer-conductor at the Proms in 1921. He was fifty-two in 1947, and was known primarily as a highly successful choral conductor. His career had included, also, ballet seasons for Diaghilev, Gilbert and Sullivan for D'Oyly Carte, and touring with the London Philharmonic Orchestra. He had established himself as a considerable educator of the young as conductor and presenter of the Robert Mayer Children's Concerts. Besides all this, in the heyday of radio Sargent became a household name through his participation in the long-running series, *The Brains Trust*. His lucidly expressed views on a wide range of subjects made a very strong impact.

> As to the identity of the Associate Conductor [wrote Hely-Hutchinson to his Controller], I feel that in 1947 we should substitute Stanford Robinson for Lambert. I opposed this suggestion two years ago because Robinson was then specifically associated with the Theatre Orchestra; but now that he is associated with the Symphony Orchestra, I think it would be unjustifiable not to allot this work to him. How much he would have to do would depend on the requirements of the individual conductors, and would probably vary with each of them. But the programmes could be built in such a way as to make it clear that he had a 'stake' in the Season as a whole. This recommendation does not imply a criticism of the work that Lambert has done in the last two years. His work on the whole has been very good, although he has not quite built himself up in the way that we hoped he would when he was originally appointed. In other words, I do not see Lambert developing into a Chief Conductor of the Proms one day . . .

Thus, in the BBC, the fate of a musician of Lambert's calibre was decided. The job of Associate Conductor went to Stanford Robinson, a BBC man who had founded the Wireless Singers (which became the BBC Singers), and had been conductor of the BBC Theatre Orchestra, later becoming assistant to Boult with the BBC Symphony Orchestra.

The BBC presented the 1947 season with a certain justifiable pride: three orchestras (BBC, LSO, LPO), three conductors (Cameron, Boult, Sargent) and an associate conductor (Stanford Robinson), eight weeks of daily concerts surveying the whole field of orchestral music – the classical repertoire and music of yesterday and today – each concert prepared with three rehearsals. No other series but the Proms was complete in this way: other concert-promoters gave a surfeit of certain works and grossly neglected others.

Not everybody was happy, however. Charles Stuart, music critic of *The Observer*, treated the whole thing (20 July 1947) as a *grande bouffe* under the

Tickets for the first and last nights of the Proms were first allocated by ballot in 1947. Revolving drums were used for the purpose.

heading 'Almanach des Gourmands'. The Saturday nights 'are as miscellaneous as the Caledonian Market – everything you can think of and nothing you really want'. He attacked the Lucullan banquet with the criticism that a concert programme should always be a unity, and that

> until Prom audiences are able to distinguish between menu and cafeteria, between a deftly composed programme and what sometimes looks like a fortuitous concurrence of musical oddments, it cannot be claimed that any significant progress has been made.

Harsh words, but they emphasise what is the most difficult aspect of the programme-building of these concerts – to make each concert a rounded significant thing in itself.

The Times of 25 July 1947 took a less jaundiced view of the Proms prospectus.

> If the Prom repertory in general is now of more consistent quality than it was 50 years ago, the devolution of the arduous season of eight weeks of daily music upon three orchestras and three and a half conductors is a great step forward towards more finished performances, made possible by the present financial prosperity of the concerts.

The same anonymous writer, however, asks

> what conceivable purpose can be served by putting Mahler's long Fourth Symphony into the second part of a programme otherwise devoted to Bach, or what is the point of concluding the second part with the most familiar overtures in the repertoire? [The answer, to the last, would be that overtures often make excellent 'enders', employing the full orchestral forces.] Part II [*The Times* continued] should surely contain the lighter things, Chabrier's *España*, for instance, or the *Prince Igor* dances, but not a movement from the *Fantastic* Symphony or an important novelty, since it offers golden opportunities for smaller works that will not fit into symphony concerts.

This was the season following the briefing from the Senior Controller (see p. 145) – a briefing which had the approval of the Director-General, Sir William Haley. It had been generally agreed by those in charge of the programmes 'to keep the Proms to their basic objective of being popular', and 'not to engage major international artists, but to give less famous but very good artists, British and foreign, a chance' (this was a Prom tradition). It was also agreed that the three services (Home, Light, and now Third as well) would try to broadcast every note of the Proms between them, and this was carried out nearly completely.

1947 was the first year that it was considered necessary to allocate tickets for the first and last nights by ballot. *The Sphere* magazine for 5 July 1947 has a picture showing the names of applicants being placed in large revolving drums and thoroughly mixed up before being drawn. At that time there were about 10,000 applicants for 6800 seats. Whatever the critics might be saying, the Proms that year were at the height of their success.

18

The Music 1945-1947

In 1945 the Proms had passed their Jubilee. It was hard to imagine a season from which Henry Wood was entirely absent – though little enough had been seen of him in 1944. Basil Cameron opened the first Prom concert after the war (Saturday 21 July 1945) with Elgar's *Cockaigne* Overture – the work with which Wood had opened more than one season of Proms, including the first BBC season in 1927. The London Symphony and the BBC Symphony Orchestra were both taking part in the opening concert, as they would also be doing on the last night of the season.

In the 1945 season everything was much as before, with the classical repertoire the basis of the programme-building. But now Wagner did not reign supreme on Monday nights as he had done consistently in Henry Wood's time. Instead Brahms mostly alternated with Tchaikovsky. There was some Wagner mixed in with other composers on Tuesdays or Thursdays. Wednesdays featured Bach, Handel and Mozart, and Friday was still Beethoven night. The custom of performing the Ninth ('Choral') Symphony on the last Friday of the season became established this year. Wood had often performed this Symphony in the early years of the Proms without its choral finale. When, in 1929, it had been performed complete for the first time at the Proms, a note was required in the printed programme requesting the audience not to applaud after the third movement.

It was an impressive season for 'novelties', partly because some of the unperformed works scheduled for the previous year had been transferred. Cameron conducted the first performance in England of Schoenberg's Piano Concerto, with Kyla Greenbaum as soloist. The suite from Britten's *Peter Grimes* was new and exciting, as the opera's première at Sadler's Wells had taken place only two months previously. This was the year when Peter Pears made his début at the Proms singing *Les Illuminations* by Britten (conducted by the composer) – the Rimbaud song-cycle originally written for the Swiss soprano Sophie Wyss, who also performed this work at a

Prom. Other composer-conductors included Vaughan Williams: the first concert performance of the suite from his film *The Story of a Flemish Farm*. His *Thanksgiving for Victory* also was heard. Alan Bush conducted the première of his characteristic *Fantasia on Soviet Themes*; and Constant Lambert, as Associate Conductor of the Proms, performed the suite from his wartime film *Merchant Seamen* and conducted a Hindemith 'first in England' – the ballet overture *Cupid and Psyché*. British composers were, all in all, very well represented that season, with, in addition, Rubbra's Third Symphony, Delius's *Appalachia* ('variations on an old slave song'), and substantial works by Bax, Rawsthorne and Bliss. Walton's suite from the Laurence Olivier film *Henry V* had its first concert performance.

In a letter to his friend the artist Michael Ayrton after the last night, in which all three conductors had taken part, Constant Lambert wrote:

> The last night of the Proms was fantastic – rarely have spectators been so dithyrambic. You have possibly read of the wild orgy in which 'the three conductors were pelted with flowers'. Old Fishface [Rawsthorne] had a good call after his concerto [for piano, No. 1] . . . I was delighted to see it had a bad notice from W. Glock [in *The Observer*].

Much of the so-called forward-looking part of the repertoire was given to Constant Lambert, both in 1945 and 1946, and this was looked upon as his main contribution to the Proms as a conductor. But his range was wide and included Liszt, Sibelius, French, Russian and English composers, and much else. He conducted his *Rio Grande* once again in 1946, and the première of John Ireland's overture *Satyricon* was also given by him.

In the 1946 season Vaughan Williams again conducted his *London* Symphony, and all the other four symphonies he had so far written were heard, as were, in both 1945 and 1946, all seven of Sibelius. It was a season which explored a great deal of new music from abroad: first performances in England of Shostakovich's Ninth Symphony and Prokofiev's Fifth, Bloch's *Symphonic Suite*, the American Paul Creston's *Poem* for harp and orchestra, Hindemith's *Symphonic Metamorphoses of themes by Weber*, Richard Strauss's Oboe Concerto (with Léon Goossens as soloist), Stravinsky's *Scherzo à la Russe* (conducted by Boult), and Milhaud's two marches – *In memoriam* and *Gloria victoribus*.

For the unveiling of a stained-glass window in memory of Henry Wood, in the Church of St Sepulchre, Holborn Viaduct – the church where Wood's musical life began and where his ashes remain – William Walton made his setting of Masefield's poem 'Where does the uttered music go?' This was performed by the BBC Singers, conducted by their chorus-master, Leslie Woodgate, in the last week of the 1946 Proms.

For many, one of the highlights of the season was the first appearance at the Proms of Handel's *Alexander's Feast* – the whole of the second part of the cantata, to words by John Dryden, celebrating the power of music. There were also four Wagner concerts, which pleased wide audiences on Tuesdays and Thursdays, at a time when Wagner was being neglected in English opera-houses. Elgar-lovers had a whole concert of his music, including two of his masterpieces – the Shakespearian symphonic study *Falstaff* and the Violin Concerto, with Yehudi Menuhin (making his Prom début that year). It was a season that seemed to revel in its renewed opportunities for engaging international artists: Elisabeth Schumann, Szigeti, Emil Telmanyi returned; and there was the Polish pianist Malcuzynski, the Belgian violinist Arthur Grumiaux, and the teenage French violinist Devy Erlih.

The programmes of the Winter Proms revival of 1947 mostly presented the familiar Prom repertoire, but it did contain Constant Lambert's brilliant scherzo 'King Pest' from his choral-and-orchestral work *Summer's Last Will and Testament*; also, a setting by Bantock of Robert Browning's 'oriental' poem 'Feristah's Fancies', and the première of a short choral symphony of Man's relation to Nature, *The Hills* by Patrick Hadley, then Professor of Music at Cambridge.

After the reprimand issued by the BBC's Senior Controller regarding the Proms of the 1946 season, which complained that the Proms had become 'too symphonic and advanced', there was a danger that the programmes might have been forced to the opposite extreme the next year, becoming popular and safe. This was certainly not the case. Instead, a more varied feast was prepared for the summer than perhaps ever before. Julian Herbage, in the Foreword to that season's prospectus, considered that the new and adequate rehearsal arrangements made possible the removal of any restrictions on the repertoire to be chosen.

> In what Promenade season of the past could one have conceived a performance of Stravinsky's *Le Sacre du Printemps* with, on the preceding night, a new concerto by a British composer, and on the following night, the first performance in England of a contemporary American symphony. Yet this type of programme-building is a commonplace of the present season.

That year, probably for the first time – and certainly not the last – the Proms were compared to a Festival.

> Could even Salzburg, in the palmy inter-war years [Herbage continued] offer

us three orchestras, three principal conductors, to say nothing of an associate conductor and composers directing their own works? An eight weeks' orchestral season in which the nightly concerts are allotted an average of three rehearsals each? It can safely be asserted that no such musical enterprise has previously been conceived.

Novelties were largely British. They included the first performance in London of a symphony by Victor Hely-Hutchinson, the BBC's Director of Music, who in fact had died in March of that year (1947) and had been succeeded by the well-known singer Steuart Wilson. Rawsthorne and Gordon Jacob were represented by new concertos, for oboe (Evelyn Rothwell, wife of Barbirolli) and bassoon (Archie Camden) respectively. Elisabeth Lutyens's *Petite Suite* had its first concert performance in London, conducted by Boult, and was far more warmly received than the Three Pieces which Wood performed in 1940: in fact, the idiom of the *Petite Suite* is far less demanding, as the work is based on some of Lutyens's film music. 'Brilliant, clear Prokofiev-like textures' (according to *The Times*) characterised a Concerto for Orchestra by an unknown Russian composer, Mikhail Starokadomsky. This 'first in England' was conducted by Sargent; another was the American William Schuman's Piano Concerto, conducted by Cameron, with Iris Loveridge as soloist.

Kathleen Ferrier made her début at the Proms that season. She had been 'discovered' in Manchester in 1941 by Sargent, who immediately booked her for a *Messiah* with the Royal Choral Society and recommended her to a London concert agency. She made a deep impression at the 1947 Proms with her performance of Brahms's *Alto Rhapsody*. (So successful was it that she was asked to repeat it in the 1948 season; and in 1949 an equal success awaited her in Brahms's *Four Serious Songs*, performed with Sargent's orchestral version of the accompaniment.) At the peak of her outstanding career, in 1953, she died of cancer.

19
A Plain of Achievement

The word 'plain' is used advisedly. It conveys the steady level of achievement maintained through a dozen seasons, from 1948 to 1959, after which (with the appointment of William Glock as the BBC's Controller of Music) the pattern of the Proms changed in certain ways. As far as basic repertoire was concerned, one could be sure during that period of hearing all the Beethoven and Brahms symphonies, all Beethoven's piano concertos and his violin concerto, both Brahms's piano concertos and his violin concerto (and usually the Double Concerto), some (if not all) of the Sibelius symphonies (particularly Nos. 2, 5 and 7); at least two Rachmaninov piano concertos and the Paganini Rhapsody, Tchaikovsky's symphonies (Nos. 4, 5, and 6) and at least two of his piano concertos. Up to and including 1959 this was the hard core around which other ingredients varied. Each year there was a substantial list of novelties (see pp. 256 ff.), except for 1952 which was a deliberate repertoire-establishing season.

Between the death of Hely-Hutchinson and the appointment of Steuart Wilson, the BBC's Acting Director of Music was Kenneth Wright, who, after the 1947 season of Proms, reported that Sir Malcolm Sargent had made an excellent start. 'He is ideal in personality, showmanship, and energy, and was very popular.' Sargent had the reputation of being an 'ambassador' of music in England and in many other countries, and he included in his programmes some of the works of British composers with whom he was in sympathy, notably Elgar, Vaughan Williams and Walton. But one of his drawbacks, if considered as a successor to Henry Wood, was his serious lack of enterprise, after the 1930s, when it came to new music – his complete lack of interest in taking his audience into new paths of musical experience. His vanity prevented him from risking any work which he felt was not assured of popular success. This perpetually subjective attitude to the new and untried, this fear of losing face, may have been partly through sheer lack of time to learn new things in the midst of a crowded schedule of conducting

and social activities. His judgement of works new to him was often in-
credibly hasty and superficial, for somebody who was undoubtedly very
musical indeed. For example, writing in 1955 to Leonard Isaacs, who was
then in charge of music for the BBC's Home Service, Sargent said, of
Alexander Tansman's *Isaiah*, which he had been asked to conduct:

> I cannot understand how any composer could allow himself to write a work so
> completely lacking in melodic interest. If you glance through the whole work,
> the soprano line is absolutely terrifying in its lack of ideas and complete lack of
> any sense of melody. The part writing, too, of course, is absolutely square-cut
> and juvenile in its conception. There is also no rhythmic variety or interest. It
> is just another of those compositions which consist really of a succession of
> modern harmonies. I don't know what the modern composers are coming to,
> but I really do feel that they are a very uninspired lot!

Nevertheless, between 1948 and 1959 Sargent was occasionally responsible for introducing new works in a fairly 'advanced' (but never fully
12-note) idiom, though these were few and far between. They included
Humphrey Searle's *Overture to a Drama* in 1949, Petrassi's *Partita* and
Racine Fricker's First Symphony in 1951, and Milhaud's Concerto for
percussion and small orchestra in 1959. But normally, in his basic and
desperate need to communicate with people in the mass, he preferred to
keep to the safe classics and the proven moderns. Mass communication is
also a basic need to the Proms. In his way, Sargent certainly fulfilled this
aspect with great skill and a masterly sense of style – not with selfless
dedication, as Wood had done, but producing something of the same
educative results. A vast number of concert-goers and radio listeners of the
1950s and 1960s discovered their early enjoyment of music through the way
that it was presented to them by Sargent.

Very different was the thoughtful and far less demonstrative approach of
Sir Adrian Boult, who (in his autobiography) wrote: 'I have always maintained that I as an executant am not, and have no right to be, a critic of any
kind, even to the extent of having preferences and favourites.' In 1931 he
performed the Variations, Op. 31, by Schoenberg with the BBC Symphony
Orchestra in a BBC studio concert, and five years later he gave its first
performance in the composer's home town of Vienna. Indeed a notable
event for an English conductor – and despite the fact that he could not enjoy
Schoenberg's 12-note idiom. But he found 'a craftsman's pleasure in seeing
that his H.S. and N.S. directions [*Hauptstimme* and *Nebenstimme*, chief
subject and subsidiary strand] were faithfully observed, serving as they did
as a check on the dynamic signs in the score, which he placed so wisely that

they almost tallied perfectly'. Boult tells us that some of Schoenberg's admirers expressed their approval; but, alas, the composer himself did not hear any of the performances. Boult's attitude to new works was the same as Wood's had been – to understand and to follow, as completely as possible, the intentions of the composer.

This too, was the attitude of Basil Cameron, who was responsible for a large proportion of the novelties at the Proms during his twenty-four seasons with them. Cameron's position as a Prom conductor was threatened behind the scenes, in early 1948, when the new BBC Director of Music, Steuart Wilson, wished to reduce the number of principal conductors to two – to concentrate rather than diffuse the personal side. As Boult wished to withdraw from the Proms, it was hoped that the two could be Sargent and Barbirolli. Cameron was then regarded by the BBC's Music Department as a dull conductor, without the personality to gain the enthusiastic adherence of the Prom audience – a judgement which, after Cameron's seven Prom seasons, must have been difficult to substantiate. However, Barbirolli proved unobtainable; so Cameron continued on equal terms with Sargent. Stanford Robinson ('Robbie') was, in 1948, called 'Assistant Conductor' rather than Associate, and it was agreed that he would be given at least one complete concert per week, plus any which the principal conductors could not do. There was also a contract for Julian Herbage, who had now retired from the BBC staff to become a freelance musician. For £500 he was to advise on the programme content of the Proms (as he had been doing for so many years); to attend all concerts and rehearsals, with special reference to the broadcasting side; also to attend auditions of artists and reporting sessions arising from them; and finally to write a detailed report at the end of a series. Programme notes were to be by two well-known writers about music, Hubert Foss and William McNaught – a month each.

The fortnight of Winter Proms in January 1948 had been given – without Sargent – by Cameron with the London Symphony Orchestra and Boult with the BBC Symphony Orchestra, with Stanford Robinson assisting. Then, at his own request, Boult did not take part in the summer season: it was Sargent conducting the BBC Symphony Orchestra, and Cameron conducting the LSO, again with Stanford Robinson. (Boult returned for a fortnight the following year.)

At the end of 1948, Cameron again found himself out of favour with the BBC's Music Department, who decided not to use him for the Winter Proms of 1949. Steuart Wilson had written to Cameron in October 1948 saying: 'We have decided that the BBC Orchestra can tackle them [the Winter Proms] single-handed, and with the dispensing of the second or-

chestra I am afraid that the necessity, or rather the luxury, of a second
conductor also disappears . . .' This obviously disturbed Cameron, who in
January 1947 had shared the one orchestra with Boult (a week each), and he
went to see the BBC's Director-General, Sir William Haley. Cameron
agreed that he had no legal claim, but because of his close connection with
the Proms for a number of years (originally as Henry Wood's first associate
conductor) he thought he had a moral right to more considerate treatment.
He felt he should at least have been consulted in the matter before being
presented with a *fait accompli*. The following year, however, saw a change of
leadership in the Music Department: Steuart Wilson resigned, and his place
was taken by the composer Herbert Murrill. Cameron returned to the
Proms in the summer.

    1948 was the twenty-first anniversary of the BBC taking over the Proms: a
Coming-of-Age celebration of what was something of a landmark in British
music. As the Concert Manager, W. W. Thompson, pointed out: 'Until that
moment (1927), singers, instrumentalists, and orchestra could either play in
concert halls or broadcast, but it was difficult for them to do both.' Previously, no microphone had ever invaded the sacred precincts of Queen's
Hall, and (as we have already seen) many thought it was the end of concert
life when it did. In fact, the appetite of audiences was whetted and attendance at concerts increased greatly.

    In the Wood–Newman days of the Proms, the planning and management
of this eight-week series of concerts rested with a very small number of
hard-working people. In the 1950s, as run by the BBC, it became more than
six-months' work for dozens of people – as one of them, Patricia Young,
explained in the magazine *Music and Musicians* in August 1953. In December there were auditions. Then the Concerts Manager and Julian
Herbage began the tremendous task of working out forty-nine consecutive
programmes, with some general guidelines (such as Beethoven on Friday
and popular works on Saturdays) and including carefully-chosen new works
by British and foreign composers. By about March, programmes were ready
for approval by the conductors, the BBC's music chiefs and Controllers.
Then orchestras, conductors and soloists had to be booked, and posters and
an attractive prospectus brought out. There were tickets to be printed,
programme notes to be commissioned and edited, and as much publicity as
possible put in motion. There was the task of providing music for all the
concerts – scores, orchestral parts – a job for a full-time orchestral librarian;
and music had to be sent to soloists and choirs. Scripts for announcers had to
be prepared; complimentary tickets for the critics and for various other
people had to be organised; and the business side at the hall – box office,

ushers, programme-sellers – had to be attended to. Orchestral porters had the job of looking after the many thousand pounds' worth of musical instruments belonging to the BBC Symphony Orchestra, and seeing to the 'orchestral layout' for all the concerts according to the conductor's wishes. The studio managers were obliged to cope as well as they could with the (then) very tricky acoustics of the Albert Hall.

Some of the 'back-room' personalities became quite well known. Edgar Mays – assistant for the orchestra and for artists – would be applauded as he raised or lowered the piano lid, or brought in batons or music for the rostrum. He also looked after conductors and artists in a firm, frank, but very well-meaning manner, bringing drinks, seeing to their bouquets, wishing them 'good luck', and pushing them on to the platform at the right moment. There was also C. B. Rees, a jovial Welshman who had been a friend of Henry Wood. He was connected with the publicity department of the Proms for many years, often writing articles, arranging interviews, and seeing to photographic sessions.

The excellent rehearsal system of 1947 was changed in the next season, the two orchestras doing alternate whole weeks. Julian Herbage felt that a greater sense of continuity was achieved in this way than in the 'never two nights running' system of the previous year, but there was strong feeling in orchestral circles that something had been lost. In the previous year, Lady Jessie Wood had written to the BBC expressing the view that the use of only one orchestra was part of the essential character of the Proms; but times had changed, and no ice was cut. After the 1950 season W. W. Thompson, the Concert Manager, felt that a plan whereby no orchestra appeared for more than three consecutive nights was the most generally favoured and produced the best results. He criticised Malcolm Sargent for 'playing down to the public' on the last night in the choice of works. 'Some attempt must be made to curb the increasing hysteria of the audience and the only way that I can see is to present a much less frivolous type of programme.'

Herbert Murrill was concerned, too, about the problem of the last night. It was, he thought, far too light-weight and provided too much opportunity for unrestricted horseplay on the part of the audience.

> Sir Malcolm, however, is prepared to encourage audience enthusiasm to the maximum point at which he can restrain it, and although Concert Manager and I feel that the point was perhaps reached and even passed this year, I do not know that Sir Malcolm would agree.

In the smaller Queen's Hall, Wood had been able to encourage a last-minute festive spirit, which never got out of hand and reached a fervent climax in the singing of *Rule, Britannia*. In the vaster spaces of the Albert Hall, with a larger, high-spirited, promenading audience, displaying slogans, Union Jacks and funny hats, and including some exhibitionistic trouble-makers armed with whistles, rattles and toy trumpets, the scene can easily become pandemonium. ('Give the toys back to Nanny!' admonished Sargent on one occasion.) The last night has now become famous as a strange British custom, which foreigners find both fascinating and amusing – a sort of tribal ritual, switching from crude clowning to the passionate declaration of out-of-date imperialist 'Land of Hope and Glory' sentiments – all this encouraged and magnified by the presence of television cameras.

It can be argued that the practice of standing or walking about during the concerts is itself an anachronism, only appropriate to the times before Henry Wood when Promenade Concerts were generally made up of light frivolous music, and the purpose was an evening out, meeting friends, chatting and drinking, with music as a sort of enhancement. But this argument is strongly countered by the promoters and by the audiences alike, as was clear in 1952, when Arthur Jacobs published a provocative article in London's *Daily Express* under the title 'Have the Proms had their day?' His point was that taking away the seats had become a meaningless custom: originally it was to accommodate the throng, but this was no longer necessary because London now had plenty of concerts at moderate prices: the Proms were no longer unique, as they once were. The article provoked a response from Sargent himself: 'There was never so much interest in the Proms as now, and I do not believe we could accommodate all the promenaders in seats. They don't want to sit, anyway; they want to promenade.' And from Paul Beard: 'Interest is as great as at any time I have known. Put back the seats and you would destroy the atmosphere.' And from the Concerts Manager, W. W. Thompson: 'Audiences are quite big enough to justify the Prom system . . . With seats we could not keep the prices so low.' For the Promenaders it was a unique chance to hear good music for two shillings – and anyway, said one of them, 'I find music most *un*enjoyable sitting bolt upright in a seat.'

It is often said that the Prom audience is without discrimination in its applause, whatever the quality of the performance (and with 200 works in the space of an eight-week season, the performances can't all be first-rate). Most of the promenaders who cheer, when the critics sneer, are young: they have not yet had time to form critical judgements; the classics are fresh to them; all is new and exciting, and they are discovering their delight in music. That is largely the emotion expressed at the end of a performance. Not always, however. The young can be much more sophisticated now than was ever possible in the early days of the Proms. Through broadcasting, the best music in the world, old and new, is available the whole year round for all who wish to hear. In more permanent form, the gramophone provides its immense riches. The teaching of music in schools, primary and other, has enormously developed. Local choral and orchestral societies have increased in scope. The Arts Council assists private and commercial enterprises . . .

With all this, it is essential that the Proms maintain their own strong distinctive character and clear *raison d'être* as a concentrated series of excellent symphony concerts, at which, for a small outlay, everybody can acquire a sound knowledge of the classical repertoire and, in a purposeful way, a good idea of more recent and very recent kinds of composition. Because the Proms are sponsored by the BBC, new music can be included without severe box-office worries, and if the programmes are skilfully planned the difficulties of communication between many contemporary composers and the public can be reduced. Much can be done to encourage British composers, and to help towards an understanding of what is being achieved in other countries. The atmosphere in which this can take place is quite different from that of the normal concert. More than one Prom conductor has remarked on the contrast between the cheerful informality, as he comes to the rostrum, and, from the moment he raises his baton, the intense silence and concentration, followed by the spontaneous burst of enthusiasm at the end. Sometimes just before the end. At a performance of Stravinsky's *Les Noces*, conducted by Pierre Boulez in the seventies, the 'deceptive' ending, with its separated chords and necessary reverberations, was spoilt by *one* over-enthusiastic Prommer. 'I could have thrown all four pianos at him,' said Boulez afterwards.

Between 1948 and 1959 attendance figures varied to some extent: for example, there was a slight falling off in 1949, but the 1950 receipts were the highest on record. In 1951 there was a particular effort to make the programmes attractive, because the Prom season followed the Festival of Britain (with its important symphonic activities) and could have been an anti-climax – which in fact it wasn't. During the 1950s there were sometimes two principal conductors, sometimes more; and often as many as five orchestras took part in a season (see p. 309 *et seq.*). The Royal Philharmonic Orchestra was added to the list in 1952. And in the Diamond Jubilee year of the Proms, 1954, Sir Thomas Beecham at the age of seventy-five appeared for two concerts with the London Philharmonic Orchestra (the orchestra which he founded in 1932). As already noted, Beecham had once conducted a Prom for Henry Wood – on 9 October 1915, when he was a mere thirty-six. The Hallé Orchestra under Barbirolli ('Glorious John', as Vaughan Williams called him) repeated its success of the previous season – a week of

Some 'associate' and 'assistant' conductors at the Proms:

Stanford Robinson

John Hollingsworth

Trevor Harvey

Maurice Miles (a pupil of Wood)

programmes, ending on the Saturday with a Viennese evening, which proved to be an immensely popular idea.

Meanwhile, there was the solid and loyal work done each year by Basil Cameron – conscientious and wide-ranging, but modest and avoiding the limelight. Sometimes he came in for special notice. John Ireland, in 1950, expressed his 'unbounded admiration' for the way Cameron had presented three of his works the *Concertino pastorale*, *A London Overture* and *The Forgotten Rite*. The same year Herbert Murrill noted one Cameron concert in particular – on a Saturday:

A London Overture – – – – – – –	–	*Ireland*
The Wife of Bath (*The Canterbury Pilgrims*) – – –	–	*Dyson*
Scherzo: L'Apprenti Sorcier – – – – – –	–	*Dukas*
Piano Concerto No. 2, in C minor – – – –	–	*Rachmaninov*
Don Juan – – – – – – – –	–	*Strauss*
Suite: Háry János – – – – – –	–	*Kodály*
Bolero – – – – – –	–	*Ravel*

'It was a model scheme for a Saturday night,' reported Murrill, 'and was presented in a manner which resulted in a crescendo of interest and enthusiasm.'

Murrill was concerned, in 1950, about the BBC's policy regarding new works. Very few of the scores sent in by composers and publishers were found to be of any use, and not much effort was made to secure first performances of works from established composers (as was normally done, for example, when the Cheltenham Festival was being planned). It was felt that the ideal number of novelties, British and foreign, would be two a week. The Head of the Third Programme stated, somewhat loftily, that his service was not especially interested in novelties from the Proms, as a vast number of unusual items were readily available from other sources. The number of new works in the following season (1951) was thirteen, including such names as Bloch, Fricker, Hindemith, Castelnuovo-Tedesco (the première of his Concerto da Camera for oboe and strings), Daniel Jones, and Petrassi.

Murrill died in 1952, and the following year saw some changes at the BBC. Previously the Music Department had been a section of the Entertainment Division: now a Music Division came into existence in its own right. It had its own Controller, Richard Howgill, and Maurice Johnstone, formerly Head of Music in the BBC's North Region, was brought to London to become Head of Music Programmes (Sound). His appointment had been recommended by Sir Malcolm Sargent – which, in fact, was somewhat ironic, as later events proved.

One of the first things that Johnstone did was to omit Henry Wood's *Fantasia on British Sea-Songs*. In the 1953 Prom prospectus it was conspicuous by its absence, having had a place in the Proms ever since 1905 (though not necessarily on the last night). He gave his reasons in an internal memorandum:

> Being a badly constructed piece of music, merely a selection, it is an unworthy end to a fine series of concerts which covers the best in music from 1700 to the present day. Its jingoism is out of date, and latterly its vestige of musicality has been destroyed by an enthusiastic but unthinking section of the audience . . . We are determined to end the Proms in a more dignified but less communal way.

He did not know what strong feelings would be aroused among the Prommers. There were protests at previous concerts from the floor of the arena; banners were carried; Prom hoardings were defaced with 'WE WANT SEA SONGS' painted in large black letters; the press made a lot of it. As was proved more recently, also, the Last Night is an institution, a curiously ingrained symbol of solidarity: it may be out-of-date, but if the BBC programme-builders interfere with it they do so at their peril. Sargent had doubts from the start about the decision to omit the Sea-songs. Disaster was avoided by an announcement that they would be played as an encore at the end of the advertised programme. Honour, on both sides, was therefore satisfied. And in the preface to the Prom prospectus of the following year, Howgill included the following statement:

> The Sea Songs were omitted from the programme last year because it was felt that the accompaniment provided by certain elements of the audience was tending to make their performance more of a nuisance than a pleasure to both the main audience in the hall and to broadcast listeners. They were nevertheless played as an encore at the end of the programme with satisfactory results. This year they have been reinstated in a modified version in the main body of the programme, there being little doubt now that the natural exuberance of the occasion will not exceed reasonable bounds.

Sargent, in 1950, had been conducting Proms for four seasons and was enjoying great success. In that year he became Chief Conductor of the BBC Symphony Orchestra in succession to Sir Adrian Boult – a controversial appointment, partly because Sargent's autocratic and *prima-donna* attitude towards orchestral players caused him to be disliked, and partly because the limited range of works which he was prepared to conduct cast doubts on his suitability for the post. He was, anyway, third choice. The BBC tried hard to get Barbirolli, but he eventually turned down the offer; and hopes of appointing the Czech-born Rafael Kubelik likewise came to nothing.

As soon as he was appointed Chief Conductor, Sargent wrote to the BBC's Senior Controller asking whether he could also be joint Head of Music and Chief Conductor of the BBC Choir (presumably ousting the then conductor, Leslie Woodgate). The BBC resisted both these suggestions – as they did his later suggestion that the Henry Wood Proms be rechristened the 'Wood–Sargent Proms'. Sargent put the BBC Symphony Orchestra's back up immediately by insisting that they all stood up when he came on to the platform – which in fact they steadfastly refused to do. The seven years that followed were full of bitterly unhappy relations between Sargent and the BBC's Music Division. Sargent had warned the BBC at the start that his appointment would not be allowed to interfere either with his important choral activities in other parts of the country or with his extensive conducting abroad. At the same time, he wanted to have full control of everything that happened at the BBC. The correspondence and memoranda in the BBC Archives make very depressing reading indeed. There was even a complaint from a member of the music staff that Sargent, with complete insensitivity, made cuts in Schubert's 'Great' C major Symphony for a BBC broadcast of that work. But the main complaint was that he was absent for such long periods from his orchestra that the sense of continuity and the maintenance of a standard of orchestral playing were lost.

In a memorandum to his Controller, Richard Howgill, in July 1954, Maurice Johnstone, wrote:

> Except when a Barbirolli or a Kletzki has been in charge of it for a few days, the Orchestra is inferior, as an artistic instrument, to the Hallé or Philharmonia . . . Music is merely Sargent's shop-window. He has no sense of public, artistic or functional responsibility. He is indifferent to the morale and welfare of the Orchestra and to the individual temperaments of his players as artists or as human beings. His absences from the Symphony Orchestra are so irregular in periodicity and length that it is frequently impossible to engage guest conductors effectively. His sense of loyalty to music-staff is non-existent and his sense of co-operation is vestigial . . .

And so on. Nevertheless, Sargent was felt to be 'an immensely skilful conductor', with performances that were 'always efficient and often vital'. This was undoubtedly true: circumstances could indeed combine to enable him to give an exhilarating performance of Walton's *Belshazzar's Feast* and a moving interpretation of Elgar's *The Dream of Gerontius*; but normally the 'great' performance eluded him, never broke through the exterior. His nickname, 'Flash Harry', almost certainly originated in orchestral circles (possibly from something Beecham once said). The superficial nature of many of his performances, together with spruceness of appearance, sartorial elegance, unchanging hair-colour, gave the appellation a certain rough appropriateness. It obviously distressed him, and he sought to change its meaning by reference to his flashing speed of travel hither and thither. But there was mitigation in the fact that his 'beloved Promenaders' took up the name with affection: 'We want Flash!'

As far as the BBC was concerned, it was not until 1957 that what had been a very unhappy situation was resolved, and Sargent's contract as Chief Conductor was not renewed. The terms on which he left were nevertheless very much in his favour. A characteristic BBC publicity statement was sent to the press:

> In order to give Sir Malcolm Sargent greater freedom for his many engage-ments it has been mutually agreed by him and the BBC that from the autumn of 1957 he will relinquish his position as conductor-in-chief of the BBC Symphony Orchestra. He will be conductor-in-chief of the Promenade Concerts and chief guest-conductor of the BBC Symphony Orchestra in sound and television at other times of the year.

This was enhanced by a letter to Sargent from the then Director-General, Sir Ian Jacob:

> ... I suppose that one day, as happens with human affairs, this arrangement might come to an end by mutual agreement, but I hope that that moment will be a very long way off ...

The BBC Symphony Orchestra needed a different, more thoughtful, dedicated approach, such as Boult had brought – and such as the BBC hoped that Sargent's successor, Rudolf Schwarz, would bring. But the Proms were well and truly Sargent's field – the kind of programmes and circumstances which could assure him the personal success he craved for. He regarded the Proms as the most important part of his work, and in the fifties and sixties his name was very closely identified with them, until illness and death in 1967 brought this to an end.

20

The Music 1948-1959

'The emphasis is on the popular, the familiar, but always the good. This short season is not for experimentation and new exploration.' So wrote C. B. Rees in the preface to the fortnight of Winter Proms in January 1948. Highlights included the Walton Symphony No. 1, conducted by the composer, and Vaughan Williams's *Job*; all six Brandenburg Concertos were played. On the popular side, Eileen Joyce played Tchaikovsky No. 1 and Pouishnoff played Rachmaninov No. 2.

In the summer, the 54th season celebrated the twenty-first anniversary of the marriage of the Proms and the BBC. There were broadcasts to listeners at home, but also to the four corners of the earth, because the BBC's General Overseas Service was now giving a special place to Prom programmes in its transmissions, sometimes 'live', sometimes in specially recorded form. This overseas broadcasting of Proms has steadily increased in range and importance since then.

Cameron and Sargent conducted, with assistance from 'Robbie'; but, at his own request, Boult did not take part. It was the season of the divided concert: Tchaikovsky–Strauss, Bach–Holst, Mozart–Brahms, Beethoven–Bax, Schubert–Liszt. Léon Goossens was soloist in the première of Cyril Scott's Oboe Concerto. Other premières were Searle's *Fuga giocosa*, springing from a Danish proverb, 'One little feather can easily become five hens'; a Fugal Overture by Bernard Stevens; and a Serenade in G by E. J. Moeran. Vaughan Williams conducted the first concert performance of his *Partita* for double string orchestra, and Colin Horsley was soloist in the première of a piano concerto by Lennox Berkeley. Foreign novelties were well represented also: Auric, Kabalevsky, Martinu, Milhaud; and the first performance of Mozart's K314 in what was probably its original form, an oboe concerto. In all it was a good season in the best Prom traditions.

After this season, Stanford Robinson came in for criticism from the Head of Music, Steuart Wilson. Robbie had had seven concerts altogether, which included a number of classical works. 'I am sorry to say', reported Wilson to his Controller, 'that he has not succeeded in convincing any observers that I have heard from that he has really expressed the heart of the music. There have not been any accidents in these performances, but there has not been any uplift either.' Again, we can see how a person's future in the BBC is decided: Robbie did not participate in the summer Proms of 1949. And Cameron, as we have seen, was excluded from the Winter Proms of 1949. Sargent did all but two of them (which were in fact given to Robbie). Notable in the fortnight was the first concert performance of *Music for a Prince* – a suite by three different English composers (Gordon Jacob, Herbert Howells and Michael Tippett) written to celebrate the birthday of Prince Charles (14 November 1948).

'The Promenade Concerts loudly proclaim that in music everything is for everybody,' wrote the composer Alan Rawsthorne in the prospectus of the 1949 summer season. 'The Proms do not proselytise; they simply make things available. And the Promenader is certainly open-minded . . .' It made the Proms sound rather like a cafeteria. Rawsthorne's 'first in England' of his Concerto for string orchestra was greeted by *The Observer* as 'hypnotic . . . nothing could be more articulate'. And *The Times* found a 'rare coherence' in Honegger's *Symphonie Liturgique* (first English performance). Humphrey Searle appeared to *The Daily Telegraph* to have 'crammed in a few pages every trick known to modern musical science' in his *Overture to a Drama*. More than one journalist noted brilliant orchestral writing, but choral parts which lacked clarity and sureness, in Berkeley's *Colonus's Praise* – the première of his setting of W. B. Yeats's translation from Sophocles. Rubbra's Fifth Symphony had a second hearing. The programme note for the première of Alan Bush's Violin Concerto had a lot to say about 'the struggle of the individual' and his 'absorption into world-society' – all symbolised by this concerto, in which Max Rostal was soloist. A novelty of particular interest was Ernest Bloch's powerful and visionary *Concerto symphonique* for piano and orchestra, the soloist being Corinne Lacomblé, with the composer conducting. Another composer-conductor was Walton, directing both his First Symphony and *Belshazzar's Feast*. Boult conducted a Wagner concert on a Monday – harking back to the tradition which had waned in recent years. It was also the year of John Ireland's seventieth birthday. Bartók's Concerto for Orchestra was establishing itself as one of that composer's outstanding works.

In short, another very good season, in which three orchestras had taken part and three principal conductors – Sargent for a month, Cameron and

Boult for a fortnight each. Instead of Robbie there were two assistant conductors, Trevor Harvey and John Hollingsworth. Harvey had been the BBC's assistant chorus-master and then musical director of the British Forces Network in Germany in 1945 and 1946. Hollingsworth had made his name in film and ballet music. The duties of an assistant conductor were to attend the rehearsals of his principal conductor and to be available at all times for any work that the principal cared to delegate. Sargent had Hollingsworth, Cameron and Boult had Harvey, and both the assistants were given parts of concerts in acknowledgement.

Sargent was again given the lion's share of the 1950 Winter Proms. Cameron did two only of the fortnight's concerts, and John Hollingsworth had two second halves. The highlight of a fairly ordinary fortnight was Dennis Brain's performance in a Strauss horn concerto. The eight-week summer season was shared by two conductors, Sargent and Cameron, assisted by Harvey and Hollingsworth. *The Times* complained about un-adventurousness, but in fact, although there was only one actual première (the Viola Concerto of Elisabeth Lutyens), it *was* an adventurous season, with plenty of novelties being performed in England or London for the first time: Bax's *Concertante* for orchestra with piano (left-hand), written for Harriet Cohen when she sprained her right wrist; an Australian legend-inspired work by Clive Douglas, under a visiting Australian conductor, Joseph Post; Bartók's Viola Concerto, written for William Primrose; a Fantasia on the 'Old 104th' Psalm-tune by Vaughan Williams (first heard nine days earlier at the Three Choirs Festival at Gloucester); Lambert's ballet suite from Purcell, *Comus*, written for Sadler's Wells; Gordon Jacob's Symphonic Suite, which had been very successful at the 1949 Cheltenham Festival; an organ concerto by the American Leo Sowerby; and the *Prelude, Fugue and Postlude* by Honegger. Vaughan Williams conducted his serene and beautiful Fifth Symphony – seven years after its première, which he had conducted at a wartime Prom in 1943. There was a striking innovation in 1950: three Saturday programmes devoted to opera and ballet music – something new to the Proms but not outside its traditions, as this example shows.

ITALIAN OPERA–RUSSIAN BALLET CONCERT

OVERTURE, La Gazza Ladra   –   –   –   –   –   –   –   *Rossini*
RECIT. AND ARIA, Madre, pietosa vergine (La Forza del Destino)   –   *Verdi*
INTERMEZZI from (a) Cavalleria Rusticana   –   –   –   –   *– Mascagni*
       (b) The Jewels of the Madonna –   –   –   *Wolf-Ferrari*
RECIT. AND ARIA, Celeste Aida (Aida) –   –   –   –   –   –   *Verdi*

TORCH DANCE AND CAVALCADE (Romeo and Juliet)–   –   –   – *Zandonai*
DUET from Act I (Madam Butterfly) –   –   –   –   –   – *Puccini*
(a) INVOCATION TO THE MOON
                                    (Turandot)   –   –   –   – *Puccini*
(b) MARCH OF THE MANDARINS

INTERVAL

OVERTURE, Prince Igor –   –   –   –   –   – *Borodin–Glazounov*
SUITE FROM THE BALLET, Cinderella –   –   –   –   – – *Prokofiev*
SUITE, The Sleeping Beauty –   –   –   –   –   – *Tchaikovsky*

Joan Hammond

James Johnston
(By permission of the Administrator of the Covent Garden Opera Trust)

The BBC Opera Chorus
(Trained by Alan G. Melville)

The BBC Opera Orchestra
Leader: John Sharpe

Conductor Stanford Robinson

By this time Stanford Robinson was the BBC's Opera Organiser and conductor of the recently-formed BBC Opera Orchestra (which had grown out of the BBC Theatre Orchestra). It should have been a successful and popular variation for some of the Saturday nights; but the new Head of Music at the BBC, Herbert Murrill, considered the inclusion of the Opera Orchestra to be 'a mistake' – 'artistically the experiment was not a complete success'. So the idea was dropped for future seasons.

The 1951 summer season was ushered in by the now regular all-night queue for the first concert. The strain of abundant social and conducting activities was taking its toll on Sargent's health. Earlier, in his late thirties, he had had an operation for a tubercular abscess; this time it was a virus infection of a lung. By 31 August he returned to conduct a Prom: the old vigour, to all appearances, was there, but he sat down to conduct. Before long he seemed to have recovered completely, and to be as busy as before.

Sir Arthur Bliss celebrated his sixtieth birthday during this season. On the eve of it, he conducted his Piano Concerto, with Mewton-Wood at his most fiery and brilliant as soloist; also his *Music for Strings*, one of his finest works. The main conductors were Sargent and Cameron, with Harvey and Hollingsworth as assistants, but Constant Lambert returned to the rostrum twice – to conduct his *Horoscope*, and to conduct Part 2 of a concert which included his *Rio Grande* and Ravel's *La Valse*. Michael Tippett conducted his vital Concerto for double string orchestra. Walton conducted his second

Façade Suite, his Violin Concerto (with Campoli), and *Belshazzar's Feast*. The première was given of Five Pieces by Daniel Jones, which were found entertaining. Of first English performances, Hindemith's Clarinet Concerto (with Frederick Thurston as soloist), Bloch's *Scherzo fantasque*, and Petrassi's Partita (1932) were the most notable. Racine Fricker's Symphony No. 1 had recently received a Koussevitzky award and was given its first London performance, after being heard at the Cheltenham Festival. The Cello Concerto No. 2 (*El Cant dels Ocells*) by Herbert Murrill was played, with his wife Vera Canning as soloist. Based on a Catalan song, and dedicated 'to Pau Casals, with respect and affection', the work had originally been written for a Henry Wood Birthday Promenade Concert earlier that year (3 March), promoted by the Henry Wood Concert Society.

In August 1952 the music critic of *The Observer*, Eric Blom, was sarcastic about the 'indiscriminate raptures' of the Prommers, and had doubts about the musical and cultural value of these concerts. Sargent sprang to the defence of his 'beloved Promenaders' and insisted that 'the young musicians of England find the Proms their most stimulating and instructive inspiration'. More drastic criticism came the same month from Noël Goodwin, in the periodical *Truth*, under the heading 'Travesty of Tradition'. He argued that the tradition of performing new and unusual works was slipping away. He complained also that the same classical works were performed each year (Sibelius's Symphonies Nos. 2, 5 and 7, but never 1, 3, 4 and 6; Mendelssohn's *Italian* Symphony, but never his others; the same handful of Haydn symphonies out of the possible 104; never the symphonies of English composers – Bliss, Britten, Bush, Moeran, Tippett; and so on). He also found that young artists, particularly young British artists, were not being represented as had traditionally been the custom; and that, despite the growing size of audiences, the BBC were making petty economies (for example, in the number of string players in the orchestras). He came to the conclusion that the Proms had ceased to play any significant part in Britain's musical life.

Criticism of this sort constantly breaks out against the Proms, and is just as constantly refuted. Basil Cameron responded to adverse criticism in 1952 by asserting that the quality of the performances had been 'astonishingly high' and that 'interest had been not merely sustained but increased'. Average attendances had been about 5000, with 'sell-outs' on about twenty-four nights. Sargent stated that nothing would tempt him away from the Proms. 'I believe that the Promenade season brings more good music to the public hearing of music-lovers than does any festival or other series of concerts in the world.'

At the time, the BBC Symphony Orchestra would give three concerts in a Prom week with seven rehearsals – not very adequate if new works had to be learned. The policy of Henry Wood, said Herbert Murrill in his introduction to the 1952 Prom prospectus, was 'no cut-and-dried formula, but a careful emergent and creative endeavour', and the BBC was 'continuing to mould and develop that policy – within the main framework – to suit the ever-changing conditions of our modern musical world'. How the Proms would have developed under that lively and intelligent Head of Music would be idle speculation: he died in that same year. The year in question (1952) there were no premières or first English performances, but a good overall variety, including sixteen works 'not previously performed at a Henry Wood Promenade Concert'. Britten's Piano Concerto and his Violin Concerto were performed in the same programme. There were also violin concertos by Fricker and the American Walter Piston. Larry Adler played the *Romance* for harmonica and strings by Vaughan Williams, who was in his eightieth year. Six of Vaughan Williams's symphonies had been written, and these were all played in the course of the season. Other programmes featured Sibelius and Tchaikovsky. Sargent and Cameron were again assisted by Harvey and Hollingsworth.

After 1952, the Winter Proms were abandoned: it was decided for the time being that they were not a viable proposition. Immediately, the London Symphony Orchestra stepped in with a week of Winter Proms at the Albert Hall. It would be twenty years before they were tried again by the BBC.

Five orchestras took part in the 1953 summer season – the BBC Symphony Orchestra, the London Philharmonic, the Royal Philharmonic and the London Symphony Orchestra, with Sargent, Cameron and Sir Adrian Boult (returning after an absence of three seasons: since 1950, when he was retired by the BBC, he had been principal conductor of the London Philharmonic Orchestra) – and in addition there was the Prom début of the Hallé Orchestra of Manchester, under its conductor Sir John Barbirolli, playing Elgar, Brahms and lighter Viennese music. This was Coronation year, celebrated at the Proms with a programme of Coronation music by Purcell, Handel and Walton. And following on from a pre-war experiment, television successfully broadcast the first night of the 1953 Proms, making the most of the then first-night carnival atmosphere – the impromptu singing and chanting before the concert; the cheers for Edgar as he raised the piano lid; the scene, with its fountain and goldfish, its massed flowers; the committed silence during a performance; the wild applause. As a television show, it was as good as a football match; and the televising of the

Last Night of the Proms the following year was even more so, with the balloons, Union Jacks, coloured streamers, slogans, and so on. Sargent was reported to have said: 'If people can get as enthusiastic about music as they do about football, that is all to the good.'

In 1953, the Proms had laid emphasis on British music in relation to the great classics, and the overall representation of British music was nearly a quarter of the whole output that season. Its range and achievement was a matter of pride. The list of novelties (see p. 280) included only three works from abroad – by Jongen, Malipiero and Frank Martin – but the season as a whole was varied and purposefully conceived.

The Diamond Jubilee of Proms in 1954 was presented by the BBC as 'a landmark in the history of British music': the Proms had undoubtedly played an important part in the twentieth-century renaissance of British music. Beecham was there with the London Philharmonic Orchestra, and Barbirolli with the Hallé, but the brunt of the work fell on Sargent and Cameron, with guest appearances by Boult. The basis of the season was, as always, the classical output – this time including the traditional full symphonic representation of Beethoven and Brahms, all six Brandenburg Concertos, the last six of Haydn's *London* Symphonies, and the seven of Sibelius. Thirty-two works were heard for the first time at the Proms, of which seven were first public performances anywhere, and five were first English or London performances (see p. 280). John Ireland's seventy-fifth birthday was celebrated; and the inclusion of Janáček's *Sinfonietta* marked the centenary of that composer's birth. Several famous works were included that in the past had had their first performance at Proms. Eight young British artists were among the thirty-four newcomers, and the Cambridge University Madrigal Society (under Boris Ord) made an appearance. Joan Sutherland made her Prom début singing Lisa's aria from Tchaikovsky's *Queen of Spades*. Britten's *Spring Symphony* was given; and the Symphony No. 3 of William Wordsworth (a direct descendant of the poet's brother). Barbirolli performed Vaughan Williams's *Sinfonia Antartica*, and the assistant Prom conductor, Maurice Miles, conducted one of the novelties – the *Sinfonia Pastorale* of Norman Fulton, which had won a prize in Bournemouth in connection with the Festival of Britain celebrations in 1951. Harriet Cohen played Fricker's Piano Concerto, and Myra Hess played Howard Ferguson's

In 1955 Sargent, as was by now customary, undertook about half the concerts with the BBC Symphony Orchestra; the LPO, LSO, RPO, and the Hallé with Barbirolli, were there again. Beecham could not be persuaded to appear. Cameron conducted a large number of the concerts, as was also

Sir Thomas Beecham, who conducted Proms in 1915 and 1954.

customary. The reconstituted Bournemouth Symphony Orchestra, under its conductor Charles Groves, gave two concerts. Sir Adrian Boult conducted the National Youth Orchestra of Great Britain, which displayed an astonishingly high level of performance. Of seventeen soloists new to the Proms only four were young, British and not yet established. Bach was now one of the composers who practically filled the Albert Hall, and certain of his works, such as the Concerto in D minor for harpsichord, played by George Malcolm, were given under the assistant conductor, John Hollingsworth, in their original instrumentation. About a dozen nationalities were included in the novelties. Weber's Symphony No. 1 in C was probably receiving its first concert performance in England. There was a roaring welcome for the première of Malcolm Arnold's rollicking *Tam O'Shanter* Overture (inspired by Burns's poem) and it had to be repeated. The composer conducted with his customary exuberance. Bliss's Violin Concerto and Rubbra's excellent Symphony No. 6 had both been commissioned by the BBC (but not for the Proms). Andrzej Panufnik's *Sinfonia Rustica*, conducted by the composer, was given a warm ovation: in Poland it had been first praised, then denounced. Mátyás Seiber's *Notturno*, dedicated to the memory of Brahms, made its appeal as a warmly romantic work, but thoroughly modern in style and technique. The 33-year-old English composer John Veal made an impression with his *Panorama*, inspired by San Francisco Bay, the city itself and the Golden Gate Bridge. Prokofiev's Piano Concerto No. 3 was already popular; but Kyla Greenbaum, with Cameron as conductor, was the soloist in his then unknown Second Piano Concerto (it was the first English performance). There was an overture *Royal Tribute* by the Canadian composer Alexander Brott – commissioned for the Coronation – symbolising 'the significance of that event in our turbulent times'.

When the Proms that year (1955) were castigated for planning two performances of Beethoven's Seventh while ignoring important modern symphonies, Sargent replied (in *The Times*) that its second performance was put in to ensure an audience for Alban Berg's Violin Concerto. André Gertler was the soloist in this, and Boult conducted – after which *The Times* commented: 'Sir Adrian is always at home to complicated modern scores, and to this one he accorded exemplary sympathy and lucidity.' Another work that season was also placed in a Beethoven context – the original and striking Violin Concerto of the Swiss composer Frank Martin, the soloist being Henry Holst. Besides all this, the love duet from Act 2 of Walton's new opera *Troilus and Cressida* was heard, under Sargent who had conducted its première at Covent Garden. Sargent also returned to an old love, Gilbert and Sullivan, to which one concert was devoted. There was also a

Wagner Night. In fact, all in all, it was an outstanding season, although ending on a curious note. On the last night, detectives mingled with the audience because the Greek-born pianist Gina Bachauer, who was soloist in John Ireland's Concerto, had received a letter in which the anonymous writer threatened to shoot her if she played at the Prom. Nothing happened, however: the concerto was performed without any unusual incident.

Julian Herbage described the quarter million people who attend the Proms each year as 'the world's greatest fellowship of music-lovers'. Traditionally they have come primarily for the classical fare, to which was added a comprehensive selection of other, more recent works. In the early days of the Proms practically every novelty was a première or first British performance; but in more recent times, concert societies, festivals, and broadcasting have been first in the field with many works which should certainly be heard at Proms. So the BBC had begun to list their novelties as 'first performance at a Henry Wood Promenade Concert' – far less attractive than being able to say 'first performance' or 'first performance in England'. To get a second or third performance, however, a work must at least have proved its quality. In the 1956 season thirty-four contemporary works were performed at the Proms for the first time, of which some were premières. Living composers that season occupied some twenty hours of programme time – or one fifth of the total Prom output.

It was the bicentenary of Mozart's birth in 1956, and the last six symphonies were played. Verdi's *Requiem* was introduced to the Proms, and a concert of contemporary American music included Copland's Symphony No. 3, new to England, and the Harvard Glee Club sang some unusual pieces by Randall Thompson. Sargent conducted the first London performance of the *Peacock* Variations by Kodály – a work that was soon to become an established favourite. Another novelty for London was the Harp Concerto of Milhaud, with Nicanor Zabaleta as soloist. There were new British works by Leighton Lucas, Fricker, Searle, Arthur Benjamin, Alun Hoddinott, Alan Bush, and Iain Hamilton (see p. 281); and Lennox Berkeley was represented by a Suite from his recent opera *Nelson*.

1957 was the centenary of Elgar's birth, and what more perfect way to celebrate it than by the first performance at a Prom of his masterpiece, *The Dream of Gerontius*. It was a work which Sargent had made very much his own, and he conducted the Croydon Philharmonic Society, the Royal Choral Society and the BBC Symphony Orchestra (with William Herbert as Gerontius). Large choral works, in fact, were becoming increasingly popular at the Proms. That year Walton's *Belshazzar's Feast* and Verdi's *Requiem* were heard again. It was fifty years since the death of Grieg and a

Basil Cameron conducting in 1959, with Clifford Curzon as soloist.

complete concert was devoted to his music. The great operatic soprano
Kirsten Flagstad came out of retirement to take part (her first appearance at
a Prom), and a compatriot, Robert Riefling, played Grieg's Piano Concerto.

The major part of the conducting was again shared by Sargent and
Cameron, with Hollingsworth as assistant, and with Boult as distinguished
guest conductor. The BBC Concert Orchestra took part for the first time
under its conductor Vilem Tausky, and the 10-year-old National Youth
Orchestra of Great Britain repeated its success of 1955. Again the list of
novelties, from England and other countries, was impressive, including two
'first public performances' of works by Jacques Ibert and Goffredo Petrassi,
both commissioned by the BBC to celebrate the tenth anniversary of the
Third Programme. Christopher Bunting was soloist in a recent work of
Hans Werner Henze for cello and orchestra – the *Ode to the West Wind*,
inspired by Shelley and composed on the island of Ischia (where Walton and
Auden also made their home). Alan Rawsthorne conducted the première of
his ballet suite *Madame Chrysanthème*.

In 1912 the first British performance of Schoenberg's *Five Orchestral
Pieces* had been given at a Prom. A very large orchestra was called for then;
but in 1949 the composer made a revised version with some reduction in the
scoring. This version was played at a Prom in 1958. A suggestion of the most
favourable way to approach this music was given by Andrew Porter in his
programme note:

> . . . not to try to find the 'reasons' for it, but to let the expressive content – the
> infinitely subtle and varied tensions and relaxations, ordering and disorder-
> ing, repetitions and variations – play directly upon our responses.

The first concert of the 1958 season, 26 July, was a tribute to the founder
of the Proms, Robert Newman, the centenary of whose birth fell on that day.
Some of Newman's favourite music was included in this concert: Wagner's
Meistersinger Overture, Tchaikovsky's *1812* Overture, the aria 'Softly
awakes my heart' from *Samson and Delilah* by Saint-Saëns. Moiseiwitsch,
whose Prom début had been in 1914, was the soloist at this concert.
Barbirolli and the Hallé Orchestra provided another kind of celebration – a
replica of the first concert given by the Hallé Concert Society, founded in
Manchester a hundred years earlier by Sir Charles Hallé. The concert had
the pleasant title 'Mr Charles Hallé's Grand Orchestral Concert'. (The
same could hardly be done with the first Prom conducted by Henry Wood: it
is doubtful whether a replica of that 1895 programme would be tolerable to
a present-day concert audience!) It was also a Puccini centenary year, and
for the first time a whole act of a Puccini opera (*Tosca*) was included. Sir

Malcolm Sargent conducted a whole concert of Sibelius – a memorial tribute to the composer, who had died the previous year – and also presented Part I of Haydn's *The Creation* for the first time at a Prom.

Although the number of new works that season was only nine (see p. 282) the range of music new to the Proms was immense, and included (besides the works already mentioned) Bartók's *Music for Strings, percussion and celesta*, Orff's *Carmina Burana*, Stravinsky's *Pulcinella*, Fricker's *Dance Scene*, and *The Bermudas* by Iain Hamilton. There was also Shostakovich's Eleventh Symphony, and Eileen Joyce gave the first British performance of his Piano Concerto, Op. 101. Boult conducted Tippett's Symphony No. 2. The Goossens family (Marie, Sidonie and Léon) took part in the Concert Piece for two harps, oboe, cor anglais and orchestra, which their brother Eugene had written for them. Aaron Copland was represented by his new *Orchestral Variations* and three episodes from his *Rodeo* ballet. There was Walton's *Partita*, Vaughan Williams's Symphony No. 9, Bruckner's Symphony No. 4, the Dances from *Don Quixote* by Roberto Gerhard, the 'Pas de Six' from Britten's ballet *Prince of the Pagodas*. It was well and truly 'Proms International' that year, and 1959 was very similar in its scope.

As Vaughan Williams had died in 1958, it was certainly appropriate that for once, in 1959, the Proms should include all nine of his symphonies (no two of which are alike) as a tribute to this very great English composer. This meant a lot of programme time, but was certainly justified in the circumstances. There was also an all-Sibelius concert, conducted by Sargent, and an all-Tchaikovsky one, conducted by Cameron, and another Viennese Night with Barbirolli. The National Youth Orchestra appeared again, under Walter Susskind.

The Proms of 1959 presented four well-spaced programmes under the heading 'Masters of the Twentieth Century'. Masterworks such as Stravinsky's *Symphony of Psalms*, Sibelius's *Tapiola*, Berg's Violin Concerto, Bartók's Piano Concerto No. 1, were included; but the intention was to avoid the more difficult contemporary styles which would not be enjoyed by a general audience, because in the planners' minds the Proms were basically a popular series of concerts, as they were for Henry Wood. The season as a whole was an extremely varied one, not lacking in adventurousness and with a good proportion of novelties (see p. 283). For the first three weeks of the season there was a printing dispute and audiences had to manage without programme notes. Order was restored just before the programmes of twentieth-century masters began.

New works that season included the première of Alwyn's Symphony No. 4; also Richard Arnell's ballet suite *Harlequin in April* (conducted by

The first night of the 1959 season, with Sir Malcolm Sargent conducting the BBC Symphony Orchestra, with Norma Procter (contralto) as soloist in a performance of Elgar's Sea Pictures. *Television cameras were at the Albert Hall.*

The last night of the 1960 season, with Sir Malcolm.

the composer), Milhaud's Concerto for percussion and small orchestra, Elizabeth Maconchy's Concerto for oboe, bassoon, and strings (with Evelyn Rothwell and Archie Camden), Rodrigo's Concerto-Serenata for harp and orchestra (with Zabaleta), and Three Pieces for cello and orchestra by Mátyás Seiber, the Hungarian-born composer who had made England his home (he died in a car accident the following year). There were important works by Ibert, Martinu, Honegger (*King David*), Panufnik (*Polonia*), and the first Prom performance of Tippett's Ritual Dances from *The Midsummer Marriage* and Searle's Second Symphony.

It is sometimes said that the Proms of the fifties were stagnating – that they were in the doldrums. But to look at them in some detail, as has been done in this chapter, surely shows that this view is untenable. There was variety, vitality and sustained interest in the programmes presented, and a generally high level of performance. The purpose of the Proms was achieved in providing a framework of standard classics together with a wide-ranging selection of more recent works from Britain and other countries. The contemporary scene was extensively represented within the bounds of what was considered to be popular taste – that is to say, works acceptable to general audiences (which is what Prom audiences are). The selection was by no means narrow. Soon it was to become wider still.

21

Wider still and wider

The appointment of William Glock as the BBC's Controller of Music in 1959 in succession to Richard Howgill caused a good deal of surprise and alarm. It was alarming in certain quarters – including the BBC's Music Division – because Glock was known to be a strong and determined personality of highly idiosyncratic tastes. The music magazine, *The Score*, which he edited, showed a special sympathy for music of the most 'advanced' and experimental kinds; and this, in an educational context, was finding a practical realisation through the annual Summer School which he organised, first at Bryanston and then at Dartington Hall – an enterprise remarkable for the range of distinguished composers, artists and teachers which it brought together. Prior to this, he had studied in Berlin with Artur Schnabel, and had shown himself to be a very fine classical pianist, particularly in Mozart. He had also spent several years writing on music – as critic for various papers, including *The Observer* (from which, it was said, he resigned after the editor's complaint that too much was being written about Bartók).

The press as a whole welcomed the BBC appointment: it felt like an exciting change, full of potential news value. The editor of the *Musical Times*, however, expressed grave doubts, and there was some genuine concern elsewhere that somebody with views that were *so* individual should be in a position to impose those views on an organisation such as the BBC, which is not a private enterprise, but a very public institution, paid for with the licence money from people's pockets. Whatever else may be achieved, the basic aim in planning BBC music programmes is to ensure, as far as possible, that listeners, whatever their tastes, will find each week in *Radio Times* much that is interesting and rewarding – and to ensure also that performances are of as high a standard as possible. The bulk of the broadcast repertoire, of course, remains constant, whoever is in charge of the music. The character of an era, such as that of William Glock in the BBC, depends on the treatment, context and spotlighting of a very small percentage of the total output. This was shown from 1960 onwards in symphony concerts organised by the BBC, in the Thursday Invitation Concerts with their striking and purposeful combining of chamber-music works old and new, and – above all – in the Proms, which reflect BBC music policy most fully.

And 'music policy' in the BBC was centred on William Glock, because very soon after his appointment he took over (in addition to his administrative job as Controller) the duties of Head of Music Programmes (Sound) when Maurice Johnstone was forced to leave. At first the building of the Prom programmes was carried out with help from Julian Herbage (as previously), but very soon Glock assumed sole responsibility, with a newly-organised BBC concerts management staff assisting in the realisation of the plans. Soon, instead of a handful of conductors and two or three orchestras for the Proms, as had normally been the case since the war, the list of conductors, orchestras and ensembles, choral groups, and so on, increased greatly, so that new works of many different kinds could be in the hands of the most appropriate performers. At the time of Glock's appointment the chief conductor of the BBC Symphony Orchestra was Rudolf Schwarz, a thoughtful, distinguished musician, but not the kind of personality that would thrive most readily under Prom conditions. Sargent, who had retired in 1957, continued as chief guest-conductor of the Orchestra and as chief conductor of the Proms, where he had the largest share of concerts, performing the music which he enjoyed conducting and with which he was so successful with Prom audiences. This was to continue; but he would have had no wish to undertake the majority of the works new to the Proms which Glock was anxious to introduce; and so, frequently, Sargent would share his concerts with other conductors. Glock found him very co-operative over this.

The task of planning the Proms became even more formidable than before. The large number of new works each season was the result of careful consideration of the availability and the suitability of different kinds of artists. In the course of a public lecture, 'The BBC's Music Policy', given in 1963 and later published, William Glock described the planning of the Proms as one of the most exacting, most creative and most important tasks that the BBC has to undertake.

> It is exacting because so many things have to be reconciled, especially the declared policy of 'representing all that is most vital in orchestral music from the eighteenth century to the present day', with the need to explore and to maintain freshness each year. [*The passage in quotes apparently refers to a declared BBC policy, but is not a quotation from Henry Wood.*] It is creative

because the ordering of such a vast repertoire of music into forty-nine
satisfying programmes demands an invention and imagination that can never
be sufficiently forthcoming. It is important because these concerts are attended by a large and uniquely receptive audience, and heard over the radio
by more listeners than at any other time. Faced with such a great enterprise it
is essential for those in charge of these concerts to review their efforts
constantly; to remember, amongst other things, that 50 years ago Sir Henry
Wood included Schoenberg's Five Orchestral Pieces within a few months of
their being written. [*This is not accurate: the Schoenberg pieces were written in
Vienna in 1909 and Wood's performance of them at a Prom was in 1912. But the
point being made was that Wood was highly adventurous in his choice of novelties.
He was, however, always considering very carefully the audience-appeal of the
novelties – and as far as Schoenberg and his followers were concerned, the works
included were few and far between: the Five Orchestral Pieces of Schoenberg in
1912 and his version of two Bach Choral-Preludes in 1928; Berg's early Six
Songs with orchestra and Webern's* Passacaglia *in 1931; three fragments from
Berg's* Wozzeck *in 1934; and in 1940 an English version of 12-note technique –
Three Pieces for Orchestra by Elisabeth Lutyens, which Wood strongly disliked.
But the range of other novelties, from Britain and other countries, which Wood
introduced, was large – and after his death this aspect of the Proms was not
neglected in the late forties and fifties, as we have shown.*] In trying to follow his
[Wood's] example, we were determined in 1960 to venture a few yards further
out to sea where contemporary music was concerned; and we also tried to
evolve a different pattern for the individual programmes – a pattern which
instead of continuing with one-composer evenings or segregating new music
from old, set out to assert as often as possible the range and variety of good
orchestral music by presenting them as a direct experience in one and the
same concert.

These quotations from Glock's lecture on policy indicate the basis of the
changes which he was to make from 1960 onwards (the programme for 1959
had all been arranged before he was appointed) – a wider range of contemporary music (and later of pre-classical music) and the mixing of
programme ingredients. With the Proms, he started with the immense
advantage of a series which was enormously successful as he found it. It was
still based on the assumption that a lot of people, particularly young people,
went to the Proms to discover and enjoy the perennial masterworks of the
orchestral repertoire, together with a generous sprinkling of novelties – in
other words, the Proms as Henry Wood saw them. So strong were the
traditions and prestige of the Proms that a particular kind of audience had
come into existence, characterised by a combination of informality and

(when it came to listening) ritualistic concentration and involvement. Where else in the world could that be found?

It was immensely important not to alienate this audience – an audience that was being held largely through the classical ingredients of the Proms, and for whom Beethoven or Tchaikovsky concerts were still a major attraction. By altering the balance of classical, romantic and twentieth-century ingredients the attendance figures could drop – and in fact they *did* drop, by about nine per cent, over the first two seasons of the Glock régime. In 1961 the programmes had been the shortest in Prom history. This was changed in the following season (six or seven minutes on the average being added to each programme), and the enterprising novelties were cleverly set in a strong traditional framework calculated to draw large audiences. Important twentieth-century works, such as Schoenberg's *Orchestral Variations* and Stravinsky's *Oedipus Rex*, were set alongside great works of the past and cast into 'rounded and vigorous programmes'. And the tide was turned. Audience figures, taken as a whole, did not drop again.

Until he became seriously ill after the 1966 season, Sir Malcolm Sargent continued as principal conductor. Basil Cameron retired after the 1964 season (the 70th): it was his twenty-fourth year as a Prom conductor, and his eightieth birthday was celebrated on 18 August, when he conducted an enterprising programme which included Stravinsky's *Symphony of Psalms*. The relationship between Sargent and Glock, throughout the seven years that they worked together, was on the whole satisfactorily co-operative. There were frequent tensions – but short-lived; quite different from the basic disagreements of the BBC's Music Division in the early fifties. Correspondence in the BBC Archives provides evidence of mutual respect and understanding. Sargent, writing to Glock in August 1962, says: 'The Proms are going excellently. You seem to have hit on the secret of the programmes to attract the public . . .' Later that year, writing to the BBC's Director of Sound Broadcasting, Lindsay Wellington, he observes:

> Glock is doing excellent work and I like him very much. He is obviously an 'enthusiast' in the dictionary sense of the word – but what a blessing to get someone who has ideas and is working directly towards them. I would always be honoured to be taken into his confidence and I assure you my motives . . . are not jealous but zealous.

In the same year, however, there was some trouble when Glock engaged a new co-principal clarinet for the BBC Symphony Orchestra at the Proms without consulting Sargent: the result was a bitter letter from Sargent to Glock. On another occasion, Sargent was worried at having to do a piece by the Mexican composer Carlos Chávez. In a letter to Glock he wrote: 'After the Schubert, Berlioz and Debussy, I would come away feeling very unclean if I did the Chavez.' Often long letters were exchanged between them about the details of Prom programmes. Definite views were expressed on both sides, but agreement was reached without difficulty. A seemingly annoyed (but perhaps half-laughing) postscript by Sargent in 1964 reads: 'Please do not alter my programmes without just letting me know. Just try that method on Monteux or Stokowski!!'

In 1964 Sargent described Glock's Prom programmes as 'a triumph'. It was also the year when serious trouble was starting with Equity about the use of amateur and professional choral groups at concerts and in broadcasts with professional orchestras. Sargent had strong feelings on the subject, as one might expect: 'Amateur choral societies are the backbone of English Music . . . Equity must do nothing to make it more expensive for them or in any way command the situation.'

With Sargent's reluctance over new works, it was often necessary for Glock to be writing to him along lines such as those of 17 February 1964:

> Would you agree to conduct a first half consisting of the Bartered Bride overture, Mozart's Violin Concerto in D, K218, with Tessa Robbins, and Tchaikovsky No. 6? Then I have thought of a second half beginning with Roberto Gerhard's Catalan Songs (which I assure you are most ingratiating), then the Saint-Saëns Carnival of the Animals and Chabrier's Marche Joyeuse. Would you agree to conducting the whole programme or prefer to delegate the second half?'

Sargent was always concerned about the practical aspects of his concerts. After the 1964 season he wrote to the orchestral manager, Paul Huband:

> We had many difficulties this year with regard to platform arrangements at concerts. Please avoid piano items at choral concerts. . . . We had several evenings when there were long waits in the hall, which destroyed the concert atmosphere, while the platform was being re-arranged.

And he did not like members of the orchestra moving about between items:

> I may say that throughout the second half the trombones and trumpets seemed to change places at every piece. I quite realise that they all wanted to be in the television and I am all in favour of this, but there is no reason at all why they should not obey the rules which we used to have, i.e. that everybody was ON who was taking part in that section and that *he remained in his seat*. The television cameras do not like empty seats anyway.

Regarding orchestral discipline, Sargent (back in 1936) had seriously damaged his relations with orchestral players through an unfortunate interview which appeared in *The Daily Telegraph* on the subject of pensions for orchestral musicians. When asked his opinion on an issue, he had said:

> As soon as a man thinks he is in his orchestra job for life, with a pension waiting for him at the end of it, he tends to lose something of his supreme fire. He ought to give of his life-blood with every bar he plays. Directly a man gets *blasé* or does not give of his very best he ought to go. It sounds cruel, but it is for the good of the orchestra.

This perhaps hastily-considered statement was never forgotten by orchestras. But he was constantly worried about slack behaviour of players. Again to the orchestral manager (in 1964):

> . . . I am always ashamed in the interval to hear Mays or somebody yelling 'Come along please – hurry up', etc. and all sorts of noises which to a foreign conductor must be extremely unfortunate and not likely for them to go away with a feeling that English orchestras know how to behave. I can assure you that in Vienna, Berlin or America the bell rings five minutes before the second half is to begin and it is taken for granted that within that time every player is in his seat, in tune and silent . . .

His concern even extended to the printed programme notes for his concerts, which he would normally ask to see at proof stage. Sometimes he would criticise them and ask for alterations. He wanted to be in control of everything.

While Sargent was enjoying great success, mostly with the standard repertoire, another kind of success was taking place in other aspects of the Proms. In this age of the long-playing record, broadcasting, the proliferation of concerts, music in schools, and much else, a new concept of the Proms could emerge. No longer did most people go to hear Beethoven, Bach, Brahms for the first time – as they had done in Henry Wood's time. The Proms could now be assumed to have far more 'knowing' audiences and, moreover, ones which expected a far higher standard of performance than had been possible in earlier days. It was Glock's working faith that these audiences would be receptive to an infinitely wider range of new and of early music, mixed in with the standard repertoire.

In the first Glock-fashioned season in 1960 – besides a long list of novelties – there was the innovation of engaging young conductors for nearly one-third of the concerts, while Sargent and Cameron were responsible for the rest. Beethoven, instead of being confined more or less to

Fridays, was spread out over fifteen mixed programmes, so in fact more Beethoven was included. There is a closer look at the music of this and succeeding Glock seasons in the next chapter.

In 1961 the Proms looked 'further abroad for works that would add colour and freshness to the programmes', and more traditional practices (such as starting more than half the programmes with overtures) were queried. Glyndebourne Opera brought its production of Mozart's *Don Giovanni* – the start of an important trend: evenings of whole operas. Four British composers were commissioned to write new works – a practice which was to continue. Of 110 artists taking part, thirty-nine (some very young) were making their Prom début, and of seventeen conductors, seven were new. By now there had been one great blessing for concert-planners – the abolition of the nine o'clock news on the Home Service. This had been a sacred and immovable event, often restricting the content of Part 1 of a concert, whether originated or relayed – even, on one occasion, cutting short the final cadence of an important Walton première!

By eliminating some of the Prom pieces, 'which had done yeoman service, and . . . urgently needed replacing', Glock was able to introduce in 1962 nearly sixty works of importance which had not previously been heard at Proms. Programmes were slightly longer than before, so as to accommodate new works more easily and provide more contrast. Looking back over the previous two seasons, Glock said:

> Where we failed to attract a good audience, the reason was usually that we had neglected to observe an important rule, which is to see that there are never less than two works in a programme that appeal to the same kind of concert-goer; or else that we have compiled a succession of perfectly agreeable pieces but without including any irresistible item, any major box-office draw.

The 1963 Proms were particularly ambitious, with Monteverdi's opera *L'Incoronazione di Poppea*, Britten's *War Requiem*, three Mahler symphonies. For the first time there were a number of eminent foreign conductors – Silvio Varviso with the Glyndebourne Opera and Georg Solti with Covent Garden Opera, Leopold Stokowski, Carlo-Maria Giulini. The accent was still on British artists and British conductors, but the Proms were becoming more and more international in character.

To increase the variety still further, chamber music was made a part of the Proms in 1964, and (for more idiomatic performances of Purcell, Bach and Handel) two chamber orchestras were included. The idea of chamber music, for 'contrast and refreshment within individual programmes' may be attractive in itself – though a string quartet can sound extremely tenuous in

Leopold Stokowski rehearsing for a Prom in 1963. Behind him is the BBC Symphony Orchestra's principal viola-player, Harry Danks.

a building of the size and acoustic of the Albert Hall; also, the fact that the Proms are fundamentally a series of concerts exploring the orchestral repertoire seems at times to have been forgotten in the search for variety and new experience. (The chamber-music element was maintained and even extended in the following season – but was before long discontinued as a regular feature.)

An important novelty in 1964 was the televising of as many as ten concerts – four by BBC 1 and six by BBC 2. It was estimated that the total audience for the Proms that year – in the hall, on the radio, and on television – was about fifty million during the season. This was the seventieth year of the Proms.

An important traditional feature in Henry Wood's time was the composer conducting his own music. This element returned in strength in 1965, when composer-conductors included Malcolm Arnold, Roberto Gerhard, Gordon Jacob, Alan Rawsthorne, Michael Tippett, Virgil Thomson, William Walton, Hans Werner Henze, and Pierre Boulez. About fifty works were new to the Proms that year, ranging from Purcell to Penderecki, and there was a remarkable choice of operas that season: Purcell's *Indian Queen*, Mozart's *The Marriage of Figaro*, Verdi's *Macbeth*, and Schoenberg's *Moses and Aaron*.

The Proms seemed deliberately to have moved further away from being an orchestral series and nearer to becoming an international music festival second to none. Great interest was aroused in 1966 by the visit of the Moscow Radio Orchestra, under its conductor Gennadi Rozhdestvensky (twelve years later to become chief conductor of the BBC Symphony Orchestra). It was the first time a foreign orchestra had visited the Proms. Some of the finest performances, also, that British orchestras had given during the year were repeated at the Proms under such conductors as Bernard Haitink, Gary Bertini, Jascha Horenstein, and others. Sir Arthur Bliss's seventy-fifth birthday and Havergal Brian's ninetieth were celebrated. The season was also the last in which Sir Malcolm Sargent took part. He had celebrated his seventieth birthday at the 1965 Proms, with a splendid programme of British music, and the opening concert of the 1966 season was his 500th appearance.

In April 1967 Sargent was writing to Glock from Australia: 'Just to comfort you with the news of my good health. I am very fit – doing two or three concerts each week and many rehearsals. All is going splendidly . . .' At the same time Glock heard from another source that Sargent was spending the morning in bed after each concert, which would be impossible during a Prom season. Sargent was going on to America and then returning to England in July, shortly before the beginning of the Proms. The Director of Sound Broadcasting agreed that deputies must be standing by: Colin Davis, conductor-designate of the BBC Symphony Orchestra, Sir Adrian Boult, and others.

As soon as Sargent returned he contracted what was described as a sharp attack of gastro-enteritis. His doctors would not allow him to conduct the BBC Symphony Orchestra in Cheltenham in mid-July. He was particularly anxious not to miss the preliminary Prom rehearsals starting on 17 July. Shakily he took the first two – not at all like his former self. Then he was forced to abandon them, although he still hoped he could conduct the first concert of the season. On the morning of that concert, however – with Colin Davis standing by – Sargent had to tell Glock that he could not conduct that evening. Shortly after that he was in hospital for removal of his gall bladder, and any hopes that he would conduct the final concerts of the season were soon dispelled.

Then came the surprise of the Last Night, the dramatic coda, when Colin Davis, after the traditional jollifications and the now-traditional speech, announced that Sargent was with them, and he would fetch him. Amid cheering and all the battery of bells, whistles and rattles, Sargent came on to the platform with Davis. Spruce, in a pin-striped suit, with the obligatory white carnation in his buttonhole, he showed that he was well in control of his movements. A girl, representing the Prommers, gave him a bouquet and a kiss. His voice, when he spoke, sounded almost like the old Sargent. The speech, punctuated by the Prommers' acclamations and other normal re-actions, was in the usual genial style. 'I feel tonight I am an intruder. I'll tell you why. I didn't win a seat in the ballot, and I haven't bought a ticket.' He regretted his absence from what would have been his twenty-first season; he paid tribute to 'my old friends and colleagues in the BBC Symphony Orchestra', and complimented Colin Davis. And then he ended: 'Next year the Promenade Concerts begin on July 20th. I have been invited to be here on that night . . . I have accepted the invitation . . . God willing, we shall all meet again then.'

He died of cancer on 3 October 1967, two and a half weeks after his Last Night appearance. At a memorial service later that month, in the crowded Westminster Abbey, Colin Davis – as Sargent had requested – conducted the slow movement of Elgar's Serenade for Strings, Holst's *Ode to Death*, Parry's *Jerusalem* ('And did those feet . . .') and Sargent's arrangement of Handel's Dead March in *Saul*. And on the day before the first night of the 1968 Prom season, an extra Prom was arranged – a Sir Malcolm Sargent Memorial Concert. This was given by the BBC Symphony Orchestra, and again conducted by Colin Davis – a programme of English works as befitted the occasion: Vaughan Williams's *Serenade to Music* (written for Henry Wood's Jubilee as a conductor), Walton's Viola Concerto, with Peter Schidlof (of the Amadeus Quartet) as soloist, and Elgar's Second Symphony (with its beautiful elegiac slow movement). At this concert the bronze bust of Sargent by William Timyn was on show at the Albert Hall.

Colin Davis conducted fourteen of the fifty-two concerts in that season – nearly a quarter, including the first and last nights. It meant that he was virtually stepping into Sargent's shoes – not without misgivings, as he made clear. For a young conductor (he was still only forty-one) this was a challenge of some magnitude which, after some difficulty, Davis turned to success, and a satisfactory and 'working' relationship with the Prommers was established. In the background was his assistant conductorship with the BBC Scottish Orchestra, learning the repertoire, making mistakes, finding his feet; his excellent work with the Chelsea Opera Group; some useful 'breaks' – in 1959 he substituted for Klemperer at the Edinburgh Festival and at the Royal Festival Hall, drawing glowing notices in *The Observer* and *The Times*; and then some real fulfilment as musical director of Sadler's Wells Opera up to 1964. This was followed by a further difficult period before William Glock demonstrated his confidence by making him chief conductor of the BBC Symphony Orchestra from September 1967. (He held the position until 1971.) The way was not always smooth, but Glock and Davis worked together harmoniously.

Davis never really identified himself with the Proms in the way that Sargent had done. Nothing could have been further from the image of a suave father-figure. In his own right, he brought a youthful vigour, an urgency combined with cheerfulness; his conducting was demonstrative, but always musically meaningful; and there was precision, rhythmic bite, freshness of approach – and also a good deal of subtlety and inwardness where necessary. Before long, he had the Prommers calling out 'We want Colin' – and meaning it. At times he seemed to be one of them, raised to the *n*th.

But he was on record as having said that the Last Night of the Proms perhaps needed to be reshaped or reconsidered very seriously – that the 'jingoism, the patriotic flag-waving and exhibitionism' were perhaps now out-of-date. It was more or less what Maurice Johnstone had been saying in 1953. 1968, however, the year after Sargent's death, did not seem the right time to change things: the traditional Last Night was now very closely bound up with memories of Sargent. But a move was made in 1969: the *Pomp and Circumstance* March No. 1, with 'Land of Hope and Glory', was

'We want Colin.' Colin Davis in 1968.

A Prom audience of the late 1960s.

absent from its usual place. As in 1953 with the Sea Songs, there was a public outcry: it was as though the BBC had wanted to banish the Royal Family. After the Proms press conference in June 1969, angry letters from the public appeared in many of the newspapers, and in the end *Pomp and Circumstance* had to be reinstated. Again it was shown that this end-of-season national demonstration, this nostalgia for the past, carried out as a ritual, in an atmosphere of carnival, switching to seriousness tinged with satire – this curious ceremony represents something very real and is clearly not to be thrown away. It is more than just letting off steam.

Not to be outdone, Glock and Davis thought up another modification for the last night – an idea which would at least give part of it a relevance to the present. In 1970 Malcolm Arnold was commissioned to write a modern equivalent of the *Fantasia on British Sea-Songs*, with audience participation (if necessary, rehearsed beforehand). The result was a *Fantasy* for audience and orchestra which included the traditional Sailor's Hornpipe, but in 5/8 rhythm – thus ensuring even more chaotic stamping than usual! It did not catch on. In 1971 a similar commission brought forth one of Malcolm Williamson's 'instant operas' – a ten-minute work called 'The Stone Wall', the plot of which imagined a war which was breaking out between England and Scotland. The audience in the arena was divided into three groups – the English, the Vikings, and the Scots – each with its own music, printed in the programme. The result was not a success. One more attempt was made the following year to produce a satisfactory modern substitute for the Sea-Songs – this time a more serious piece, *Celebration* by Gordon Crosse (with words by William Blake) – which the participating audience undoubtedly found musically rewarding; but again the work was not considered specially appropriate to the occasion. In 1973 the *Fantasia on British Sea-Songs* was back again and in its full version as originally performed by Henry Wood (see p. 51). In Sargent's day a shorter, Sargent-edited version had become customary, ending with his arrangement of *Rule, Britannia* . . .

> This does not mean [wrote Glock in the introduction to the 1973 prospectus] that the experiments of the past three years will be abandoned for ever, or that they were regarded as a mistake. The truth is that conducting this final concert of the Proms is one of the most nerve-racking assignments imaginable, and Colin Davis thought he had now done his share and would like to hand over to someone else. I'm sure there could be no better choice than Norman Del Mar, but it is only right to ask him to decide on his own kind of programme for the occasion.

Wood, Cameron, Sargent, Boult: all made a strong *personal* impact on the

Sir Adrian Boult in the mid-1960s.

Proms and the Prom audiences, an impact which continued beyond the Psalmist's three score years and ten – Wood and Sargent into their seventies, Cameron and Boult into their eighties. In the 1960s the personal element became widely diffused among many conductors, particularly after the 'mainstays', Cameron and Sargent, were gone, and Boult was doing less and less. Davis was making his mark; but as a whole the Proms had become many different conductors interpreting an ever-increasingly wide range of music.

Apart from the changing personalities out in front, there were changes behind the scenes. In the late sixties and throughout the seventies the two principal 'realisers' of the Proms – those who have the job of putting into effect the plans made each year by the BBC's Controller of Music – have been Christopher Samuelson and Freda Grove (Concerts Manager and Concerts Organiser respectively) with their staff in the concerts management department. After the retirement in 1970 of the late Edgar Mays (whose work has already been described) the BBC's orchestral supervisor was Bill Edwards, who became just as familiar a figure on the platform of the Albert Hall, seeing to adjustments in the orchestral lay-out between items, opening the piano lid for a concerto (to the traditional audience reaction), and so on – besides looking after a host of soloists and conductors – among them Sir Adrian Boult, whom he always accompanied to and from the rostrum when in his late years this conductor needed help. Bill Edwards retired in June 1979, having celebrated fifty years of service with the BBC.

From 1966, visits by foreign orchestras became a regular and important feature of the Proms. It began, as we have seen, with the Moscow Radio Orchestra: assisted by some talented young artists of the Soviet Union, it gave four concerts. These were followed, in 1967, by the Concertgebouw of Amsterdam, under Bernard Haitink, and the Polish Radio Orchestra under Jan Krenz. Then in 1968 four concerts by the USSR State Orchestra; in 1969 the Czech Philharmonic. It was an enhancement of the international character of the Proms which became particularly important in the 1960s and has continued since.

By now the form of the concerts had broken away completely from the familiar overture–concerto–symphony pattern. The utmost variety of character was aimed at from one evening to the next, and the overall character of each week was carefully considered. Spaced out over the whole season were a number of special events: in 1968 these included nothing less than Berlioz's immense opera *The Trojans* (which was on a Sunday, beginning at 4.30 and continuing through the evening, with a 'supper break' from 6 to 7 p.m.) and Bach's *St Matthew Passion*. Events of this kind were possible through orchestras and conductors being able to repeat some of the finest concerts they had given during recent months. Among international artists heard at the Proms that year were not only world-famous names such as Curzon, Ashkenazy, Oistrakh, Isaac Stern, Rostropovich, but also many highly-gifted younger artists, such as Jean-Rodolphe Kars, Philip Hirschhorn and Michael Roll. An ever-wider range of artists was being used for an ever-wider range of music that was being admitted to the Proms.

In 1969 the Proms spread backwards as well as forwards: after two important seventeenth-century Italian works which had been heard the previous year – Monteverdi's *Vespers of 1610* and Cavalli's opera *L'Ormindo* – it was now the turn of medieval music, for the first time at the Proms, with a motet by Dunstable, five pieces by Dufay, and a Mass by Machaut. Thus the range was now 600 years – not merely eighteenth century to the present day, as had been the Proms' normal brief, but Machaut to Messiaen and beyond. That year there was even dancing (in Stravinsky's *Renard*), a 'Pop' element – a new work by Luciano Berio written for the Swingle Singers, with orchestra – and a generous helping of Stockhausen, synthesising normal and electronic sounds. The following year 'Pop' was extended to The Soft Machine.

Since the Sargent Memorial Concert in 1968, it has been the custom to start each season a day earlier, usually with some large, important work – in 1969 it was Berlioz's *Grande Messe des Morts*; and in 1970 Messiaen's awe-inspiring oratorio *La Transfiguration de notre Seigneur Jésus Christ*. This new custom forestalls the traditional 'opening night' on the Saturday and somewhat damps its festive spirit. Enough of that, no doubt, on the last night.

In the controversial manifesto, *Broadcasting in the Seventies*, published by the BBC in 1969, various cuts in expenditure were proposed with regard to music broadcasting, including the disbanding of certain BBC orchestras and the BBC Chorus. Strong public reaction and widespread discussion in the press caused the BBC to abandon proposed cuts and to leave well alone. It was a proof that, in the age of television, radio is very much alive; and it showed in a realistic way that the broadcasting of music on a fully comprehensive scale is immensely important – one of the major justifications, in fact, for maintaining a complex and costly radio service. And of all the radio enterprises, the Proms, with their large audiences and their internationally wide-ranging programmes, their extensive press coverage, their world fame, were in themselves a major justification.

In the 1970 season, for the first time at the Proms, there was an extra late-night concert, experimentally providing an entire programme of 'avant-

Rehearsing for an entire concert of avant-garde music, 13 August 1970.

Interior of the Albert Hall in the 1970s, with the 'flying saucers'.

garde' music – including a specially commissioned work from Tim Souster (who had for a time been on the BBC's music staff), his *Triple Music II* for three orchestras with three conductors, and – the main feature of the programme – The Soft Machine, a pop group with a certain intellectual following in Europe, but who fell rather flat at this Prom with a 40-minute offering of seemingly aimless doodling.

That late-night experiment, beginning at 10 o'clock, led to the extremely interesting Round House concerts which began the following year. The idea, as Glock explained, was to achieve a kind of informality that would be difficult to achieve in the Albert Hall. And so, after a perfectly normal concert of Haydn, Brahms, Beethoven, with the BBC Symphony Orchestra conducted by Colin Davis, there was just time (if you were lucky) to get from South Kensington to Chalk Farm. There, in a building originally designed as a railway-engine shed, and now primarily a theatrical 'performing area' for unusual stage productions, you could hear Pierre Boulez conducting a section of the BBC Symphony Orchestra. Other famous artists taking part included the pianist Jean-Rodolphe Kars, the versatile singer Cleo Laine, who can range from jazz to Schoenberg, the King's Singers, the Philip Jones Brass Ensemble. The Round House Proms were established as a regular ingredient of each season.

In 1971 the Proms ventured out also to the Royal Opera House, Covent Garden, for a performance of Mussorgsky's *Boris Godunov* under Prom conditions (an idea explored further and independently by the Royal Opera House), and to Westminster Cathedral for the *Missa solemnis* of Beethoven. That performance was followed by a concert at the Albert Hall featuring Stockhausen's *Mantra* and a late-evening Raga. The Raga was presented by the famous sitar-player Imrat Khan, and it was the first time that Indian music had been heard at the Proms. On that night, taxi-drivers were given the approximate finishing time of the *Missa solemnis* (9.10 p.m.) and informed that many people might wish to reach the Albert Hall by 9.30 (just possible). The Covent Garden experience could not be repeated, but Boris Christoff (who sang the leading role) said afterwards that performing to the Prom audience had been a tremendously moving experience. There was another visit to Westminster Cathedral in 1972, for the Monteverdi *Vespers of 1610*, and the second of the Round House concerts that year was a somewhat sensational 'happening' – John Cage's *HPSCHD* (computer terminology for *Harpsichord*), which required seven harpsichords, fifty-two tape recorders to reproduce computer-generated sounds, sixteen film projectors for multi-layered visual effects, and it went on for far longer than the scheduled ninety minutes. That season there was, besides Cage, a strong representation of twentieth-century American music: this included a new Concerto by Elliott Carter and George Crumb's *Echoes of Time and the River*. (The latter's *Star Child* was to make a deep impression in 1979.)

In the course of the fourteen years that William Glock was in charge of music for the BBC, every complexion of twentieth-century music was presented, not only the most 'difficult' and controversial. But, naturally, the most controversial aspects tend to be remembered most vividly. Soon after his appointment, Glock brought into the BBC a number of other musicians who were in sympathy with what he was trying to do: the aim was, in idealistic terms, the integration of the music of our time as a natural part of the concert and broadcasting life of the country, closing the gap that had become very evident between the tastes of the concert-going (and radio-listening) public and the work of many of the most influential composers of the twentieth century. The gap remains far from closed, but Glock's services to music through the BBC (for which he was knighted in 1970) have undoubtedly made the gap less wide than before. From the early sixties, the staff of the BBC's Music Division included Stephen Plaistow, a one-time chairman of the British section of the International Society for Contemporary Music; Alexander Goehr, son of the exiled German conductor Walter Goehr and a composer with a non-English background (he later became the Cambridge Professor of Music); Leo Black, with contemporary-music connections through the world of publishing; Hans Keller, Austrian born, an authority on the music and the theories of Schoenberg. It was felt that Schoenberg had been very under-represented by the BBC. Keller was first made music talks producer, and before long he was Glock's chief assistant, first for chamber music and then for orchestral and choral music. Writing in the BBC Handbook of 1965 about the problems and responsibilities of music planning – that is, the planning of the whole extensive output of the BBC's Music Division, of which the Proms are a comparatively small part – he said:

> There is not a single musician alive to whom all contemporary music is comprehensible. To make matters even more problematic, the crisis works both ways: not only are advanced styles incomprehensible to traditionalists, but more conservative styles tend to be incomprehensible to advanced minds. It is a fact that highly competent, perhaps even outstanding avant-gardists have come to the conclusion that the music of this country's greatest living composer is rubbish. It is useful to remind oneself of such facts when one feels like shouting 'Rubbish!' oneself – whether one is a listener or a programme-builder.

In Mozart's day, Keller continued, people wanted contemporary music, and only contemporary music. Today, a complex situation exists.

> It is, in fact, the BBC's duty to be both popular and unpopular at the same time – unpopular in discharging its duty towards the contemporary composer who, if he doesn't happen to have written the *War Requiem*, usually has to confine himself to a minority audience, however enthusiastic; and popular in catering for the musical tastes of various majorities.

Radio 3 broadcasts a tremendous amount of 'good music' across the whole spectrum. In planning, the greatest difficulty is with contemporary music, where, as Keller pointed out, 'you can't do anything without being told by somebody that you ought to have done something else; and for all you know you ought.' With foreign composers, you can choose works which have already proved themselves. With British composers, it is extremely difficult for the BBC to sort out the many new scores that it receives from composers, publishers, and performers. Advice and help from outside authorities can be useful, but the ultimate decision is always the responsibility of the BBC, whether it be a committee decision or one made solely by the Controller of Music.

Not only the choice of music but also the question of who performs it can be problematic. Groups such as the London Sinfonietta, who are geared to performing works in 'difficult' contemporary idioms, are rare. It was fortunate for William Glock that he could arrange to work with the French conductor and composer Pierre Boulez. They had many ideas in common about changing the norm of concert-giving; both in fact were idealists along similar lines. In 1965 Boulez began to be a regular guest conductor at the Proms, presenting that year one programme of Stravinsky, Berg, Webern, Debussy – the composers who had most powerfully influenced him in his own composing work (the extension of the twelve-note technique to the mathematical organising of pitch, rhythm, volume), an example of which, *Le Soleil des eaux*, was also included. The following year he gave three concerts, again with the BBC Symphony Orchestra, and among a wide range of contemporary works was the first performance in Britain of his *Éclat*. What Boulez as conductor achieved in a wide range of music was great clarity of detail, always with a clear overall sense of context, of the overall structure. But the interpretations were controversial – for some a revelation, for others clinical or cold. A work by Debussy could be clear and lucid, but at the same time (for many) a misrepresentation – as that great Debussy authority Ernest Ansermet himself found. The members of the BBC Symphony Orchestra were also strongly divided in their reactions to Boulez,

Pierre Boulez conducting a concert of music by Stravinsky, 25 August 1972.

particularly when it came to romantic works (for example, Wagner or Brahms). And controversy surrounded his appointment as chief conductor of the BBC Symphony Orchestra in 1971, in succession to Colin Davis (who had been appointed musical director of the Royal Opera House, Covent Garden). There can be no doubt that Boulez made a considerable difference to British musical life, giving audiences the opportunity to explore new paths, making available areas of music style which, whatever their final value may be, should certainly be admitted and experienced.

Boulez's position as the BBC's chief conductor continued until 1975, forming a kind of bridge between two régimes. William Glock retired from the BBC in December 1972 and was succeeded by Robert Ponsonby, whose previous experience had included five years as artistic director of the Edinburgh Festival, followed by freelance work in the USA, an administrative post with the Independent Television Authority, and, from 1964 to 1972, the position of general administrator of the Scottish National Orchestra.

22

The Music 1960-1973

From 1960 there was a 'new look' about the Proms as devised by William Glock. It was extension rather than revolution. A certain section of the press did more harm than good by giving the impression that the Proms in the late fifties were moribund or ossified, and that they sprang into instant life as soon as Glock came along. We have seen that this impression is completely false. The 1957, 1958 and 1959 series were all full of life, variety and novelty, and were highly successful in audience terms. They were, in their way, carrying out faithfully the brief of the Proms as established by Henry Wood and as interpreted by his successors. The press gave a great many Prom-goers the suggestion that continuity was broken and that now everything was different – in ways which in fact most people did not want. This had its effect on the audience figures of 1960 and 1961, which were substantially lower, but there was recovery the year after, when the blend of items in the programmes as a whole was very carefully calculated to be appealing, and at the same time included a great deal that was new to the Proms.

There were thirty-five works new to the Proms in 1960, and these included not only twentieth-century works, but also, perhaps surprisingly, Beethoven's *Missa solemnis*, Berlioz's *Grande Messe des Morts*, and Mozart's Piano Concerto in C (K503). Five twentieth-century works in particular set the tone of the season, and provided a foretaste of things to come: Stravinsky's *Oedipus Rex*, Schoenberg's Variations, Op. 31, Webern's Six Orchestral Pieces, Op. 6, Debussy's *Jeux*, and Luciano Berio's *Perspectives*. The audience's reaction to *Perspectives* – it was the first time that electronic music had been given in Britain at a public concert – was very mixed, and the press mostly felt that the future of electronic music was as incidental sound for plays and films, or as one of many ingredients in a musical composition.

The *Musical Times* stressed the chance given to young conductors in the 1960 season, and praised Colin Davis's performance of *Oedipus Rex*:

A queue extending from the Albert Hall down past the Royal College of Music, and snaking round into Prince Consort Road.

His handling of the tricky score, vintage Stravinsky of the middle twenties, was masterly, and he had male choir and orchestra in complete control. He was helped by a strong Sadler's Wells team consisting of Ronald Dowd, Patricia Johnson, Raimund Herincx, Roger Stalman and Alberto Remedios.

This was also the year of the first British performance of *Three Places in New England* by Charles Ives, the American composer whom Glock did much to promote, and of Berg's *Altenberglieder*. There were premières of Thea Musgrave's *Triptych* and an overture *Derby Day* by William Alwyn, a BBC commission. (The commissioning of works for the Proms from British composers became a regular and important form of promotion and encouragement during Glock's regime.) Graham Treacher conducted Schoenberg's last complete work, *De Profundis*, a setting of the Hebrew text of Psalm 130, bringing into contrast speaking and singing voices. It made a deep impression, and was performed twice. Milhaud's *La Création du Monde* and Satie's *Parade*, two outstanding works from the Paris of around 1920 also had first Prom performances.

Although the classical repertoire remained the basis of the Proms, after 1960 the representation in that field from year to year became more selective, less 'comprehensive', as many other kinds of music were included. No less than fifty-six works new to the Proms were heard in 1961, but they included a Handel overture, four Haydn symphonies and three major works of Mozart (the Sinfonia Concertante in E flat, K297b, the Requiem Mass, and the opera *Don Giovanni*). The BBC commissions included works by composers particularly admired by Glock: *Symphonies* for solo piano, wind, harps and percussion by Elisabeth Lutyens; *Hecuba's Lament* by Alexander Goehr (an orchestral work stemming from *The Trojan Women* by Euripides); and a Divertimento for string orchestra by Anthony Milner. The programmes that year set out 'to invent more freely, to look further abroad for works that would add colour and freshness', and indeed there was no lack of variety. 'Since the Prom audience is the most enterprising in the world', wrote William Glock, 'it need cause no astonishment that the largest attendance of the whole season was for a programme which included Schoenberg's Violin Concerto.' The present writer remembers that concert. The first part, up to the interval, consisted only of Beethoven, conducted by Sir Malcolm Sargent. Then, in Part 2, Sir Eugene Goossens conducted the Schoenberg Violin Concerto (with Tibor Varga as soloist) and two works by Debussy. A fairly large number of people had left in the interval and the arena was noticeably less full when the Schoenberg began; a few more left the hall during the performance. Those who remained were enthusiastic. But it would be misleading to give the impression that the largest attendance of the season was *because* of the Schoenberg work. Most people had come to hear Beethoven. Glock was aware of this, but did not want to repeat a considerable number of the great classics each season, because he wanted the series to explore the whole repertoire of orchestral music and to consist of programmes that were 'balanced, varied, original and satisfying'. Undoubtedly this started to be achieved in 1961.

So rich in interesting events did the seasons become that in a comparatively short space one can do little more than mention highlights. Colin Davis gave a vital performance of Stravinsky's *Les Noces*, and a number of enterprising programmes conducted by Basil Cameron in the 1961 season included Bruckner's Symphony No. 7, Schoenberg's Piano Concerto, and Stravinsky's *Rite of Spring*. George Malcolm appeared as a sensitive conductor of Britten's *Cantata Academica*, as also of Bach and Beethoven. Among the programmes conducted by John Pritchard was the complete Mozart opera *Don Giovanni*, given as a concert performance by the Glyndebourne Opera directly after the end of their season. It was a star-studded cast, which included Richard Lewis and Geraint Evans, and the success was phenomenal. The performance was without scenery or costumes, but the principal singers were 'appropriately' dressed – tails for Don Giovanni, dinner jacket for Leporello, lounge suit for Masetto – and there was some semblance of acting.

Don Giovanni was followed in 1962 by another Glyndebourne Opera performance – Mozart's *Così fan tutte* – again conducted by Pritchard. There were four BBC commissions that year: the *Fantasia on an In Nomine of John Taverner* by Maxwell Davies was conducted by the composer; Norman Del Mar conducted the other three, which were *The Phoenix and the Turtle* for chorus and orchestra by Thea Musgrave, the *Scenes and Arias* (to medieval words) by Nicholas Maw, and the *Medieval Diptych* for baritone and orchestra by Alan Rawsthorne. There were also premières of Lennox Berkeley's Five Pieces for violin and orchestra, and the suite from Arnold Cooke's ballet *Jabez and the Devil*. This was the season when representative music by the important French organist and composer Olivier Messiaen made an impression on the Proms – not in the hands of Pierre Boulez, as was later to happen, but under the direction of the young British conductor, John Carewe, who gave the *Cinq Rechants* for unaccompanied chorus, and *Oiseaux exotiques* for piano and orchestra (the soloist being Aloys Kontarsky); also, five movements of Boulez's *Le Marteau sans Maître* (now a modern classic). More Stravinsky works, too, made their first Prom appearance: *Agon* and *Le Baiser de la Fée*; and Colin Davis conducted a special concert for Stravinsky's eightieth birthday on 28 August.

In 1963 the press gave much coverage to the foreign conductors at the Proms that year – in particular to the octogenarian Leopold Stokowski (who was English-born, but a naturalised American since 1915). Stokowski gave two programmes which included Mahler's Symphony No. 2 and his own orchestral version of Mussorgsky's *Pictures from an Exhibition* (a version which inexplicably leaves out two essential quick movements). There were 'gala evenings' (as Glock called them), including two Glyndebourne Opera productions in concert form (Mozart's *The Marriage of Figaro* and Monteverdi's *L'Incoronazione di Poppea*), the 150th anniversary of Verdi's birth, marked by Giulini conducting the Verdi *Requiem*, and the 150th anniversary of Wagner's birth, with a special Wagner concert given by Solti and singers and orchestra from Covent Garden. There was the first British performance of Britten's *Cantata Misericordium*, Op. 69, which had just been written for the centenary celebrations of the International Red Cross in Geneva (Peter Pears and Thomas Hemsley were the soloists). Britten's *War Requiem* had an outstanding performance (as yet only its third in London), conducted by Meredith Davies and the composer – the three soloists on this occasion being English (Heather Harper, Pears, and Hemsley).

Three British composers were commissioned to write works for the 1963 season: these were Lennox Berkeley's *Four Ronsard Sonnets* (conducted by the composer), Francis Burt's *Phantasmagoria* ('a fantastic series of illusive images'), and Peter Racine Fricker's *O longs désirs* for soprano and orchestra (settings of five sixteenth-century love sonnets). Luigi Nono conducted the first London performance of his *Sul ponte di Hiroshima*, and Sargent conducted Roberto Gerhard's Piano Concerto (with Malcolm Binns as soloist).

The 70th anniversary of the Proms was celebrated on 10 August 1964 with a special anniversary concert. It was not a superlative orchestral programme as one might have expected, but a superlative concert performance of Verdi's *Otello*, given by Covent Garden Opera under Solti. Other 'gala evenings' that year included Glyndebourne Opera again – Mozart's *Idomeneo*, conducted by Pritchard – and Mahler's Eighth Symphony ('Symphony of a Thousand'), conducted by Charles Groves. There was another Covent Garden occasion with Solti, Acts 1 and 3 of Wagner's *Die Walküre*. And following the success of *The Creation* under Sargent in 1962, an evening in 1964 was devoted to Haydn's *The Seasons*, this time conducted by Colin Davis. Several important works of Haydn were given a first Prom performance that season. 'Amazingly enough', wrote Glock, 'there is still a need to champion Haydn.'

Basil Cameron's eightieth birthday concert on 18 August was followed the next day by a concert conducted by Sargent to mark the twentieth anniversary of Sir Henry Wood's death. The programme included the Bach-Klenovsky *Toccata and Fugue in D minor* and the *Serenade to Music* which Vaughan Williams had written for Wood's Jubilee as a conductor in 1938; and there was also a brand-new tribute to Wood, commissioned by the BBC – the Concerto Grosso No. 3 by William Alwyn (who had played flute in Wood's orchestra). The composer conducted. Another 'remembrance' concert – on 4 August, the fiftieth anniversary of the outbreak of the first world war – consisted of Vaughan Williams's Sixth Symphony and Britten's *War Requiem*.

Other BBC-commissioned works that year were an *Aubade* by Richard Rodney Bennett in memory of the Prom conductor John Hollingsworth, who had recently died; a cantata by Bernard Naylor, *Sing O my love*; a Cello Concerto by the South African-born Priaulx Rainier; and a choreographic suite, *Creation Epic*, by Reginald Smith Brindle, an exponent of twelve-note technique.

An important première took place on 13 August: Mahler's Symphony No. 10, in F sharp major, which had been left uncompleted by the composer but was now realised in a full-length performing version by Deryck Cooke – a version much discussed and now world-famous. For the Prom performance Berthold Goldschmidt conducted the London Symphony Orchestra. The following year Mahler's Fourth and Sixth Symphonies were included, and in 1966 the Tenth was repeated, this time under Walter Susskind; in the course of that season, also, Mahler's major vocal works were heard – *Das Lied von der Erde, Kindertotenlieder*, and songs from *Des Knaben Wunderhorn* – and Jascha Horenstein conducted the Ninth Symphony. Mahler's music had by now become a fully relevant part of the English musical scene, and the Proms had played their part in achieving that acceptance.

Stokowski, in 1964, repeated his personal success of the previous year. Another octogenarian, Pierre Monteux, was to have conducted Debussy, Berlioz and Tchaikovsky, but he died in July, the month before the Proms started: his place was taken by Rudolf Kempe. Charles Mackerras conducted a performance of Handel's great cantata *Alexander's Feast*, with a Handel organ concerto between the two parts of the work, as was the custom in the composer's time. Other important vocal works that season were Berlioz's oratorio, *The Childhood of Christ* (conducted by Sargent), Arthur Bliss's cantata *The Beatitudes* (conducted by the composer), and Schoenberg's 'monodrama' *Erwartung* (conducted by Norman Del Mar).

The extension of the chamber music element in 1965 led to some problems of juxtaposition in the programme planning. For example, one

programme began with Bach's Brandenburg Concerto No. 3, followed by
Chopin's Piano Concerto No. 2 and Beethoven's Symphony No. 4; then,
after the nineteenth-century orchestral sound there was a Telemann con-
certo 'to clear the air' before the sparse chamber-music textures of
Stravinsky's *Abraham and Isaac*; after which the programme ended with a
Bach organ solo. Not, surely, a convincing mixture as a whole. But there
were planning difficulties of other sorts too. Another programme consisted
of Elgar's arrangement of an Overture in D minor by Handel, Mozart's
Sinfonia Concertante, K364, Tchaikovsky's 'Pathétique' Symphony, and
Messiaen's *Trois petites liturgies de la Présence Divine* (not so 'petites' – the
work is over half-an-hour long) – and this was surely asking for trouble, for
many people would regard the first three works as in themselves constituting
a complete and satisfying concert, and the last item would seem irrelevant,
avoidable, an 'outsider' in the circumstances. One might also query whether
a programme consisting of three symphonies (Haydn's 'La Poule',
Beethoven's 'Eroica' and Nielsen's 'The Inextinguishable') was good Prom
planning. But these are minor quibbles in a season which contained a truly
amazing variety and richness. Glyndebourne Opera presented Verdi's *Macbeth* and Mozart's *Marriage of Figaro*. Covent Garden brought their sensationally successful production of Schoenberg's *Moses and Aaron* (though
without the visual side much was lost). Purcell's quasi-opera *The Indian
Queen* was followed (in Part 2 of the concert) by three Brandenburg
Concertos.

Elgar's *Dream of Gerontius*, conducted by Sargent, was preceded by a
sensitive *Stabat Mater* for women's chorus and small orchestra by Bernard
Naylor, conducted by Louis Halsey. Hans Werner Henze conducted his
cantata *Novae de infinito laudes*, after a conventional Part 1 consisting of
Weber (overture), Mozart (piano concerto) and Beethoven (symphony). Sir
John Barbirolli and the Hallé Orchestra returned to the Proms with three
substantial programmes (including Schubert's Great C major Symphony
and Mahler's No. 6), and one of their famous Viennese evenings.
Composer-conductors included Walton (*Façade*), Alan Rawsthorne (a
second Prom performance of his *Medieval Diptych*), Virgil Thomson (some
film music), Michael Tippett (his Piano Concerto, with John Ogdon). It was
the season of the *Stabat Mater* – besides Bernard Naylor's there was the
setting by Palestrina, and two very different ones by Polish composers,
Penderecki and Szymanowski.

By 1966, the Proms were openly becoming a festival 'with all that implies
in freedom of choice, in standards of performance, and in events of particular interest' (to quote Glock in the preface to the 1966 Prom prospectus).

It was a festival, however, which still depended on the standard orchestral repertoire as its foundation.

No one in his senses [wrote Glock] would plan such a series of concerts without including, for example, a large number of works by Beethoven; indeed it may be doubted if the Proms could survive if Beethoven had not provided a backbone to the repertory which is a source of strength in almost any context, and which does not spoil our appetite for new, or for very old, works which may appear in the same programme. Where a combination of Rachmaninov and Byrd would be anathema, and of Dvořák and Boulez hardly less happy, this is never so with Beethoven. Or with Bach. Both are needed for their own magnificence and also for their mixing qualities . . .

There were several American and several Russian ingredients that year. Two works of bold originality by Charles Ives – *The Fourth of July* (one of four recollections of American childhood) and his complex Fourth Symphony – aroused particular interest and much press comment. Edgar Varèse had recently died in New York; he was described by Glock as 'one of the heroes of 20th-century music' for his pioneering work in new styles. Two works of Varèse were conducted by Frederik Prausnitz – *Déserts* and *Equatorial* (first performance in England), the aim of the latter being 'to unlock the realm of pure sound'. Another American composer strongly advocated by Glock, Elliott Carter, was represented by his Variations for orchestra.

The Moscow Radio Orchestra, under its conductor Gennadi Rozhdestvensky, brought a new work by Shostakovich, *The Execution of Stefan Razin*, for its first performance in the West. The soloist was a Russian bass, Vitaly Gromadsky, and the choral parts were sung in Russian by the BBC Chorus. The other programmes of the Moscow Orchestra were a fine selection of Russian works (Tchaikovsky, Prokofiev, Scriabin, Rachmaninov) with some Haydn, Mahler and Britten. Sir Arthur Bliss conducted his Piano Concerto (with John Ogdon as soloist) at his seventy-fifth birthday concert on 2 August. The ninetieth birthday of that incredible composer Havergal Brian was also celebrated two days later with a performance of his Symphony No. 12, conducted by Norman Del Mar. That work had been written in 1957, when he was eighty-two, and many more symphonies followed before he was ninety.

There were many special events in that 1966 season: Glyndebourne's *Magic Flute* was conducted by Hans Gierster; Solti and the Covent Garden Company performed Acts 2 and 3 of Wagner's *Parsifal*; Handel's oratorio *Solomon* was conducted by Charles Mackerras, who also gave a memorable performance of Bach's Mass in B minor; Sargent conducted Delius's *Mass of Life* and Elgar's *Dream of Gerontius*; Barbirolli, with the Hallé Orchestra, gave Bruckner's Ninth Symphony in its original version; Antal Dorati conducted Beethoven's *Missa Solemnis*. Part 1 of Berlioz's massive opera *The Trojans* was sung in English, with a cast that included Janet Baker, Raymond Herincx and Ronald Dowd; Colin Davis conducted.

There were two works commissioned by the BBC for that year. One was a motet *Veni Creator Spiritus*, for mixed choir and brass, by Edmund Rubbra: it was the year of his sixty-fifth birthday. The other was *Ceremony* for cello and orchestra, by Gordon Crosse, whose *Elegy* had made a strong impression in the previous season.

In 1967 Sargent was too ill to take part. Colin Davis, as we have seen, took over many of his Prom assignments, including the first and last nights. The visiting orchestras from abroad were the Amsterdam Concertgebouw (three concerts under Bernard Haitink, one under Colin Davis), and the Polish Radio Symphony Orchestra. The latter, under Jan Krenz, included a work which aroused considerable interest – the *Jeux vénitiens* of Witold Lutoslawski, the senior Polish composer, held in high esteem by the young avant-garde.

The English Opera Group gave a performance in costume of Britten's church parable *The Burning Fiery Furnace*. Another evening showed Britten's remarkable gifts as an interpreter, when he conducted a performance of Bach's *St John Passion* with Peter Pears as Evangelist. The season also included the very different *St Luke Passion* of Penderecki, which Glock included as 'an act of faith', and which (as he said) 'many are convinced is an authentic and profoundly moving work'. This year the opera from Glyndebourne was Mozart's *Don Giovanni*, under Pritchard, and from Covent Garden Beethoven's *Fidelio* under Solti. Colin Davis, recognised as an excellent Berlioz conductor, was responsible for a performance of *The Trojans at Carthage*. In lighter vein, the Gilbert and Sullivan evening, normally a Sargent speciality, was this time in the hands of Marcus Dods, conducting the BBC Concert Orchestra and a strong 'G and S' team of singers. Also on a Saturday, Messager's *Véronique* provided an example of French operetta at its best.

Barbirolli and the Hallé Orchestra again made their contribution to the season, one of their programmes including Vaughan Williams's Symphony No. 8, which is dedicated to Barbirolli ('Glorious John'). Another English symphony, Robert Simpson's No. 3, made a strong impression. The Third Symphony of Roberto Gerhard explored new forms of contrast, as its subtitle 'Collages' suggests. More and more the influence of Pierre Boulez was

Sir John Barbirolli at a Prom rehearsal in 1966.

felt at the Proms. Of particular interest this season were his penetrating performances of Debussy's *Jeux*, Stravinsky's *Les Noces* and *The Rite of Spring*, the three fragments from Berg's *Wozzeck*. In one of his concerts, also, Stockhausen's *Gruppen* for three orchestras and three conductors was included. *The Observer* spoke of a 'gripping *Gruppen*'. It was a gripping season generally.

Glock was trying to achieve more ambitious programmes each year. In 1968 about one in three of the works played were new to the Proms. The commissioning of works specially for the Proms continued to be important. In 1967 there had been only two – *Oxus*, a scena for tenor and orchestra by Humphrey Searle (to a text by Matthew Arnold), and *Touchstone*, a 'portrait' for orchestra by Thomas Wilson, conveying the contradictory nature of a Shakespearian clown. In 1968 there were four commissioned works, and Glock tried an unusual experiment: two of them – a Violin Concerto by the Australian-born Don Banks and *In Alium* by John Tavener – together with a Concerto for Orchestra by Thea Musgrave were played in the first part of a concert; then, during the interval, the audience could choose, by ballot, which of these works they would like to hear played again in the second part of the concert (before a performance of Stockhausen's *Kontakte*). Some of the audience may not have wished to hear any of the pieces again; but the ballot choice was for Tavener's *In Alium*, a strange Messiaen-ish piece using live and recorded sound (with loudspeakers placed round the hall); it later enjoyed some success at the Festival of the International Society for Contemporary Music held in Hamburg the following year. The other BBC commissions of 1968 were a Concerto for two pianos and orchestra by Alan Rawsthorne, a characteristic work in its fine craftsmanship, and Harrison Birtwistle's *Nomos*, in which an amplified wind quartet is contrasted and combined with the surrounding instrumental textures.

Following the B minor Mass and the St John Passion of the previous year came Bach's St Matthew Passion in 1968, conducted by Karl Richter. There was a large ingredient of early music – notably the Glyndebourne version of the opera *L'Ormindo* by Cavalli (the Italian composer of operas and church music in the generation after Monteverdi). It was edited and conducted by Raymond Leppard, whose stylistically controversial performing editions of music of that period have become well known. John Eliot Gardiner conducted the Monteverdi *Vespers of 1610*. There was Purcell, Bach, and Handel with the English Chamber Orchestra, conducted by Charles Mackerras; and the Martindale Sidwell Choir sang Byrd motets. Also, starting that year at the Proms, the Accademia Monteverdiana (under its conductor Denis Stevens) contributed sixteenth-century Italian music by Andrea and

Giovanni Gabrieli – and in later Proms, Monteverdi, early English music (Dunstable, Byrd, Purcell), early French (Charpentier, Leclair, Pierre Robert), and early Flemish (Willaert, Lasso, Josquin des Prés).

Hans Schmidt-Isserstedt was one of the distinguished conductors from abroad in 1968, and his concerts included the first British performance of Blacher's Cello Concerto (with Siegfried Palm as soloist). Bernard Haitink conducted a memorable performance of Britten's *Spring Symphony*. Boulez, with the BBC Symphony Orchestra, gave some more works by the iconoclastic American composer Edgar Varèse (*Arcana* and *Ionisation*), followed by the rarely-heard cantata *Le Roi des Étoiles* of Stravinsky and his *Requiem Canticles*. Another Boulez concert of important twentieth-century works included Messiaen's *Chronochromie*, Boulez's own *Le Marteau sans maître*, and Berg's Three Orchestral Pieces, Op. 6; and in the same concert Aloys Kontarsky played Stockhausen's highly controversial *Piano Piece No. 10*. Another concert included an example of Boulez's idiosyncratic interpretation of heavy romantic music – Mahler's Symphony No. 5. The Moscow Radio Orchestra's visit in 1966 was followed in 1968 by the State Orchestra of the USSR, conducted by Evgeny Svetlanov and David Oistrakh, in both Russian and standard works. Unfortunately, the recent events in Prague were very much in people's minds at that time. There were demonstrations with banners outside, and some verbal hostility from some members of the Prom audiences. The occasion led to Mstislav Rostropovich, one of the soloists with this orchestra, being visibly moved to tears during his performance of the Dvořák Cello Concerto.

The Covent Garden contribution in 1968 was Verdi's *Don Carlos*, and the other Glyndebourne production was Mozart's *Die Entführung aus dem Serail*. There was also a complete Haydn programme, with Mario Rossi conducting the BBC Symphony Orchestra, and a complete Walton programme in which the composer and John Pritchard shared the conducting. Concerts devoted to several works by one composer were now uncommon at the Proms.

From 1960 onwards, many of the major works of Schoenberg were finding their way into the Proms – the Violin Concerto, the Piano Concerto, *Erwartung, Moses and Aaron*; in 1968 it was his uncompleted cantata *Jacob's Ladder*.

Anniversaries have been a regular feature of the Proms. In the 1969 season there was a concert to mark the 150th anniversary of the birth of Prince Albert – a concert of music which he would have enjoyed, especially in the present improved acoustic of the Albert Hall. The programme included Handel's *Water Music* and Mendelssohn's *Hymn of Praise*. That

year was also the centenary of the death of Berlioz. An outstanding event of
the previous year had been *The Trojans*, conducted by Colin Davis; and the
1969 season opened on a Friday with his vigorous interpretation of the
Grande Messe des Morts – a concert which also marked the centenary of
Henry Wood's birth. Davis also conducted the centenary concert performance of Berlioz's opera *Beatrice and Benedict*, the music interspersed with
spoken dialogue. There were many other large-scale events in 1969: Bach's
B minor Mass (conducted by Mackerras); Mozart's *Don Giovanni* from
Glyndebourne, conducted by Reinhard Peters with Ruggiero Raimondi as
. Giovanni; Verdi's opera *The Sicilian Vespers* was heard, in a BBC concert
production conducted by Mario Rossi, with the BBC Concert Orchestra
and Chorus; and the Verdi Requiem under Lorin Maazel. John Eliot
Gardiner was making his mark with Monteverdi – Vesper Psalms and
Motets, and the Prologue and two acts of *Orfeo*. Messiaen's enormous
Turangalîla Symphony was given for the first time at the Proms. And it was
another good year for Mahler: his Second Symphony (*The Resurrection*) was
given under Bernard Haitink, his Seventh under Jascha Horenstein, and his
Fifth under Vaclav Neumann (in the course of three concerts given by the
Czech Philharmonic Orchestra).

The famous Wandsworth School Boys' Choir, trained by their remarkable
choirmaster, the late Russell Burgess, performed two of Benjamin Britten's
dramatic cantatas, *The Children's Crusade* and *The Golden Vanity*, in costume. One of the most talked-about works of the season was the *Sinfonia* of
Luciano Berio, written for the Swingle Singers and orchestra: the composer
conducted. A very favourable impression was made by the imaginative early
work of John Tavener, *The Whale*, heard in the same concert as Stravinsky's
Renard (a burlesque in song and dance). And some controversy was aroused
with one of the BBC's commissioned works – *Yeibichai* by Wilfrid Mellers,
for chorus, orchestra, and jazz trio, with soprano and scat singer. 'The
glamorous compound was immediate in its effect,' said *The Daily Telegraph*.

In fact, the five works commissioned by the BBC for the Proms that year
show the range of styles brought forth by that enterprising aspect of the
Proms. Besides the Mellers work, there was Malcolm Arnold's Concerto for
two pianos and orchestra (the soloists being Phyllis Sellick and Cyril Smith).
The composer, who conducted, said disarmingly about the work: 'While not
attempting to plumb the depths of the great truths of life and death, I hope
the concerto will sound brilliant and give some pleasure.' It did, on both
counts, particularly in the jazzy finale. There was also a *Scherzo* for wind
orchestra and percussion by Alan Bush, personal and vital in style. *Worldes
Blis* by Peter Maxwell Davies provoked mirth with a piano turned on its side

The Golden Vanity *by Benjamin Britten was performed at the Proms in costume in 1969.*

Benjamin Britten at the Proms. He conducted a performance of Purcell's The Fairy Queen, *8 September 1971.*

like a harp and old metal tubes used as bells, and an old anvil. It demanded a very concentrated kind of listening, which it did not always get; there were boos, catcalls, and a lot of people went out during the performance. Hugh Wood's Cello Concerto (with Zara Nelsova) made a strong impression (as did also his *Scenes from Comus* in 1965). *The Observer* commended the composer's powers of extended musical thought, and referred to 'flesh and solid bone'. It would be pleasant to feel that out of all the forty-five works commissioned for the Proms by William Glock during his régime, one or two at least had entered the general repertoire of orchestral music and were heard regularly; but, disappointingly and often despite favourable reactions and good reviews, this has not happened.

In 1970 Glock wrote in the preface to the Proms prospectus that the main advance that year lay in the design of the programmes rather than in their content – the design which, in fact, owes much to radio programmes with their freedom from traditional concert patterns. But, come what may, the basic repertoire must be there. Twenty-one pieces by Beethoven (it was the bicentenary of his birth), thirteen by Bach, twelve by Mozart, for example, were included that season. A typical programme design now could be:

Monteverdi   Music for the Nativity Vespers
Beethoven   Piano Concerto No. 3, in C minor
Stravinsky   *Petrushka* (1947 version)

The range was from music of medieval Florence to Terry Riley, from Rameau's *Hippolyte et Aricie* to *The Lindbergh Flight* by Kurt Weill. *Pierrot Lunaire* was brought to the Proms for the first time, and more Charles Ives – *Tone Roads Nos. 1 and 3* and *The Pond* (these heard for the first time in England) and his astonishing Fourth Symphony (previously heard in 1966). The mixture of chamber music and full orchestral colour was persisting: one concert this season started with the Beaux Arts Trio playing Schubert's Piano Trio in B flat (D898) followed by Colin Davis conducting Act 3 of Wagner's *Tristan und Isolde* (with Ronald Dowd as Tristan and Amy Shuard as Isolde).

Sir Adrian Boult, then aged eighty-one, gave a memorable performance of Elgar's *Dream of Gerontius* and later (in the course of an all-English programme) of his Symphony No. 1 in A flat. He also conducted one of his specialities – an all-Brahms concert. But a tragic note was struck with the death of a well-loved Prom figure, Sir John Barbirolli, at the age of only seventy-one. It fell to Sir Charles Groves to conduct a memorial concert on 28 August – one of the concerts that had been planned for Barbirolli.

A double bill of Mozart opera, conducted by Mackerras, brought together *The Impresario* and *Zaide* (first Prom performances), and Handel's *Messiah* in its entirety, conducted by Colin Davis, was heard for the first time at these concerts. So too was the complete *Daphnis and Chloë* ballet music by Ravel, in Boulez's characteristically clear and vivid interpretation. From Glyndebourne came Tchaikovsky's *Eugene Onegin*, under John Pritchard; and from Covent Garden Wagner's *Das Rheingold* – the last of Solti's Covent Garden appearances at the Proms.

The BBC commissions went to the 64-year-old Elisabeth Lutyens, who produced *Essence of our happinesses* (to words by John Donne), and with Richard Lewis as soloist this turned out to be one of the composer's most acceptable works; to Sebastian Forbes – an *Essay* for clarinet and orchestra, the soloist being Gervase de Peyer; and to Tim Souster, whose *Triple Music II* was for three orchestras (the first, sixty strings; the second, thirty-four wind instruments; the third, various keyboards, percussion and harps), each with its own conductor.

As previously mentioned, the Proms of 1971 ventured for the first time to other parts of London besides the Albert Hall – the Round House, Covent Garden, and Westminster Cathedral. Again there was a monumental opening at the Albert Hall on a Friday, this time with Mahler's Symphony No. 8. Again the concerts that season covered an enormous range of music – as Glock put it, from Josquin to George Newson, from Schütz to Stockhausen, from the *Archduke* Trio to *Siegfried*, and with Indian music, with ten works by Stravinsky, with Bach's *St Matthew Passion* (this time under August Wenzinger from Switzerland). Some of the programmes were very unusual in shape: for example, the one on 12 August, which consisted of three parts, each lasting about an hour, with two intervals (each of half-an-hour). Part 1 consisted of music by Roberto Gerhard and Bach, followed by a BBC commission, the *Beat Music* of Roger Smalley, a Stockhausen pupil, performed by Intermodulation (not an attempt to reproduce Rock on the concert platform, but an abstraction of certain elements from it). Part 2 was Stravinsky's *The Soldier's Tale*, staged – that is, spoken, danced and played – and in Part 3 there were Tippett's *Songs for Dov* and Berio conducted his *Laborintus II*. 'BERIO IN STEREO' chanted the Prommers.

Stereophonic broadcasting was by then well established – a wonderful enhancement to the radio reception of the Proms and other music programmes. Today we take it for granted. It began as a regular thing on 1 August 1966 with a Prom relay in stereo of *Parsifal* from Covent Garden.

Sir Adrian Boult conducted three of Sir Arthur Bliss's works in 1971, as a tribute on his eightieth birthday. Frederik Prausnitz shared another concert with Boult. Prausnitz conducted American music – Ruggles, Ives and

Sessions – and Boult conducted Beethoven. The Leningrad Philharmonic Orchestra came for the first time, but their four programmes were somewhat routine in content. Bruckner symphonies were now making regular appearances: that year Haitink conducted No. 2 and Horenstein No. 5. Early music was conducted by Roger Norrington – Schütz, Monteverdi, C. P. E. Bach; and a three-part concert was given by the Early Music Consort, directed by the late David Munrow, the Cantores in Ecclesia, directed by Michael Howard, and the London Bach Orchestra, conducted by Martindale Sidwell. The BBC Welsh Orchestra came to the Proms that season for the first time.

Following *L'Ormindo* in 1968, Glyndebourne presented another Cavalli opera, *La Calisto*, in 1971; again it was edited and conducted by Raymond Leppard. They also brought Mozart's *Così fan tutte*, with John Pritchard conducting. Scottish Opera, under its conductor Alexander Gibson, was presented also – Acts 1 and 3 of Wagner's *Siegfried*. The attractive production of Purcell's *The Fairy Queen* from the Aldeburgh Festival came to the Proms in September that year, conducted by Benjamin Britten, for whom the music of Purcell meant so much.

Every performance by Boulez is a clearly-defined personal interpretation – for better or for worse, according to taste, but always of distinct interest. In 1971, now as chief conductor of the BBC Symphony Orchestra, a wide range of music was performed in his five Prom concerts: not only his own music and Debussy, Ravel, Stravinsky; but also Schumann, Berlioz, Mahler (No. 9). Particularly telling was his concert consisting of the suite from Stravinsky's *Le Rossignol*, Schoenberg's Piano Concerto (with Alfred Brendel) and *Bluebeard's Castle* by Bartók – to each of which he was able to bring a vital viewpoint, with memorable results. He was in his element, too, in leading the National Youth Orchestra of Great Britain through a very demanding programme of twentieth-century works, including Stravinsky's Symphonies for Wind Instruments, Webern's Six Pieces (Op. 6) and Debussy's *La Mer*. And his mastery of the most *avant-garde* styles was demonstrated in the late-night Round House concert which, besides Messiaen (*Seven Haikai*) and two Ligeti works, included George Newson's *Arena* – a BBC-commission for mixed media, comprising solo clarinet, speaker, the singers Cleo Laine and Jane Manning, a choir, the King's Singers, a section of the BBC Symphony Orchestra, film projections, coloured lights. Press comment was not encouraging. But about another commissioned work that season – *Scenes and Prophecies* by Bernard Naylor – the critic of *The Financial Times* commented that Naylor 'uses traditional harmony in a way that makes it seem entirely new and expressive'. This is a notable impression to have made in the composers' world of the time, when a Prom commission from Glock would for many have meant a challenge to write something as far off the beaten track as possible!

There were two foreign orchestras at the Proms in 1972: the NHK Symphony Orchestra of Japan (on a Sunday at the awkward time of 5 p.m.) gave Prommers the rare opportunity of hearing two orchestral works by Japanese composers, besides interpretations of Brahms and Mozart; and the Munich Philharmonic, under Rudolf Kempe, played Mahler (No. 2), Bruckner (No. 4), Strauss, Mendelssohn, Dvořák, in the course of three concerts. Sir William Walton's seventieth birthday concert was given by André Previn and the London Symphony Orchestra. (Walton is said to be one of Previn's favourite composers.) The distinguished soloists were Jill Gomez, Richard Lewis, Peter Pears and John Shirley-Quirk – to perform Act 2 of *Troilus and Cressida* – and the concert ended with a fine performance of *Belshazzar's Feast*.

George Malcolm directed the Northern Sinfonia (from the harpsichord) in all six Brandenburg Concertos. There was another performance of the 'Symphony of a Thousand' – Mahler's No. 8 – conducted, as in the previous season, by Colin Davis. Another Glyndebourne version of an early opera edited and conducted by Raymond Leppard was heard: this time Monteverdi's *Il ritorno d'Ulisse in Patria*, with a distinguished cast headed by Janet Baker and Richard Lewis. The Fires of London, directed by Peter Maxwell Davies, gave a highly effective interpretation of Schoenberg's *Pierrot Lunaire*, with the soloist, Mary Thomas, in Pierrot costume. And Boulez interpreted Peter Maxwell Davies's *Blind Man's Buff* in a programme which included his own *Cummings ist der Dichter* and Heinz Holliger's virtuoso oboe work, *Siebengesang*, in which the composer was the brilliant soloist. Other Boulez concerts that year included Beethoven's *Missa solemnis*, Wagner's *Parsifal*, Mahler's Sixth Symphony, Messiaen's *Poèmes pour Mi* (the soloist being Felicity Palmer), and *Seven Haikai* which uses piano, xylophone and marimba in its orchestral colouring; and two American works – Elliott Carter's complex Concerto for Orchestra, and John Cage's 'anti-art' impression entitled *First Construction in Metal*. Chamber, orchestral and choral works by Mozart were brought together when Daniel Barenboim took part as pianist in the Piano Quartet in G minor (K478), and as soloist in the B flat Piano Concerto (K456), and then conducted the John Alldis Choir, soloists, and the English Chamber Orchestra in the *Requiem* (K626).

After the Aldeburgh performance of *The Fairy Queen* in 1971, there was considerable interest in Purcell's *King Arthur*, which was given a staged performance in the 1972 season – as seen at the Aldeburgh Festival that year in Colin Graham's production, and conducted by Philip Ledger. Stanford Robinson, with the BBC Concert Orchestra, the BBC Choral Society, and well-known singers such as Patricia Kern and Alexander Young, gave an evening of Gilbert and Sullivan, as they had successfully done in the previous two seasons.

As usual, in 1972 there were a great many works new to the Proms. A programme by the London Sinfonietta, conducted by David Atherton, had four of them – Birtwistle's *Down by the Greenwood side*, Kurt Weill's *Kleine Mahagonny*, Schoenberg's Chamber Symphony, Op. 9, and Tavener's *Celtic Requiem*. The BBC commissions went to John Lambert and the pianist-composer Ronald Stevenson. Lambert's *Formations and Transformations* made a positive impression, with press comments such as 'beguiling', 'craftily scored', 'fluid internal relationships'. But comment on Stevenson's Piano Concerto No. 2 (*The Continents*) was as a whole rather scathing about the composer's 'polyglot' music which 'seeks to voice humanity'. In another vein, *Hexameron* (a series of variations by Liszt and other composers of his time) was given a spectacular production at the Proms, with the pianist David Wilde impersonating Liszt.

In his last year as the BBC's Controller of Music, Glock decided once again to try a short season of Winter Proms. It lasted a week – from Friday 29 December to Friday 5 January 1973 – and included a very enterprising range of music: Boulez conducting an all-Stravinsky programme and a complete performance of Berlioz's *Damnation of Faust*; an all-Mozart concert; an evening when the London Sinfonietta, conducted by David Atherton, played works by Hugh Wood and Roberto Gerhard, and a commissioned piece from the up-and-coming Robin Holloway – *Evening with Angels*. Maazel conducted Bartók and Tchaikovsky, Haitink gave Mahler's Sixth and Boult Elgar No. 1. John Alldis conducted David Bedford's *Star clusters, Nebulae and Places in Devon*. There was an unusual concert of early choral music at Westminster Cathedral. But the only really successful concert, in terms of attendance, was a 'Fanfare for Europe' celebration in which Karajan and the Berlin Philharmonic Orchestra played two Beethoven symphonies (Nos. 4 and 5).

In the 1973 prospectus of the Proms, Glock pointed out that operas would in future have to be fewer – 'not because of any change in our belief that they provide an invaluable ingredient of the Proms', but because regrettably they were becoming too expensive. If prices of admission were to be kept down, while artists' fees rose uncontrollably, some things would have to be sacrificed. Nevertheless, the season offered an extremely enterprising repertoire

A rehearsal for Stockhausen's **Carré** *for four orchestras, 7 September 1972.*

Sir William Glock at his last Proms press conference in June 1973.

and the prospect of high-quality performances. Glock's own account of what guided his planning of the Proms is well worth quoting:

> It is always hard to describe the planning of the Proms, and the aspirations that lie behind it. Part of the problem is to do justice to the basic repertory of orchestral music, but without resorting to banal or overworked patterns – by which I mean not only the familiar sequence of Overture, Concerto, Symphony, but also a succession of famous works, without the relief of something unobvious or a little antiseptic. Let me give a few examples. The 1973 Proms include three evenings entirely devoted to Beethoven – on the face of it, a relapse from the very sensible rule of recent years that his works should be spread as widely as possible over the season as a whole. But one of the three concerts begins with Roger Woodward's volcanic performance of the *Hammerklavier* sonata, another includes the much neglected Triple Concerto, and the third has Beethoven's last two cello sonatas, played by Jacqueline du Pré and Daniel Barenboim, before ending with the Ninth Symphony. And the same applies to the two Haydn evenings (if only there could be half a dozen!), one consisting of three symphonies, Nos. 60, 83 and 102, interspersed with Bartók; the other of the String Quartet in F, Op. 77, No. 2, the *Clock* Symphony and the *Nelson* Mass – supreme works that have almost certainly never appeared together before in a public concert. Generally speaking, the search for programmes that are convincing and yet unexpected is an important part of the whole process, and of course we don't always succeed, or anything like it. One example that seems to come off is the concert on 6 September, with Boris Christoff singing Glinka and Mussorgsky, and then Beethoven's *Eroica* as the second half. Another is the programme on 12 September of Holst, Elgar and Vaughan Williams, with Michael Tippett's new Piano Sonata to make the audience sit up, but without breaking the sense of the evening as a whole.

It was also Glock's aim to arrange about a dozen outstanding occasions during the season. In 1973 the operatic ones were a Covent Garden performance in concert form of Beethoven's *Fidelio*, conducted by Colin Davis; a Glyndebourne performance, under John Pritchard, of Strauss's *Capriccio*; another Glyndebourne performance, this time of Mozart's *The Magic Flute*, conducted by Bernard Haitink; and to celebrate the sixtieth birthday of Benjamin Britten, the Sadler's Wells Opera Company, under Charles Mackerras, gave that composer's neglected *Gloriana*, originally produced in 1953 in honour of the coronation of Queen Elizabeth II. The B minor Mass, the *St John Passion*, *Messiah* – all these were special occasions. The Monteverdi *Vespers*, which had been so successful the previous season, had another performance in Westminster Cathedral, again with John Eliot Gardiner conducting; but the amount of pre-classical music was not as great as usual this season. It did, however, include an excellent late-evening concert of plainsong and polyphonic church music in Brompton Oratory (about a mile from the Albert Hall), conducted by the Oratory's Director of Music, John Hoban.

There were two other anniversaries in 1973. One, a Rachmaninov Centenary Concert, with the London Symphony Orchestra conducted by André Previn: the main work was Rachmaninov's remarkable choral symphony, *The Bells*. And at Lennox Berkeley's seventieth birthday concert, with the BBC Northern Symphony Orchestra under its conductor Raymond Leppard, the composer's Third Symphony was performed; the BBC also commissioned a work from him – the *Sinfonia Concertante* for oboe and chamber orchestra (with Janet Craxton).

Other BBC commissions were to three composers of different generations. The young Nicola LeFanu (daughter of the composer Elizabeth Maconchy) produced *The Hidden Landscape*, an orchestral piece suggesting (in no obvious way) an identification with Nature's many moods. Thea Musgrave, Scottish-born in 1928, wrote a Viola Concerto, which *The Observer* described as 'a triumph' and *The Times* as 'a model of clarity'. Controlled improvisation was one element of the work, and there were new groupings within the orchestra and in relation to the soloist. The other commissioned work was *Ploërmel* by Priaulx Rainier, for wind instruments and percussion; it originated with an idea about bells and their resonances, leading to the development of some intriguing, rich musical textures.

Unusually, there was a two-piano Prom, without orchestra: the Kontarsky brothers at a Round House late-evening concert played Debussy's *En blanc et noir*, Boulez's *Structures* (Book 2), and, with electronic treatment, Stockhausen's metaphysical *Mantra*.

Boulez, as had become customary, conducted a wide range of music, from Schumann to Berio. The Berio work was a Concerto for two pianos, immensely varied in texture and establishing quite unusual relationships between soloists and orchestra. Boulez also conducted his . . . *explosante-fixe* . . . written in memory of Stravinsky. Another Boulez concert was all-Stravinsky, including a wide range of styles – *Agon*, *Renard*, and *Les Noces*. There was the first Prom performance, again under Boulez, of Schoenberg's *Gurrelieder* (Songs of Gurra) – an 'early' work, still heavily Wagnerian, written for four solo singers, three male choruses, one mixed chorus, and an exceptionally large orchestra.

And so, in every way, the final season of Glock Proms showed no diminuendo in enterprise or imagination. Looking back over his fourteen seasons, 1960 to 1973, it appears that the Proms completely changed in character. They became, and have remained, a unique *international* festival into which more and more new musical experiences can be poured. Today it is safe to assume that people do not come to the Proms to hear the standard classics for the first time, with a few novelties thrown in for good measure. The standard orchestral repertoire, after all, is being broadcast the whole time – this was specially true in the last years of the sixties when the Third radio network was the Music Programme; long-playing records offer everything and a multiplicity of interpretations; orchestral concerts are not rare. The Proms can be devised for knowing audiences whose experience of orchestral music is calling out to be enriched on a foundation that is already established. How different from Henry Wood's Proms in the early years of the century, when for most of the audience those concerts were the be-all and end-all – where you came to make your first acquaintance with Beethoven's Seventh or the *Tannhäuser* Overture. Has the spirit and purpose changed? The music may range over five centuries rather than two-and-a-bit; and instead of a 'one-man-show' with one orchestra, we have a proliferation of orchestras and conductors. Wood's aim was to present the best music that was available at the time to as wide an audience as possible, at a price that all could afford. In their present richness, the Proms still have the same objective, and with the sponsorship of broadcasting it can still be realised. It was a remarkable achievement of Glock to have been able to alter and expand the scope of the Proms to such an extent – to such extremes – without the concerts as a whole becoming any less successful than they were before.

23

Interlude: The Prommers

For whom is all this trouble taken? The nucleus of the audience is (as it has always been) the promenaders (or 'Prommers') – that large sea of faces in the arena which the conductor surveys from his rostrum when he turns to acknowledge applause. There are others, too, at the Albert Hall, less in evidence, but with a god-like view, who roam the Gallery. For those of the audience who sit in stalls, loggia or balcony, the experience is roughly like that of a normal concert, except that Roman-like they can 'watch the animals' in the arena! For the Prommers, however, the experience is unique.

Since 1977, towards the end of each Prom season, the BBC has arranged a Prommers' Meeting at which aspects of these concerts can be discussed with the Controller of Music, Robert Ponsonby, and some of his staff. Thus, a direct link is established between the 'hard core' of the audience and the actual programme-makers. The present writer sent a questionnaire to about a hundred Prommers whose names and addresses were known to the BBC: of these well over half responded – and a summary of this exercise is given below.

In the early days of the Proms, the size and shape of Queen's Hall created an atmosphere far more intimate than that of the massive Albert Hall. Pictures of promenaders in Victorian and Edwardian times show other differences – not only in the dress of the audience (see illustration, p. 10): it is clear that Prommers were not predominantly youthful then, as they are now. The ages of those who replied to the questionnaire ranged from fourteen to fifty-seven, but the majority were between twenty and thirty. A large number of these get season tickets and clock up an impressive number of concerts per season – sometimes forty or more out of the fifty-four possible. Having raked together the money for the season ticket, often with difficulty, they may find that the average price of each concert is less than 50p. ('The cheapest series of concerts in the world.')

The questionnaire asked: *Are you satisfied with the range and variety of the*

programmes? Do you think they now go too far in a search for new experiences?
Do you prefer to be on 'safer' ground more of the time? Are you open-minded
about music you don't know, or do you tend to avoid it? What do you look for?

Most were satisfied with the choice offered. The answers were definitely
in favour of adventure, with few exceptions – justifying Glock's view of
programme-building rather than a policy of standard and proven works
only, such as was advocated by Sargent. Not everybody liked the constant
bringing-together of a wide mixture of styles – ultra-modern works and
(say) a Beethoven symphony in the same concert – but for many it had
opened up new horizons. For example, John Barnard, a physicist: 'Although
my attitude to much twentieth-century music was very cool before I started
to Prom regularly, the policy of mixed programmes enabled me to "discover" the works of composers like Bartók, Shostakovich, Britten and
Tippett, from whom I had previously shied away . . . So far as new music is
concerned, I am always now interested to hear it.' Isobel Squire, a student:
'I have enjoyed some music which I might otherwise have dismissed
without a hearing' – citing works by Maxwell Davies and Lutoslawski. It
seems that the informal atmosphere of the Proms is ideal for this kind of
experience, in a way quite different from ordinary concerts. For Jules
Holden, a computer operator, the Proms are 'the cheapest way of getting an
unbiased musical education'. With a season ticket a Prommer may well
explore certain concerts that he might not otherwise have 'risked'. Few, it
seemed, wanted to return to the wholly Beethoven or the wholly Tchaikovsky concerts, or to the frankly 'popular' Saturdays. Several wanted to
hear more of the little-known works of the great masters; others wanted
more of certain English composers now unfashionable, such as John Ireland
and Cyril Scott, or of neglected Continental composers such as Goldmark
and Raff. Some, although open-minded, felt that the proportion of new
atonal music should not be too high. And Judy Dustin, a chartered librarian,
noted that in 1979 over fifty per cent of the composers presented were of the
twentieth century. 'I think that's too much,' she says. (In 1978 it was about
the same proportion.) More than one thought that the most effective
concerts were the ones which contained unconventional music: this could
mean Monteverdi and Fayrfax, or unfamiliar nineteenth-century works, as
well as contemporary music. The Gamelan music of Indonesia in 1979 was
mentioned by several as a particularly interesting venture. Most Prommers
are looking for 'enjoyment', communication, and a widening of experience.

Are you particularly keen on the first and last nights? Do you queue sometimes
for a long time? How do you account for the special appeal of the Last Night for
so many?

A number of really 'hard-core' Prommers camp on the pavements outside the Albert Hall for as many as eight nights, sometimes more, to get the best positions in the arena for the Last Night celebrations. At its best, this final concert (particularly Part 2) is a party, a relaxation, a letting-down of hair, an 'end of term', after many evenings of standing quietly, concentrating on the music during the eight-week season. A curious, make-believe spirit of flag-waving, nostalgic pseudo-patriotism and other excesses has become a sort of tradition, kept within reasonable limits before the invasion of television – but now, as many Prommers complain, attracting rather a large number of exhibitionistic rowdies, who are not interested in the music. Elizabeth Hyde, a schoolgirl, finds it 'a last fling to make the season go out with a bang rather than a whimper. Also, the *whole auditorium* joins in: mass feeling which is *so* satisfying – and it's beautiful; there's no other word for it.' She is not alone.

The first night is also an event for which there is much queuing. It is now a more serious occasion musically, important also to many Prommers as an occasion for reunion with old friends; its spirit is quite different from that of the last night (but the difference was less marked when the Proms began with a popular concert on the Saturday). Many Prommers say they now avoid the last night, because its character has so degenerated in recent years – and this despite the fact that all arena and gallery season-ticket holders are admitted to the arena and the 'day-trippers' are banished to the gallery. Most seem to enjoy the queuing, even when it goes on for a long time. In the ordinary way, to queue from 9 a.m. on the day of a concert that one particularly wants to attend is quite common. For the very popular Viennese Night people sometimes sleep on the pavement for two or more nights.

Do you find that the attraction of the Proms is not only musical but social? How important to you is this aspect? Have you made lasting friends – possibly with a group which meets at other times during the year?

Overwhelmingly, the replies were in the affirmative. Many lasting friendships, and sometimes marriages. The queuing is for many a particularly important social activity, complete with country dancing, singing, and even the performing of chamber music. The season as a whole is a wonderful opportunity to meet new congenial friends, renew previous acquaintances, and have a splendid time generally. Simon Yorke, in the timber trade, says he's made friends with lots of people, including 'three computer guys, a milkman, a BR ticket inspector, a physicist, and a lawyer'. For some, while the season lasts, it is a complete way of life, and often extends beyond the eight weeks, with people meeting in groups for other entertainments throughout the year, for reunion dinners, or pub get-togethers. Some join

James Loughran and the BBC Scottish Symphony Orchestra at a Prom, 30 August 1969.

Last night of the Proms, 1976. Sir Charles Groves receives the customary acclaim from streamer-throwing Prommers.

the Henry Wood Proms Circle. There is even a well-organised group which writes and rehearses an opera (the 'Groperetta') during the season and gives performances on the steps of the Albert Hall on the last afternoon for the entertainment of the last-night queue. Collections are made by the Prommers for the Malcolm Sargent Cancer Fund for Children and for the Musicians' Benevolent Fund. A handful of 'regulars' each year make around 400 white carnation buttonholes which are worn on the last night by the musicians, chorus, Albert Hall stewards, and BBC camera crews.

How important to you are the conductors and the soloists? Or do you go to the concerts purely to hear the music you're interested in?

As expected, most said they go to hear the music first and foremost. Several stressed the importance of all aspects of the performance. Remarkably few conductors were singled out – showing rather strikingly how diluted the personality side of the Proms has become since the death of Sir Malcom Sargent. But Lesley Melliard, a teacher, referring to a visit of the Israel Philharmonic with Zubin Mehta and Daniel Barenboim, said: 'With a line-up like that, they could have been playing the Magic Roundabout music and I'd still have gone!' Sir Adrian Boult, James Loughran and Bernard Haitink were praised by more than one, and some naturally had their favourite soloists, such as Dame Janet Baker or Alfred Brendel.

Do you mind paying as much as 40p (sometimes) for a printed programme at a concert if it gives all the words of the sung works, besides the programme notes?

Many said they never bought a programme: either it was too expensive or they simply felt they did not require it; or they read somebody else's. Others did not mind the cost: even if it were as expensive as the price of admission – reckoning a proportion of the season ticket price (£20 in 1979) over perhaps forty concerts – the overall expenditure was still felt to be very reasonable. One Prommer said that the programme notes for the standard works never varied from season to season: this is untrue.

If you could stand or sit for the same price, would you prefer to stand? Is it an essential part of the relaxed, informal atmosphere of these concerts?

Yes. Yes. The answers were virtually unanimous. To be able to choose where to stand, according to what is being performed, is obviously considered a great advantage.

Any other remarks or suggestions regarding the Proms?

A large number of serious Prommers are furious at the behaviour of the 'intruders', the 'trippers' who invade the first and last nights. They resent the fact that there is a shortage of season tickets because so many people buy them for use *only* on the first night, the Viennese night, and (especially) the last night. Jane Harrison, a student: 'If a system was introduced whereby one's season ticket was stamped as one went in, admission to the last night could be limited to those who had been to (say) thirty per cent of the concerts to which their ticket would admit them.' It was suggested by some that the first and last nights should not be on television, and that information about which Proms are being recorded for television should not be published.

'Bring back the Prom Badges!' was a fairly frequent cry. 'We are Prommers. We want to show that we're proud of this.'

Nina Drucker, a writer: 'As a Prommer, I dislike concerts with two intervals: too tiring and uncomfortable.'

Miss P. J. Blackman, a Post Office employee: 'Though my preference is for newer music, I think there is a lack of "family" concerts to which children could be brought. The old type of Saturday concerts was an ideal introduction for young people.'

Nick Martin, in management services: 'What about an out-of-season Promenaders' Ball (or Viennese Ball) in smart dress? This could be a good television light music evening – and could give publicity to the coming season.'

Clare Goehr, a student, complained about the frequent proximity of television cameras. 'On one occasion,' she said, 'all I could hear was a cameraman talking to the producer and the camera hissing away. It's very disturbing!!'

Nigel Stevens, a computer systems designer, kindly provided some examples of Prommers' wit. It has become customary for groups of Prommers in the arena, and sometimes in the gallery, to comment in speaking-chorus (as in ancient Greek drama) during pauses at concerts. At a Prom in 1977 Christopher Seaman was conducting the BBC Scottish Symphony Orchestra at a time when members of the Merchant Navy were taking industrial action and withholding their labour. The Orchestra assembled on stage and awaited the conductor. A lengthy pause ensued, to be broken by a speaking-chorus from the arena: 'IS SEAMAN ON STRIKE?'

The speaking-chorus was again in evidence when stereo broadcasting was first introduced at the Proms. The Prommers arranged their own transmission test as follows:

All: 'HERE IS A STEREO TRANSMISSION TEST.'
Stage Right: 'LEFT CHANNEL.'
Stage Left: 'RIGHT CHANNEL.'
Stage Right: 'LEFT CHANNEL.'
Stage Left: 'RIGHT CHANNEL.'
All: 'END OF STEREO TEST.'

24

The International Festival continues, 1974-1979

When Robert Ponsonby became the BBC's Controller of Music in 1973, he took over from Sir William Glock the planning and programme-building of the Proms and other important public concerts. This kind of personal responsibility for programme detail is not necessarily part of the Controller's duties, but Glock had taken it upon himself from the start, cannibalising the job of Head of Music Programmes when Maurice Johnstone left shortly after Glock's appointment. But whether the Controller actually builds the programmes himself or has it done for him, it is very important, in the internal set-up of the BBC, that these programmes should finally have the full approval and backing of the Controller, because the Proms, in their range and standard of performance, reflect most pointedly the BBC's musical policy.

Some explanation is necessary. Before Glock, the Controller's job had been concerned entirely with policy matters and the administration of the BBC's Music Division, which was then broader in its scope. The details of programme-planning were delegated to various 'Heads' (serious music, light music, television music) and 'Organisers' (for Home Service, Third Programme, External Services, BBC Transcription Services, and various music routines); and outside London, BBC Heads of Music in each of the regions (Midland, North, West, Wales, Scotland, Northern Ireland) were responsible for some of the BBC orchestras, regional music-making, and programme contributions to the national networks. A Controller was needed to co-ordinate all these activities, which collectively made up the BBC's music output. He was a central point of reference, extremely knowledgeable in matters of policy and BBC procedures, and a sorter-out of difficulties – somebody in the hierarchy of the BBC whose status as Controller would mean that his views and wishes carried weight at important management meetings and discussions which affected the workings of the Music Division.

That was the situation when Glock was appointed in 1959 – a unified Music Division, under one Controller, and responsible for all aspects of music broadcasting except gramophone programmes (this exception has always been a BBC anomaly – that music programmes from records, which form a very important and substantial part of music broadcasting as a whole, should be planned and realised in a different department of the BBC, quite separate from the Music Division). Glock was certainly more interested in programmes than in administration; for him the most important things were the Proms, the other BBC public concerts, and the BBC Symphony Orchestra. Many changes occurred during his régime, and the unified structure of the Music Division was to a considerable extent lost, partly through various pressures in replanning the radio networks, and partly through the relative importance (or unimportance) which Glock attached to certain aspects of the Music Division's work. Before long, the connection with operatic and other music programmes on BBC Television was lost: in view of the immense audiences (many times larger than those of radio) for any programme broadcast on television, this was for the Controller of Music a serious loss indeed. From then on, television music was planned and carried out by the television department, without a representative in the Music Division. When the 'Music Programme' was established in the sixties, it had its own Controller, to whom the Music Controller was a supplier (another BBC anomaly! See also p. 139). In 1969 the BBC published its controversial document *Broadcasting in the Seventies*, as a result of which four radio networks were established: the Music Programme became Radio 3, a mixed cultural programme, and Radio 2 became a continuous light music programme. The Music Division's connection with light music was then lost – again regrettable from the point of view of unification and co-ordination. Often the line of demarcation is difficult to define between so-called serious and light music (for Mozart it did not exist). The Proms, for example, have regularly had their Viennese Nights and Gilbert and Sullivan.

The situation when Ponsonby took over as Controller was therefore very different from that inherited by Glock. The responsibility was now for originated music on Radio 3 (but not gramophone programmes), with an occasional programme for Radio 4 (which is basically a speech network, with news and current affairs, plays, discussions, light entertainment). The regional connection continued, and the link with the External (Overseas) Services. But the Music Division was without television or light music connections, and was working always *vis-à-vis* the Controller of Radio 3, who has to make decisions on the policy and content of this service as a whole. Hence the importance of a strong music policy which, as already stated, is seen most clearly and publicly in the scope and variety of the Proms, in the form put forward each year by the Controller of Music.

Ponsonby's attitude to contemporary music is perhaps more circumspect than Glock's. He respects what certain composers are doing, without necessarily liking the results. He believes that the need to present 'happenings' at the Proms – such as Cage's *HPSCHD* – is now past. It was necessary to have them, but now, he believes, there are positive signs of consolidation of style and outlook among the 'advanced' composers. He concedes that many good musicians, besides many keen, average, thoughtful concert-goers, can still get very little out of Schoenberg and Webern. Nevertheless, since the departure of Glock, the Proms have certainly not become timid or lacking in enterprise and novelty; and Ponsonby will not be content with lower standards in the events offered. It is significant that in 1959 he resigned the directorship of the Edinburgh Festival on a matter of principle: not enough money was being made available to maintain the level and scope of that international festival. He is not the sort of person to permit things to go downhill.

The situation, as far as the Proms are concerned, is a healthy one. They are the most discussed musical enterprise of the BBC, and the most successful in audience figures at the concerts, in audience response to the broadcasts, in fame and prestige at home and abroad, and musically in the comprehensiveness of their repertoire (all of which is broadcast). If the character of Radio 3 remains as it is now, as the main network for the broadcasting of serious music, and if the BBC can continue to pay for the BBC Symphony Orchestra, BBC Symphony Chorus and BBC Singers – all of whom are employed solely for broadcasting – then everything could continue in its present satisfactory state. But without these essential performing ingredients, the Proms would not be a viable proposition.

From the start, from the 1974 season onwards, Robert Ponsonby has continued to see the Proms as an international festival, as they were for Glock, and has aimed at making each new season seem fresh and compelling. His earlier experiences of planning, for the Edinburgh Festival and then for the Scottish National Orchestra, must have been immensely valuable. Already in 1974 there were innovations: the inclusion of music for brass band, for the first time at the Proms; and two of the concerts were given at a North London church – St Augustine's, Kilburn, which has good acoustics. This was in addition to Westminster Cathedral and the Round House, which as before were occasionally used for appropriate concerts. The organ at the Albert Hall had just been modernised, and this enabled Ponsonby to include more solo organ music than before – including Hans Haselböck extemporising on a theme of Bruckner. A new feature that year – which has continued to prove very satisfactory each season since – was the series of informal pre-Prom talks at the Royal College of Art or the Royal College of Music (both in close proximity to the Albert Hall). These talks, at 6.30 p.m. and about thirty minutes long, with some discussion, are designed to illuminate new and unfamiliar music. If possible it is the composer talking about his own work to be played at the concert that evening, or somebody else closely connected with the music – often the conductor.

Two orchestras from abroad visited the Proms in 1974 – the Sydney Symphony Orchestra, under their conductor Willem van Otterloo, included a work by the Australian composer Don Banks (*Prospects*), and the Los Angeles Philharmonic, with Zubin Mehta, included a Charles Ives 'novelty', *Decoration Day*, and Bruckner's Eighth Symphony. As usual the BBC Symphony Orchestra shouldered most of the load. Boult, then eighty-five, shared the opening Friday concert with Pierre Boulez and conducted the 'Great' C major Symphony of Schubert. Many other orchestras took part, including the BBC's Northern and Welsh, and the National Youth Orchestra of Great Britain was conducted by Christopher Seaman in music by Tchaikovsky, Prokofiev and Brahms – more regular fare than they gave under Boulez in 1971! Alan Hacker, at a Boulez concert, gave a performance of Mozart's Clarinet Concerto on a basset-clarinet, the deeper instrument for which it is thought to have been originally composed. Charles Mackerras conducted the BBC Symphony Orchestra in a programme to celebrate (according to the prospectus) the '80th anniversary' of the first Henry Wood Promenade Concert – but in fact it was the 79th! It began appropriately with the *Rienzi* Overture – the same item which opened the first concert in 1895 (see p. 33).

The most unusual concert was certainly that given by the Black Dyke Mills Band and the Grimethorpe Colliery Band, conducted by Elgar Howarth, playing music by Elgar, Holst, Grainger, and the *Grimethorpe Aria* by Harrison Birtwistle. Sharing this concert was the BBC Concert Orchestra, under Ashley Lawrence, playing music by Delius and Grainger, including one of the latter's finest works, *A Lincolnshire Posy*; and the evening ended with Gilbert and Sullivan's *Trial by Jury*. The most unusual occurrence of the season happened during a performance of Carl Orff's *Carmina Burana*, under André Previn. It made a wonderful story for the newspapers, who spread themselves with headlines such as 'Unknown singer saves the day', 'Singer wakes up to a dream', and so on. What actually happened was that the baritone soloist, Thomas Allen, fainted during one of his solos and was carried out. Patrick McCarthy, who was listening in the arena with a score of the music, knew the part well because he had sung it in a performance in Birmingham. He left the arena and rushed round to the Artists' Entrance, found the BBC's concerts organiser, Freda Grove, and said 'I am a professional singer. I can sing the baritone part.' He was then allowed on to the platform, where he sang the rest of Thomas Allen's part, and at the end the audience gave him an ovation. Moreover, the whole incident was recorded for television.

The sequel came at the concert on the following day. This time it was somebody in the audience who was overcome by the heat and passed out. A speaking-chorus in the arena was not slow in its reaction: 'A PROMENADER HAS FAINTED' suddenly resounded through the hall. 'PLEASE ASK ONE OF THE SOLOISTS TO TAKE HIS PLACE.' This was, in fact, a good season for the speaking-choruses. When Charles Ives's *Decoration Day* had been played by the Los Angeles Symphony Orchestra, the comment from the arena, as the players were leaving the platform before the interval, was: 'NOT BAD FOR COLONIALS!'

1974 was the centenary of Schoenberg's birth. Apart from the short *Accompaniment to a Film Scene*, the three works heard that season were *Gurrelieder*, repeated from the previous season, conducted by Boulez; the Chamber Symphony No. 1, Op. 9; and *Verklärte Nacht* – all, in fact, early works. The operas were Holst's *Savitri* (it was also the centenary of Holst's birth), in an English Opera Group production conducted by Steuart Bedford, with Janet Baker. There were two Mozart operas: *Le Nozze di Figaro* from Glyndebourne, conducted by Pritchard, and *La Clemenza di Tito* from Covent Garden, conducted by Colin Davis. Charles Mackerras, who did so much to promote the operas of Janáček while he was musical director of the English National Opera Company, brought its interpretation of *Katya Kabanova*. This first season of Ponsonby's showed in every way the kind of variety and interest that Prom audiences had come to expect. Sir William Glock was connected with the 1974 season in a different capacity – that of executant with members of the Lindsay String Quartet in Mozart's E flat Piano Quartet (K493).

The commissioned works of 1974 – in part inherited from the previous régime – included one of Malcolm Williamson's best compositions, the *Hammarskjöld Portrait*, a study of commitment and suffering in a public figure; *Domination of Black* by Robin Holloway, a young composer coming to terms with German romanticism; and a Viola Concerto by Martin Dalby, the three movements of which, the composer tells us, are symbolically linked to 'Birth, Copulation, and Death'. The soloist in this last work was the composer's viola teacher, Frederick Riddle, and this concerto was a gift for his sixtieth birthday. The commissions of the following year included a Cello Concerto by Arnold Cooke (then aged sixty-nine) – a work displaying, as always with this composer, fine craftsmanship and melodic strength – and two works from the younger generation: the young conductor Andrew Davis (who was by now making a very strong impression at the Proms) conducted the BBC Symphony Orchestra in Edward Cowie's *Leviathan*, the dense textures of the music according with the definition of the Hebrew title ('That which gathers itself into folds'); and John Poole conducted David Bedford's choral-and-orchestral *Twelve Hours of Sunset* (starting from the idea of an aeroplane journey travelling due West – the 'strange feelings of suspension, timelessness and perpetual evening' which the piece attempts to convey).

The Albert Hall, Westminster Cathedral, the Round House, St Augustine's – the venues for the Proms were the same in 1975 as in the previous year. It was a season when more than thirty living composers were represented, more than half of them British. Michael Tippett was seventy, and he conducted his Piano Concerto (with Paul Crossley as soloist). His *Fantasia Concertante* on a theme of Corelli was also heard, and (at St Augustine's) his Sonata for four horns, and a Magnificat and Nunc Dimittis. Other anniversaries marked were those of Bizet, Johann Strauss the Younger, and Ravel (a centenary tribute, with several works during the season).

That 1975 season opened with an impressive 'Viennese Week-end': Mahler's 'Symphony of a Thousand' (No. 8) and Schoenberg's parable for our times, *Moses and Aaron*, were both conducted by Pierre Boulez, with characteristic clarity and vitality. In between, on the Saturday, was a popular Viennese Night, with the Hallé under James Loughran, a many-sided successor to Barbirolli. Besides the Schoenberg opera, there were several others: Covent Garden brought Britten's *Peter Grimes*, conducted by Colin Davis, with Jon Vickers outstanding in the title rôle; Glyndebourne brought Stravinsky's *The Rake's Progress*, conducted by Bernard Haitink; the English National Opera Strauss's *Die Fledermaus*, zestfully conducted by Mackerras; and Kent Opera Monteverdi's *The Coronation of Poppea*, stylistically well integrated under Roger Norrington.

The Black Dyke Mills and Grimethorpe Colliery Bands repeated their success of the previous year, in a concert which after the interval again consisted of Gilbert and Sullivan excerpts, with the BBC Concert Orchestra. There were visits, too, from both the National Youth Orchestra of Great Britain (under Christopher Seamen) and the International Youth Orchestra (under Claudio Abbado). The New York Philharmonic

Sir Colin Davis.

Andrew Davis.

Orchestra, Boulez's 'other orchestra', played Elliott Carter's *Concerto for Orchestra* and Mahler's Symphony No. 9, under Boulez. This was Boulez's last year as Chief Conductor of the BBC Symphony Orchestra, and he gave his final concert with that orchestra on 30 July when, besides Berio's *Ora* and Stockhausen's *Kontrapunkte*, he gave a performance of one of the most representative examples of the personal idiom which he himself had created – his own *Pli selon pli*. Boulez was to continue, with Colin Davis, as a chief guest conductor of the BBC Symphony Orchestra. The other orchestra from abroad was the Cleveland Orchestra, under its conductor Lorin Maazel, playing a well-chosen programme of Charles Ives's *Three Places in New England*, Bartók's *Miraculous Mandarin*, and Beethoven's *Eroica* Symphony.

Early music was given by the BBC Northern Singers, under Stephen Wilkinson (Byrd and Palestrina); and the Monteverdi Orchestra, under John Eliot Gardiner, performed Handel and Rameau (including a section of the latter's opera *Les Fêtes d'Hébé*). John Poole conducted the BBC Singers in Tallis's marvellous 40-part motet, *Spem in alium*, and a Magnificat by the early sixteenth-century John Taverner, which was followed by *Últimos Ritos* by the 31-year-old John Tavener of our own times – an attempt to capture ritualistically the essence of the mystical experience, using a large and strangely constituted orchestra, choirs, four soloists and tape.

Two works of Hans Werner Henze were heard: the première of his *Ragtime* and *Habanera* from a Symphony for Brass, and the 'recital for four musicians', *El Cimarrón* – the four musicians being bass-baritone, flautist, guitarist, and percussionist, all of them stretched to the utmost. This work, in which the composer acted as adviser and producer, involved an important element of extemporisation and lasted about eighty minutes. It was given at the Round House – one of three enterprising concerts of the music of our time.

One thing we take for granted when we go to an orchestral concert is that all the members of the orchestra will be there on the platform ready to play. Normally they are – but not absolutely always. If one or two of the string players are absent, the concert could begin without them. But what happens when the first oboe, or the second trombone, is missing, and his part is essential for the completeness of the music? A delay could be caused. It was – at a Prom on 14 August 1975. Bernard Haitink was conducting the BBC Symphony Orchestra, and the first work in the programme was the complete incidental music of Mendelssohn for *A Midsummer Night's Dream*. The first flute, essential for this performance, was stranded by a violent storm. The concert was held up for nearly half an hour. When the flautist eventually arrived, she was greeted with applause and comments from the audience: 'We've just finished re-scoring' – 'You've missed your cue'. The flautist, who plays very near the beginning, was given a minute or two to settle down and breathe again normally. Besides the delay in the hall when this kind of thing happens, there is the gap in the broadcast that has to be filled from the studio with an emergency programme on records, and the timings of the other scheduled programmes during the evening are all haywire.

Another unforeseen delay was caused on an occasion when Prince Charles unexpectedly visited a Prom. The first item was for eighteen strings only; but the full orchestra had to assemble on the platform at the beginning for an unscheduled performance of the National Anthem. Then woodwind, brass and percussion went out, leaving only the reduced number of strings. Comment was not slow in coming from the arena: 'Now look what Your Royal Highness has done!'

In the 1976 prospectus Robert Ponsonby wrote:

> This year's programmes attempt, as always, to balance what is acknowledged to be great music with the best of what is unfamiliar. The task is increasingly difficult, for whereas, two years ago, the programmes covered a span of over 500 years – from Dufay's death in 1475 – this year we draw upon seven centuries – from the anonymous *The Play of Daniel* to the commissioned works of 1976. Obviously the number of concerts can't be significantly increased. Consequently, as more and more early music becomes available, what was hitherto accepted as the indispensable centre of the repertoire will have to be the object of more rigorous scrutiny. I am inclined to think that some very popular works, when they are not indisputably great and when they can easily be heard outside the Proms, should no longer earn a place in the programmes. This year there is no Tchaikovsky B flat minor and no Rachmaninov Concerto. But there are four of Beethoven's piano concertos, his Violin Concerto and the Brahms B flat. These works illustrate the distinction which has to be made, I believe, between the very popular and the very great.

This statement led to a good deal of press comment, some of it unfavourable – some critics calling it 'subjective' or 'snobbish'. One popular newspaper proclaimed 'Popular gems get banned by autocratic Ponsonby'. Ponsonby was unrepentant about the value judgement involved and about the policy (inherited from Henry Wood) of educating public taste. As he himself expressed it:

> . . . I believe that where works of art are concerned it is inevitable and right
> that we resort to consensus: to the 'received' view that, for example, Chartres
> Cathedral is a greater work of art than the Duomo of Milan, Gainsborough a
> greater portrait-painter than Winterhalter, Shakespeare's Henry IV plays
> greater than Marlowe's Edward II – and that the 'Emperor' Concerto is
> greater than Rachmaninov's Second.

Criticisms from press and public, Ponsonby pointed out, 'box the compass'.
There were complaints in 1976 of not enough enterprise, but also of neglect
of the classics; of too few Bruckner and Mahler symphonies; of too few
'20th-century masterpieces'; but also 'At least you've spared us Stockhausen and Boulez'. Some wanted more organ music; some wanted less
early polyphony.

All this is healthy, of course. If people stopped caring what they heard,
then the BBC really would have to start worrying. The Proms make
available a vast range of music from which it is hoped everybody will find
satisfying programmes according to individual tastes. Old and new, familiar
and unfamiliar may be mixed in the same programme as a matter of policy,
but the Prom audiences have the reputation of being 'the most open-minded
in the world'.

A tragic note was struck in 1976 with the deaths of Rudolf Kempe and
David Munrow, both of whom were due to conduct important concerts at
the Proms that year. Kempe had been appointed chief conductor of the BBC
Symphony Orchestra only the previous September, and the opening concert of the Proms on 16 July, with Beethoven's *Missa Solemnis*, which
Kempe was to have conducted, became a memorial concert for him. David
Munrow, the persuasive broadcaster and director of the Early Music Consort of London, was to have directed two Proms during the season, including that thirteenth-century musical drama *The Play of Daniel*; but he died in
May, at the age of only thirty-three. In a different way, also, there were two
other casualties that season: commissioned works from the Australian
composers David Lumsdaine and Richard Meale (a Piano Concerto) were
not ready in time. It was, however, a rich and adventurous series with many
high points of interest. The Glyndebourne contribution was Debussy's
Pelléas et Mélisande, conducted by Bernard Haitink, who also gave a moving
interpretation of Britten's *War Requiem* (with Galina Vishnevskaya and
Peter Pears, two of the soloists for whom the work was originally written);
Scottish Opera, conducted by Alexander Gibson, contributed Verdi's masterpiece, *Falstaff*; Colin Davis, with soloists and orchestra from Covent
Garden, gave Act I of Wagner's *Die Walküre*; and, on a lighter note,

Bernard Haitink.

Rudolf Kempe.

Mackerras and the English National Opera Company provided Sullivan's *Patience, or Bunthorne's Bride.*

Another feature of the 1976 season was American music, to mark the bicentenary of the Declaration of Independence: Ives's *The Fourth of July*, the Eighth Symphony and the Double Concerto of Roger Sessions, Gershwin's Variations on 'I got rhythm', Copland's *Quiet City* and Four Dance Episodes from his ballet *Rodeo (or the Courting at Burnt Ranch)*, a sonata by Elliott Carter, and George Crumb's *Ancient Voices of Children*. Forming a link with England, four works by Benjamin Britten were included, all dating from 1939 and 1940 when he was living in the United States: *Les Illuminations, Canadian Carnival, Sinfonia da Requiem,* and *Diversions on a theme* for piano (left hand) and orchestra. Another Anglo-American connection was the first British performance of Richard Rodney Bennett's *Zodiac* (in twelve sections, each representing a Sign of the Zodiac): this was commissioned by the Washington State Symphony Orchestra for the Bicentennial celebrations. The dedication was 'to the distinguished English composer Elisabeth Lutyens, on her 70th birthday'. Lutyens herself contributed another of the Prom 'novelties' that season – her *Music for Orchestra II*. Two commissioned works were heard: *Scherzos* for four pianos by Brian Chapple, a work which had its initial impulse in the sounds of many pianists practising at the Royal Academy of Music; and the 40-year-old David Blake's Violin Concerto, renewing tradition through the art and landscape of Italy.

1977 was a double jubilee year – the Queen's Silver Jubilee and the 50th anniversary of the BBC's take-over of the Proms. It was a difficult time for the BBC financially, and when the Proms were being planned there was uncertainty over many aspects of the future of broadcasting (the report by the Annan Committee had not yet been published, and an improvement in the broadcasting licence fee was still awaited). However, everything went through as planned. The season began with a festival-within-a-festival – three attractive programmes of English music for the Queen's Jubilee, including Purcell's celebratory cantata *Hail, bright Cecilia* ('a Song for St Cecilia's Day, 1692'), Elgar's Second Symphony, Vaughan Williams's *Serenade to Music*, and Walton's *Belshazzar's Feast.* This was followed by the Fires of London performing a commissioned work – *The Martyrdom of St Magnus* by Peter Maxwell Davies, a full-length chamber opera which had recently had its first performance in the Orkney Islands, in St Magnus Cathedral, Kirkwall. It was one of three Jubilee commissions that year. The others were Edwin Roxburgh's *Montage* for orchestra, an abstract work with philosophical undertones which the composer compared to a space trip; and John Buller's *Proença*, for large orchestra, mezzo-soprano and electric guitar, using early Provençal texts. Buller's work was described by *The Daily Telegraph* critic as 'forty minutes of absorbingly imaginative music'.

Four of the concerts had the title 'Contemporary Masterworks', and these four together were offered for the price of three concerts. The idea was not pursued in the following year – wisely, perhaps, because it is hard to see why the particular masterworks were singled out from a good many other important twentieth-century works in the programmes, except by their mere length, which in each case formed a whole concert in itself. They were Henze's *The Raft of the 'Medusa'*, a 'popular and military oratorio' dedicated to Che Guevara; Tippett's first and perhaps greatest opera, *The Midsummer Marriage*, in which (if anywhere) he achieves fulfilment of 'a vision of wholeness'; Messiaen's *Turangalîla* Symphony ('the play of love' – love that is fatal, irresistible, transcending all); and Luciano Berio's *Coro* (different modes of setting to music – displaying diverse techniques from many cultural sources).

The full repertoire performed in 1977 is given in Appendix C (see p. 371). It included three British premières – by the Hungarian Sándor Balassa, Tristan Keuris of the Netherlands, and England's Richard Rodney Bennett. In an interview (published in *The Composer*, summer 1975) Ponsonby was asked whether the music of living British composers should be featured in BBC programmes more than that of living composers from other countries. His answer was:

> Yes, I think it should. From time to time publishers press me to include works by unknown foreign composers in the BBC's programmes. I am inclined to reply that when the country of origin of the composer concerned takes interest in his or her work, then it will be time for the BBC to consider whether to broadcast it in Britain.

In the case of Balassa and Keuris, the former won an international prize with a Requiem, and Keuris's Sinfonia had been broadcast by Netherlands Radio and included in the 1976 ISCM Festival.

About this time, the Composers' Guild of Great Britain was vigorously querying whether the building of the programmes of the Proms – in particular with regard to the new works – should be in the hands of the one person for a long period. A single viewpoint must always be governed by *some* prejudices. Perhaps somebody different should do it each time, or a group of people. Ponsonby maintains, however – and BBC management has confirmed – that it is preferable for one person to be responsible for the final co-ordination of the programmes, and the policy that lies behind them. At the same time, many ideas come from members of the BBC's Music Division and from other sources, and in the difficult question of value-judgements which have to be made over a wide variety of musical styles, many opinions, inside and outside the BBC, are considered. A Proms Group consisting of Ponsonby and senior members of his staff meet from time to time; and there is an annual post-mortem.

A feature of 1978 was the absence of commissioned works and a deliberate stress on 'second hearings' (often more difficult to get than first perfor-mances): these included *Diaphony* for organ and orchestra by Justin Con-nolly – the opposition of two sound-blocks, organ and orchestra, each complete in itself; *Seven Poems by e. e. cummings* for soprano and orchestra by Edward Harper – a work first heard in Glasgow; and Edward Cowie's Piano Concerto. Robin Holloway's *Romanza* for violin and orchestra, how-ever, was heard for the first time and made a definite impression – four linked movements, beautifully shaped and lyrical in style.

'Over the years,' wrote Ponsonby in the preface to the 1978 prospectus, 'the policy evinced in the Proms programmes has not deviated much from that established by Sir Henry: the regular introduction of new works, particularly by British composers, into programmes largely devoted to the great accepted masterpieces.' What has changed, however, is the number of the novelties each season, which has considerably enlarged, as can be seen from Appendix A (p. 256), and the range of great classics is now far more selective, far less comprehensive. For those who 'like what they know' there is far less than in Wood's time; on the other hand, the audiences (through records, broadcasting, and so on) have come to 'know' and 'like' far more. The unknown or little-known works are from all periods. The rarities of 1978 included Liszt's *Christus*, an immense oratorio in fourteen parts, which the composer called his last will and testament; and Rameau's opera of 1764, *Les Boréades*, buried in the Bibliothèque National, Paris, unperformed and unpublished, for over two hundred years, and brought to light and to performance by John Eliot Gardiner in 1975, and in 1978 at the Proms.

Of immense interest in 1978 was the visit of the Chicago Symphony Orchestra, with its conductor Sir Georg Solti, and the central attraction was the first public performance in Britain of Michael Tippett's Fourth Sym-phony, commissioned by that orchestra who (with Solti) gave its première the previous October. With it, in the second part of that concert, was Tchaikovsky's 'Pathétique' Symphony – thus bringing together two works in which a tremendously powerful personal vision is conveyed.

Gennadi Rozhdestvensky became chief conductor of the BBC Symphony

Sir Adrian Boult in his last year at the Proms, 1977, leaves by the Artists' Entrance of the Albert Hall, accompanied by Bill Edwards. (Robert Ponsonby is standing on the right in the doorway. Christopher Samuelson is on the left, with camera.)

From left: Walter Susskind, Peter Maxwell Davies, Robert Ponsonby, Sir Charles Groves, Rudolf Schwarz, Yehudi Menuhin and James Loughran, outside Broadcasting House after the press conference for the 1978 Proms.

Orchestra that year, while still remaining musical director of the Moscow Chamber Opera and professor of conducting at the Moscow Conservatory. His first official concert in that capacity was on 9 September 1978 in a concert which combined classical, English and Russian works – Mozart's Symphony No. 32; Britten's *Diversions on a theme*, originally written for the Austrian pianist Paul Wittgenstein, who lost his right arm in the first world war; and Shostakovich's Symphony No. 4 in C minor. The pianist in the Britten work was Rozhdestvensky's wife, Victoria Postnikova. Boulez was not deserting the Proms: that season he had one concert as a guest conductor with the BBC Symphony Orchestra in a programme of the Berg Violin Concerto (with Pierre Amoyal) and Mahler's *Das Lied von der Erde*. The new chief guest conductor of the orchestra, Michael Gielen, conducted two programmes which included Schoenberg's 'drama with music' *Die glückliche Hand* ('The Knack'), and Bruckner's Eighth Symphony. Bernard Haitink conducted Glyndebourne's new production of Mozart's *Così fan tutte* and Mahler's Symphony No. 2. Younger conductors such as Andrew Davis and Simon Rattle had by now fully proved their value and were given important concerts – Andrew Davis being entrusted (as in 1977) with the first night of the season, a performance of the Verdi *Requiem*, and Stravinsky's *Oedipus Rex* on another occasion. Lawrence Foster conducted the young musicians from all over the world who formed the Jeunesses Musicales World Orchestra – another achievement of Sir Robert Mayer, then approaching his hundredth birthday.

There were various anniversaries which shaped programmes – Schubert, Janáček, Messiaen, Stockhausen. Singcircle was the first British group to perform Stockhausen's *Stimmung*, in a concert which also included Indian music performed by Imrat Khan. Other important contemporary works that season were the Symphony of Maxwell Davies, commissioned by the Philharmonia Orchestra who performed it under Simon Rattle; *Mi-parti*, the latest composition of Lutoslawski to reach England; and the Violin Concerto of Priaulx Rainier, in which the soloist was Yehudi Menuhin. It was the year of Lennox Berkeley's seventy-fifth birthday, and his recently-composed Fourth Symphony was heard.

The appearance at the Proms of Britain's regional orchestras – including those of the BBC – was considered important by Ponsonby: from 1974 onwards, the Bournemouth, Hallé, Northern Sinfonia, Scottish National, and the BBC Northern, Scottish and Welsh Symphony Orchestras all came regularly to the Proms. The BBC Concert Orchestra, conducted by James Matheson, gave the original version of Verdi's *Macbeth*, with Peter Glossop as Macbeth and Rita Hunter as Lady Macbeth. Another important operatic

Sir Charles Mackerras.

Gennadi Rozhdestvensky.

event of 1978 was Gluck's *Orfeo*, conducted by Christopher Seaman, with Janet Baker in the title rôle.

An experiment was tried of adding the Riverside Studios to the list of outside venues for the Proms, but the results were not considered acoustically satisfactory. Meanwhile, the Round House, Westminster Cathedral and St Augustine's, Kilburn, continued to be excellent alternatives to the Albert Hall for a small number of concerts which particularly required a different acoustic and atmosphere.

The Last Night continued to be something of a problem. Sargent coped with the situation as well as anybody. Colin Davis showed spirit, but never really came to terms with it. And after Davis felt he had done his share of last nights, various conductors were tried more or less successfully – Norman Del Mar, Sir Charles Groves, James Loughran. It's rather like teachers having to cope with an unruly class. There are some who by a combination of personality, air of authority and sense of purpose, can keep order. Others can't. But the ritualistic Last Night seems to be an integral part of the whole.

Ponsonby's introduction to the 1979 schedule gave a further statement on the present policy of the Proms, which is basically 'importance and promise of importance', fully in the Henry Wood tradition.

> Among the works being performed importance is represented by the acknowledged great masters, promise by younger living composers whose music we have thought it right to incorporate. With the artists a similar principle has applied: we welcome a considerable number of the great names of our time, as well as some particularly gifted young interpreters.

The 1979 season developed a large-scale recurring programmatic strand – the music of Northern Europe. Sibelius, who suffered something of an eclipse in the Glock régime, was well represented, with the Second and Third Symphonies, *Tapiola* (his great blending of the legendary and the symphonic), and his rarely-heard early *Kullervo* symphony, with which he originally made his name in his own country. There was Nielsen's Symphony No. 4 ('The Inextinguishable'), the Cello Concerto of Vagn Holmboe, and the ever-popular Grieg Piano Concerto, this time with Emil Gilels as soloist. Poland and Russia were also well represented: the rich tapestry of Szymanowski's *Symphonie concertante*, Op. 60, in a programme by the National Youth Orchestra of Great Britain (conducted by David Atherton); Riccardo Muti and the Philharmonia Orchestra gave Penderecki's Symphony No. 1; and Lutoslawski himself conducted the BBC Symphony Orchestra in the first British performance of his *Les Espaces du sommeil*, and the following day he conducted the London Sinfonietta in his *Paroles tissées*.

Norman Del Mar.

There were symphonies by Prokofiev, Rachmaninov, and Shostakovich. Stravinsky's three great early ballets were heard and his *Symphony in Three Movements*. *Les Noces* was due to be given also, but the sickness which was crippling British industrial life and public services – the epidemic of industrial disputes – spread to the Proms, and the performance had to be cancelled. The reason: the four percussion players from the BBC Symphony Orchestra were demanding 'solo' fees.

A real innovation for the Proms in 1979 was the presentation of gamelan music and dancing of Indonesia: the Sasono Mulio Gamelan of Surakarta came to London from the Oriental Music Festival, which had just taken place in Durham. Their performance was offset at that concert by works which arguably had something akin with them – the ritualistic, the decorative, rather than the emotional. These were Peter Maxwell Davies's *A Mirror of Whitening Light*, reflecting the cliff-top atmosphere of the composer's Orkney home, with the sea as 'a huge alchemical crucible'; Ravel's Piano Concerto in G (doubtless with particular reference to the mesmeric and highly decorated slow movement); and the *Trois Petites Liturgies de la Présence Divine* by Messiaen, who (like Debussy) has been directly influenced by gamelan sounds. And another direct influence: it was a good idea to include music from *The Prince of the Pagodas*, Britten's full-length ballet, which in places represents almost literally the typical sound-patterns of the gamelan. (In one of the concerts conducted by Rozhdestvensky, a *Cantus to the memory of Benjamin Britten* by the Estonian composer, Arvo Pärt received its first British performance.)

There were two commissioned works that season, both of which had considerable success: the 'multi-faceted, dramatic' Third Symphony of Oliver Knussen, who was still in his twenties; and *La Vita Nuova* by Nicholas Maw – Italian Renaissance poetry, set in a modern expressive style characteristic of the composer. The Maw work was performed at a Round House concert at which was heard the première of Anthony Payne's *The Stones and Lonely Places Sing*, a personal form of tone-poem, legendary in mood, for a small group of players. The British première of an already famous American work, George Crumb's *Star-Child*, was partnered with Holst's *The Planets* and drew to the Albert Hall a capacity audience. The Crumb work is for large orchestra, with a much-expanded percussion department, two children's choirs, chorus, and soprano solo. Four conductors are needed.

Glyndebourne Opera offered the rarely-heard *La fedeltà premiata* by Haydn, and the Welsh National Opera contributed their impressive production of Britten's *Billy Budd*. The dramatic cantata *King David* by

Honegger proved to be a most effective Prom work. So too, in this day and age, did John Ireland's Piano Concerto, revived after nearly twenty years: it had been a steady Prom favourite, and then was dropped when Glock came to power.

In 1979 there were twenty-eight orchestras and ensembles at the Proms – including the Israel Philharmonic (under Zubin Mehta), the New Irish Chamber Orchestra (under John Beckett), and Pierre Boulez's highly-trained Ensemble InterContemporain. And there were forty-four conductors (including composer-conductors), sixteen choirs, and 118 soloists (35 instrumental, 83 vocal). A far cry from all those one-man, one-orchestra years of Henry Wood! Now richness is all. A personal unifying force is missing: but what one man (or two, or three) could be sufficiently expert in the interpretation of the vast range of musical styles now covered by the Proms?

Of the fifty-four concerts in the 1979 season, all were broadcast complete – the majority on Radio 3, some on Radio 4 or Radio 2. This is now the normal pattern of Prom broadcasting. There were nine television broadcasts, including three simultaneous broadcasts with Radio in stereo. And the BBC World Service carried twenty-one live relays and took more than thirty recordings, which were spread out over the transmissions until the end of November, making a World Service Proms season of more than four months.

Of the wide range of twentieth-century works included during a season, comparatively few would be likely to prove disturbing to audiences today. *The Rite of Spring*, once so aggressively challenging to Tchaikovsky-attuned ears, could be used with equanimity many years ago by Walt Disney in his universally popular film *Fantasia*. The same applies to Bartók; and nobody now is likely to be mystified by Debussy or Strauss or Mahler. But what about the Orchestral Variations, Op. 31, of Schoenberg? This work will be appreciated for its variety, colour, vitality, technique. For many, however, the idiom will be uncomfortable, if not repellent – and the same applies to most serial-based and non-tonal idioms. These have their adherents, but the concert appeal continues to be decidedly 'minority'. It takes all sorts to make Prom audiences; there is no one typical Prom audience situated somewhere between the intellectual exercises of the Round House at one extreme and the exhibitionistic high-jinks of the televised Last Night (Part 2) at the other. There is, as we have seen, a contingent of 'hard-core' Prommers who form groups and make a cult of the Proms, a sort of way of life – as much a social as a musical thing, with various ramifications during the whole year.

The Proms depend on the BBC being able to sponsor this kind of series of concerts. The variety and scope of the music offered depends on the outlook of the person or persons by whom the programmes are built. Nothing can be taken for granted. The Proms are not a self-supporting organisation. What they offer, to young and old alike, at the lowest possible price, is a wider and more generous choice of musical experiences, brought together within a period of about two months, than you could find anywhere else in the world. As we enter the 1980s the Proms are showing no signs of losing their vitality, purpose and relevance. There have been immense changes between 1960 and 1979, but the pattern is still arguably what it has always been: great classics, important repertoire works, and a number of new pieces. All future developments, it seems, must be variations on this basic theme.

APPENDIX A
'Novelties' at the Proms 1895-1979

P = Première (first performance anywhere) L = First London performance
E = First performance in England C = First concert performance
All other works are first performances at a Prom. (In certain cases, the form of a title is given as in the original programme.) The word 'novelty' is used in all the above senses – as Henry Wood used it.

Composer	*Work*	
	1895	
ANDERSEN, JOACHIM	Flute solo 'Fantasia on the Dutch National Anthem'	E
BUNNING, HERBERT	'The Shepherd's Call'	L
CHOPIN orch.	Nocturne in F minor	P
HAROLD VICARS		
CLUTSAM, GEORGE	Carnival Scenes	P
D'ERLANGER, F.	Suite Symphonique No. 2	P
FREWIN, T. H.	The Battle of the Flowers	P
HALVORSEN	Boyard's March	E
KISTLER, CYRILL	Chromatic Concert Valses from the opera *Eulenspiegel*	L
	March, 'Festklange'	E
LUCAS, CLARENCE	Minuet from *Anne Hathaway*	P
MACKENZIE, A. C.	Recitation with music 'Eugene Aram'	L
MASSENET	Meditation from *Thaïs*	L
	Overture, *Phèdre*	L
MOSZKOWSKI	Introduction and ballet music *Boabdil*	L
PITT, PERCY	Suite in Four Movements	P
RIMSKY-KORSAKOV	Overture *La Nuit de Mai*	L
SCHARWENKA, XAVER	Prelude to the opera *Mataswintha*	E
SCHLOESSER, LOUIS	Grand March, 'Les Enfants de la Garde'	P
SCHUBERT orch.	Military March	P
HAROLD VICARS		
STANFORD, C. V.	Suite of Dances	P
STRAUSS, RICHARD	Prelude to First Act of *Guntram*	E
SVENDSEN	Andante Funèbre for orchestra	E
TCHAIKOVSKY	Marche Solennelle	E
VICARS, HAROLD	Prelude *Rosalind*	E

1896

CHABRIER	Joyeuse Marche	E
	Slavonic Dance from opera *Le Roi malgré lui*	E
CHAMINADE	Suite d'Orchestre 'Callirhoe'	L
DUBOIS, THÉODORE	Three Orchestral Pieces from *Xavière*	E
FRANCHETTI, A.	Symphony in E minor	E
FREWIN, T. H.	Ballade for orchestra 'Mazeppa'	P
GLAZOUNOV	Scènes de Ballet	E
GUILMANT, ALEXANDRE	Marche Fantaisie for organ, harp, and orchestra	L
ITASSE, LÉON	Rhapsodie Espagnole	E
KISTLER, CYRILL	Festmarsch for orchestra	E
MACBETH, ALLAN	Serenata for strings	L
MASSENET	Overture *Le Cid*	E
	Rhapsodie Mauresque and Marche du Cid	E
MOSZKOWSKI	Suite from the ballet *Laurin*	E
NICODÉ, JEAN LOUIS	Symphonic variations in C minor	L
PADEREWSKI orch. ERNEST FORD	Minuet in A	P
PITT, PERCY	Coronation March	P
RIMSKY-KORSAKOV	Capriccio Espagnol	E
	Scheherazade	E
RUBINSTEIN, ANTON	Valse Caprice in E flat	L
SARASATE, PABLO	Violin solo 'Zigeunerweisen'	L
SCHUBERT orch. FELIX MOTTL	Phantasie in F minor	L
TCHAIKOVSKY	Suite 'Casse-Noisette'	E
WEST, JOHN	Recitation with music, 'King Robert of Sicily' (Longfellow)	P

1897

BECKER, REINHOLD	Huldigungsmarsch ('Frauenlob')	E
BUNNING, HERBERT	Suite Villageoise	L
CUI, CÉSAR	Suite-Miniature	E
DVOŘÁK	Tone poem, 'The Water-goblin'	P
FREWIN, T. H.	Sketches for orchestra, 'The Seven Ages of Man'	P
HARTMANN, EMIL	Overture, *Runenzauber*	E
NAPRAVNIK, E.	Romance and Fandango	E
PITT, PERCY	Concertino in C minor for clarinet and orchestra	P
SEROFF, ALEXANDER	Danse Cosaque	E
SQUIRE, W. H.	Entr'acte, *Summer Dreams*	P
TCHAIKOVSKY	Suite No. 4, 'Mozartiana'	E

1898

ANSELL, JOHN	'Cello solo, 'Serenade'	P
COLERIDGE-TAYLOR	Four Characteristic Waltzes	L
DONJON, I.	Flute solo, 'Invocation'	P
DOPPLE, F.	Flute solo, 'Das Waldvöglein'	P
ELGAR, EDWARD	Three Bavarian Dances	L
FREWIN, T. H.	Overture, *Bellona*	P

GERMAN, EDWARD	Bourrée and Gigue (*Much Ado about Nothing*)	C
GOMEZ, F.	Clarinet solo, 'Caprice'	P
HALVORSEN	Norwegian Folk-song for strings	E
LISZT	Hungarian Rhapsody No. 6 in G	L
LUCAS, CLARENCE	Overture, *Othello*	P
MASSENET	Suite, 'Scènes Hongroises'	L
MONIUSZKO, S.	Mazur, from the opera *Halka*	E
REED, W. H.	Valse Brillante	P
RUBINSTEIN orch. D'INDY	Melody in F	P
SAINT-SAËNS	Fantasia, *Samson and Delilah*	P
SQUIRE, W. H.	Entr'acte *Sweet Briar*	P
STRAUSS, RICHARD	Festmarsch	E
TCHAIKOVSKY	Entr'acte and Airs de Ballet from the opera *Le Voevoda*	E
	Symphony in Four Tableaux after Byron's *Manfred*	E
	Fantasy, *The Tempest*	L
	Polonaise from *Eugene Onegin*	C
VALENTIN, KARL	Festmarsch	E
WEBER arr. GOMEZ	Clarinet Quartet, 'Invitation à la Valse'	P

1899

BALAKIREV	Overture on Three Russian Themes	E
BLEICHMANN, JULES	Suite de Ballet	E
BLOCKX, JAN	Five Flemish Dances	E
BOUTOUX, DANL	Bass clarinet solo, 'Intermezzo'	L
COVERLEY, ROBERT	Four Sketches for orchestra	E
CUI, CÉSAR	Premier Scherzo	E
DITTERSDORF, CARL VON	Symphony 'The Transformation of Acteon into a Stag'	E
DVOŘÁK	Symphonic poem 'Die Waldtaube'	L
	Symphonic poem 'Heldenlied'	L
GOLDMARK, CARL	Introduction to Act II, *Der Kriegsgefangene*	E
GOMEZ—PERCY PITT	Clarinet solo 'Tango'	P
HAYDN, MICHAEL	Symphony in C major, opus 1 no. 3	E
HOFMANN, H.	Flute solo 'Andante from Serenade'	P
HORROCKS, AMY	Orchestral Ballade 'The Romaunt of the Page'	P
D'INDY, VINCENT	Chanson et Danses	E
IPPOLITOFF-IVANOFF	Suite for orchestra	E
LEO, LEONARDO	Sinfonia from oratorio *Sant' Elena al Calvario*	E
LIADOV, ANATOLE	Valse-Badinage (A Musical Snuffbox)	E
LUCAS, CLARENCE	Overture 'As you like It'	P
MASCHERONI, E.	Grand Valse 'Espagnole'	P
MASSENET	'Le Sommeil de Cendrillon' and 'Menuet' from *Cendrillon*	E
	Ballet music from *Hérodiade*	L
MIGUEZ	Symphonic poem 'Ave Libertas'	E
MOSZKOWSKI	Polish Folk-dances for orchestra	E
OLSEN, OLE	Symphonic poem 'Asgardsreien'	E
PITT, PERCY	Air de Ballet for strings	P
	Suite 'Cinderella'	P
RABAUD, HENRI	Eglogue, 'Poème Virgilien'	E

RAMEAU—MOTTL	Suite de Ballet	*E*
REED, W. H.	Overture 'Touchstone'	*P*
SAINT-SAËNS	Prelude and Cortège from *Déjanire*	*E*
SIMONETTI, ACHILLE	Madrigale	*E*
SQUIRE, W. H.	Entr'acte 'Slumber Song'	*P*
SUTCLIFFE, WALLACE	Two dances for orchestra	*P*
	Bassoon solo: Old English Air 'The Ploughboy'	*P*
TCHAIKOVSKY	Suite for orchestra No. 2	*E*
	Overture 'Les Caprices d'Oxane'	*E*
	Symphony No. 3 in D	*E*
	Danse Cosaque from opera *Mazeppa*	*E*
	Chant sans Paroles, opus 2 no. 3	*E*
HAYDN WAUD, J.	Comedy Overture	*P*
WEBER—FELIX WEINGARTNER	Invitation to the Waltz (for orchestra)	*E*
DE WOLKOFF, N.	Cosatschok	*E*
SOKOLOFF GLAZOUNOV LIADOV	Polka for strings 'Les Vendredis'	*E*

1900

ASHTON, ALGERNON	Turkish march 'Bag and Baggage'	*L*
BEETHOVEN	Duet in G for two flutes	*E*
FOX, GEORGE	Fantasia 'The Boy and the Butterfly'	*P*
GERMAN, EDWARD	Three dances from *Nell Gwyn*	*C*
GLAZOUNOV	Ballet music *Ruses d'Amour*	*E*
GLUCK—MOTTL	Suite de Ballet, No. 2	*E*
HOLBROOKE, JOSEF	Variations on 'Three blind Mice'	*P*
JACOBS, J. H.	Viola solos 'Rêverie' and 'A la Hongroise'	*P*
LALO, EDOUARD	Suite No. 2 'Namouna'	*E*
MATTEI, TITO	Lord Roberts' March	*C*
MONASTERIO, J.	Violin solo 'Rondo Lievaneuse'	*E*
RACHMANINOV	Piano Concerto No. 1 in F sharp minor	*E*
REED, W. H.	Valse élégante	*P*
RIMSKY–KORSAKOV	Symphony No. 2 'Antar'	*E*
RONALD, LANDON	Suite de Ballet	*P*
STRAUSS, RICHARD	Serenade in E flat for wind instruments	*E*
TCHAIKOVSKY	Piano Concerto No. 2 in G	*E*
TINEL, EDGAR	Overture 'Godoleva'	*E*
WEST, ALFRED	Mafeking Night	*C*

1901

ALFVEN, HUGO	Symphony No. 2 in D	*E*
AMES, JOHN	March from *The Last of the Incas*	*P*
BELL, W. H.	Symphonic prelude 'A Song in the Morning'	*L*
BLOCH, JOSEF	'Suite Poétique'	*E*
CELEGA, NICOLO	Symphonic poem 'The Heart of Fingal'	*E*
COBB, GERARD	Romanze for orchestra	*L*
ELGAR	'Chanson de Nuit' and 'Chanson de Matin'	*L*
	Elevation in B flat ('Sursum Corda')	*L*

ELGAR	Military Marches 'Pomp and Circumstance' Nos. 1 and 2	L
FLOERSHEIM, OTTO	Miniature suite 'A Love Tale'	E
GLAZOUNOV	'Cello solo 'Chant du Ménestrel'	E
	Ballet *The Seasons*	E
	Ouverture Solennelle	E
KLUGHARDT, A.	Festival Overture	E
LIAPUNOV, SERGE	Ouverture Solennelle	E
LUCAS, CLARENCE	Overture *Macbeth*	E
MACDOWELL, E.	Indian Suite	E
O'NEILL, NORMAN	Overture 'In Autumn'	P
PITT, PERCY	Suite de Ballet 'Dance Rhythms'	P
ROZE, RAYMOND	Suite 'Sweet Nell of Old Drury'	C
SCHUMANN, GEORGE	Dance of Nymphs and Satyrs (*Amor and Psyche*)	E
SIBELIUS, JEAN	Suite 'King Christian II'	E
STEGGALL, R.	Dramatic prelude 'Oreithyia'	P
TCHAIKOVSKY	Suite 'The Swan Lake'	E
	Schäferspiel from *La Dame de Pique*	E
VOLBACH, FRITZ	Symphonic poem 'Es waren zwei Königskinder'	E
	Symphonic poem 'Ostern'	E
WAGNER, SIEGFRIED	Introduction to Act III, and Valse at the Fair from *Herzog Wildfang*	E
WEINGARTNER, F.	Symphony No. 2 in E flat	E
CUNNINGHAM WOODS, F.	Suite in F for small orchestra	E

Winter Season 1901

ALTES, HENRY	Offertoire for organ and flute	P
BLAKE, ERNEST	Symphonic poem 'Alastor'	P
HUBER, HANS	Symphony No. 2 in E minor	E
KOESSLER, HANS	Symphonic Variations	E
REED, W. H.	Symphonic poem 'Among the Mountains of Cambria'	P
SCHUMANN, GEORGE	Overture 'Liebesfrühling'	E
SCHYTTE, LUDWIG	Piano Concerto	E

1902

AVERKAMP, ANTON	Symphonic ballad 'Elaine and Lancelot'	E
BRUNEAU, ALFRED	Four preludes from 'L'Ouragon'	E
ENNA, AUGUST	Overture 'Cleopatra'	E
ERKEL, FRANZ	Overture 'Hunyády László'	L
FAURÉ, GABRIEL	Suite 'Pelléas et Mélisande'	C
FRANCK, CÉSAR	Symphonic Variation for piano and orchestra	E
FRISCHEN, JOSEF	Mood picture 'Herbstnacht', and 'A Rhenish Scherzo'	E
GOETZ, HERMANN	Overture 'Francesca da Rimini'	L
HOLBROOKE, JOSEF	Symphonic poem 'The Skeleton in Armour'	L
D'INDY, VINCENT	Trilogy 'Wallenstein'	E
JÄRNEFELT, A.	Symphonic poem 'Korsholm'	E
SCHILLINGS, MAX	Symphonic prologue 'King Oedipus'	E
SINDING, CHRISTIAN	Violin Concerto No. 1 in A	L
SMYTH, ETHEL	Dances from 'Der Wald'	C
TCHAIKOVSKY	Symphony No. 1 in G minor	L

TCHAIKOVSKY	Symphony No. 2 in C minor	*L*
	Piano Concerto No. 3 in E flat	*L*
	March, Entr'acte and Overture from *Hamlet*	*L*
THUILLE, LUDWIG	Romantic Overture	*E*
WOOD, ARTHUR H.	Suite	*L*

1903

ARENSKY, ANTON	Piano Concerto	*E*
BAINTON, EDGAR	Symphonic poem 'Pompilia'	*P*
BANTOCK, GRANVILLE	Suite 'Russian Scenes'	*L*
BECKER, HUGO	'Cello Concerto in A	*L*
BLAKE, ERNEST	Introduction to an operatic poem *The Bretwalda*	*P*
BOUGHTON, RUTLAND	Symphonic poem 'Into the Everlasting'	*P*
BOWDEN, YORK	Symphonic poem 'The Lament of Tasso'	*P*
COWEN, FREDERICK	Indian Rhapsody	*L*
COX, GARNET WOLSELEY	Pastoral suite 'Ewelme'	*P*
FARJEON, HARRY	Piano Concerto in D	*L*
FORSYTH, CECIL	Viola Concerto in G Minor	*P*
GATTY, NICHOLAS	Concert-Allegro for piano and orchestra	*P*
HANDEL	Concerto in F for two wind orchestras and strings	*E*
HOLBROOKE, JOSEF	Concerto Dramatique in F minor for piano and orchestra	*L*
D'INDY, VINCENT	Entr'acte *L'Etranger*	*E*
LENORMAND, RENÉ	Piano Concerto in F	*E*
MAHLER, GUSTAV	Symphony No. 1 in D	*E*
NESVERA, JOSEF	Overture from opera *Waldesluft*	*E*
PITT, PERCY	Three Old English Dances from *King Richard II*	*C*
RAFF, JOACHIM	'Cello Concerto	*L*
REED, W. H.	'Suite Vénitienne'	*P*
RIMSKY-KORSAKOV	Night on Mount Triglav, from *Mlada*	*E*
SCHILLINGS, MAX	Prelude 'Der Pfeifertag'	*E*
SCOTT, CYRIL	Symphony No. 1 in A minor	*P*
SIBELIUS	Symphony No. 1 in E minor	*E*
STRAESSER, EWALD	'Cello Concerto in D	*E*
STRAUSS, RICHARD	Song 'Das Thal'	*E*
	Symphonic fantasia 'Aus Italien'	*E*
SUK, JOSEF	Suite 'A Fairy Tale'	*E*
WAGNER	Scena and Aria 'Halloh! Lasst alle Hunde los!' from *Die Feen*	*E*
WALLACE, WILLIAM	Orchestral suite 'Pelléas and Mélisande'	*L*
WILCOCKE, JAMES	Piccolo solo 'Le Chardonneret'	*P*
WOLF–FERRARI	Chamber Symphony in B flat	*E*

1904

BOSSI, ENRICO	Organ Concerto in A minor	*E*
BOWEN, YORK	Concert Overture	*P*
	Piano Concerto No. 1 in E flat	*P*
CLUTSAM, GEORGE	Suite 'Harlequinade'	*P*

CONVERSE, F.	Romance 'The Festival of Pan'	E
COWEN, FREDERICK	Two pieces for orchestra, 'Childhood' and 'Girlhood'	L
DEBUSSY	Prelude à 'L'Après-midi d'un faune'	E
D'ERLANGER, F.	Andante Symphonique for 'cello and orchestra	E
GARDINER, BALFOUR	English Dance for orchestra	P
VAN GOENS	Cello Concerto No. 2 in D minor	E
GOLDMARK, CARL	Overture 'In Italien'	E
GOUVY, THEODORE	Serenade for flute and strings	E
HANDEL	Cantata 'Dank sei Dir'	E
	Concerto Grosso No. 12 (opus 6, no. 1)	L
JUON, PAUL	Symphony in A	E
LOTTER, ADOLF	'The Coon's Patrol'	P
MACPHERSON, CHARLES	Suite 'Hallowe'en'	P
MACPHERSON, STEWART	Violin Concerto in G minor	P
MILES, NAPIER	Lyric overture 'From the West Country'	L
O'NEILL, NORMAN	Ballad 'Death on the Hills'	L
	Overture 'Hamlet'	P
SCHUTT, EDUARD	Piano Concerto No. 1 in G minor	L
SCOTT, CYRIL	Rhapsody No. 1 for orchestra	P
SINDING, CHRISTIAN	Piano Concerto in D flat	E
TCHAIKOVSKY	Intermezzo 'The Battle of Poltava' from *Mazeppa*	E
	Air 'One moment, pray' from *La Dame de Pique*	L
VASSILENKO, SERGE	Poème Epique	E
VOLBACH, FRITZ	A Spring Poem, for orchestra	E
WALTHEW, R.	Caprice Impromptu for violin and orch.	P
WEBER	Theme and Variations for corno di bassetto and orchestra	E
ZILCHER, HERMANN	Concerto in D minor for two violins and orchestra	E

1905

BANTOCK, GRANVILLE	'Helena' Variations	L
BRUCH, MAX	Suite on Russian Folk-melodies	E
DAVIS, J. D.	Suite 'Miniatures'	P
DRAESEKE, FELIX	Jubilee Overture	E
FORSYTH, CECIL	'Four studies from Victor Hugo'	E
	Chant Celtique for viola and orchestra	P
FRANCHETTI, A.	Symphonic impression 'Nella Foresta Nera'	E
HARTY, HAMILTON	Symphony in D minor (Irish)	E
HAUSEGGER, S. VON	Symphonic poem 'Barbarossa'	E
LISZT	Hungarian Storm March	L
MAHLER, GUSTAV	Symphony No. 4 in G	E
PURCELL	Three pieces for strings	L
SCHUBERT	Overture 'Des Teufels Lustschloss'	L
SIBELIUS	Legend 'The Swan of Tuonela'	L
STRAUSS, RICHARD	Symphony in F minor	L
TCHAIKOVSKY	Closing scene from *Eugene Onegin*	C
	Three pieces for violin and orchestra	E
	Introduction and Dances from *The Opritchnik*	E
	Symphonic ballade 'Le Voyevode'	E

| WALLACE, WILLIAM | Symphonic poem 'Sir William Wallace' | P |
| WOLF, HUGO | 'Weylas Gesang' | E |

1906

ARENSKY	Variations on a Theme by Tchaikovsky	E
BANTOCK,	Hymn to Aphrodite from *Sappho*	L
GRANVILLE	Prelude to *Sappho*	P
BLOCKX, JAN	Symphonic Triptych	E
BOEHE, ERNST	Episode 'Ausfahrt und Schiffbruch' (from *Odysseus Fahrten*)	E
BORODIN	Finale from the opera-ballet *Mlada*	L
BRUNEAU, ALFRED	Entr'acte Symphonique 'Messidor'	E
BUSONI	Suite from Gozzi's *Turandot*	E
	Eine Lustspiel-Ouvertüre	E
DORLAY, GEORGES	Symphonic poem 'St George'	L
ENNA, AUGUST	Symphonic poem 'Märchen'	L
FIBICH, ZDENKO	Overture 'A Night at Karlstein'	E
FOULDS, JOHN	Music poem 'Epithalamium'	P
GLIÈRE	Symphony in E flat	E
HALFORD, GEORGE	Overture 'In Memoriam'	L
HENRIQUES, FINI	Suite in F major for oboe and strings	E
HOLBROOKE, JOSEF	Symphony No. 1, 'Les Hommages'	P
LALO	Violin Concerto in G minor on Russian Themes	L
LIADOV	Eight Russian Folk-songs for orchestra	E
	Tableau musical 'Baba-Yaga'	E
MUSSORGSKY	Gopak (*Sorochinski Fair*)	E
O'NEILL, NORMAN	Overture 'In Springtime'	L
PETRI, EGON	Concertstück in C minor for piano and orchestra	E
RICCI, VITTORIO	Two Forest Scenes	E
SIBELIUS	Tone poem 'En Saga'	L
	Symphonic poem 'Finlandia'	L
	Suite 'Karelia'	E
WAGNER	Isolde's narrative (*Tristan and Isolde*)	C
VAUGHAN WILLIAMS	Norfolk Rhapsody No. 1	P

1907

ARENDS, H.	Viola Concertino	E
AUSTIN, FREDERIC	Rhapsody for orchestra 'Spring'	P
BACH	Cantata 'Amore traditore' for bass and orchestra	E
BANTOCK,	Orchestral poem 'Lalla Rookh'	P
GRANVILLE		
BARKER, F. C.	Violin Concerto	P
BARNS, ETHEL	Concertstück in D minor for violin and orchestra	P
BRIAN, HAVERGAL	English Suite	L
	Overture 'For Valour'	P
BRIDGE, FRANK	Symphonic poem 'Isabella'	P
COX, GARNET	Suite No. 2 'The Mysterious Rose-garden'	P
WOLSELEY		
DAVIES, WALFORD	'Holiday Tunes'	P
DELIUS, FREDERICK	Piano Concerto in C minor	E
DORLAY, GEORGES	Flute solos 'Légende' and Scherzo Brillant	P

ELGAR	March 'Pomp and Circumstance' No. 4	P
HALL, MARSHALL	Symphony in E flat ('An Elizabeth Comedy')	P
HARTY, HAMILTON	Comedy Overture	L
	Aria 'Ode to a Nightingale'	P
D'INDY, VINCENT	Symphonie Montagnarde for piano and orchestra	E
ISAACS, EDWARD	Piano Concerto in C sharp minor	L
LISZT—BURMEISTER	Concerto Pathétique in E minor for piano and orchestra	E
MOZART	Concerto in F for three pianos and orchestra	E
PEZEL, JOHANN	Two Suites for two trumpets and three trombones	E
QUILTER, ROGER	Serenade for small orchestra	P
RAVEL	Introduction and Allegro	E
REGER, MAX	Serenade in G for orchestra	E
SCOTT, CYRIL	Overture 'Princess Maleine'	P
SIBELIUS	Dance Intermezzo No. 2	E
	Violin Concerto	E
	Overture 'Karelia'	E
COLERIDGE- TAYLOR	Entr'acte from 'Nero' (No. 1 in G)	C
VERHEY, THEO	Flute Concerto in D minor	P
VREULS, VICTOR	Poème for cello and orchestra	E
WHITE, FELIX H.	Overture 'Shylock'	P

1908

BELL, W. H.	Prelude 'Agamemnon'	P
BOWEN, YORK	Piano Concerto No. 3 in G minor	P
BREWER, HERBERT	Two pieces for orchestra 'Age and Youth'	P
DEBUSSY	Song 'Le Jet d'Eau'	E
DUPARC, HENRI	Song 'Phidylé'	E
GARDINER, B.	Symphony in E flat	P
PHILLIPS, M.	Song with orchestra 'Fidelity'	P
LUARD-SELBY, B.	A Village Suite	P

1909

BATH, HUBERT	Two Sea Pictures for orchestra	P
BERLIOZ	Aria 'The Danish Huntsman'	L
BORSDORF, OSKAR	Concert Overture in D major	P
CAETANI, R.	Prélude Symphonique in E flat	P
CHADWICK, G.	Suite for orchestra, Symphonic Sketches	E
COATES, ERIC	Four New Shakespearian Songs with orchestra	L
DAVIES, WALFORD	Solemn Melody for organ and strings	C
	Songs of Nature (From 'Songs of a Day')	C
DORLAY, GEORGES	Symphonic poem 'The Lay of the Bell'	P
DVOŘÁK	Humoreske	E
GRAENER, PAUL	Symphonic piece 'From Valleys and Heights'	P
HADLEY, HENRY	Symphonic poem 'Salome'	E
HAYDN, JOSEPH	Violin Concerto No. 1 in C	E
	Violin Concerto No. 2 in G	E
HERBERT, VICTOR	'Cello Concerto in E minor	E
LIAPUNOV, SERGE	Rhapsody for piano and orchestra	E
MAHLER, GUSTAV	Adagietto for strings and harp	E

MATTHAY, TOBIAS	Concert Piece No. 1 in A minor for piano and orchestra	*L*
MUSSORGSKY	Humorous scene 'The Peep-Show'	*E*
	Scena *King Saul*	
NOREN, HEINRICH	Variations and Double Fugue 'Kaleidoscope'	*E*
PADEREWSKI	Piano Concerto in A minor	*L*
RAVEL, MAURICE	Rapsodie Espagnole	*E*
REGER, MAX	Variations and Fugue upon a Merry Theme	*E*
	Symphonic prologue to a Tragedy	*E*
REINECKE, CARL	Flute Concerto in D major	*E*
RUBINSTEIN, A.	Fantasy for piano and orchestra	*E*
SCHEINPFLUG, PAUL	Overture to a Comedy of Shakespeare	*E*
SCHUMANN	Concertstück for four horns and orchestra	*E*
SIBELIUS	Suite for orchestra 'Swan-White'	*E*
SINIGAGLIA, LEONE	Danze Piemontesi, opus 31, nos 1 and 2	*E*
STANFORD, C. V.	Two Songs with Orchestra, opus 82	*P*
arr. HENRY J.	Fantasia on Welsh Melodies	*P*
WOOD	Fantasia on Scottish Melodies	*P*

1910

AUSTIN, ERNEST	Variations for string orchestra 'The Vicar of Bray'	*P*
BAX, ARNOLD	Tone poem 'In the Faery Hills'	*P*
BRUNEAU, ALFRED	Suite 'L'Attaque du Moulin'	*E*
BRYSON, ERNEST	A study for orchestra 'Voices'	*P*
DAVIES, WALFORD	Festal Overture in B flat	*L*
FOOTE, ARTHUR	Suite in E major for strings	*E*
HATHAWAY, J. W. G.	A sketch for orchestra 'Sunshine'	*P*
HURLSTONE, W.	Suite 'The Magic Mirror'	*L*
MACK, ALBERT	Song with orchestra 'The Song of the Shulamite'	*P*
MARTIN, EASTHOPE	Two Eastern Dances for orchestra	*P*
MUSSORGSKY–WOOD	Song of the Flea	*E*
O'NEILL, NORMAN	Four dances from *The Blue Bird*	*C*
PAUR, EMIL	Symphony in A major, 'In der Natur'	*E*
PITT, PERCY	Serenade for small orchestra	*P*
JERVIS-READ, H. V.	Two Night-pieces for orchestra	*P*
ROGISTER, J.	Fantaisie Concertante for viola and orchestra	*E*
VAUGHAN WILLIAMS	Fantasia on English Folk-song	*P*

1911

ALFVEN, HUGO	Swedish Rhapsody ('Midsommarvaka')	*E*
BACH–MAHLER	Suite for orchestra	*E*
COATES, ERIC	Miniature Suite for orchestra	*P*
DEBUSSY	Suite 'Children's Corner'	*E*
ENESCO, GEORGES	Rumanian Rhapsody No. 1 in A major	*E*
	Suite for orchestra	*E*
GARDINER, BALFOUR	Shepherd Fennel's Dance	*E*
HARTY, HAMILTON	Three pieces for oboe and orchestra	*P*
MENDELSSOHN–FORSYTH	Suite for orchestra 'Five Songs without Words'	*P*
MOUQUET, JULES	Suite for flute and orchestra 'The Flute of Pan'	*L*
O'NEILL, NORMAN	Variations on an Irish Air	*P*

RAFF, arr. H. J. WOOD	Cavatina	P
RAVEL	Pavane pour une Infante Défunte	L
ROOTHAM, CYRIL	Orchestral Rhapsody 'A Passer-by'	P
ROZE, RAYMOND	Symphonic poem 'Anthony and Cleopatra'	P
SANDERS, FRANCIS	Canon by Schumann, arranged for orchestra	P
SCHUMANN—HANS PFITZNER	Eight choruses for female voices (Frauenchore)	E

1912

ASHTON, ALGERNON	Three English Dances	P
BACH	Piano Concerto No. 2 in E major	E
BAINTON, EDGAR	Celtic Sketches for orchestra	L
BOSSI, ENRICO	'Intermezzi Goldoniani' for strings	L
BRIDGE, FRANK	Suite 'The Sea'	P
DALE, BENJAMIN	Concert Piece for organ and orchestra	P
DUBOIS, THÉODORE	Fantaisie Triomphale for organ and orchestra	E
ELGAR	Four Songs with orchestra	P
	Suite 'The Crown of India'	L
ENESCO, GEORGES	Rumanian Rhapsody No. 2 in D	E
FOULDS, J. H.	Music-pictures (Group III)	P
GLAZOUNOV	Introduction and Dance from *Salome*	E
HARRISON, JULIUS	Variations 'Down among the Dead Men'	P
JUON, PAUL	Concerto in D minor for piano, violin, cello, and orchestra	E
KORBAY, FRANCIS	Hungarian Overture	P
KORNGOLD, ERICH	Prelude, Serenade, and Entr'acte from the pantomime *The Snowman*	L
	Overture to a play	E
O'NEILL, NORMAN	Three Eighteenth-century Pieces by J. H. Fiocco, orchestrated and arranged by O'Neill	P
POLDOWSKI	Nocturne for orchestra	P
QUILTER, ROGER	Suite from *Where the Rainbow Ends*	P
SCHOENBERG	Five Orchestral Pieces	E
SINIGAGLIA, LEONE	Suite for orchestra 'Piemonte'	E
COLERIDGE-TAYLOR	Violin Concerto in G minor	P
WOLF-FERRARI	Introduction to Acts II and III, *The Jewels of the Madonna*	C

1913

BACH	Aria for soprano with obbligato of three flutes 'Hört doch der sanften Flöten Chor'	E
BACH, orch. H. J. WOOD	Toccata in F	P
BAX, ARNOLD	Two orchestral sketches, 'Pensive Twilight' and 'The Dance of Wild Irravel'	P
BRIAN, HAVERGAL	Comedy-overture 'Dr Merryheart'	P
CLUTSAM, GEORGE	Introduction and Dance from *King Harlequin*	C
COATES, ERIC	Idyll for orchestra	P
DEBUSSY	'Ibéria', Images pour orchestre No. 2	E
DOHNÁNYI	Suite for orchestra in F sharp minor	E

DORLAY, GEORGES	Concerto Passioné for cello and orchestra	P
DUNHILL, THOMAS	Prelude 'The King's Threshold'	P
FAIRCHILD, BLAIR	Esquisse for orchestra, 'Tamineh'	P
FAURÉ	Ballade for piano and orchestra	E
GLAZOUNOV	Piano Concerto in F minor	E
GOOSSENS, EUGENE	Variations on an Old Chinese Theme	P
GRAINGER, PERCY	Irish Tune from County Derry	L
	Shepherd's Hey	L
HAHN, REYNALDO	Suite for wind instruments, two harps and piano, 'Le Bal de Béatrice d'Este'	L
KEYSER, HARRY	Preludes to Acts IV and V *Othello*	P
LEKEU, G.	Fantasia on Two Popular Airs of Anjou	E
MANDL, RICHARD	Hymn to the Rising Sun, for strings, harp, and organ	L
MOZART–PITT	Andante for wind instruments	P
PITT, PERCY	Aria for strings	P
PURCELL	Scene 'From Rosy Bowers', from *Don Quixote*	E
RACHMANINOV, orch. H. J. WOOD	Prelude in C sharp minor, opus 3, No. 2	P
RAVEL	Valses Nobles et Sentimentales	E
SCOTT, CYRIL	Two Poems for orchestra	P
STRAVINSKY	Suite for orchestra 'The Firebird'	E
VASSILENKO, SERGE	Suite 'Au Soleil'	E
WILLIAMS, VAUGHAN	Suite 'The Wasps' (Aristophanes)	C
ZOELLNER, H.	Aria 'O buzzing golden bee' (*The Sunken Bell*)	E

1914

ASHTON, ALGERNON	Three Scottish Dances	P
BARTÓK, BÉLA	Suite No. 1 for orchestra	E
BORSDORF, OSKAR	Dramatic fantasy 'Glaucus and Ione'	P
BOUGHTON, RUTLAND	'Love and Night' for orchestra	P
BRIDGE, FRANK	Dance Rhapsody for orchestra	P
BRUCKSHAW, KATHLEEN	Piano Concerto in C major	P
COWEN, FREDERIC	Second Suite de Ballet 'The Language of Flowers'	P
DAVIES, WALFORD	'Conversations' for piano and orchestra	P
DAVIS, J. D.	Two Pieces for 'cello and orchestra	P
ELGAR	Adagio 'Sospiri'	P
FRANCK, CÉSAR	Symphonic poem 'Les Éolides'	E
GARDINER, BALFOUR	'In May-time'	P
GEEHL, HENRY	Suite for orchestra 'Fairyland'	P
GOOSSENS, EUGENE	Symphonic poem 'Perseus'	P
HOLBROOKE, JOSEF	Imperial March	P
PITT, PERCY	Suite de Ballet 'Sakura'	P
SACRATI, F.	Aria 'E dove t'aggiri' (*Proserpina*)	L
SCHMITT, FLORENT	Suite for orchestra	E
STRAVINSKY	Scherzo Fantastique for orchestra	E
COLERIDGE-TAYLOR	Rhapsody for orchestra 'From the Prairie'	L
VIVALDI–SILOTI	Concerto in D minor for orchestra	E
WALTHEW, R.	Overture 'Friend Fritz'	P

1915

BAGRINOVSKY, M.	Fantastic Miniatures for orchestra	E
BATH, HUBERT	African Suite	P
BRIDGE, FRANK	Lament, for stringed orchestra	P
COATES, ERIC	Song Cycle 'The Mill o' Dreams'	P
CORDER, PAUL	Preludes to Acts I and II, *Rapunzel*	P
COWEN, F. H.	Fantasy of Life and Love	P
DEBUSSY	*Le Martyre de Saint Sébastien* (Fragments Symphoniques)	E
	'Printemps' for piano duet and orchestra	E
JONGEN, JOSEPH	Fantasia on two popular Walloon Carols	E
LOEFFLER, CHARLES	Symphonic poem 'The Death of Tantagiles'	E
MASCAGNI	Introduction 'The Sun' (*Iris*)	E
MÉHUL, orch. H. J. WOOD	French National Song 'Le Chant du Départ'	P
PHILLIPS, MONTAGUE	Song with orchestra 'Lethe'	P
RACHMANINOV	The Island of the Dead	E
SMYTH, ETHEL	Overture 'The Boatswain's Mate'	C

1916

BACH–GOUNOD, arr. H. J. WOOD	'Méditation' upon the 1st Prelude of the Well-tempered Clavichord	P
BACH–H. J. WOOD	Orchestral Suite No. 6	P
COATES, ERIC	Suite 'From the Countryside'	L
DORLAY, GEORGES	Symphonic Fantasia 'Struggle and Hope' for piano and orchestra	P
GLAZOUNOV	Paraphrase on the Hymns of the Allied Nations	E
	Song of the Haulers on the Volga	E
GRAINGER, PERCY	Clog Dance 'Handel in the Strand'	P
MACDOWELL, EDWARD	Two poems for orchestra, 'Poème Erotique', and 'Scotch Poem'	E
MACKENZIE, A. C.	Ancient Scots Tunes set for strings	C
MUSSORGSKY	Intermezzo in B minor for orchestra	E
	Persian dance from 'Khovanstchina'	E
MUSSORGSKY– TOUSHMALOV	Suite 'Pictures from an Exhibition'	E
O'NEILL, NORMAN	Hornpipe for full orchestra	L
PROKOFIEV, SERGE	Humorous Scherzo for four bassoons	P
PROWINSKY	A Passing Serenade	P
REBIKOV, VLADIMIR	Suite for orchestra 'The Christmas Tree'	E
RIMSKY–KORSAKOV	Suite for orchestra 'Pan Voyevoda'	E
SCRIABIN	Scherzo for orchestra	E

1917

ALBÉNIZ	Nivian's Dance from the opera *Merlin*	E
AUBERT, LOUIS	Suite Brève	E
BRIGHT, DORA	Suite Bretonne for flute and orchestra	P
BUCK, PERCY	'Croon' for orchestra	P
BUTTERWORTH, G.	Rhapsody 'A Shropshire Lad'	L

CARR, HOWARD	Suite for orchestra 'The Jolly Roger'	*L*
GRANADOS	Five Spanish Dances	*E*
IRELAND, JOHN	Prelude 'The Forgotten Rite'	*P*
LIADOV	Legend for orchestra 'Kikimora'	*E*
LOEFFLER, C.	A Pagan Poem (after Virgil)	*E*
O'NEILL, NORMAN	'Before Dawn', a Swinburne ballet for women's voices and orchestra	*P*
PALMGREN	A Finnish Lullaby for strings	*L*
PHILLIPS, MONTAGUE	Phantasy for violin and orchestra	*P*
SPEAIGHT, JOSEPH	Two Pieces for orchestra, 'Queen Mab Sleeps' and 'Puck'	*P*
WALDO WARNER, H.	Three Elfin Dances	*L*

1918

ARCADELT— H. J. WOOD	Ave Maria, for orchestra	*P*
AUSTIN, ERNEST	'Stella-Mary Dances'	*P*
BACH	Violin Concerto in G minor	*E*
BACH—SANDERS	Passacaglia in C minor	*P*
CARPENTER, JOHN ALDEN	Suite 'Adventures in a Perambulator'	*E*
CARR, HOWARD	Sketches for orchestra 'Three Heroes'	*P*
JAQUES-DALCROZE	'An Allegory' for orchestra	*C*
DUPARC, HENRI	'Aux Etoiles'	*E*
GILBERT, HENRY F.	Comedy Overture on Negro Themes	*E*
LAURENCE, F.	Legend for orchestra	*P*
MALIPIERO, G. F.	Impressioni dal Vero	*E*
ROOTHAM, CYRIL	Overture to the opera *The Two Sisters*	*P*
SKILTON, C. S.	Two Indian Dances	*E*
SPEAIGHT, JOSEPH	Tone poem 'Joy and Sorrow'	*P*

1919

ALBÉNIZ	'Córdoba' from 'Chants d'Espagne'	*E*
BAINTON, EDGAR	Two Pieces for orchestra	*P*
BAX, ARNOLD	Scherzo for orchestra	*P*
BERNERS, LORD	Fantaisie Espagnole	*P*
BUTTERWORTH, GEORGE	Idyll for orchestra 'The Banks of Green Willow'	*P*
CARR, HOWARD	Rondo 'The Jovial Huntsmen'	*P*
CASELLA, ALFREDO	Suite 'Le Couvent sur l'Eau'	*E*
COATES, ERIC	Suite 'Summer Days'	*P*
DEBUSSY	'La Cathédrale Engloutie' for orchestra	*E*
DUNHILL, THOMAS	Dance Suite for Strings	*P*
D'ERLANGER, F.	Symphonic prelude 'Sursum Corda'	*P*
GARDINER, B.	'The Joyful Homecoming'	*P*
GOLESTAN, STAN	Rhapsodie Roumaine	*E*
GOOSSENS, EUGENE	Prelude for orchestra 'Philip II'	*P*
GRAINGER, PERCY	Children's march 'Over the Hills and Far Away'	*L*
HADLEY, HENRY	Rhapsody 'The Culprit Fay'	*E*
HOWELL, DOROTHY	Symphonic poem 'Lamia'	*P*

LOEFFLER, C.	Fantaisie Symphonique 'La Villanelle du Diable'	*E*
MOZART, orch. F. G. SANDERS	Fantasia in F minor for orchestra	*P*
MUSSORGSKY	Songs of the Nursery, for voice and orchestra	*E*
POLDOWSKI	'Pat Malone's Wake' for piano and orchestra	*L*
PRATELLA, F. BALILLA	'War', Three dances for orchestra	*E*
QUILTER, ROGER	Children's Overture	*P*
SCHMITT, FLORENT	'Rêves' No. 1 for orchestra	*E*
SMITH, DAVID STANLEY	Overture 'Prince Hal'	*P*
TCHEREPNIN	Quartet for four horns	*P*
WIDOR	Sinfonia Sacra for organ and orchestra	*E*
	Symphony in F minor for organ and orchestra	*E*

1920

BAX, ARNOLD	Symphonic Variations in E, for piano and orchestra	*P*
BOWEN, YORK	Concerto in E minor for violin and orchestra	*P*
CASELLA, ALFREDO	Pagine di Guerra (Pages of War)	*E*
CATOIRE, GEORGE	Concerto in A flat for piano and orchestra	*E*
DORLAY, GEORGES	Mirage (Valse Intermezzo)	*P*
FAURÉ	Fantaisie for piano and orchestra	*E*
	Suite for orchestra, 'Masques et Bergamasques'	*E*
FOGG, ERIC	Suite from the ballet, *The Golden Butterfly*	*P*
GIBBS, ARMSTRONG	Suite for orchestra, 'Crossings'	*C*
GOOSSENS, EUGENE	Symphonic poem, 'The Eternal Rhythm'	*P*
HOWELLS, HERBERT	Merry-eye, for orchestra	*P*
LAWRENCE, F.	The Dance of the Witch Girl, for orchestra	*P*
PALMGREN, S.	Piano Concerto No. 2	*E*
PHILLIPS, MONTAGUE	Concerto No. 2 in E for piano and orchestra	*P*
PROKOFIEV	Concerto No. 1, in D flat, for piano and orchestra	*E*
RONALD, LANDON	Orchestral suite, 'The Garden of Allah'	*C*
STRONG, TEMPLETON	Suite for orchestra, 'The Night'	*E*

1921

BACH–GOOSSENS	Suite in G (from the French Suites)	*P*
BAINTON, EDGAR	Symphonic poem, 'Paracelsus'	*L*
BANTOCK, G.	Coronach for strings, harp, and organ	*L*
BARTÓK	Rhapsody for piano and orchestra	*E*
BLISS, ARTHUR	Mêlée Fantasque for orchestra	*P*
BUTTERWORTH, GEORGE	Two English Idylls	*P*
CARPENTER, JOHN ALDEN	Concertino for piano and orchestra	*E*
DIEREN, B. VAN	Les Propous des beuveurs – 'Introit'	*P*
HOWELL, DOROTHY	*Koong Shee* (A ballet)	*P*
HUGHES, HERBERT	Parodies for voice and orchestra	*P*
JARNEFELT	Suite for orchestra, 'The Promised Land'	*E*
JONGEN, JOSEPH	Symphonic tableau 'Lalla Rookh'	*E*

MACEWAN, DÉSIRÉE	'Clam-Var' for orchestra	P
O'CONNOR–MORRIS, GEOFFREY	Concerto in A minor for violin and orchestra	L
OFFENBACH	Serenade ('The Goldsmith of Toledo')	E
O'NEILL, NORMAN	Prelude and Call ('Mary Rose')	C
SANTOLIQUIDO, F.	Symphonic sketch, 'Crepuscolo sul Mare'	E
	'Il Profumo delle Oasi Sahariane'	E
SARGENT, MALCOLM	Orchestral poem, *An Impression on a Windy Day*	L
TICCIATI, F.	Poema Gregoriano for piano and orchestra	P
YSAŸE, THÉOPHILE	Piano Concerto in E flat	E

1922

AUBERT, LOUIS	Habanera for orchestra	E
BLOCH, ERNEST	Hebrew rhapsody 'Schelomo' for 'cello and orchestra	E
BÖNESEN, HAKON	Aria 'Ujarak's Departure' (*Kaddara*)	E
BRIDGE, FRANK	A Christmas dance, 'Sir Roger de Coverley'	P
ENNA, AUGUST	Aria 'It seems to me' (*Comedians*)	E
FARRAR, ERNEST	Suite for orchestra 'English Pastoral Impressions'	L
GIBBS, ARMSTRONG	Ballet music from *The Betrothal*	C
GREENBAUM, HYAM	'Parfum de la Nuit' (Three Miniatures for solo oboe and small orchestra	P
HOLBROOKE, JOSEF	Prelude 'Bronwen'	L
HOWELLS, HERBERT	Procession for orchestra	P
MCEWEN, J. B.	'A Winter Poem'	P
MIGOT, GEORGES	'Le Paravent de Lacque' and 'Cinq Images'	E
MILHAUD, DARIUS	Suite Symphonique No. 2	E
MONTEVERDI arr. B. MOLINARI	Sonata sopra Sancta Maria for organ and orchestra	E
PHILLIPS, MONTAGUE	Four Dances (*The Rebel Maid*)	C
PIERNÉ, GABRIEL	'Paysages Franciscains' (Three Pieces for orchestra)	E
ROUSSEL, ALBERT	'Pour une Fête de Printemps'	E
SARGENT, MALCOLM	Nocturne and Scherzo	L
SCARBOROUGH, E.	Orchestral fantasy 'Promise'	P
WALL, ALFRED M.	Concert overture 'Thanet'	L

1923

ARENSKY	'Song of the Water-nymph'	E
BRETON, TOMÁS	Violin Concerto in A minor	P
CASSADÓ, JOAQUÍN	Spanish Fantasy for piano and orchestra, 'Hispania'	E
DAVIES, WALFORD	A Memorial Suite in C for piano and orchestra	P
DOHNÁNYI	Violin Concerto in D minor	E
FOULDS, J. H.	Keltic Suite	L
GIBBS, ARMSTRONG	Poem for orchestra 'A Vision of Night'	P
GILBERT, HENRY F.	Symphonic poem 'The Dance in Place Congo'	E
GREENBAUM, HYAM	A Sea Poem	P
HEATH, JOHN R.	Scherzo for wind instruments and percussion	P
HOLST, GUSTAV	Fugal Concerto for flute, oboe, and strings	C
	Fugal Overture	C
HOWELL, DOROTHY	Piano Concerto in D minor	P

KORNGOLD, ERICH	Suite 'Much Ado about Nothing'	E
MACKENZIE, A. C.	Ballet music 'St John's Eve'	P
MIASKOVSKY	Poem for orchestra 'Alastor'	E
PICK– MANGIAGALLI, R.	Symphonic poem 'Sortilegi' for piano and orchestra	E
REGER, MAX	Piano Concerto in F minor	E
SAINT–SAËNS	Suite 'Le Carnaval des Animaux'	E
SAINTON, PHILIP	Two Orchestral Pictures	P
SMYTH, ETHEL	Four Chorale Preludes	P
SPELMAN, T. M.	Suite 'Barbaresques'	P

1924

No New Works

1925

D'ALBERT, EUGÈNE	Suite 'Aschenputtel'	E
BARTÓK	Dance Suite	E
CARR, HOWARD	Prelude 'The Shrine in the Wood'	P
	Symphonic march 'The Sun God'	P
COATES, ERIC	Two Light Syncopated Pieces	P
DYSON, GEORGE	Serenade, 'Won't you look out of your window?'	P
FOULDS, J. H.	Suite 'Saint Joan'	C
GRAENER, PAUL	Variations on a Russian Folk-song	E
HALES, HUBERT J.	Concert overture 'Twelfth Night'	P
HAY, E. NORMAN	Tone poem 'Dunluce'	P
IBERT, JACQUES	'The Ballad of Reading Gaol' for orchestra	E
KUFFERATH, C.	Symphonic poem 'Mirages'	E
MCEWEN, J. B.	Prelude	L
PFITZNER, HANS	Three Preludes from *Palestrina*	E
SAINTON, PHILIP	'Harlequin and Columbine' (An orchestral study)	P
SCHREKER, FRANZ	Suite 'The Birthday of the Infanta'	E
SMYTH, ETHEL	Intermezzo and Overture from *Entente Cordiale*	C
SPAIN–DUNK, SUSAN	Idyll for string orchestra	P
	Romantic Piece for flute solo and strings	P
TAYLOR, DEEMS	Suite 'Through the Looking Glass'	E
TCHEREPNIN	Suite 'The Romance of a Mummy'	E

1926

AKIMENKO, FEODOR	'Ange' (Poème – Nocturne)	E
AUSTIN, FREDERIC	Suite from the music to the Insect Play	P
BLISS, ARTHUR	Introduction and Allegro for full orchestra	P
BOUGHTON, RUTLAND	Overture 'The Queen of Cornwall'	L
COATES, ERIC	Phantasy for orchestra 'The Three Bears'	P
DOHNÁNYI	Ruralia Hungarica	E
HADLEY, HENRY	Symphonic poem 'The Ocean'	E
HANSON, HOWARD	Symphonic poem 'Pan and the Priest'	P
HINDEMITH, PAUL	Concerto for orchestra	E
D'INDY, VINCENT	'La Queste de Dieu' (Symphonie Descriptive)	C

JACOB, GORDON	Viola Concerto in C minor	C
MALIPIERO, F.	'Il Molino della Morte'	E
MANÉN, JOAN DE	Concerto Espagnol for violin and orchestra	E
MARX, JOSEPH	Romantic Concerto in E for piano and orchestra	E
SPAIN–DUNK, SUSAN	Concert overture 'The Kentish Downs'	P
TAILLEFERRE, GERMAINE	Ballade for piano and orchestra	E

1927

ALWYN, WILLIAM	Five Preludes for orchestra	P
BRIDGE, FRANK	Impression for orchestra 'There is a Willow grows aslant a Brook'	P
DUPRÉ, MARCEL	Cortège et Litanie for organ and orchestra	E
HELY–HUTCHINSON, V.	Variations for orchestra (Intermezzo, Scherzo, and Finale)	E
HINDEMITH	Piano Concerto No. 1	E
O'DONNELL, B. WALTON	Amráin na N'Gaedeal, 'Songs of the Gael' (A Gaelic Fantasy)	C
SPAIN–DUNK, SUSAN	Poem for orchestra 'Elaine'	P
WALTON, WILLIAM	Overture 'Portsmouth Point'	L
WOOD, THOMAS	A Seaman's Overture	L

1928

BACH–SCHOENBERG	Two Choralvorspiele for orchestra	E
BAINTON, EDGAR	Eclogue for orchestra	C
BENJAMIN, ARTHUR	Concertino for piano and orchestra	P
CASELLA, ALFREDO	Partita for piano and orchestra	E
FOGG, ERIC	'June Twilight' for orchestra	L
GOLDMARK, RUBIN	A Negro Rhapsody	C
HOWELL, DOROTHY	Overture 'The Rock'	P
JACOB, GORDON	Overture 'Clogher Head'	P
KODÁLY, ZOLTÁN	Suite 'Háry János'	E
SAMPSON, GODFREY	Symphony in D	P
SIBELIUS	Symphonic poem 'Tapiola'	E
SOWERBY, LEO	Overture 'Comes Autumn Time'	E
STRAUSS, RICHARD	Parergon to the Sinfonia Domestica, for piano and orchestra	E
TANSMAN, A.	Piano Concerto	E

1929

ANROOIJ, P. VAN	'Piet Hein' (A Dutch Rhapsody)	E
ARNE, THOMAS	Piano Concerto No. 5 in C minor	C
BAX, ARNOLD	Three Orchestral Pieces: Overture, Elegy, and Rondo	P
BERKELEY, LENNOX	Suite for orchestra	E
BERNERS, LORD	Suite from 'The Triumph of Neptune'	E
BLISS, ARTHUR	Concerto for two pianos and orchestra	E
CONVERSE, FREDERICK	'Flivver Ten Million' (A joyous epic for orchestra)	E
HELY–HUTCHINSON, V.	A Carol Symphony	L

HONEGGER, ARTHUR	Concertino for piano and orchestra	L
	'Rugby', Mouvement Symphonique	E
HOWELLS, HERBERT	'In Green Ways' (Song-group for soprano and orchestra)	L
LAMBERT, CONSTANT	Music for Orchestra	C
MIASKOVSKY	Symphonic poem 'Silentium'	E
MOERAN, E. J.	Rhapsody No. 2	L
SAINTON, PHILIP	Ballet *The Dream of a Marionette*	P
SOWERBY, LEO	Suite 'From the Northland': Impressions of the country round Lake Superior	E
TOMMASINI, V.	Prelude, Fanfare, and Fugue	E
WALTON, WILLIAM	Viola Concerto	P
WILSON, STANLEY	Piano Concerto	P

1930

BRIDGE, FRANK	Rhapsody for orchestra 'Enter Spring'	L
DUPRÉ, MARCEL	Symphony for orchestra and organ	E
GOOSSENS, EUGENE	Oboe Concerto	P
GRAINGER, PERCY	English Dance for orchestra and organ	E
HONEGGER	'Cello Concerto	E
IRELAND, JOHN	Piano Concerto	P
JANÁČEK, LEOS	Wallachian Dances for orchestra	E
KODÁLY	'Summer Evening' (Nyari Este)	E
KRENEK, ERNST	Potpourri for orchestra	L
MACONCHY, ELIZABETH	Suite 'The Land'	P
SMYTH, ETHEL	Anacreontic Ode for baritone and orchestra	C
VILLA-LOBOS, H.	Chôros (No. 8) for full orchestra	E

1931

BERNERS, LORD	'Luna Park'	C
ELGAR	Nursery Suite	P
DELIUS	'A Song of Summer'	P
FOGG, ERIC	Bassoon Concerto in D major	P
POULENC, F.	Aubade for piano and orchestra	E
WALSWORTH, IVOR	Rhapsodic Dance	C
WEBERN, ANTON	Passacaglia for orchestra	E

1932

BAINTON, EDGAR	'Epithalamion'	L
BEETHOVEN—JOAN DE MANÉN	Konzertstück in C major for violin and orchestra	E
RAVEL	Piano Concerto for the left hand	E

Winter Season 1932–1933

| HINDEMITH | Philharmonic Concerto | E |
| SMYTH, ETHEL | Fête Galante (A Dance Dream) | L |

1933

DELIUS	Idyll for soprano, baritone, and orchestra	P
GERHARD, ROBERTO	Six Catalan Folk-songs for soprano and orchestra	E
GOOSSENS, EUGENE	'Kaleidoscope'	E
HONEGGER	Symphonic Movement No. 3	E

1934

BACH–PICK- MANGIAGALLI	Two Preludes for strings	L
BACH RESPIGHI	Prelude and Fugue in D	E
CONVERSE, FREDERICK	'California'	E
COOKE, ARNOLD	Concert Overture No. 1	L
DALE, BENJAMIN	An English Dance	C
KODÁLY	Dances of Galanta	E
MOERAN, E. J.	Farrago	L
SINIGAGLIA, L.	Rondo for violin	P
TAPP, FRANK	'Metropolis'	P
TAYLOR, DEEMS	'Circus Day'	E
TOCH, ERNST	Symphony for piano and orchestra	P
VAUGHAN WILLIAMS	'The Running Set'	P

Winter Season 1934–1935

SMYTH, ETHEL	*Entente Cordiale*	P

1935

BARTÓK	Hungarian Peasant Songs	E
BERKELEY, LENNOX	Overture	E
BLISS, ARTHUR	Suite from Film Music – 1935	C
BUSH, ALAN	Dance Overture	C
FOGG, ERIC	'September Night'	C
HOWELLS, HERBERT	Elegy for strings	L
JACOB, GORDON	Passacaglia on a Well-known Theme	L
LARSSON, LARS-ERIK	Saxophone Concerto	E
SAINTON, PHILIP	Serenade Fantastique for viola and orchestra	P
SHOSTAKOVICH	Symphony No. 1	L
STEPHEN, DAVID	'Coronach'	L

TAILLEFERRE,
  GERMAINE
	Concerto for two pianos, mixed chorus, saxophones, and
	  orchestra
		E

1936

BACH–CASELLA	Chaconne for full orchestra	E
BANTOCK, GRANVILLE	Comedy overture 'The Frogs'	P
DOHNÁNYI	Minutes Symphoniques	E
GREENWOOD, JOHN	'Salute to Gustav Holst'	C
IBERT	Concertino da Camera for saxophone and orchestra	E

IRELAND, JOHN	'A London Overture'	P
MACONCHY, ELIZABETH	Piano Concerto	E
MARSICK, ARMAND	Tableaux Grecs	E
SIBELIUS	Ballad for mezzo-soprano and orchestra 'The Ferryman's Bride'	E
VOGEL, VLADIMIR	'Ritmica Ostinata'	E
WHYTE, IAN	Three Scottish Dances	L

1937

AUSTIN, FREDERIC	Overture 'The Sea Venturers'	L
BAX, ARNOLD	'London Pageant'	C
ROSSINI—BRITTEN	Suite 'Soirées Musicales'	C
GIBBS, ARMSTRONG	Essex Suite for strings	L
HANDEL	Five Choruses from the operas	C
PURCELL—JULIAN HERBAGE	Suite from *King Arthur* for strings	L
IBERT	'Escales'	L
JACOB, GORDON	Variations on an Original Theme	L
KODÁLY	Ballet Music	E
MALIPIERO, F.	Violin Concerto	E
RUBBRA, EDMUND	Fantasia for violin and orchestra	P
TAILLEFERRE, GERMAINE	Harp Concerto	E

1938

BLISS, ARTHUR	Film Music 'Conquest of the Air'	C
BRITTEN, BENJAMIN	Piano Concerto	P
JACOB, GORDON	'Helen of Kirconnell'	E
LAMBERT, CONSTANT	Suite from the Ballet *Horoscope*	C
LEWIS, ANTHONY	Overture for unaccompanied chorus	P
MILHAUD	Suite Provençale	E
POOT, MARCEL	Allegro Symphonique	L
RACHMANINOFF	Prelude to the opera *The Avaricious Knight*	E
ROUSSEL	Rapsodie Flamande	E
WALTON, WILLIAM	Façade (Second Suite)	E

1939

| BARBER, SAMUEL | Essay for orchestra | E |
| BLISS, ARTHUR | Piano Concerto | E |

(Season curtailed through outbreak of war.)

1940

BERKELEY, LENNOX	Introduction and Allegro for two pianos and orchestra	P
HARRIS, WILLIAM H.	Once upon a time	P
LUTYENS, ELISABETH	Three Pieces for orchestra	P

(Season again curtailed.)

1941

No New Works

1942

BENJAMIN, ARTHUR	Rondo for orchestra, 'Prelude to Holiday'	E
BRITTEN	Sinfonia da Requiem	E
BUSH, ALAN	Symphony in C	P
CIMAROSA–BENJAMIN	Oboe Concerto	E
COPLAND, AARON	Ballet suite, *Billy the Kid*	E
DEMUTH, NORMAN	Valses Graves et Gaies	P
DUNHILL, T. F.	Triptych, Three Impressions for viola and orchestra	P
FARJEON, HARRY	Symphonic Poem, 'Pannychis'	P
GIPPS, RUTH	Symphonic Poem, 'Knight in Armour'	P
HARRIS, WILLIAM H.	Heroic Prelude	P
IRELAND, JOHN	Epic March	P
LUCAS, LEIGHTON	Suite Française	P
LUCAS, MARY ANDERSON	Circus Suite	P
MACONCHY, ELIZABETH	Dialogue for piano and orchestra	P
MOERAN, E. J.	Violin Concerto	P
ROWLEY, ALEC	Three Idylls for piano and orchestra	P
RUBBRA, EDMUND	Symphony No. 4	P
SHOSTAKOVICH	Symphony No. 7 (Leningrad)	E

1943

ALEXANDROV	Overture on Russian Folk Tunes	E
BERKELEY, LENNOX	Symphony No. 1	P
BRITTEN	Scottish Ballad for two pianos and orchestra	E
BUDASHKIN	Festival Overture	E
BUSCH, WILLIAM	'Cello Concerto	P
CHÁVEZ, CARLOS	Sinfonia India	E
COPLAND, AARON	A Lincoln Portrait	E
DUNHILL, T. F.	Waltz Suite	P
GOOSSENS, EUGENE	Symphony No. 1	E
GUNDRY, INGLIS	Heyday Freedom	P
KABALEVSKY	Suite from *Colas Breugnon*	E
KHACHATURYAN	Lezginka	E
MOERAN, E. J.	Rhapsody, for piano and orchestra	P
PISTON, WALTER	Sinfonietta	E
ROWLEY, ALEC	Burlesque Quadrilles	P
RUBBRA, EDMUND	Sinfonia Concertante for piano and orchestra	P
SCHUMAN, WILLIAM	Symphony No. 3	E
SHEBALIN	Overture	E
STRINGFIELD, LAMAR	Symphonic Patrol, A Negro Parade	E
VAN WYK, ARNOLD	Saudade, for violin and orchestra	P
VAUGHAN WILLIAMS	Symphony in D	P
WEBER	Concertstück	E
WEISGALL, HUGO	American Comedy 1943	E

1944

BANTOCK, GRANVILLE	Two Hebridean Sea Poems	P
BARBER, SAMUEL	Violin Concerto	E
GOOSSENS, EUGENE	Fantasy Concerto, for piano and orchestra	E
PHILLIPS, MONTAGUE	In Praise of my Country	P

(Season curtailed by flying bombs.)

1945

BRITTEN	Four Interludes and Passacaglia, *Peter Grimes*	L
BUSH, ALAN	Fantasia on Soviet Themes	P
DUNHILL, T. F.	Overture, May-Time	P
EVANS, DAVID MOULE	Poem for Orchestra, September Dusk	P
HADLEY, PATRICK	Travellers, for soprano, chorus and orchestra	L
HINDEMITH	Ballet Overture, Cupid and Psyche	E
MARTINU	Memorial to Lidice	L
NOBLE, TERTIUS	Introduction and Passacaglia	E
RAWSTHORNE	Fantasy Overture for Orchestra, Cortèges	P
SCHOENBERG	Piano Concerto	E
SCHUMAN, WILLIAM	A Free Song, for chorus and orchestra	E
VEPRIK	Song of Jubilation	E
WALTON	Suite from Henry V	C
WHYTE, IAN	Festival March	P
VAUGHAN WILLIAMS	Suite, The Story of a Flemish Farm	C
	Thanksgiving for Victory	C

1946

BLISS	Suite, Adam Zero	C
BLOCH	Suite Symphonique	E
BRITTEN	Piano Concerto No. 1 in D (revised version)	L
CRESTON	Poem, for harp and orchestra	E
HINDEMITH	Symphonic Metamorphoses on Themes of Weber	E
IRELAND	Overture, Satyricon	P
LUCAS, LEIGHTON	Litany, for orchestra	C
MILHAUD	Deux Marches	E
PROKOFIEV	Symphony No. 5	E
SHOSTAKOVICH	Symphony No. 9	E
STRAUSS, RICHARD	Oboe Concerto	E
STRAVINSKY	Scherzo à la Russe	E
WALTON	Where Does the Uttered Music Go? (for unaccompanied chorus)	C

Winter Season 1946–1947

| HADLEY, PATRICK | Cantata, The Hills | P |

1947

CHAGRIN	Prelude and Fugue for Orchestra	P
DURUFLÉ, MAURICE	Trois Danses	E
GOOSSENS, EUGENE	Three Pictures, for flute, strings and percussion	E
HAYDN	Concerto in C, for organ	E
HELY-HUTCHINSON	Symphony, for small orchestra	L
JACOB, GORDON	Concerto, for bassoon, strings and percussion	P
LEWIS, ANTHONY	Elegy and Capriccio, for trumpet and orchestra	P
LUTYENS, ELISABETH	Petite Suite	L
NOVÁK, VITESLAV	Triptych on a Chorale Theme from St Wenceslas	P
PISTON, WALTER	Symphony No. 2	E
RAWSTHORNE	Concerto, for oboe and strings	L
RUBBRA, EDMUND	Festival Overture	L
SCHUMAN, WILLIAM	Piano Concerto	E
STAROKADOMSKY, M.	Concerto for orchestra	E

1948

AURIC, GEORGES	Overture	E
BERKELEY, LENNOX	Piano Concerto in B flat	P
COOKE, ARNOLD	Processional Overture	L
GRAINGER, PERCY	Danish Folk Music Suite	E
JAUBERT	Suite Française	E
KABALEVSKY	Piano Concerto No. 2	E
MILHAUD	Suite Française	E
MOERAN, E. J.	Serenade in G for orchestra	P
MOZART	Oboe Concerto in C	E
RAWSTHORNE	Violin Concerto	L
SCOTT, CYRIL	Oboe Concerto	P
SEARLE, HUMPHREY	'Fuga giocosa' for orchestra	P
STEVENS, BERNARD	Fugal Overture	P
VAUGHAN WILLIAMS	Partita for double string orchestra	C

1949

BERKELEY, LENNOX	Colonus's Praise	P
BLOCH	Concerto Symphonique for piano and orchestra	L
BUSH, ALAN	Violin Concerto	P
GOOSSENS, EUGENE	Fantasy for piano and orchestra	P
	Sinfonietta	L
HONEGGER	Symphony No. 3	E
JACOB, GORDON	Fantasia on the Alleluia Hymn	L
LUCAS, LEIGHTON	Chaconne in C Sharp Minor	C
RAWSTHORNE	Concerto for string orchestra	E
SEARLE, HUMPHREY	Overture to a Drama	P
STRAUSS, RICHARD	Duet Concertino for clarinet, string orchestra and harp	L

1950

BARTÓK	Viola Concerto	L

BAX	Concertante for Orchestra with Piano Solo (Left hand)	L
DOUGLAS, CLIVE	Warra-Wirrawaal	E
FRANKEL, BENJAMIN	Overture, May Day	L
HONEGGER	Prelude, Fugue and Postlude	E
JACOB, GORDON	Symphonic Suite (Suite No. 2)	L
LUTYENS, ELISABETH	Viola Concerto	P
PURCELL— LAMBERT	Ballet Suite, Comus	C
SOWERBY, LEO	Organ Concerto in C	E
VAUGHAN WILLIAMS	Fantasia on the Old 104th Psalm-tune	L

1951

BLOCH	Scherzo Fantasque for piano and orchestra	E
BUSH, ALAN	Symphonic Suite, Piers Plowman's Day	E
CASTELNUOVO— TEDESCO	Concerto da Camera	E
FRICKER, P. RACINE	Symphony No. 1	L
HINDEMITH	Clarinet Concerto	E
JACOB, GORDON	Galop Joyeux	L
JOHNSTONE, MAURICE	A Cumbrian Rhapsody, Tarn Hows	L
JONES, DANIEL	Five Pieces for Orchestra	P
SAINTON, PHILIP	Sérénade Fantastique	L

1952

No premières. Stress on 'second hearings'.

1953

ARNOLD, MALCOLM	Concerto, for piano duet and strings	L
BENJAMIN, ARTHUR	Harmonica Concerto	P
BERKELEY, LENNOX	Flute Concerto	P
HAMILTON, IAIN	Symphony No. 2	L
HOWELLS, HERBERT	A Kent Yeoman's Wooing Song	P
JACOB, GORDON	Violin Concerto	P
JOHNSTONE, MAURICE	The Oak and the Ash	L
JONGEN, JOSEPH	Symphonie Concertante, for organ and orchestra	L
MALIPIERO	Symphony No. 7	E
MARTIN, FRANK	Petite Symphonie Concertante, for harp, harpsichord, piano and strings	E
TIPPETT	Fantasia Concertante on a Theme of Corelli, for strings	L
WALTON	Coronation Te Deum	L
WHETTAM, GRAHAM	Concertino for oboe and strings	C

1954

ALWYN, WILLIAM	Harp Concerto	P
APIVOR, DENIS	A Mirror for Witches	P
BENJAMIN, ARTHUR	Symphony	L
BLISS	A Song of Welcome	P

BURKHARD, PAUL	Overture, The Hunting Parson	*E*
CANNON, PHILIP	Symphonic Study, Spring	*P*
FULTON, NORMAN	Sinfonia Pastorale	*L*
GARDNER, JOHN	A Scots Overture	*P*
JOLIVET	Concertino, for trumpet, strings and piano	*E*
LEIGHTON, KENNETH	Violin Concertino	*P*
MACONCHY, ELIZABETH	Concertino, for bassoon and strings	*P*
RACHMANINOV	Symphonic Dances	*E*

1955

ALWYN, WILLIAM	Autumn Legend for cor anglais and strings	*L*
ARNOLD, MALCOLM	Overture 'Tam O'Shanter'	*P*
BROTT, ALEXANDER	Overture, Royal Tribute	*E*
COOKE, ARNOLD	Oboe Concerto	*L*
JACOB, GORDON	'Cello Concerto	*P*
MENOTTI	Overture, Amelia Goes to the Ball	*E*
PANUFNIK	Sinfonia Rustica	*E*
PROKOFIEV	Symphony No. 7	*L*
	Piano Concerto No. 2	*E*
VEALE, JOHN	Panorama	*L*
WALTON	Duet, Act 2, Troilus and Cressida	*C*
WEBER	Symphony No. 1 in C	*E*

1956

ADDISON, JOHN	Suite from ballet Carte Blanche	*C*
BENJAMIN, ARTHUR	Concerto quasi una Fantasia, for piano and orchestra	*L*
BERKELEY, LENNOX	Suite, Nelson	*C*
BUSH, ALAN	Concert Suite, for 'cello and orchestra	*L*
COPLAND, AARON	Symphony No. 3	*E*
FRICKER, P. RACINE	Concertante for three pianos, strings and percussion	*L*
GREENWOOD, JOHN	Viola Concerto	*P*
HAMILTON, IAIN	Symphonic Variations	*L*
HODDINOTT, ALUN	Concerto, for clarinet and strings	*L*
KODÁLY	Variations on a Hungarian Folk-song ('Peacock')	*L*
LUCAS, LEIGHTON	Concert Champêtre	*E*
MARTINU	Suite Concertante for violin and orchestra	*E*
MILHAUD	Harp Concerto	*E*
SAEVERUD	Siljuslatten	*E*
SEARLE, HUMPHREY	Piano Concerto No. 2	*L*
SURINACH	Sinfonietta Flamenca	*E*
THOMPSON, RANDALL	The Last Words of David	*E*
	Tarantella	*E*

1957

ARNOLD, MALCOLM	Divertimento	*L*
BATE, STANLEY	Piano Concerto No. 3	*P*
BLACHER, BORIS	Fantasy for orchestra	*E*
FRICKER, P. RACINE	Litany, for double string orchestra	*L*

HAMILTON, IAIN	Overture, Bartholomew Fair	E
HENZE, HANS WERNER	Ode to the West Wind, for 'cello and orchestra	E
HOLMBOE, VAGN	Epitaph	E
IBERT	Bacchanal	C
JACOB, GORDON	Piano Concerto No. 2	L
JONES, DANIEL	Symphony No. 4 (In memory of Dylan Thomas)	L
MARTIN, FRANK	Overture, Athalie	E
MARTINU	Piano Concerto No. 4	E
PANUFNIK	Rhapsody for Orchestra	C
PETRASSI, GOFFREDO	Invenzione Concertata	C
RAWSTHORNE	Dance Suite, Madame Chrysanthème	P
REIZENSTEIN, FRANZ	Overture, Cyrano de Bergerac	L

In the 1950s the stress was placed less on premières and first English performances and became WORKS NOT PREVIOUSLY PERFORMED AT A HENRY WOOD PROMENADE CONCERT. From now on, these are given.

1958

ALWYN, WILLIAM	Elizabethan Dances	
APIVOR, DENIS	Pianoforte Concerto	C
ARNOLD, MALCOLM	Symphony No. 3	
BACH	Motet, Jesu, priceless treasure	
	Cantata No. 140, Wachet auf, ruft uns die Stimme	
BARTÓK	Music for Strings, Percussion and Celesta	
BRITTEN, BENJAMIN	Pas de Six (The Prince of the Pagodas)	
BRUCKNER	Symphony No. 4, in E flat (Romantic)	
BUSH, GEOFFREY	Symphony No. 1	L
BUTTERWORTH, ARTHUR	Symphony	L
COPLAND, AARON	Orchestral Variations (1957)	E
	Three Dance Episodes from Rodeo	
DELIUS	Serenade (Hassan)	
FINZI, GERALD	The Fall of the Leaf	L
FRICKER, RACINE	Dance Scene	
GERHARD, ROBERTO	Dances from Don Quixote	
GOOSSENS, EUGENE	Concert Piece for Two Harps, Oboe, Cor Anglais and Orchestra	
HAMILTON, IAIN	The Bermudas, for Baritone, Chorus and Orchestra	
HAYDN	The Creation (Part I)	
HAYDN (attrib.)	Oboe Concerto in C	
HODDINOTT, ALUN	Harp Concerto	L
JOHNSTONE, MAURICE	Dover Beach, for Baritone and Orchestra	
MARTIN, FRANK	Etudes, for String Orchestra	E
ORFF, CARL	Carmina Burana, for Soli, Chorus and Orchestra	
PUCCINI	Tosca, Act III	
REIZENSTEIN, FRANZ	Concerto Populare (The Concerto to end all Concertos)	
RUBBRA, EDMUND	Soliloquy, for Violoncello and Orchestra	
SCHOENBERG	Five Orchestral Pieces (Revised Version)	

SHOSTAKOVICH	Symphony No. 11	
	Pianoforte Concerto, Op. 101	E
STRAVINSKY	Ballet Suite, Pulcinella (after Pergolesi)	
TCHAIKOVSKY	Love Duet (Romeo and Juliet)	
TIPPETT, MICHAEL	Symphony No. 2	
VAUGHAN WILLIAMS	Symphony No. 9	
WALTON, WILLIAM	Partita	
WILLIAMS, GRACE	Penillion	L

1959

ALWYN, WILLIAM	Symphony No. 4	P
ARNELL, RICHARD	Suite from the Ballet, Harlequin in April	C
BARTÓK	Pianoforte Concerto No. 1	
BERKELEY, LENNOX	Symphony No. 2	L
BOWEN, YORK	Pianoforte Concerto No. 4 in A minor	C
HANDEL	Harp Concerto in B flat	
HANDEL–JACOB	Overture, Theodora	
HAYDN	The Creation (Parts II and III)	
HONEGGER	King David, for Narrator, Soloists, Chorus and Orchestra	
IBERT	Symphonie Concertante for Oboe and Strings	E
JONES, DANIEL	Symphony No. 5	
LEIGHTON, KENNETH	Burlesque	C
MACONCHY, ELIZABETH	Concerto for Oboe, Bassoon and Strings	C
MARTINU	Oboe Concerto	E
MILHAUD	Concerto for Percussion and Small Orchestra	L
PANUFNIK, ANDRZEJ	Suite, Polonia	
RODRIGO	Concerto-Serenata for Harp and Orchestra	E
SEARLE, HUMPHREY	Symphony No. 2	
SEIBER, MÁTYÁS	Tre Pezzi, for Violoncello and Orchestra	L
STRAUS, OSCAR	Selection, A Waltz Dream	
STRAUSS	Suite, Le Bourgeois Gentilhomme	
STRAUSS, JOHANN	New Pizzicato Polka (Op. 449)	
TCHAIKOVSKY	Pézzo Capriccioso, for Violoncello and Orchestra	
TIPPETT, MICHAEL	Ritual Dances (The Midsummer Marriage)	
WHETTAM, GRAHAM	Dance Concertante for Two Pianofortes (three hands) and Orchestra	L
WILLIAMSON, MALCOLM	Pianoforte Concerto	L

1960

ALWYN	Overture: Derby Day (Commissioned by the BBC)	P
BARTÓK	Sonata for two pianos and percussion	
BEETHOVEN	Mass in D (Missa Solemnis)	
BERG	Altenberglieder	E
BERIO, LUCIANO	Perspectives	E
BERKELEY, LENNOX	Four Poems of St Teresa of Avila	
BERLIOZ	Grande Messe des Morts	
BLACHER	Variations on a theme of Paganini	
BLISS	Pastoral: Lie Strewn the White Flocks	

BRITTEN	Nocturne	
DEBUSSY	Ballet: Jeux	
GERHARD	Violin Concerto	
GOOSSENS	Phantasy Concerto for violin and orchestra	C
HAMILTON, IAIN	Scottish Dances	C
HODDINOTT	Concerto for piano and wind	
IVES	Three Places in New England	E
LUTOSLAWSKI	Musique Funèbre	
MEYERBEER– LAMBERT	Les Patineurs	
MILHAUD	La Création du Monde	
MOZART	Piano Concerto No. 25 in C (K. 503)	
MUSGRAVE, THEA	Triptych	P
PROKOFIEV	Suite: Lieutenant Kijé	
SATIE	Parade	
SCHOENBERG	De Profundis	
	Variations, Op. 31	
SEARLE	Poem for twenty-two strings	
STRAUSS	Metamorphosen	
STRAVINSKY	Anne's Scena (The Rake's Progress)	
	Ode	
	Oedipus Rex	
	Symphony in C	
	Symphony in three movements	
TIPPETT	Sosostris's Aria (The Midsummer Marriage)	
VIVALDI	Concerto in D for flute and strings (Il Cardellino)	
WEBERN	Six Pieces, Op. 6	

1961

ARNOLD, MALCOLM	Oboe Concerto No. 1	
BARTÓK	Rhapsody No. 1, for violin and orchestra	
BAX	Mater ora Filium, for a cappella chorus	
BERLIOZ	The Flight into Egypt (The Childhood of Christ)	
	La Mort d'Ophélie	
	Sara la Baigneuse	
BERWALD	Symphony in C (Singulière)	
BOULEZ	Improvisation sur Mallarmé, No. 2: Une dentelle s'abolit	
BRITTEN	Cantata Academica	
	Prelude and Fugue, for strings in eighteen parts	
BRUCKNER	Mass in E minor	
CHOPIN	Variations on 'Là ci darem'	
COPLAND	Statements, for orchestra	
DEBUSSY	Images (complete)	
DUKAS	Fanfare: La Péri	
DVOŘÁK	Serenade in E, for strings	
FALLA	El Amor Brujo (complete)	
	Seven Popular Spanish Songs	
GABRIELI	Two Canzonas from Symphoniae Sacrae (Nos 3, 5)	
GERHARD	Two songs from 'The Duenna'	C
GLINKA	Waltz Fantasy in B minor	
GOEHR, ALEXANDER	Hecuba's Lament (Commissioned by the BBC)	P

HAMILTON, IAIN	Écossaise	*L*
HANDEL	Overture: Ezio	
HAYDN	Symphony No. 67, in F	
	Symphony No. 91, in E flat	
	Symphony No. 93, in D	
	Symphony No. 95, in C minor	
HINDEMITH	Six Songs from Das Marienleben	
LALO	Symphonie espagnole (complete)	
LISZT	Organ Solo: Prelude and Fugue on B.A.C.H.	
LUTYENS, ELISABETH	Symphonies for solo piano, wind, harps and percussion (Commissioned by the BBC)	*P*
MAHLER	Kindertotenlieder	
	Songs to poems by Rückert	
MENDELSSOHN	Symphony No. 5, in D (Reformation)	
MILNER, ANTHONY	Divertimento for string orchestra (Commissioned by the BBC)	*P*
MOZART	Don Giovanni	
	Requiem Mass (K. 626)	
	Sinfonia Concertante in E flat (K. 297b)	
MYASKOVSKY	Symphony No. 21, in F sharp minor	
RAVEL— GOOSSENS	Le Gibet (Gaspard de la Nuit)	*E*
ROUSSEL	Symphony No. 3	
SCHOENBERG	Violin Concerto	
	Verklärte Nacht	
SCHUBERT	Serenade, Op. 135, for contralto, women's chorus and piano	
SCHUMANN	Symphony No. 2, in C	
SHOSTAKOVICH	Symphony No. 6	
	Cello Concerto	
	Polka and Russian Dance (The Age of Gold)	
STRAVINSKY	Les Noces	
TALLIS	Motet in forty parts: Spem in alium nunquam habui	
VERDI	Overture: La Forza del Destino	
	Overture: Luisa Miller	
	Ballet Music: Otello	
WALTON	Symphony No. 2	
WEBERN	Five Orchestral Pieces, Op. 10	
WILLIAMSON, MALCOLM	Organ Concerto (Commissioned by the BBC)	*P*

1962

BACH—WEBERN	Ricercare (The Musical Offering)	
BEETHOVEN	Elegiac Song: Sanft wie du lebtest (Op. 118)	
BERKELEY, LENNOX	Five Pieces for Violin and Orchestra	*P*
BERLIOZ	The Damnation of Faust	
	Te Deum	
	Ballet Music from The Trojans	
BOULEZ	Movements from Le Marteau sans Maître	
BRAHMS— SCHOENBERG	Quartet in G minor	*E*
BRITTEN	Hymn to St Cecilia	

BRITTEN—BERKELEY	Mont Juic	
BRUCKNER	Symphony No. 9, in D minor	
BUSONI	Tanzwalzer	
COOKE, ARNOLD	Suite from the Ballet, Jabez and the Devil	*P*
DEBUSSY	La Damoiselle élue	
	Music for King Lear	
DEBUSSY—RAVEL	Danse	
GABRIELI	Canzonas Nos 14 and 16 (Symphoniae Sacrae)	
GERHARD, ROBERTO	Symphony No. 1	
HANDEL	Overture: Alexander's Feast	
	Israel in Egypt	
	Par che mi nasca in seno (Tamerlano)	
HAYDN	Mass in B flat (Theresa)	
HENZE	Five Neapolitan Songs	
MAHLER	Symphony No. 3	
	Adagio (Symphony No. 10)	
MAW, NICHOLAS	Scenes and Arias (Commissioned by the BBC)	*P*
MAXWELL DAVIES, PETER	Fantasia on an In Nomine of John Taverner (Commissioned by the BBC)	*P*
MESSIAEN	Cinq Rechants	
	Oiseaux Exotiques	
MONTEVERDI	Magnificat (Vespers of 1610)	
MOZART	Cosi fan tutte	
	Introduction, Papageno's Aria and Quintet (The Magic Flute, Act I)	
	Mass in C (K. 317) (The Coronation)	
	Misera dove son (K. 369)	
	Munich Kyrie (K. 341)	
MUSGRAVE, THEA	The Phoenix and the Turtle (Commissioned by the BBC)	*P*
PURCELL	Suite from Abdelazer	
RAWSTHORNE, ALAN	Medieval Diptych (Commissioned by the BBC)	*P*
SHOSTAKOVICH	Festival Overture	*E*
STRAUSS	Three Hymns, Op. 71	*E*
STRAVINSKY	Agon	
	Le Baiser de la Fée	
	Greeting Prelude	*L*
TCHAIKOVSKY	Manfred Symphony	
	Arioso from Mazeppa	
VERDI	Overture: I Masnadieri	
WALTON	Gloria in Excelsis Deo	
	The Quest	
WEBER	Clarinet Concerto No. 2, in E flat	
	Bassoon Concerto in F	

1963

BACH	Der Geist hilft unsrer Schwachheit auf	
BARTÓK	Cantata Profana	
BENNETT, RICHARD	A London Pastoral	
BERKELEY, LENNOX	Four Ronsard Sonnets (Commissioned by the BBC)	*P*
BLISS	The Enchantress	
BRAHMS	Liebeslieder Waltzes (orchestrated by the composer)	

BRITTEN	Simple Symphony	
	Cantata Misericordium, Op. 67	E
	War Requiem	
BRUCKNER	Ave Maria	
	Symphony No. 3, in D minor	
BURT, FRANCIS	Fantasmagoria per orchestra (Commissioned by the BBC)	P
CIMAROSA	Il maestro di cappella	
FRICKER, RACINE	Song Cycle: O longs désirs (Commissioned by the BBC)	P
GERHARD	Piano Concerto	
HAYDN	Mass in B flat (Creation)	
HINDEMITH	Symphony in E flat	
MAHLER	Symphony No. 2	
	Symphony No. 6, in A minor	
MONTEVERDI	L'Incoronazione di Poppea	
MOZART	The Marriage of Figaro	
	Mass in C minor (K. 427)	
	Concert Rondo (K. 382)	
	Vesperae solennes de confessore (K. 339)	
NONO, LUIGI	Sul ponte de Hiroshima	L
PURCELL	Come ye sons of art away	
	Welcome to all the pleasures	
REZNIČEK	Overture: Donna Diana	
ROSSINI	Overture: Il Signor Bruschino	
	Overture: La Cenerentola	
SCHOENBERG	Friede auf Erden	
SHOSTAKOVICH	Symphony No. 4	
	Symphony No. 12	
STRAUSS, JOHANN	Overture: Waldmeister (The Woodruff)	
STRAVINSKY	Ballet: Orpheus	
	Mass	
SULLIVAN	Trial by Jury	
TCHAIKOVSKY	Mozartiana	
TIPPETT	The Midsummer Marriage (Act II)	
VERDI	Overture: I Vespri Siciliani	
	Four Sacred Pieces	
WAGNER	Götterdämmerung (Act III)	
WALTON	Variations on a theme by Hindemith	
WEBER	Overture: Abu Hassan	
WEBERN	Variations, Op. 30	

1964

ALWYN, WILLIAM	Concerto Grosso No. 3 (Tribute to Henry Wood) (Commissioned by the BBC)	P
BACH	Cantata No. 105: Herr, gehe nicht ins Gericht	
	Organ Solos: Fantasia in G major (S. 572)	
	Fugue on the Magnificat (S. 733)	
	Prelude and Fugue in C major (S. 545)	
BEETHOVEN	Mass in C major	
BENNETT, RICHARD RODNEY	Aubade (In memory of John Hollingsworth) (Commissioned by the BBC)	P
BERLIOZ	The Childhood of Christ	

BLISS	The Beatitudes	
BRINDLE, REGINALD SMITH	Creation Epic (Choreographic Suite for Orchestra) (Commissioned by the BBC)	*P*
BRITTEN	Choral Dances from Gloriana	
BRUCKNER	Symphony No. 5, in B flat major	
BUSH, ALAN	Dorian Passacaglia and Fugue	
BYRD	Magnificat and Nunc Dimittis (Great Service)	
DEBUSSY	Trois Chansons de Charles d'Orléans	
GLAZUNOV	Violin Concerto in A minor	
GOEHR, ALEXANDER	Little Symphony (In memoriam Walter Goehr)	
HANDEL	Alexander's Feast	
	Dixit Dominus	
HAYDN	Horn Concerto No. 1, in D major	
	Mass in D minor (Nelson)	
	The Seasons	
	String Quartet in C major, Op. 76 No. 3 (Emperor)	
	Te Deum No. 2, in C major	
HINDEMITH	Concert Music for piano, brass, and two harps	
	Concert Music for viola d'amore and small orchestra	
	Lied: Die Zeit vergeht (Cardillac)	
HOLST	The Hymn of Jesus	
LUTYENS	Wittgenstein Motet	
MAHLER	Symphony No. 8, in E flat major	
	Symphony No. 10, in F sharp major (Deryck Cooke's realisation)	*P*
MENDELSSOHN	Octet for strings	
MOZART	Eine kleine Nachtmusik (K. 525) (with two minuets)	
	Idomeneo	
MUSSORGSKY– SHOSTAKOVICH	Shaklovity's Aria (Khovanshchina)	
NAYLOR, BERNARD	Cantata: Sing O my love (Commissioned by the BBC)	*P*
NIELSEN	Symphony No. 5	
POULENC	Les Biches	
PURCELL	Dido and Aeneas	
RAINIER, PRIAULX	Cello Concerto (Commissioned by the BBC)	*P*
SCHOENBERG	Erwartung	
SCHUBERT	Nachtgesang im Walde	
SPONTINI	Aria: O re dei cieli (Agnes von Hohenstaufen)	
STRAUSS	Elektra's Monologue	
STRAVINSKY	Octet for wind instruments	
	Pulcinella	
TCHAIKOVSKY	Joan's Narration (The Maid of Orleans)	
TIPPETT	Concerto for Orchestra	
VAUGHAN WILLIAMS	Dona Nobis Pacem	
VERDI	Otello	
WAGNER	Die Walküre (Acts I and III)	
WALTON	Suite from Henry V	
WILLIAMSON, MALCOLM	Concert Suite: Our Man in Havana	

1965

BACH	Organ Solos: Concerto No. 1, in G major (S. 592)
	Fantasia and Fugue in G minor (S. 542)
	Prelude and Fugue in C major (S. 547)
	Partita in E major for violin
BOULEZ	Le soleil des eaux
BRAHMS	Requiem
BRITTEN	Our Hunting Fathers
BRUCKNER	Mass No. 3, in F minor
	Symphony No. 8, in C minor
CROSSE, GORDON	Elegy
DVOŘÁK	Romance for violin and orchestra (Op. 11)
GERHARD	Hymnody
HAMILTON, IAIN	Cantos for Orchestra (Commissioned by the BBC) *P*
HANDEL	Concerto Grosso in B flat major (Op. 3 No. 2)
	Concerto Grosso in A major (Op. 6, No. 11)
HAYDN	Mass No. 7, in C major (Mass in time of war)
	Nocturne No. 8, in C major
HENZE, HANS WERNER	Cantata: Novae de infinito laudes
JACOB, GORDON	Festival Overture
LEHÁR arr. RYAN	Suite: The Merry Widow
LISZT	Symphonic Poem: Hungaria
MACONCHY, ELIZABETH	Variazioni Concertanti for oboe, clarinet, bassoon, horn and *P*
	string orchestra (Commissioned by the BBC)
MESSIAEN	Organ Solo: Les anges; Dieu parmi nous (La Nativité du Seigneur)
	Trois petites liturgies de la Présence Divine
MOZART	Serenade No. 10, in B flat major (K. 361)
NAYLOR, BERNARD	Stabat Mater, for women's chorus and small orchestra
NIELSEN	Symphony No. 4 (1916) (L'inestinguibile)
PAGANINI	Moses Fantasy
PALESTRINA	Stabat Mater
PENDERECKI	Stabat Mater
POULENC	La figure humaine
PURCELL	The Indian Queen
ROSSINI	Overture: La pietra del paragone
SCHOENBERG	Moses and Aaron
SHOSTAKOVICH	Symphony No. 8
SIBELIUS	Lemminkaïnen and the maidens of Saari
STRAUSS	Horn Concerto No. 2, in E flat major
STRAVINSKY	Abraham and Isaac
	Dumbarton Oaks
	Symphonies of Wind Instruments
SZYMANOWSKI	Stabat Mater
TELEMANN	Concerto in B flat major, for three oboes, three violins and continuo
THOMSON, VIRGIL	Acadian songs and dances (Louisiana Story)
TIPPETT	Piano Concerto
VERDI	Macbeth
WALTON	Façade (complete)

WEBER	Concertino in C minor – E flat major, Op. 26, for clarinet and orchestra	
WILLIAMSON, MALCOLM	Concerto Grosso (Commissioned by the BBC)	P
WOOD, HUGH	Scenes from Comus (Commissioned by the BBC)	P

1966

ARNOLD, MALCOLM	Concerto for two violins and strings	
	Cornish Dances	
BACH	Chaconne in D minor (Partita No. 4)	
	Mass in B minor	
BERG	Symphonic pieces from the opera 'Lulu'	
BERLIOZ	The Fall of Troy	
BOULEZ	Éclat	E
BRIAN, HAVERGAL	Symphony No. 12	
BYRD	Motets: Civitas sancti tui, Non vos relinquam orphanos, Beata viscera Mariae Virginis, Assumpta est Maria, Senex puerum portabat, Gaudeamus omnes in Domino	
CARTER, ELLIOTT	Variations for orchestra	
CAVALLI	Messa concertata	
CROSSE, GORDON	Ceremony for cello and orchestra, Op. 19 (Commissioned by the BBC)	P
DELIUS	A Mass of Life	
GERHARD	Concerto for Orchestra	
GLINKA	Overture: Prince Kholmsky	
HANDEL	Solomon	
	With thunder armed, Great God, arise } (Samson)	
	Let their celestial concerts all unite }	
IVES, CHARLES	The 4th of July	E
	Symphony No. 4	
MAHLER	Des Knaben Wunderhorn	
	Symphony No. 9, in D flat major	
MOZART	Ave, verum corpus (K. 618)	
	Die Zauberflöte	
	Six Nocturnes for voices and woodwind	
	Symphony No. 34, in C major (K. 338)	
ORR, ROBIN	Symphony in one movement	
PROKOFIEV	Symphony No. 2	
RAWSTHORNE	Cello Concerto	
ROSSINI	Overture: La cambiale di matrimonio	
RUBBRA	Motet: Veni, Creator Spiritus, for mixed choir and brass, Op. 130 (Commissioned by the BBC)	
SCHOENBERG	Four Songs, Op. 22	
SCHULLER, GUNTHER	Middle Movement from 'Movements for flute and strings'	E
SCHÜTZ	German Magnificat (1671)	
	Sion spricht	
	Saul, Saul	
	Herr, nun lässet Du Deinen Diener (Musikalische Exequien, Part III)	
	'Uppsala' Magnificat	

SHOSTAKOVICH	The Execution of Stepan Razin (First performance in Western Europe)	
SKRYABIN	Prometheus (The Poem of Fire)	
SMETANA	Šárka (Má Vlast)	
TIPPETT	The Vision of St Augustine	
VARÈSE	Ecuatorial	E
	Desérts	
WAGNER	Parsifal (Acts II and III)	
WALTON	The Twelve	
WEBERN	Cantata No. 1, Op. 29	
	Cantata No. 2, Op. 31	

1967

BACH	St John Passion
	Toccata and Fugue in F major (S. 540)
	Prelude and Fugue in D major (S. 532)
BEETHOVEN	Fidelio
BERKELEY, LENNOX	Serenade for string orchestra
BERLIOZ	The Trojans at Carthage
BLISS	Suite: Miracle in the Gorbals
BRAHMS	Serenade No. 2, in A major
BRITTEN	The Burning Fiery Furnace
CHARPENTIER, M. A.	Te Deum
GERHARD	Symphony No. 3 (Collages)
HANDEL	Saul (Act 3)
HAYDN	Recit. and Aria: Indarno m'affano, from L'incontro improvviso
HOLST	Choral Fantasia
LISZT	Mephisto Waltz No. 1
LUTOSLAWSKI	Jeux Vénitiens
LUTYENS, ELISABETH	And suddenly it's evening, for tenor and eleven instruments
MAHLER	Wer hat dies Liedlein erdacht?
MESSAGER	Véronique
MESSIAEN	Et exspecto resurrectionem mortuorum
MONTEVERDI	Final duet (Il ritorno d'Ulisse)
	Orfeo's aria and Messenger Scene (Orfeo)
	Instrumental dances and last scene (Il ballo delle ingrate)
	Beatus Vir (1st setting)
	Audi coelum (Vespers 1610)
	Gloria
	Ballo: Movete al mio bel suon
	Piange e sospira
	Presso un fiume tranquillo
	Hor che'l ciel e la terra
PALESTRINA	Missa Assumpta est Maria
PENDERECKI	St Luke Passion
PIJPER	Six Symphonic Epigrams
PURCELL	Voluntary on the 100th psalm tune
RAVEL	Introduction and Allegro for harp, with flute, clarinet, and string quartet
SCHUBERT	Octet

SCHUBERT	Impromptu in G flat major	
	Symphony No. 3 in D major	
	Mass in E flat major	
SEARLE, HUMPHREY	Oxus; Scena for tenor and orchestra (Commissioned by the BBC)	*P*
SIMPSON, ROBERT	Symphony No. 3	
SMALLEY, ROGER	Missa Brevis	
STOCKHAUSEN, KARLHEINZ	Gruppen	
STRAUSS, J.	Tritsch-Tratsch Polka	
	Champagne Polka	
SULLIVAN	Excerpts from The Sorcerer	
VIVALDI	Concerto in D minor for two violins, 'cello, strings and continuo (L'estro armonico)	
VOLKONSKY	The Lament of Shchazï	
WILSON, THOMAS	Touchstone: Portrait for orchestra (Commissioned by the BBC)	*P*

1968

ARNOLD	Overture: Peterloo	*P*
BACH	Cantata No. 79: Gott, der Herr, ist Sonn' und Schild	
	Prelude and Fugue in C minor	
	St Matthew Passion	
BANKS, DON	Violin Concerto (Commissioned by the BBC)	*P*
BAX–BARBIROLLI	Oboe Quintet (arranged for oboe and string orchestra)	
BERG	Three Orchestral Pieces	
BERKELEY	Signs in the Dark	
BERLIOZ	Nuits d'été	
BIRTWISTLE	Nomos (Commissioned by the BBC)	*P*
BLACHER	Cello Concerto	*E*
BLISS	Morning Heroes	
BOULEZ	Le marteau sans maître	
BRAHMS	Piano Quintet in F minor	
BRITTEN	Folk Song arrangements:	
	Come you not from Newcastle?	
	O Waly, Waly	
	Oliver Cromwell	
	Overture: The Building of the House	
BRUCKNER	Symphony No. 6, in A major	
BUSONI	Berceuse élégiaque	
BYRD	Motets: Sing joyfully	
	Ne irascaris Domine	
	Civitas sancti tui	
	Laudibus in sanctis	
CAVALLI	L'Ormindo	
COUPERIN	Excerpts from Messe pour les couvents	
DALLAPICCOLA	Piccola musica notturna	
DELIUS	Requiem	
GABRIELI, ANDREA	Kyrie	
	Canzona à 4	
	O frassi sparsi	

GABRIELI, GIOVANNI	Deus qui beatum Marcum	
	Canzona à 10	
	Surrexit Christus	
	Canzona 'Fa sol la re'	
	Dormira dolcemente	
	Omnes gentes	
HAYDN	Mass in B flat major (Harmoniemesse)	
	Scena di Berenice	
MAHLER	Symphony No. 5	
MESSIAEN	Chronochromie	
MONTEVERDI	Vespers	
MOZART	Die Entführung aus dem Serail	
MUSGRAVE	Concerto for orchestra	
NIELSEN	Symphony No. 1, in G minor	
POULENC	Piano Concerto	
PURCELL	Te Deum and Jubilate	
RAWSTHORNE	Concerto for two pianos and orchestra (Commissioned by the BBC)	P
RIMSKY–KORSAKOV	Two excerpts from The Legend of the Invisible City of Kitezh	
ROSSINI	Introduction, Theme and Variations for clarinet and orchestra	
SCARLATTI, DOMENICO	Stabat Mater	
SCHOENBERG	Jacob's Ladder	
SCHUBERT	Gesang der Geister über den Wassern	
SESSIONS	Symphony No. 4	E
SHOSTAKOVICH	Violin Concerto No. 2	
STOCKHAUSEN	Kontakte	
	Piano Piece No. 10	
STRAVINSKY	Ebony Concerto	
	The King of the Stars	
	Requiem Canticles	
TAVENER, JOHN	In alium (Commissioned by the BBC)	P
VARÈSE	Arcana	
	Ionisation	
VERDI	Don Carlos	
WALTON	Philharmonic Overture N.Y. '68	E
WEILL	The Seven Deadly Sins	
	Symphony No. 2	E
WOLPE	Chamber Piece No. 1	E

1969

ANON. (15th century)	Basse danse I and II	
ARNOLD	Concerto for two pianos and orchestra (Commissioned by the BBC)	P
BACH	Cantata No. 202: Weichet nur (Wedding Cantata)	
BEDFORD, DAVID	Two poems for chorus on words of Kenneth Patchen (1966)	E
BENNETT	Piano Concerto	
BERIO	Sinfonia	E
BERKELEY	Magnificat	
BERLIOZ	Beatrice and Benedict	

BLISS	Royal Fanfare (Tribute to Prince Albert's 150th Anniversary)	
BOULEZ	Pli selon pli	
BRITTEN	Children's Crusade	
	The Golden Vanity	
BUSH, ALAN	Scherzo for wind with percussion (Commissioned by the BBC)	P
BYRD	The Queen's Alman	
COOKE, ARNOLD	Variations on a theme of Dufay	P
DAVIES, PETER MAXWELL	Worldes Blis (Commissioned by the BBC)	P
DUFAY	Adieu ces bons vins de la lannoys	
	Adieu m'amour	
	Donnes l'aussault	
	Mon cuer me fait	
	Resveilles vous	
DUNSTABLE	Veni sancte spiritus	
DVOŘÁK	Biblical Songs	
GERHARD	Alegrias: divertissement flamenco	
	Symphony No. 4	
GOEHR, ALEXANDER	Three pieces for wind instruments, harp and percussion from 'Arden must die'	
HANDEL	Semele	
	Water Music: Suite No. 1, in F major	
HAYDN	Symphony No. 82, in C major (The Bear)	
MACHAUT	La Messe de Nostre Dame (c. 1364)	
MAHLER	Symphony No. 7	
MARTINU	Symphony No. 6	
MELLERS	Yeibichai, for chorus, orchestra, and jazz trio, with soprano and scat singer (Commissioned by the BBC)	P
MENDELSSOHN	Hymn of Praise	
MESSIAEN	Turangalîla Symphony	
MONTEVERDI	Magnificat for double choir (1640)	
	Orfeo: Prologue, Act I and Act II	
	Vesper Psalms and Motets (1640 and 1651)	
MOZART	Clarinet Quintet in A major (K. 581)	
	Quintet in E flat major for piano and wind (K. 452)	
PARRY orch. ELGAR	Jerusalem	
PURCELL	Now does the glorious day appear	
RACHMANINOV	Symphony No. 1, in D minor	
SCHUBERT	Als ich sie erröthen sah	
	An die Musik	
	Auf dem Wasser zu singen	
	Du liebst mich nicht	
STOCKHAUSEN	Gesang der Jünglinge	
	Mikrophonie II	
STRAVINSKY	Concerto for piano and wind	
	Mavra	
	Renard: Burlesque in song and dance	
	Suite: The Soldier's Tale	
TAVENER, JOHN	The Whale	
TIPPETT	Sonata for four horns	

VAUGHAN WILLIAMS	Symphonic Impression: In the Fen Country	
VERDI	The Sicilian Vespers	
WOOD, HUGH	'Cello Concerto (Commissioned by the BBC)	*P*

1970

ANON.	Istampitta ghaetta	
	Lamento di Tristan	
	Trotto	
ARNOLD	Concerto No. 2, for horn and string orchestra	
	Fantasy for audience and orchestra (Commissioned by the BBC)	*P*
KEES VAN BAAREN	Concerto for piano and orchestra	*E*
BACH	Cantata No. 34: O ewiges Feuer	
	Cantata No. 116: Du Friedefürst, Herr Jesu Christ	
BEETHOVEN	Cantata on the death of Emperor Joseph II	
	Diabelli Variations	
	Leonora	
BERLIOZ	Funeral March (Hamlet)	
	Songs: La belle voyageuse	
	Zaide	
BERNERS	A Wedding Bouquet	
BIRTWISTLE	Verses for Ensembles	
BOYCE	Symphony No. 5, in D major	
BRAHMS	Clarinet Quintet in B minor	
BYRD	Ave verum corpus	
	Haec dies	
	Laudate pueri	
	Vide Domine afflictionem nostram	
CARTER, ELLIOTT	Double Concerto for piano and harpsichord	*E*
CAVALLI	Magnificat	
CROSSE, GORDON	Violin Concerto No. 2	
DVOŘÁK	Serenade in D minor	
FORBES, SEBASTIAN	Essay for clarinet and orchestra (Commissioned by the BBC)	*P*
GERHARD	Epithalamion	
	Leo	
HANDEL	Messiah	
HAYDN	Symphony No. 84, in E flat major	
	Symphony No. 87, in A major	
IVES	The Pond	*E*
	Tone Roads No. 1	*E*
	Tone Roads No. 3	*E*
LANDINI	Deh! dimmi tu	
	Ecco la primavera	
	Giunta vaga bilta	
	La bionda trecca	
	Questa fanciull' amor	
LUTYENS	Essence of our Happinesses (Commissioned by the BBC)	*P*
MESSIAEN	La Transfiguration de notre Seigneur Jésus Christ	*E*
MILNER, ANTHONY	Roman Spring	

MOZART	The Impresario
	Zaide
PERGOLESI	Stabat Mater
PIERO, MAESTRO	Con bracchi assai
PURCELL	Ode on St Cecilia's Day (1692)
RAMEAU	Hippolyte et Aricie, Acts III and IV
RAVEL	Ballet: Daphnis and Chloë (complete)
RILEY, TERRY	Keyboard Studies
SCHOENBERG	Pierrot Lunaire
	Song of the Wood Dove (Gurrelieder)
SCHUBERT	Piano Trio in B flat major (D. 898)
SOUSTER, TIM	Triple Music II (Commissioned by the BBC)	P
STRAUSS, RICHARD	Serenade in E flat major for thirteen wind instruments
STRAVINSKY	Berceuses du chat
	Pribaoutki
SULLIVAN	Excerpts from The Grand Duke
TCHAIKOVSKY	Eugene Onegin
TIPPETT	The Shire Suite
VAUGHAN WILLIAMS	Magnificat
WAGNER	Das Rheingold
	Tristan und Isolde, Act III
WEILL	The Lindbergh Flight	E
ZACHARA DA TERAMO	Rosetta

1971

ARNOLD	Symphony No. 6
BACH, C. P. E.	Magnificat
BACH, J. S.	Cantata No. 11: Lobet Gott
	Goldberg Variations
	Motet: Jesu meine Freude
	Prelude and Fugue in E flat major, S. 552 (St Anne)
BARTÓK	Duke Bluebeard's Castle
BEETHOVEN	Piano Trio in B flat major, Op. 97 (The Archduke)
BERG	Seven early songs
BERIO	Laborintus II
BOULEZ	Eclat/multiples
BRUCKNER	Symphony No. 2, in C minor
CAVALLI	La Calisto
CONNOLLY	Cinquepaces
GABRIELI, GIOVANNI	O magnum mysterium
GERHARD	Libra
HAMILTON	Piano Concerto
HAYDN	Symphony No. 64, in A major
	Symphony No. 77, in B flat major
	Symphony No. 85, in B flat major (La Reine)
HEUBERGER	Duet: In's Chambre séparée (Der Opernball)
HOLST	Capriccio
IVES	Last movement of Second Orchestral Set
JOSQUIN DES PRÉS	Ave Maria
	Veni sanctus spiritus
LEHÁR	Aria: Du bist meine Sonne! (Guiditta)

LEHÁR	Aria: Vilja (The Merry Widow)	
	Duet: Heia, Mädel, aufgeschaut (The Merry Widow)	
LIGETI	Aventures	
	Nouvelles aventures	
MESSIAEN	Poèmes pour Mi (orchestral version)	E
	Seven Haïkaï	
MONTEVERDI	Gloria à 7 voci	E
	Motets: Adoramus te Christe	
	Laetatus sum	
MOZART	Adagio in E major, K. 261, for violin and orchestra	
	Rondo in C major, K. 373, for violin and orchestra	
	Symphony No. 26, in E flat major, K. 184	
MUSGRAVE	Horn Concerto	
MUSSORGSKY	Boris Godunov	
NAYLOR	Scenes and Prophecies (Commissioned by the BBC)	P
NEWSON, GEORGE	Arena (Commissioned by the BBC)	P
PRAETORIUS	Dances from Terpsichore (1612)	
PURCELL	The Fairy Queen	
RUGGLES	Sun-treader	
SCHUBERT	Fantasia in C major (The Wanderer)	
SCHÜTZ	Ach Herr, du Schöpfer	
	Domini est terra	
	Es erhub sich	
	Ich danke dem, Herrn	
SESSIONS	Rhapsody for orchestra	
SHOSTAKOVICH	Symphony No. 14	
SMALLEY	Beat Music (Commissioned by the BBC)	P
STOCKHAUSEN	Mantra	
STRAUSS, JOHANN	Duet: One thing I never can forgive (Vienna Blood)	
STRAVINSKY	Eight Instrumental Miniatures	
	The Soldier's Tale	
	Suite: Le rossignol	
TIPPETT	Symphony No. 1	
	Songs for Dov	
WAGNER	Siegfried, Acts I and III	
WALTON	Improvisations on an Impromptu by Benjamin Britten	
WILLIAMSON	The Stern Wall (Commissioned by the BBC)	P
	Music at the Court of Spain	
	Raga (Late evening)	

1972

BACH	Cantata No. 67: Halt im Gedächtnis Jesum Christ
	Cantata No. 191: Gloria in excelsis Deo
	The Christmas Oratorio
	Concerto for oboe and violin in C minor
	Prelude and Fugue in B minor, S. 544
BERLIOZ	Benvenuto Cellini
BIRTWISTLE	Nenia on the Death of Orpheus
	Down by the Greenwood Side
BOULEZ	E. E. Cummings ist der Dichter
CAGE	First Construction in Metal

CAGE	Hpschd	E
CARDEW	The Great Learning, Paragraph One	
CARTER	Concerto for Orchestra	E
CROSSE	Celebration (Commissioned by the BBC)	P
CRUMB, GEORGE	Echoes of Time and the River	E
GABRIELI, ANDREA	Magnificat for three choirs	
GABRIELI, GIOVANNI	In ecclesiis benedicite Domino	
	Canzona noni toni	
	Canzona septimi	
	Jubilate Deo a 8 (1613)	
GIBBONS	Hosanna to the Son of David	
	The Silver Swan	
	What is our life?	
HAYDN	Orfeo ed Euridice, Act IV	
	Symphony No. 52, in C minor	
HOLLIGER	Siebengesang	
ISHII, MAKI	Kyoso	E
JANAČEK	Glagolitic Mass	
LAMBERT, JOHN	Formations and Transformations (Commissioned by the BBC)	P
LISZT	Hexameron (6 pianos and orchestra)	E
MAXWELL DAVIES	Blind Man's Buff	
MESSIAEN	Seven Haikai	E
MIYOSHI	Concerto for Orchestra	E
DE MONTE, C.	Plaude decus mundi	
MONTEVERDI	Il ritorno d'Ulisse in patria	
MOZART	Piano Quartet in G minor, K. 478	
PURCELL	King Arthur	
RAINIER, PRIAULX	Requiem	
RAWSTHORNE	Theme and Variations for two violins	
SCARLATTI, A.	Magnificat (Vespers of St Cecilia)	
SCHOENBERG	Chamber Symphony No. 1, in E, Op. 9	
SCHUBERT	Chorus of Huntsmen (Rosamunde)	
	Nachthelle	
SCHÜTZ	Psalm 100: Jauchzet dem Herren alle Welt	
STEVENSON	Piano Concerto No. 2 (The Continents) (Commissioned by the BBC)	P
STOCKHAUSEN	Carré	E
STRAUSS, JOHANN	Csárdás (Die Fledermaus)	
	Csárdás (Ritter Pásmán)	
	Galop: Banditten	
	Polka: Freikugeln	
	Spanish March	
STRAUSS, JOSEPH	Feuerfest: Polka française	
	Polka: Plappermäulchen	
	Waltz: Mein Lebenslauf ist Lieb und Lust	
STRAVINSKY	Ballet: The Firebird	
	Le Rossignol	
	Symphonies of wind instruments (original version)	
	Symphony No. 1, in E flat	
TALLIS	O Lord, give thy holy spirit	
	O sacrum convivium	
TAVENER	Celtic Requiem	

THOMSON	The Plough that Broke the Plains	
TIPPETT	Fantasia on a theme of Handel	
	Symphony No. 3	
VIVALDI	Violin Concerto in E flat major, Op. 8, No. 5 (La Tempesta di mare)	
	Concerto for two violins in A minor, Op. 3, No. 8	
	Concerto for three violins in F major	
WAGNER	Parsifal, Act I	
WALTON	Troilus and Cressida, Act II	
WEILL	Kleine Mahagonny	
ZIMMERMANN	Canto di Speranza	*E*
	Music for Maximilian I	

1973

BACH	Prelude and Fugue in D major for organ, S. 532	
BANCHIERI	Fantasia: In echo	
BARTÓK	Two Portraits, Op. 5	
BEETHOVEN	Sonatas for cello and piano:	
	Op. 102, No. 1, in C major	
	Op. 102, No. 2, in D major	
	Piano Sonata in B flat major, Op. 106 (Hammerklavier)	
BERIO	Concerto for two pianos and orchestra	
BERKELEY	Sinfonia Concertante for oboe and chamber orchestra	*P*
	(commissioned by the BBC)	
	Symphony No. 3	
BIRTWISTLE	The Triumph of Time	
BOULEZ	'. . . explosante fixe . . .'	*E*
	Structures, Book II (1961)	
BRITTEN	Gloriana	
BULL	Organ offertory: Salve Regina	
BYRD	Mass in Five Parts	
CHARPENTIER	Ouverture pour le Sacre d'un Evêque	
CROSSE	Memories of Morning: Night	
DEBUSSY	En blanc et noir	
FRESCOBALDI	Processional: Toccata Quinta	
GABRIELI	Canzona a 8	
GERHARD	Libra	
GLINKA	Overture: A Life for the Tsar	
	Finale: Act IV (A Life for the Tsar)	
HAMILTON	Amphion: Violin Concerto No. 2	
HANDEL	Concerto Grosso in G major, Op. 3, No. 3	
HAYDN	String Quartet in F major, Op. 77, No. 2	
	Symphony No. 60, in C major (Il distratto)	
HINDEMITH	Mass	
HOLST	Hammersmith: Prelude and Scherzo	
LAPPI	Canzona: La Serafina	
LECLAIR	Violin Concerto in A major, Op. 10, No. 2	
LEFANU	The Hidden Landscape (commissioned by the BBC)	*P*
LIGETI	Chamber Concerto	
LOCKE	Music for His Majesty's Cornets and Sackbuts	
LUTYENS	De Amore	*P*
MAXWELL DAVIES	Revelation and Fall	

MENDELSSOHN	A Midsummer Night's Dream: Incidental Music, Op. 61	
MOZART	Symphony No. 21, in A major K. 134	
MUSGRAVE	Viola Concerto (commissioned by the BBC)	P
POULENC	Gloria	
PURCELL	Fantasias in 5, 6 and 7 parts for strings	
PURCELL—M. DAVIES	Fantasia and two Pavans	
RACHMANINOV	Vocalise	
	The Bells: Choral Symphony	
RAINIER	Ploërmel (commissioned by the BBC)	P
RAVEL	Three poems of Mallarmé	
ROBERT, PIERRE	Psalm: Deus noster refugium	
SCHOENBERG	Gurrelieder	
SHOSTAKOVICH	Symphony No. 15	
STRAUSS	Capriccio	
STRAVINSKY	Ballet: Apollo	
TIPPETT	Piano Sonata No. 3	
TITELOUZE	Recessional: Ave maris stella	
VARÈSE	Poème électronique	E
VAUGHAN WILLIAMS	Toward the Unknown Region	
VICTORIA	Motet: Vidi speciosam	

1974

AGRICOLA, ALEXANDER	Carmen	
ANON.	Nobilis Humilis	
ARNOLD	Concerto for flute and string orchestra	
BANKS	Prospects	E
BARTÓK	Village Scenes	
BERG	Der Wein	
BERIO	Allelujah II	
	Recital I (For Cathy)	
BIRTWISTLE	Grimethorpe Aria	
BRIAN	Festival Fanfare	
BRITTEN	Cantata Rejoice in the Lamb	
	Six Metamorphoses after Ovid	
BRUMEL	Da pacem Domine	
BYRD	Libera me de morte aeterna	
CREQUILLON	Canzon Onques amor	
CROSSE	Ariadne	
DALBY	Viola Concerto (commissioned by the BBC)	P
DUFAY	Ballade, Se la face ay pale	
	Mass, Se la face ay pale	
	Rondeau, Ce moys de may	
DVOŘÁK	Four Slavonic Dances from Op. 72	
ELGAR	Severn Suite	
GRAINGER	Brigg Fair	
	I'm seventeen come Sunday	
	A Lincolnshire Posy	
HAMILTON	Voyage for horn and orchestra	
HANDL	Missa super Undique flammatis	
HOLLOWAY	Domination of Black	

HOLST	A Moorside Suite	
	Savitri	
IVES	Decoration Day	
JANÁČEK	Katya Kabanova	
	Taras Bulba	
JOSQUIN DES PRÉS	Diligam te Domine	
LIGETI	Concerto for flute, oboe and orchestra	
LISZT	Fantasia and Fugue on the Chorale Ad nos, for organ	
MAXWELL DAVIES	Hymn to St Magnus	
	Suite The Devils	
MOUTON, JEAN	En venant de Lyons	
	Libera animam meam	
MOZART	La Clemenza di Tito	
	Per questa bella mano, K. 612	
	Fantasy in F minor, K. 608, for organ	
	Piano Quartet in E flat major, K. 493	
NIELSEN	Clarinet Concerto	
	Overture Helios	
PROKOFIEV	Symphony No. 6, in E flat minor	
RAVEL	L'Heure Espagnole	
RZEWSKI	Les Moutons de Panurge	
SCHOENBERG	Accompaniment to a Film Scene	
SENFL, LUDWIG	Lamentatio	
SMALLEY	Monody	
SOUSTER	Zorna	P
STOCKHAUSEN	Across the Boundary	
STRAUSS, JOHANN	Entrance March The Gypsy Baron	
	Im Krapfenwald'l (Cuckoo) Polka	
	Vergnügnungszug (Excursion Train) Galop	
STRAVINSKY	Ballet Jeu de cartes	
	Choral Variations on 'Vom Himmel Hoch'	
	Suites Nos. 1 and 2 for small orchestra	
TIPPETT	A Child of our Time	
	Praeludium for brass, bells and percussion	
VAUGHAN WILLIAMS	Mass in G minor	
	Ten Blake Songs	
VECCHI, ORAZIO	Saltarello detto Trivella	
VERDELOT, PHILIPPE	Da pacem Domine	
WILLIAMSON	Hammarskjöld Portrait (commissioned by the BBC)	P

1975

ANON.	Worldes Blis	
BIRTWISTLE	Two 14th-16th Century melodies	
BAINBRIDGE, SIMON	People of the Dawn	P
BARTÓK	Contrasts	
BEDFORD, DAVID	Twelve Hours of Sunset (commissioned by the BBC)	P
BENNETT, RICHARD RODNEY	Soliloquy	
BERIO	Ora	
BERKELEY	Voices of the Night	
BERNSTEIN	Overture: Candide	

BIRTWISTLE	La plage	
BLISS	Suite: Kenilworth	
BRIDGE	Two Songs (Tagore)	
BRITTEN	Missa Brevis	
	Peter Grimes	
	Suite on English Folk Tunes (A time there was), Op. 90	
BRUCKNER	Christus factus est	
	Ecce sacerdos magnus	
	Tota pulchra es	
BRUMEL, ANTOINE	Gloria from the Missa Et ecce terrae motus	
BULLER, JOHN	Finnegan's Floras	
BUXTEHUDE	Motet: Benedicam Dominum	
BYRD	Browning à 5	
	Christ rising	
	Domine quis habitabit?	
	Fantasia à 5	
	From Virgin's womb	
	Justorum animae	
	Laudate Dominum	
	Memento homo	
COOKE, ARNOLD	Cello Concerto (commissioned by the BBC)	P
COPLAND	Piano Concerto	
COWIE, EDWARD	Leviathan (commissioned by the BBC)	P
GABRIELI, G.	O quam gloriosa	
GERHARD	Cancionero de Pedrell	
	Sardana No. 1 (1946)	
GESUALDO	Ave dulcissima Maria	
GOEHR	Metamorphosis/Dance	
HAMILTON, IAIN	Epitaph for this World and Time	
HANDEL	Concerto Grosso No. 28, in F major (a due chori)	
	Silete venti	
HARRIS	Symphony No. 3	
HAYDN	Symphony No. 49, in F minor (La passione)	
	Violin Concerto in C major	
HAYNE, VAN GHISEGHEM	Chanson: De tous biens plaine	
HENZE	El Cimarrón	
	Ragtime and Habanera (Symphony for brass)	P
IRELAND	A Downland Suite	
ISAAC	Agnus Dei from the Missa La bassa danza	
	Canzona: A la bataglia	
JANÁČEK	Children's Rhymes	
JOSQUIN DES PRÉS	Credo Super de tous biens plaine	
	Fanfare: Vive le roy	
	Motet: Inviolata, integra, et casta es, Maria	
LAMBERT	Concerto for piano and nine instruments	
LISZT	Variations on a theme of Bach: Weinen, Klagen, Sorgen, Zagen, for organ	
LOCKE, MATTHEW	Music for His Majesty's Sackbuts and Cornetts	
LUTOSLAWSKI	Concerto for Orchestra	
MCCABE, JOHN	Notturni ed Alba	
MADERNA	Serenata (1954)	

MARTIN	Polyptyque
MATHIAS, WILLIAM	Laudi
MAXWELL DAVIES	Stone Litany
MESSIAEN	Transports de joie
	Versets pour la fête de la Dédicace
MOUTON, JEAN	Motet: Nesciens mater
MOZART	Adagio in F major, K. 411
MUSGRAVE	Space Play
OBRECHT	Motet: Haec Deum caeli
OCKEGHEM	Motet: Intemerata Dei mater
PALESTRINA	Assumpta est Maria
	Laudate Dominum
	Ricercare del ottavo tono
	Ricercare del primo tono
	Soave fia il morir
	Surge illuminare
PROKOFIEV	Suite: The Love of Three Oranges
RAMEAU	La Poésie from *Les Fêtes d'Hébé*
RAVEL	Suite: Le tombeau de Couperin
RUGGLES	Portals
SCHEIDT	Courant dolorosa
SCHUBERT	Mass in A flat (Missa solemnis)
SCHÜTZ	O bone Jesu, fili Mariae
	Veni Sancte Spiritus
SEARLE	Labyrinth
SIBELIUS	Scènes historiques: Suite No. 1
STOCKHAUSEN	Kontrapunkte
STRAUSS II, J.	Die Fledermaus
	Egyptian March
	Galop: Banditen
	Polka: Leichtes Blut
	Tik-Tak Polka
	Waltz: Memories of Covent Garden
STRAUSS, JOSEF	Polka: Die Libelle
STRAVINSKY	The Rake's Progress
	Three pieces for clarinet solo
TAVERNER	Magnificat à 6
TAVENER, JOHN	Últimos Ritos
TINCTORIS, JOHANNES	Kyrie from the Missa 3 Vocum
TIPPETT	Magnificat and Nunc dimittis
TYE	Mass: Westron Wynde
WALTON	Sonata for strings
WEILL	Songs from *Happy End* and from *The Threepenny Opera*

1976

ANON.	The Play of Daniel
	Salzburg Festival Mass
ARNOLD, HODDINOTT, MAW, JONES, WILLIAMS, TIPPETT	Severn Bridge Variations on a Welsh folk song
BARTÓK	Hungarian Peasant Songs

BENNETT, RICHARD RODNEY	Zodiac	*E*
BERG	Chamber Concerto	
BERIO	Chemins IV	
	Sequenza VII	
BIRTWISTLE	Meridian	
BLAKE, DAVID	Violin Concerto (commissioned by the BBC)	*P*
BRIAN, HAVERGAL	Symphony No. 9	
BRITTEN	Fanfare for St Edmundsbury	
BROWNE, JOHN	Stabat Mater	
BRUMEL	Missa Et ecce terrae motus	
BYRD	Fantasia a 6	
	Laetentur coeli	
CARTER, ELLIOTT	Sonata for flute, oboe, cello and harpsichord	
CHAPPLE, BRIAN	Scherzo for four pianos (commissioned by the BBC)	*P*
COPLAND	Quiet City	
CRUMB	Ancient Voices of Children	
DALLAPICCOLA	Commiato	
DAVIES, MAXWELL	Dark Angels	
	Eight Songs for a Mad King	
DEBUSSY	Pelléas et Mélisande	
DOSTAL	Aria: Ich bin verliebt (Clivia)	
FALLA	Ballet: The Three-Cornered Hat	
	Concerto for harpsichord and five instruments	
FRICKER, RACINE	Symphony No. 5 for organ and orchestra	
GABRIELI, G.	Canzon quatri toni	
GERSHWIN	Variations on I got rhythm	
GESUALDO	Hei mihi, Domine	
	O vos omnes	
GIBBONS	O clap your hands	
	O Lord in thy wrath	
GUY, BARRY	Songs from Tomorrow (commissioned by the BBC)	*P*
HAMILTON	Aurora	
HANDEL	As pants the hart for cooling streams	
HAYDN	Symphony No. 44, in E minor (Trauer)	
HEUBERGER	Overture: Der Opernball	
JOSQUIN DES PRÉS	Allegiez moi	
	Benedicta es coelorum Regina	
	El grillo	
	Mille regretz	
	Qui habitat	
	Scaramella	
KNUSSEN, OLIVER	Océan de terre	*E*
LIGETI	Two Etudes for organ:	
	Coulée	
	Harmonies	
LUTYENS	Music for Orchestra II	
MACKEBEN	Waltz: Münchner g'schichten	
MAHLER	Das klagende Lied	
MONTEVERDI	Deus tuorum militum	
MULDOWNEY, DOMINIC	Solo/Ensemble	

MUSGRAVE	Triptych
RAMEAU	Suite from Les Boréades
REICHA	Scène for cor anglais and orchestra
SCHÜTZ	Calicem salutaris
	Ego enim inique egi
	Ego sum tui plaga doloris
	Quid commisisti
	Quo, nate Dei
SESSIONS	Concerto for violin and cello
	Symphony No. 8
SMETANA	Aria: Wie fremd und todt (The Bartered Bride)
STRAUSS	Eine deutsche Motette
STRAVINSKY	Concerto in D, for string orchestra
SULLIVAN	Patience
SUSATO	Suite of dances from the Danserye (1551)
TAVENER	Canciones Españolas
VERDI	Falstaff
WILLIAMSON	Suite: Our Man in Havana

1977

ARNOLD	Overture: Beckus the Dandipratt	
BACH	Cantata No. 118: O Jesu Christ mein's Lebens Licht	
BALASSA	Quartet for Percussion	E
BARRAQUÉ	Chant après chant	
BARTÓK	Dance Suite	
BENNETT, RICHARD RODNEY	Actaeon for Horn and Orchestra	P
BERIO	Coro (first performance of revised version)	
BIRTWISTLE	Melencolia I	
BODY, JACK	Marvel not, Joseph	E
BOULEZ	Rituel: In memoriam Maderna	
BRITTEN	A Hymn to the Virgin	
	Cantata: Phaedra	
BULLER, JOHN	Proença (commissioned by the BBC)	P
CAMPRA	Messe des Morts	
DAVIES, MAXWELL	The Martyrdom of St Magnus	
	St Thomas' Wake: Foxtrot	
DIEPENBROCK	Marsyas: incidental music	E
DUPARC	L'invitation au voyage	
	Le manoir de Rosemonde	
	Au pays où se fait la guerre	
	La vie antérieure	
GABRIELI, G.	Buccinate in neomania	
GOEHR	Pastorals	
GRIFFITHS, DAVID	Salve Regina	
HARRIES, DAVID	The Three Men	
HAYDN	Symphony No. 57 in D major	
HENZE	The Raft of the 'Medusa'	E
JOSQUIN DES PRÉS	Tulerunt Dominum	
KEURIS, TRISTAN	Sinfonia	E
LIGETI	San Francisco Polyphony	

LISZT	Prelude and Fugue on Bach	
MESSIAEN	Couleurs de la cité céleste	
	Oiseaux exotiques	
MEWS, DOUGLAS	The May Magnificat	
MOZART	Serenade No. 11 in E flat major (K. 375)	
MUSGRAVE, THEA	Rorate coeli	
PARSONS, ROBERT	Ave Maria	
PROKOFIEV	Symphony No. 3 in C minor	
PURCELL	Hail bright Cecilia: a song for St Cecilia's Day, 1692	
REUBKE	Sonata on the 94th Psalm	
ROXBURGH, EDWIN	Montage (commissioned by the BBC)	P
SCHOENBERG	Chamber Symphony No. 1	
SCHUBERT'	Overture in C minor	
	Quintet in A major (The Trout)	
SCHUMANN	Four Songs, Op. 141	
SCHÜTZ	Ich beschwöre euch	
	Wie lieblich sind deine Wohnungen	
SHOSTAKOVICH	Symphony No. 4	
STANFORD	Magnificat for double choir	
STOCKHAUSEN	Adieu	
STRAUSS, JOSEF	Polka: Eingesendet	
	Polka: Plappermäulchen	
STRAUSS	Songs: Zueignung	
	Ruhe, meine seele	
	Waldseligkeit	
	Wiegenlied	
	Meinem Kinde	
	Befreit	
SULLIVAN arr. MACKERRAS	Suite from the Ballet: Pineapple Poll	
TIPPETT	The Midsummer Marriage	
XENAKIS	Phlegra	

1978

BACH	Cantata: Christ lag in Todesbanden
BARBER	Mutations on Bach
BEETHOVEN	Piano Sonata in E flat major, Op. 7
BERKELEY	Symphony No. 4
BUXTEHUDE	Mit Fried und Freud ich fahr dahin (Funeral music)
CONNOLLY, JUSTIN	Diaphony for organ and orchestra (commissioned by the BBC)
COWIE, EDWARD	Piano Concerto
CROSSE, GORDON	Some Marches on a Ground
DALLAPICCOLA	Tre poemi
DAVIES, MAXWELL	Symphony
DEBUSSY	Syrinx
FERNEYHOUGH, BRIAN	Missa Brevis
GESUALDO	Dolcissima mia vita arr. Stravinsky
	Assumpta est Maria
GLUCK	Orfeo
HAMILTON, IAIN	Scena: Cleopatra
HARPER, EDWARD	Seven poems by e. e. cummings
HAYDN	Cello Concerto in C major

HINDEMITH	Der Schwanendreher: concert for viola and orchestra	
HOLLOWAY, ROBIN	Romanza for violin and orchestra	P
IVES	From the steeples and mountains	
JANÁČEK	Mládí (Youth): wind sextet	
LIGETI	Volumina	
LISZT	Oratorio: Christus (complete)	
LUTOSLAWSKI	Mi-parti	
MARTIN, FRANK	Monologe aus Jedermann	
MESSIAEN	Quatuor pour la fin du temps	
MOZART	Davidde penitente (K. 469)	
MUSSORGSKY	A night on the bare mountain	
PACHELBEL	Cantata: Christ lag in Todesbanden	
PANUFNIK	Sinfonia di Sfere	
PURCELL	Anthem: Praise the Lord, O Jerusalem	
RACHMANINOV	Ordinary of the Vigil of the Russian Orthodox Church ('Vespers')	
RAINIER, PRIAULX	Violin Concerto	
RIMSKY-KORSAKOV arr. GLAZUNOV and STEINBERG	Suite: The Golden Cockerel	
RUGGLES, CARL	Angels	
SCHOENBERG	Die glückliche Hand: Drama with music	
SCHUBERT	Symphony No. 1	
	Psalm 23	
	Psalm 92: Lied für den Sabbath	
STOCKHAUSEN	Refrain	
	Stimmung	
	Zyklus	
STRAUSS	Symphonic poem: Macbeth	
STRAVINSKY	Ragtime	
TIPPETT	Symphony No. 4	
	Suite in D major (A Birthday Suite for Prince Charles)	
VERDI	Macbeth (original version)	
VIVALDI	Gloria in D major	
WEBERN	Concerto for nine instruments, Op. 24	
WILLIAMS, GRACE	Ballads for Orchestra	

1979

ANON.	Angelus ad Virginem	
BACH	Cantata No. 21: Ich hatte viel Bekümmernis	
	Cantata No. 30: Freue dich, erlöste Schar	
	Sinfonia from Cantata No. 42 and from Cantata No. 174	
BERIO, LUCIANO	Chemins II for viola and small orchestra	E
BIRTWISTLE, HARRISON	. . . agm . . . music for sixteen voices and three instrumental groups	E
BRITTEN	Antiphon	
	Billy Budd	
CARTER, ELLIOTT	A Symphony of Three Orchestras	
CROSSE, GORDON	Epiphany Variations	E
CRUMB, GEORGE	Star-Child	E

DALBY, MARTIN	The Tower of Victory	
DAVIES, MAXWELL	Five Klee Pictures	
	A Mirror of Whitening Light	
FAYRFAX, ROBERT	Magnificat Regale	
FORBES, SEBASTIAN	Sonata for Eight	
HARVEY, JONATHAN	I love the Lord	
HAYDN	La Fedeltà premiata	
HODDINOTT, ALAN	Organ Concerto	
HOLMBOE, VAGN	Cello Concerto	
JANÁČEK	Ballad of Blanik	
KNUSSEN, OLIVER	Symphony No. 3 (commissioned by the BBC)	P
LEIGHTON, KENNETH	Crucifixus pro nobis	
LUTOSLAWSKI	Les Espaces du sommeil	E
	Paroles tissées	
MCCABE, JOHN	Clarinet Concerto	
MARCLAND, PATRICK	Variants	E
MAW, NICHOLAS	La Vita Nuova (commissioned by the BBC)	P
MESSIAEN	Trois petites liturgies de la Présence Divine	
MONTEVERDI	Ab aeterno	
	Ardo avvampo	
	Ballo: Tirsi e Clori	
	Magnificat a 6 (1610)	
	Messa a 4 (1651)	
	Vago augeletto	
MUSSORGSKY	Pictures from an Exhibition (arranged for brass instruments by Elgar Howarth)	
PÄRT, ARVO	Cantus to the memory of Benjamin Britten	E
PAYNE, ANTHONY	The Stones and Lonely Places Sing	P
PENDERECKI	Symphony No. 1	
POULENC	Mass in G major	
RAVEL	L'Enfant et les Sortilèges	
SCHOENBERG	Variations on a recitative, Op. 40	
	Three Pieces for chamber orchestra (1910)	
SCHUMANN	Scenes from Goethe's *Faust*	
	Konzertstück in F major for piano and orchestra	
SIBELIUS	Kullervo	
STRAUSS, RICHARD	Two Songs, Op. 34	
STRAVINSKY	Four Russian Peasant Songs (1954)	
SZYMANOWSKI	Symphonie Concertante, Op. 60, for piano and orchestra	
TAL, JOSEPH	Symphony No. 3	E
TAVENER, JOHN	Settings of six Russian folk-songs for soprano and chamber ensemble	
WESLEY, S. S.	The Wilderness	
WILLIAMSON, MALCOLM	Concerto for two pianos and string orchestra	
WOOLDRIDGE, DAVID	Five Italian Songs	P
ZIMMERMANN, BERND ALOIS	Oboe concerto	

Gamelan Music with dancers

APPENDIX B
Orchestras and Conductors 1895-1979

(a) Orchestras

1895–1907
Queen's Hall

1908
Queen's Hall
New Symphony

1909–14
Queen's Hall

1915–26
The New Queen's Hall
(same orchestra,
renamed)

1927–9
Sir Henry J. Wood
and his Symphony O

1930–9
BBC Symphony

1940–1
London Symphony

1942–3
London Philharmonic
BBC Symphony

1944
London Philharmonic
London Symphony
BBC Symphony

1945–6
London Symphony
BBC Symphony

1946–7
(*winter season*)
BBC Symphony

1947
(*summer*)
BBC Symphony
London Philharmonic
London Symphony

1947–8
(*winter*)
BBC Symphony
London Symphony

1948
(*summer*)
BBC Symphony
London Symphony

1948–9
(*winter*)
BBC Symphony

1949
(*summer*)
BBC Symphony
London Philharmonic
London Symphony

1949–50
(*winter*)
BBC Symphony
London Philharmonic
London Symphony

1950
(*summer*)
BBC Symphony
London Symphony
London Philharmonic
BBC Opera O

1950–1
(*winter*)
BBC Symphony

1951
(*summer*)
BBC Symphony
London Philharmonic
London Symphony

1951–2
(*winter*)
BBC Symphony

1952
(*summer*)
BBC Symphony
London Philharmonic
London Symphony
Royal Philharmonic

1953–4
BBC Symphony
Hallé
London Philharmonic
London Symphony
Royal Philharmonic

1955
BBC Symphony
Bournemouth
  Symphony
Hallé
London Philharmonic
London Symphony
National Youth O
  of GB
Royal Philharmonic

1956
BBC Symphony
Hallé
Liverpool
  Philharmonic
London Philharmonic
London Symphony

1957
BBC Symphony
BBC Concert
London Philharmonic
London Symphony
National Youth O
  of GB
Royal Philharmonic

1958
BBC Symphony
BBC Concert

Hallé
London Philharmonic
London Symphony

1959
BBC Symphony
Hallé
London Symphony
National Youth O of GB
Royal Philharmonic

1960
BBC Symphony
London Symphony
Royal Liverpool
  Philharmonic
Royal Opera House,
  Covent Garden

1961
BBC Symphony
BBC Northern
London Philharmonic
London Symphony
Royal Philharmonic

1962
BBC Symphony
BBC Northern
BBC Scottish
London Philharmonic
London Symphony
Philharmonia
Royal Philharmonic

1963
BBC Symphony
BBC Northern
BBC Scottish
London Philharmonic
London Symphony
Philharmonia
Royal Philharmonic
Royal Opera House,
  Covent Garden

1964
BBC Symphony
BBC Northern
English Chamber
London Mozart
  Players
London Philharmonic
London Symphony
Philharmonia
Royal Liverpool
  Philharmonic
Royal Opera House,
  Covent Garden

1965
BBC Symphony
BBC Scottish
English Chamber
Hallé
London Mozart
  Players
London Philharmonic
London Symphony
Royal Opera House,
  Covent Garden
Royal Philharmonic

1966
BBC Symphony
BBC Concert
BBC Northern
English Chamber
Hallé
London Philharmonic
London Symphony
Moscow Radio
New Philharmonia
Royal Opera House,
  Covent Garden
Royal Philharmonic
Scottish National

1967
BBC Symphony
BBC Concert
BBC Scottish
  Symphony
Bournemouth
  Symphony
Amsterdam
  Concertgebouw
English Chamber
Hallé
London Bach
London Philharmonic
London Symphony
New Philharmonia
Polish Radio
  Symphony

Royal Opera House,
  Covent Garden
Royal Philharmonic

1968
BBC Symphony
BBC Concert
BBC Northern
  Symphony
Accademia
  Monteverdiana
English Chamber
Hallé
London Philharmonic
London Symphony
New Philharmonia
Royal Opera House,
  Covent Garden
Royal Philharmonic
Scottish National
State O of the USSR

1969
BBC Symphony
BBC Concert
BBC Scottish
  Symphony
Academy of
  St Martin-
  in-the-Fields
Accademia
  Monteverdiana
City of Birmingham
  Symphony
Czech Philharmonic
English Chamber
Hallé
London Philharmonic
London Sinfonietta
London Symphony
Monteverdi O
Musica Reservata
New Philharmonia
Royal Liverpool
  Philharmonic
Royal Philharmonic
Scottish National

1970
BBC Symphony
BBC Concert
BBC Northern
  Symphony
BBC Training
Academy of
  St Martin-
  in-the-Fields
Accademia
  Monteverdiana

Amsterdam
  Concertgebouw
Bournemouth
  Symphony
English Chamber
Hallé
Hurwitz Chamber
London Philharmonic
London Sinfonietta
London Symphony
Monteverdi O
New Philharmonia
Royal Opera House,
  Covent Garden
Royal Philharmonic

1971
BBC Symphony
BBC Concert
BBC Scottish
  Symphony
BBC Welsh
English Chamber
Leningrad Philharmonic
London Bach
London Philharmonic
London Sinfonietta
London Symphony
Monteverdi O
National Youth O
  of GB
New Philharmonia
Royal Liverpool
  Philharmonic
Royal Opera House,
  Covent Garden
Royal Philharmonic
Scottish National

1972
BBC Symphony
BBC Concert
BBC Northern
  Symphony
Accademia
  Monteverdiana
Bournemouth
  Symphony
English Chamber
London Bach
London Philharmonic
London Sinfonietta
London Symphony
Monteverdi O
Munich Philharmonic
NHK Symphony
New Philharmonia
Northern Sinfonia

Royal Opera House,
  Covent Garden
Royal Philharmonic
Scottish National
Steinitz Bach Players

1972–3
(*winter*)
BBC Symphony
Berlin Philharmonic
English Chamber
London Philharmonic
London String Players
London Symphony

1973
BBC Symphony
BBC Concert
BBC Northern
  Symphony
BBC Scottish
  Symphony
Accademia
  Monteverdiana
Amsterdam
  Concertgebouw
English Chamber
Richard Hickox O
London Mozart
  Players
London Philharmonic
London Sinfonietta
London Symphony
Monteverdi O
National Youth O
  of GB
New Philharmonia
Royal Liverpool
  Philharmonic
Royal Opera House,
  Covent Garden
Royal Philharmonic
Sadler's Wells
Scottish National
Serenata of London

1974
BBC Symphony
BBC Concert
BBC Northern
  Symphony
BBC Welsh
Accademia
  Monteverdiana
English Chamber
English National Opera
Hallé
London Philharmonic
London Sinfonietta

London Symphony
Los Angeles
Philharmonic
Monteverdi O
National Youth O
of GB
New Philharmonia
Royal Liverpool
Philharmonic
Royal Opera House,
Covent Garden
Royal Philharmonic
Scottish National
Sydney Symphony

1975
BBC Symphony
BBC Concert
BBC Northern
Symphony
BBC Scottish
Symphony
BBC Welsh Symphony
Academy of
St Martin-
in-the-Fields
Bournemouth
Symphony
City of Birmingham
Symphony
Cleveland O
English Chamber
English National Opera
Hallé
International Youth O
Kent Opera
London Philharmonic
London Sinfonietta
London Symphony
Menuhin Festival O
Monteverdi O
National Youth O
of GB
New Philharmonia
New York Philharmonic
Royal Opera House,
Covent Garden

1976
BBC Symphony
BBC Northern
Symphony
BBC Scottish
Symphony
BBC Welsh Symphony

English Chamber
English National Opera
Hallé
London Philharmonic
London Sinfonietta
London Symphony
Monteverdi O
National Youth O
of GB
New Philharmonia
Northern Sinfonia
Royal Liverpool
Philharmonic
Royal Opera House,
Covent Garden
Royal Philharmonic
St John's, Smith Square
Scottish National

Ensembles
Cantores et Musici
Londinenses
Chilingirian String
Quartet
The Fires of London
Heinrich Schütz
Baroque Ensemble
Kent Opera Wind
Ensemble
Lindsay String Quartet
London Philharmonic
Chamber Ensemble
London String Players
Nash Ensemble
Philip Jones
Brass Ensemble
Symphonie Sacrae

1977
BBC Symphony
BBC Northern
Symphony
BBC Scottish
Symphony
BBC Welsh Symphony
Bournemouth
Sinfonietta
Bournemouth
Symphony
City of Birmingham
Symphony
Cologne Radio
Symphony
English Chamber
Hallé

London Philharmonic
London Sinfonietta
London Symphony
Monteverdi O
National Youth O
of GB
New Philharmonia
Purcell O
Rotterdam
Philharmonic
Royal Liverpool
Philharmonic
Royal Opera House,
Covent Garden
Royal Philharmonic
St John's, Smith Square
Scottish National
Welsh Philharmonia

Ensembles
The Fires of London
London Baroque
Players
The London
Percussion Ensemble
Northern Brass
Ensemble
Philip Jones Brass
Ensemble
The Taverner Players

1978
BBC Symphony
BBC Concert
BBC Northern
Symphony
BBC Scottish
Symphony
BBC Welsh Symphony
Academy of
Ancient Music
Bournemouth
Symphony
Chicago Symphony
English Chamber
Hallé
Jeunesses Musicales
World O
London Philharmonic
London Sinfonietta
London Symphony
Monteverdi O
Northern Sinfonia
Philharmonia
Richard Hickox O

Royal Philharmonic
St John's, Smith Square

Ensembles
Ars Nova
Nash Ensemble
Philip Jones
Brass Ensemble
Singcircle

1979
BBC Symphony
BBC Concert
BBC Northern
Symphony
BBC Scottish
Symphony
BBC Welsh Symphony
The Academy of
Ancient Music
Academy of
St Martin-
in-the-Fields
Bournemouth
Symphony
English Baroque
Soloists
English Chamber
Hallé
Israel Philharmonic
London Philharmonic
London Sinfonietta
London Symphony
Musicians of London
National Youth O
of GB
New Irish Chamber
Philharmonia
Royal Liverpool
Philharmonic
Royal Philharmonic
Sasono Mulio
Gamelan of
Surakarta
Scottish Chamber
Scottish National
Welsh Philharmonia

Ensembles
Ensemble
InterContemporain
Nash Ensemble
Philip Jones
Brass Ensemble

(b) Conductors

1895–1901
Henry J. Wood

1902
Henry J. Wood
Arthur Payne

1903–7
Henry J. Wood

1908
Henry J. Wood
Edouard Colonne

1909–10
Henry J. Wood

1911–14
Sir Henry Wood

1915–26
Sir Henry Wood
(9 Oct. 1915
Thomas Beecham)

1927–40
Sir Henry Wood

1941
Sir Henry Wood
Basil Cameron

1942–4
Sir Henry Wood
Basil Cameron
Sir Adrian Boult

1945–6
Basil Cameron
Sir Adrian Boult
Constant Lambert

1946–7
(*winter season*)
Basil Cameron
Sir Adrian Boult

1947
(*summer*)
Sir Adrian Boult
Basil Cameron
Dr Malcolm Sargent
Stanford Robinson

1947–8
(*winter*)
Basil Cameron
Sir Adrian Boult
Stanford Robinson

1948
(*summer*)
Basil Cameron
Sir Malcolm Sargent
Stanford Robinson

1948–9
(*winter*)
Sir Malcolm Sargent
Stanford Robinson

1949
(*summer*)
Sir Adrian Boult
Basil Cameron
Sir Malcolm Sargent
Trevor Harvey
John Hollingsworth

1949–50
(*winter*)
Basil Cameron
Sir Malcolm Sargent
John Hollingsworth

1950
(*summer*)
Sir Malcolm Sargent
Basil Cameron
Stanford Robinson
Trevor Harvey
John Hollingsworth

1950–1
(*winter*)
Basil Cameron
Sir Malcolm Sargent

1951
(*summer*)
Sir Malcolm Sargent
Basil Cameron
Trevor Harvey
John Hollingsworth

1952
(*winter*)
Sir Malcolm Sargent
Basil Cameron

1952
(*summer*)
Sir Malcolm Sargent
Basil Cameron
Trevor Harvey
John Hollingsworth

1953–4
Sir Malcolm Sargent
Sir Adrian Boult
Sir John Barbirolli
Basil Cameron
Trevor Harvey
John Hollingsworth

1954
Sir Malcolm Sargent

Basil Cameron
Sir John Barbirolli
Sir Thomas
  Beecham Bt
Sir Adrian Boult
John Hollingsworth
Maurice Miles

1955
Sir Malcolm Sargent
Basil Cameron
Sir John Barbirolli
Sir Adrian Boult
Charles Groves
John Hollingsworth

1956
Sir Malcolm Sargent
Basil Cameron
Sir Adrian Boult
John Hollingsworth
Vilem Tausky
George Weldon

1957
Sir Malcolm Sargent
Basil Cameron
Sir Adrian Boult
John Hollingsworth
Hugo Rignold
Vilem Tausky

1958
Sir Malcolm Sargent
Basil Cameron
Sir John Barbirolli
Sir Adrian Boult
Vilem Tausky
Maurice Miles

1959
Sir Malcolm Sargent
Basil Cameron
Sir John Barbirolli
Walter Susskind
John Hollingsworth
Maurice Miles

1960
Sir Malcolm Sargent
Basil Cameron
Meredith Davies
Colin Davis
Norman Del Mar
Alexander Gibson
Sir Eugene Goossens
George Hurst
Maurice Miles
John Pritchard
Stanford Robinson

1961
Sir Malcolm Sargent
Basil Cameron
Bryan Balkwill
Sir Arthur Bliss
Sir Adrian Boult
John Carewe
Meredith Davies
Colin Davis
Reginald Goodall
Sir Eugene Goossens
George Hurst
Bernard Keeffe
Charles Mackerras
George Malcolm
John Pritchard

1962
Sir Malcolm Sargent
Basil Cameron
Lennox Berkeley
Sir Adrian Boult
John Carewe
Colin Davis
Norman Del Mar
Peter Gellhorn
George Hurst
Peter Maxwell Davies
John Pritchard
Rudolf Schwarz
Sir William Walton
David Willcocks

1963
Sir Malcolm Sargent
Basil Cameron
Lennox Berkeley
Benjamin Britten
Meredith Davies
Colin Davis
Norman Del Mar
Peter Racine Fricker
Peter Gellhorn
Carlo Maria Giulini
Charles Groves
George Hurst
George Malcolm
Luigi Nono
John Pritchard
Maurits Sillem
Georg Solti
Leopold Stokowski
Silvio Varviso
David Willcocks

1964
Sir Malcolm Sargent

Basil Cameron
William Alwyn
Sir Arthur Bliss
Sir Adrian Boult
Reginald Smith
  Brindle
Benjamin Britten
Alan Bush
John Carewe
Meredith Davies
Colin Davis
Norman Del Mar
Peter Gellhorn
Roberto Gerhard
Berthold Goldschmidt
Charles Groves
Louis Halsey
George Hurst
Rudolf Kempe
Charles Mackerras
John Pritchard
Stanford Robinson
Georg Solti
Leopold Stokowski
Vilem Tausky
David Willcocks

1965

Sir Malcolm Sargent
Malcolm Arnold
Sir John Barbirolli
Harry Blech
Pierre Boulez
Sir Adrian Boult
Colin Davis
Norman Del Mar
Antal Dorati
Lamberto Gardelli
Peter Gellhorn
Louis Halsey
Hans Werner Henze
George Hurst
Gordon Jacob
Rudolf Kempe
Istvan Kertesz
James Loughran
Charles Mackerras
John Pritchard
Alan Rawsthorne
Gennadi
  Rozhdestvensky
Martindale Sidwell
Maurits Sillem
Georg Solti
Virgil Thomson
Michael Tippett
Sir William Walton

1966

Sir Malcolm Sargent
Malcolm Arnold
Sir John Barbirolli
Gary Bertini
Sir Arthur Bliss
Pierre Boulez
Colin Davis
Norman Del Mar
Antal Dorati
Peter Gellhorn
Alexander Gibson
Hans Gierster
Bernard Haitink
Jascha Horenstein
George Hurst
Istvan Kertesz
Raymond Leppard
Charles Mackerras
George Malcolm
Roger Norrington
Frederik Prausnitz
Gennadi
  Rozhdestvensky
Gunther Schuller
Georg Solti
Leopold Stokowski
Walter Susskind

1967

Claudio Abbado
John Alldis
Sir John Barbirolli
Lennox Berkeley
Pierre Boulez
Sir Adrian Boult
Benjamin Britten
Henryk Czyz
Colin Davis
Norman Del Mar
Marcus Dods
Edward Downes
Peter Gellhorn
Charles Groves
Bernard Haitink
George Hurst
Jan Krenz
Raymond Leppard
James Loughran
Roger Norrington
Frederik Prausnitz
John Pritchard
Mario Rossi
Hans Schmidt-
  Isserstedt
Martindale Sidwell
Constantin Silvestri
Georg Solti

Denis Stevens
Karlheinz Stockhausen
Michel Tebachnik
Henry Washington

1968

Colin Davis
John Alldis
Malcolm Arnold
David Atherton
Sir John Barbirolli
Gary Bertini
Sir Arthur Bliss
Pierre Boulez
Sir Adrian Boult
Norman Del Mar
Marcus Dods
Edward Downes
John Eliot Gardiner
Peter Gellhorn
Alexander Gibson
Charles Groves
Bernard Haitink
George Hurst
Philip Ledger
Raymond Leppard
James Loughran
David Oistrakh
Frederik Prausnitz
John Pritchard
Karl Richter
Mario Rossi
Hans Schmidt-
  Isserstedt
Martindale Sidwell
Georg Solti
Denis Stevens
Evgeny Svetlanov
Sir William Walton

1969

Colin Davis
John Alldis
Malcolm Arnold
David Atherton
Sir John Barbirolli
John Beckett
Luciano Berio
Sir Arthur Bliss
Pierre Boulez
Sir Adrian Boult
Russell Burgess
Alan Bush
Meredith Davies
Peter Maxwell Davies
Norman Del Mar
Marcus Dods
Christoph von
  Dohnányi

Antal Dorati
Edward Downes
John Eliot Gardiner
Peter Gellhorn
Alexander Gibson
Reginald Goodall
Charles Groves
Bernard Haitink
Jascha Horenstein
Michael Howard
Eliahu Inbal
Zdenek Kosler
Raymond Leppard
James Loughran
Lorin Maazel
Charles Mackerras
Václav Neumann
Reinhard Peters
André Previn
Mario Rossi
Hans Schmidt-
  Isserstedt
Rudolf Schwarz
Denis Stevens
Walter Susskind

1970

Colin Davis
Malcolm Arnold
David Atherton
Serge Baudo
Pierre Boulez
Sir Adrian Boult
Justin Connolly
Meredith Davies
Norman Del Mar
Edward Downes
Lawrence Foster
John Eliot Gardiner
Peter Gellhorn
Reginald Goodall
Charles Groves
Bernard Haitink
Jascha Horenstein
Michael Howard
Elgar Howarth
George Hurst
Emanuel Hurwitz
Eugen Jochum
Raymond Leppard
James Loughran
Charles Mackerras
Neville Marriner
David Munrow
Gervase de Peyer
Frederik Prausnitz
André Previn
John Pritchard

Stanford Robinson
Michael Rose
Christopher Seaman
Georg Solti
Denis Stevens
Bryden Thomson
Sir Michael Tippett
Edo de Waart

1971
Colin Davis
Malcolm Arnold
David Atherton
Daniel Barenboim
Luciano Berio
Pierre Boulez
Sir Adrian Boult
Benjamin Britten
Andrew Davis
Norman Del Mar
Edward Downes
Lawrence Foster
Rafael Frühbeck
  de Burgos
John Eliot Gardiner
Alexander Gibson
Charles Groves
Bernard Haitink
Irwin Hoffman
Jascha Horenstein
Michael Howard
Erich Leinsdorf
Raymond Leppard
James Loughran
Charles Mackerras
Evgeny Mravinsky
Thea Musgrave
Roger Norrington
Frederik Prausnitz
John Pritchard
Stanford Robinson
Mario Rossi
Gennadi
  Rozhdestvensky
Martindale Sidwell
August Wenzinger

1972
Pierre Boulez
Gilbert Amy
David Atherton
Daniel Barenboim
Sir Adrian Boult
Cornelius Cardew
Andrew Davis
Colin Davis
Norman Del Mar
Richard Dufallo
Harold Farberman

Lawrence Foster
John Eliot Gardiner
Peter Gellhorn
Alexander Gibson
Charles Groves
Bernard Haitink
George Hurst
Elmer Iseler
Hiroyuki Iwaki
Rudolf Kempe
Bernhard Klee
Philip Ledger
Erich Leinsdorf
Raymond Leppard
James Loughran
Charles Mackerras
George Malcolm
Peter Maxwell Davies
Kenneth Montgomery
André Previn
John Pritchard
Stanford Robinson
Christopher Seaman
Martindale Sidwell
Paul Steinitz
Denis Stevens
Michel Tabachnik
Bryden Thomson
Michael Tilson
  Thomas
Sir Michael Tippett
Lukas Vis
Stephen Wilkinson
Hans Zender
Pinchas Zukerman

1972–3
(winter)
Pierre Boulez
John Pritchard
Charles Mackerras
Lorin Maazel
Bernard Haitink
John Alldis
Herbert von
  Karajan
Roger Norrington
Sir Adrian Boult

1973
Pierre Boulez
John Alldis
Daniel Barenboim
Sir Adrian Boult
Peter Maxwell Davies
Andrew Davis
Colin Davis
Norman Del Mar
Marcus Dods

Antal Dorati
Janos Fürst
John Eliot Gardiner
Alexander Gibson
Sir Charles Groves
Bernard Haitink
Richard Hickox
John Hoban
Michael Howard
Elgar Howarth
François Huybrechts
Bernhard Klee
Raymond Leppard
James Lockhart
James Loughran
Leon Lovett
Charles Mackerras
Bruno Maderna
Thea Musgrave
John Poole
André Previn
John Pritchard
Christopher Seaman
Sir Georg Solti
Denis Stevens

1974
Pierre Boulez
David Atherton
Steuart Bedford
Luciano Berio
Sir Adrian Boult
Boris Brott
Peter Maxwell Davies
Andrew Davis
Colin Davis
Norman Del Mar
Lawrence Foster
John Eliot Gardiner
Alexander Gibson
Sir Charles Groves
Bernard Haitink
Michael Howard
Elgar Howarth
Rudolf Kempe
Michael Lankester
Ashley Lawrence
Raymond Leppard
James Loughran
Leon Lovett
Charles Mackerras
Diego Masson
Zubin Mehta
Willem van Otterloo
John Poole
Simon Preston
André Previn
John Pritchard

Christopher Seaman
Denis Stevens

1975
Pierre Boulez
Colin Davis
Claudio Abbado
David Atherton
Steuart Bedford
Paavo Berglund
Sir Adrian Boult
Boris Brott
Aaron Copland
Andrew Davis
Norman Del Mar
Michael Dobson
Mark Elder
Louis Frémaux
John Eliot Gardiner
Sir Charles Groves
George Guest
Bernard Haitink
Vernon Handley
Elgar Howarth
Gordon Kember
Rudolf Kempe
Bernhard Klee
Ashley Lawrence
Raymond Leppard
James Loughran
Lorin Maazel
Charles Mackerras
Neville Marriner
Yehudi Menuhin
Harry Mortimer
David Munrow
Roger Norrington
John Poole
John Pritchard
Christopher Seaman
Sir Michael Tippett
Stephen Wilkinson
Kerry Woodward

1976
Pierre Boulez
Andrew Davis
Colin Davis
Christopher Adey
David Atherton
Simon Bainbridge
Gary Bertini
Wilfried Boettcher
Sir Adrian Boult
Boris Brott
John Carewe
Nicholas Cleobury
Peter Maxwell Davies
Andrew Davis

Antal Dorati
Edward Downes
Mark Elder
Lawrence Foster
Lionel Friend
Rafael Frühbeck
  de Burgos
John Eliot Gardiner
Alexander Gibson
Sir Charles Groves
Bernard Haitink
Raymond Leppard
James Loughran
John Lubbock
Charles Mackerras
Riccardo Muti
Roger Norrington
John Poole
John Pritchard
Simon Rattle
Ole Schmidt
Christopher Seaman
Walter Susskind
Vilem Tausky
John Tavener
Hans Vonk
David Wulstan

1977
Pierre Boulez
Charles Mackerras
Claudio Abbado
Richard Armstrong
David Atherton
Steuart Bedford
Paavo Berglund
Luciano Berio
Sir Adrian Boult

Boris Brott
Nicholas Cleobury
Andrew Davis
Colin Davis
Peter Maxwell Davies
Norman Del Mar
Edo De Waart
Mark Elder
Louis Frémaux
Lionel Friend
John Eliot Gardiner
Alexander Gibson
Peter Godfrey
Sir Charles Groves
Bernard Haitink
Elgar Howarth
James Loughran
John Lubbock
Kenneth Montgomery
Riccardo Muti
Christopher Nicholls
Roger Norrington
Andrew Parrott
Murray Perahia
Simon Rattle
Christopher Seaman
Walter Susskind
Hans Vonk
Stephen Wilkinson
Kerry Woodward

1978
Gennadi
  Rozhdestvensky
Pierre Boulez
Michael Gielen
Charles Mackerras
John Alldis

David Atherton
Serge Baudo
Boris Brott
Andrew Davis
Norman Del Mar
Lawrence Foster
Lionel Friend
John Eliot Gardiner
Sir Charles Groves
Bernard Haitink
Richard Hickox
Christopher Hogwood
Raymond Leppard
James Loughran
John Lubbock
John Matheson
Riccardo Muti
John Poole
Simon Preston
Simon Rattle
Karl Anton
  Rickenbacher
Gregory Rose
Christopher Seaman
Sir Georg Solti
Walter Susskind
Brian Wright
Hans Zender

1979
Gennadi
  Rozhdestvensky
Michael Gielen
Sir Charles Mackerras
Claudio Abbado
Richard Armstrong
David Atherton
Daniel Barenboim

John Beckett
Paavo Berglund
Pierre Boulez
Iona Brown
Colin Davis
Norman Del Mar
Edward Downes
Mark Elder
Peter Eötvös
Lionel Friend
Sebastian Forbes
Lawrence Foster
Janos Fürst
John Eliot Gardiner
Sir Alexander Gibson
Sir Charles Groves
Bernard Haitink
Günter Herbig
Malcolm Hicks
Christopher Hogwood
Elgar Howarth
Michael Lankester
James Loughran
Witold Lutosławski
Zubin Mehta
Riccardo Muti
Martin Neary
John Poole
Simon Preston
Simon Rattle
Howard Snell
Bryden Thomson
Michael Tilson Thomas
Sir Michael Tippett
Tamás Vásáry
Walter Weller
Brian Wright

APPENDIX C
Some typical programmes and repertoires*

From 1896

Saturday, September 19th

PART I

Ballet music from *Colomba*	A. C. MACKENZIE
Recit. and Aria: Ah! che assorta	VENZANI

MISS EVANGELINE FLORENCE

Recit. and Aria: Lend me your aid (*Irene*)	GOUNOD

MR HERBERT GROVER

Hymne à Sainte Cécile	GOUNOD

Solo violin: MR ARTHUR W. PAYNE
Grand organ: MR PERCY PITT

Cornet Solo: Si tu m'aimais	DENZA

MR HOWARD REYNOLDS

Rhapsody No. 4	LISZT
Violin Solo: All'Ungherese	LISZT-WITHELMJ

PERCY FROSTICK

Suite: The Language of Flowers	FREDERICK COWEN
No. 2 Lilac: First emotions of love	
No. 5 Yellow Jasmine: Elegance of Grace	
Song: The Wolf	SHIELD

MR CHARLES SANTLEY

Slavonic Dance (*Le Roi malgré lui*)	CHABRIER

(First performance in England)

PART II

Grand Fantasia: Carmen	BIZET
Song: The Queen's Shilling	ELLEN WRIGHT

MR CHARLES SANTLEY

*A few other examples, including the very first programme of 1895, are given in the main text.

Fest-Marsch .... CYRIL KISTLER
(First performance in England)
Song: Lo! here the gentle lark .... BISHOP

MISS EVANGELINE FLORENCE
Flute obbligato: MR ALBERT FRANSELLA

Cornet Quartet: Polka de Paris .... LEVY

THE PARK SISTERS

Song: My Queen

MR HERBERT GROVER

Marche Romaine .... GOUNOD

Monday, September 21st – Wagner Night
PART I

A Faust Overture .... WAGNER
Siegfried Idyll .... WAGNER
Elsa's Dream (*Lohengrin*) .... WAGNER

MADAME FANNY MOODY

Symphonic poem: Les Préludes (repeated by desire) .... LISZT
Overture: Die Feen (*The Fairies*) .... WAGNER
The King's Prayer (Lohengrin) .... WAGNER

MR CHARLES MANNERS

Ride of the Valkyries (*Die Walküre*) .... WAGNER
Good Friday Music (*Parsifal*) .... WAGNER
Siegfried's Death-March (*Götterdämmerung*) .... WAGNER
Symphonic Poem No. 2: Tasso–Lamento e Trionfo .... LISZT

PART II

Grand Fantasia: The Gondoliers .... SULLIVAN
Song: Mia Piccirella (*Salvator Rosa*) .... GOMEZ

MADAME FANNY MOODY

Cornet Quartet: Once again .... SULLIVAN

THE PARK SISTERS

Song: A hundred fathoms deep .... JUDE

MR CHARLES MANNERS

Solo Cornet: Non è ver .... TITO MATTEI

MR HOWARD REYNOLDS

March: Gablenz .... STRAUSS

Tuesday, September 22nd
PART I

Overture: William Tell .... ROSSINI

Largo in G (for solo violin, harp and organ) .... HANDEL

Solo violin: MR ARTHUR W. PAYNE
Solo harp: MISS MIRIAM TIMOTHY
Grand organ: MR PERCY PITT

Songs: (a) Ye Banks and Braes o' Bonnie Doon
      (b) O whistle and I'll come to you, my lad

MISS ISABEL MACDOUGALL

Overture: Tannhäuser .... WAGNER
Song: The Message .... BLUMENTHAL

MR HERBERT GROVER

Suite No. 1: Peer Gynt (*by desire*) .... GRIEG
Cornet Quartet: Serenade .... SCHUBERT

THE PARK SISTERS

Rhapsody No. 4 .... LISZT
Shepherd's Call .... H. BUNNING
Song: Scots wha hae

MR CHARLES SANTLEY

Three Dances (*Henry VIII*) .... EDWARD GERMAN

PART II
Grand Fantasia: H.M.S. Pinafore .... SULLIVAN
Song: The deil's awa wi' the Exciseman

MR CHARLES SANTLEY

Cornet Solo: When other lips (*The Bohemian Girl*) .... BALFE

MR HOWARD REYNOLDS

Song: Cam ye by Athol .... arr. by LAWRIE

MISS ISABEL MACDOUGALL

Serenata for Strings .... ALLAN MACBETH
      (*First performance in London*)
Song: My dream .... TOSTI

MR HERBERT GROVER

Valse (*Faust Ballet*) .... ERNEST FORD

Wednesday, September 23rd

MUSICAL DEVELOPMENT DURING THE REIGN OF H.M. THE QUEEN

PART I

God save the Queen .... arr by SIR MICHAEL COSTA
Overture: Britannia .... A. C. MACKENZIE
Coronation March (*Specially composed for this occasion*) .... PERCY PITT
A Hymn of Praise (Lobgesang) .... MENDELSSOHN

1st soprano: MADAME FANNY MOODY
2nd soprano: MISS ISABEL MACDOUGALL

Tenor: MR BEN DAVIES
Specially selected Choir of 400 voices and Choir Boys from
the London Training School for Choristers

PART II

Grand Fantasia: Tannhäuser	WAGNER
Song: The Two Grenadiers	SCHUMANN

MR CHARLES MANNERS

Cornet Solo: Should auld acquaintance

MR HOWARD REYNOLDS

Song: Swallow Song (*Esmeralda*)	GORING THOMAS

MADAME FANNY MOODY

Song: Yes! let me like a soldier fall	WALLACE

MR BEN DAVIES

Violin Solo: Reverie	VIEUXTEMPS

PERCY FROSTICK

Song: Pretty Polly Oliver

MISS ISABEL MACDOUGALL

Cornet Quartet: The Lost Chord	SULLIVAN

THE PARK SISTERS

Song: I'm a roamer (*Son and Stranger*)	MENDELSSOHN

MR CHARLES MANNERS

Valse-Ballabile (*Suite de Ballet*)	ALBERT RENAUD

From 1904

Saturday, August 20th – Popular Night

PART I

Suite de Ballet No. 1	GLUCK–MOTTL
Symphonic Dance in A	GRIEG
'Divinités du Styx'	GLUCK
Prelude 'L'Après-Midi d'un Faune'	CLAUDE DEBUSSY
(*First performance in England*)	
Symphony No. 1, in D minor, for Organ and Orchestra	GUILMANT
Overture: 'Tannhäuser'	WAGNER
Funeral March of a Marionette	GOUNOD
'O Tu Palermo'	VERDI
Largo in G	HANDEL

Solo violin: MR HENRI VERBRUGGHEN
Solo harp: MR ALFRED KASTNER
Grand organ: MR F. B. KIDDLE

Military March in D 'Pomp and Circumstance'	ELGAR

PART II

Grand Fantasia 'Lucia di Lammermoor'	DONIZETTI
'The Enchantress'	HATTON
Grand Organ Solo: Prelude and Fugue in A minor	BACH
'The Lads of Donegal'	ERIC BARING
March 'Washington Post'	SOUSA

MISS ETHEL HIRSCHBEIN
(Her first appearance at these Concerts)
MR FREDERICK RANALOW
Grand organ solos: MR H. C. TONKING

Monday, August 22nd – Wagner Night

PART I

Good Friday Music (*Parsifal*)	WAGNER
Introduction to Act III (*Tannhäuser*) – Original version	WAGNER
'Senta's Ballad' (*Flying Dutchman*)	WAGNER
Klingsor's Magic Garden and Flower Maidens' Chorus (*Parsifal*)	WAGNER
Ride of the Valkyries (*Die Walküre*)	WAGNER
Introduction to Act III (*Tristan und Isolde*)	WAGNER

Cor Anglais solo: MR H. H. STANISLAUS

'Lohengrin's Narration' (*Lohengrin*)	WAGNER
Prelude 'Lohengrin'	WAGNER
Huldigungsmarsch	WAGNER

PART II

Grand Fantasia: 'Les Huguenots'	MEYERBEER
'She Wandered down the Mountain Side'	CLAY
'From Boyhood Trained' (*Oberon*)	WEBER
March 'Hoch Hapsburg'	KRAL

MADAME EMILY SQUIRE
MR H. EVAN WILLIAMS
Cor Anglais solo: MR H. H. STANISLAUS

Tuesday, August 23rd – Popular Night

PART I

Overture: 'Benvenuto Cellini'	BERLIOZ
Dream Pantomime (*Hänsel und Gretel*)	HUMPERDINCK
(a) 'Where Corals Lie' } (*Sea Pictures*) (b) 'The Swimmer'	ELGAR
Concerto in C major, Op. 20, for 'Cello and Orchestra	EUGEN D'ALBERT
Carnival Overture	DVOŘÁK
Alt Heidelberg du feine, A Spring Poem for Orchestra	FRITZ VOLBACH
(First performance in England)	
'Lohengrin's Narration'	WAGNER
Prelude 'Lohengrin'	WAGNER

Hymne à Sainte Cécile .... GOUNOD

Solo violin: MR HENRI VERBRUGGHEN
Solo harp: MR ALFRED KASTNER
Grand organ: MR PERCY PITT

Overture: '1812' .... TCHAIKOVSKY

PART II

Grand Fantasia: 'H.M.S. Pinafore' .... SULLIVAN
'Love's Despair' .... ALLITSEN
Violoncello Solos (a) 'Romanze' .... MACDOWELL
                (b) 'Serenade' .... VICTOR HERBERT
'An Evening Song' .... BLUMENTHAL
March 'Forward' .... DOPPLER

MISS ADELAIDE LAMBE
MR HAROLD WILDE
Solo violoncello: MR HERBERT WITHERS

Wednesday, August 24th – Tchaikovsky Night

PART I

Symphony No. 4, in F minor .... TCHAIKOVSKY
'Far greater in his lowly state' .... GOUNOD
Violin Concerto .... TCHAIKOVSKY
'Pilgrim's Song' .... TCHAIKOVSKY
Overture: 'Le Voyevode' .... TCHAIKOVSKY

PART II

Grand Fantasia: 'Der Vogelhändler' .... ZELLER
'Slave Song' .... TERESA DEL RIEGO
Violin Solo 'Zigeunerweisen' .... SARASATE
'An Indian Brave's Song' .... ERIC BARING
March 'Liberty Hall' .... SOUSA

MISS WINIFRED LUDLAM
MR FREDERICK RANALOW
Solo violin: MISS MARIAN JAY

Thursday, August 25th – Popular Night

PART I

Overture: 'Zampa' .... HÉROLD
Hungarian Rhapsody No. 2, in D minor and G major .... LISZT
'Roberto, o tu che adoro' (*Roberto il Diavolo*) .... MEYERBEER
Concerto in D minor for Violoncello and Orchestra .... JULES DE SWERT
Overture: 'Hänsel und Gretel' .... HUMPERDINCK
Ballet Music 'Rosamunde' .... SCHUBERT
Wotan's Abschied und Feuerzauber (*Die Walküre*) .... WAGNER
Overture: 'Tannhäuser' .... WAGNER

PART II

Grand Fantasia: 'Cavalleria Rusticana' .... MASCAGNI
'A Song of Thanksgiving' .... ALLITSEN

Cornet Solo 'The Flight of Ages' .... BEVAN
'Don Juan's Serenade'.. TCHAIKOVSKY
Valse 'España' .... WALDTEUFEL

MISS CHRISTINE BYWATER
MR ROBERT MAITLAND
Solo violoncello: MR JACQUES RENARD
Solo cornet: MR HARRY BRYAN

Friday, August 26th: Mozart–Beethoven Night

PART I

Overture: 'Magic Flute' .... MOZART
Overture: 'Nozze de Figaro' .... MOZART
'Non temer' .... MOZART
Overture: 'Don Giovanni' .... MOZART
Wanderer Fantasie, for Pianoforte and Orchestra .... SCHUBERT–LISZT
'Oh! Cara Immagine' (*Il Flauto Magico*) .... MOZART
Symphony No. 7, in A .... BEETHOVEN

PART II

Grand Fantasia: 'Mikado' .... SULLIVAN
'Villanelle' .... E. DELL'ACQUA
Pianoforte Solo: Rhapsodie, No. 11 .... LISZT
'When the World is Fair' .... COWEN
Marche Hongroise (*Faust*) .... BERLIOZ

MISS LILLIE WORMALD
MR JOHN HARRISON
Solo pianoforte: MR HERBERT PARSONS

From 1912

Saturday, August 31st

PART I

Overture: Der Freischütz .... WEBER
Two Songs Without Words (a) Spring Song ⎫
                         (b) The Bee's Wedding ⎬ .... MENDELSSOHN
Aria: 'Softly sighs' (*Der Freischütz*) .... WEBER
Waldweben (Forest Murmurs) (*Siegfried*) .... WAGNER
Symphonic Poem 'La Jeunesse d'Hercule' .... SAINT-SAËNS
Pizzicato (*Sylvia*) .... DÉLIBES
Theme and Variations (Suite No. 3, in G) .... TCHAIKOVSKY
Humoreske .... DVOŘÁK
Recit. and Aria 'O vision entrancing' (*Esmeralda*) .... GORING THOMAS
Menuet des Follets ⎫
Danse des Sylphes ⎬ (*Faust*) .... BERLIOZ
Marche Hongroise ⎭

PART II

Waltz (*Der Rosenkavalier*) .... RICHARD STRAUSS
Bassoon Solo: Lucy Long .... FRED. GODFREY

March from *The Crown of India* .... ELGAR

MISS ESTA D'ARGO
MR HUBERT EISDELL
(His first appearance at these Concerts)
Solo bassoon: MR WILFRED JAMES
(of the Queen's Hall Orchestra)

Monday, September 2nd
PART I

Prelude to Act III (*Die Meistersinger*)	WAGNER
Prelude: Lohengrin	WAGNER
(a) Elizabeth's Prayer } (*Tannhäuser*)	WAGNER
(b) Elizabeth's Greeting	
Siegfried Idyll	WAGNER
Overture: Tannhäuser	WAGNER
Prelude to Act III (*Tristan und Isolde*)	WAGNER

Cor Anglais solo: MR JAMES MCDONAGH

Overture: Rienzi	WAGNER
Entrance of the Gods into Walhalla (*Das Rheingold*)	WAGNER
Wotan's Abschied und Feuerzauber (*Die Walküre*)	WAGNER

PART II

Symphonic Dance in A	GRIEG
Malagueña (*Boabdil*)	MOSZKOWSKI

MISS CARRIE TUBB
MR THORPE BATES

Tuesday, September 3rd
PART I

Overture: Hänsel und Gretel	HUMPERDINCK
Suite: Carmen	BIZET
Recit. and Aria: 'O love, from thy power' (*Samson and Delilah*)	SAINT-SAËNS
Five Orchestral Pieces	ARNOLD SCHÖNBERG

(First performance in England)

Concerto in A minor for Pianoforte and Orchestra	GRIEG
Two Hungarian Dances in G minor and D	BRAHMS
New Songs with Orchestra (a) 'Sigh no more, ladies' }	W. A. AIKIN
(b) Sonnet XVIII	
Huldigungsmarsch	WAGNER

PART II

Comedy Overture: The Pierrot of the Minute	BANTOCK
Entr'acte and Valse (*Coppélia*)	DÉLIBES

MISS VIOLET OPPENSHAW
MR GERVASE ELWES
Solo pianoforte: MR SYDNEY ROSENBLOOM
(His first appearance at these Concerts)

Wednesday, September 4th

PART I

Overture: Le Nozze di Figaro .... MOZART
Norwegian Rhapsody .... LALO
Songs with Orchestra (a) 'Lusinghe più care' ⎫ .... HANDEL
                        (b) A Pastorale   ⎬ .... CAREY
'Mock Morris', for Strings .... PERCY GRAINGER
(First performance at these Concerts)
Concerto No. 3, in C minor, for Pianoforte and Orchestra .... BEETHOVEN
Aria: 'Cielo è mar' (*La Gioconda*) .... PONCHIELLI
Symphony No. 3, in A minor ('Scotch') .... MENDELSSOHN

PART II

Overture: Iphigenia in Aulis .... GLUCK
Danze Piemontesi No. 2, in G.. SINIGAGLIA

MISS ADA FORREST
MR JOHN ROBERTS
(His first appearance at these Concerts)
Solo pianoforte: MR ISADOR EPSTEIN

Thursday, September 5th

PART I

Overture: William Tell .... ROSSINI
Aria: 'Batti, batti' (*Don Giovanni*) .... MOZART
Suite: Peer Gynt .... GRIEG
Music-Pictures (Group III) .... J. H. FOULDS
(First performance)
Concerto No. 3, in B minor, for Violin and Orchestra .... SAINT-SAËNS
Intermezzo (*Cavalleria Rusticana*) .... MASCAGNI
Aria: 'Largo al factotum' (*Il Barbiere di Siviglia*) .... ROSSINI
Overture: Mireille .... GOUNOD

PART II

Overture: Patrie .... BIZET
Marche du Cid .... MASSENET

MISS HELEN HENSCHEL
(Her first appearance at these Concerts)
MR PETER DAWSON
Solo violin: MR HUGO HUNDT
(Of the Queen's Hall Orchestra)

Friday, September 6th

PART I

Overture: King Stephen .... BEETHOVEN
Recit. and Aria: 'Non più di fiori' (*Titus*) .... MOZART

Corno di Bassetto Obbligato: MR F. GOMEZ

Concerto No. 17, in E flat, for Two Pianofortes and Orchestra .... MOZART
  (No. 10, B. & H.)

Recit. and Aria: 'From my eyes salt tears are streaming" .... BACH
  (From the *Church Cantata*, No. 21)
Symphony No. 3, in E flat (Eroica)... BEETHOVEN

PART II

Overture: The Bartered Bride.. SMETANA
Overture: Le Roi d'Ys... LALO

MISS MYRA DIXON
MR GERVASE ELWES
Pianists: MR CECIL BAUMER and
MISS RACHEL DUNN
(*Her first appearance at these Concerts*)

From 1915

Saturday Evening, October 9th

Conductor
Mr Thomas Beecham

PART I

Overture: Oberon .... WEBER
Mignon's Song, 'Connais-tu le pays?' (*Mignon*) .... AMBROISE THOMAS
Suite: Peer Gynt .... GRIEG
Introduction and Rondo Capriccioso for Violin and Orchestra .... SAINT-SAËNS
Symphonic Poem: 'With the Wild Geese' .... HAMILTON HARTY
(*Conducted by the Composer*)
Prologue (*Pagliacci*)... LEONCAVALLO
Symphonic Poem: Thamar .... BALAKIREV
Marche Hongroise (*Faust*) .... BERLIOZ

PART II

Valse Triste.. SIBELIUS
Marche Héroïque .... SAINT-SAËNS
French National Anthem – La Marseillaise

MISS CARMEN HILL
MR CHARLES TREE
Solo violin: MR ARTHUR BECKWITH

Tuesday Evening, October 12th

Conductor
Sir Henry Wood

PART I

Hungarian Rhapsody No. 2, in D minor and G .... LISZT
Largo in G .... HÄNDEL

Solo violin: MR ARTHUR BECKWITH
Solo harp: MR ARTHUR JONES
Organ: MR FREDK. B. KIDDLE

The Jewel Song (*Faust*) .... GOUNOD

Ballet Egyptien .... LUIGINI
Symphonic Poem ('Les Djinns') for Pianoforte and Orchestra .... CÉSAR FRANCK
Solemn Melody for Organ and Strings .... WALFORD DAVIES

Solo violoncello: MR C. WARWICK-EVANS
Organ: MR FREDK. B. KIDDLE

Aria: 'Onaway! awake, beloved' (*Hiawatha*) .... COLERIDGE-TAYLOR
Symphonic Variations: Istar .... D'INDY
Carillon: 'Chantons, Belges, Chantons' .... ELGAR

PART II

Fêtes (No. 2, from Three Nocturnes for Orchestra) .... DEBUSSY
Japanese National Anthem

MISS LOUISE DALE
MR JOSEPH CHEETHAM
Recitation: MME TITA BRAND CAMMAERTS
Solo pianoforte: MOISEIWITSCH

From 1921

Saturday, October 8th

Overture: Tannhäuser .... WAGNER
Præludium .... JÄRNEFELT
Vocal Scena: Adonaïs .... LANDON RONALD
Gavotte: Mignon .... AMBROISE THOMAS
Rhapsodie Espagnole for Pianoforte and Orchestra .... LISZT–BUSONI
Suite: King Christian II .... SIBELIUS
Barcarola: Sulla poppa (*La Prigione d'Edimburgo*) .... RICCI
Symphonic Poem: Danse Macabre .... SAINT-SAËNS
(a) Moresque (Dance Interlude) ⎰
(b) Valsette (Wood-Nymphs) ⎱ .... ERIC COATES
(Conducted by the Composer)
Bassoon Solo: Lucy Long .... arr. by FREDERICK GODFREY
Marche Slave .... TCHAIKOVSKY

MISS LOUISE TRENTON
MR HERBERT HEYNER
Solo pianoforte: MR WILLIAM MURDOCH
Solo bassoon: MR WILFRED JAMES

Monday, October 10th

'MASTERSINGERS' Selections

Prelude: The Mastersingers .... WAGNER
Aria: Elizabeth's Prayer (*Tannhäuser*) .... WAGNER
Hans Sachs' Monologue (*Mastersingers*) .... WAGNER
Trial Songs (a) By Silent Hearth (*Mastersingers*) ⎰
             (b) Now begin ⎱ .... WAGNER
The Siegfried Idyll .... WAGNER
Albumblatt in A, for Solo Violin and Orchestra .... WAGNER

Solo violin: MR CHARLES WOODHOUSE

Duet: Good evening, Master (*Mastersingers*) .... WAGNER
Introduction to Act III ⎫
Dance of the Apprentices ⎪
Procession of the Masters ⎬ (*Mastersingers*) .... WAGNER
Homage to Sachs ⎭
Overture: The Wasps .... VAUGHAN WILLIAMS
Overture: The Judges of the Secret Court .... BERLIOZ

MISS DORIS VANE
M. LAURITZ MELCHIOR
MR HAROLD WILLIAMS

Tuesday, October 11th

Song of the Volga Boatmen... GLAZOUNOV
Aria: Nobil Signor (*Gli Ugonotti*) .... MEYERBEER
Love Scene (*Feuersnot*) .... RICHARD STRAUSS
Pianoforte Concerto No. 1, in B flat minor .... TCHAIKOVSKY
An Impression on a Windy Day .... MALCOLM SARGENT

(Conducted by the Composer)

Aria: My power is absolute (*Boris Godounov*) .... MUSSORGSKY
Le Poème de l'extase .... SCRIABIN
Symphonic Poem, 'Easter', for Organ and Orchestra .... VOLBACH
Valse (The Sleeping Beauty) .... TCHAIKOVSKY

MISS DOROTHY WEBSTER
MR ROBERT RADFORD
Solo pianoforte: SPIVAKOVSKY
Organ: MR FREDK. B. KIDDLE

Wednesday, October 12th

Symphonic Prelude to Part II ('Redemption') .... CÉSAR FRANCK
Aria: Ah! fors' è lui (*Traviata*) .... VERDI
Concertino for Piano and Orchestra .... JOHN ALDEN CARPENTIER
Song with Orchestra: Adelaide .... BEETHOVEN
Symphony No. 41, in C ('Jupiter') .... MOZART
Variations on a Theme of Haydn .... BRAHMS
Scherzo Capriccioso .... DVOŘÁK

MISS GWLADYS NAISH
MR ERNEST HARGREAVES
Solo pianoforte: MISS ISABEL GRAY

Thursday, October 13th

Prelude to Act III (*Lohengrin*).. WAGNER
Idyll for Orchestra: Love Dreams .... LISZT
Aria: Depuis le jour (*Louise*) .... CHARPENTIER
Meditation (*Lux Christi*)... ELGAR
Violin Concerto in D .... TCHAIKOVSKY
Mêlée Fantasque for Orchestra .... ARTHUR BLISS

(Conducted by the Composer)

Aria: Pogner's Address (*Mastersingers*) .... WAGNER
Symphonic Poem: Vltava .... SMETANA
Welsh Rhapsody .... EDWARD GERMAN
March: Pomp and Circumstance No. 4, in G .... ELGAR

MISS LOUISE DALE
MR GEORGE BAKER
Solo violin: M. CESAR THOMSON

Friday, October 14th

Overture: Coriolan .... BEETHOVEN
Aria: Voi che sapete (*Figaro*) .... MOZART
Violin Concerto in D .... BEETHOVEN
Aria: O ruddier than the cherry (*Acis and Galatea*) .... HANDEL
Symphony No. 8, in B minor ('Unfinished') .... SCHUBERT
Suite in G for Orchestra .... BACH
Rumanian Rhapsody No. 1, in A .... ENESCO

MISS HILDA BLAKE
MR JOSEPH FARRINGTON
Solo violin: MISS ISOLDE MENGES

Repertoire 1927
(the first BBC year)

SYMPHONIES

BEETHOVEN	No. 4 in B flat
	No. 5 in C minor
	No. 6 in F (Pastoral)
	No. 7 in A
BRAHMS	No. 1 in C minor
	No. 3 in F
	No. 4 in E minor
DVOŘÁK	No. 5 in E minor (From the New World)
HAYDN	No. 7 in C major (le Midi)
	No. 22 in E flat (The Philosopher)
	No. 88 in G (Letter V)
	No. 104 in D major (The London)
MOZART	No. 29 in A
	No. 35 in D
	No. 39 in E flat
	No. 40 in G minor
SCHUBERT	No. 8 in B minor (Unfinished)

CONCERTOS

BACH	No. 1 in D minor for Pianoforte
	Brandenburg Concerto No. 1 in F
	No. 3 in G
	No. 5 in D
	Sinfonia for Organ and Orchestra to the Cantata No. 29 'Wir danken Dir'

BEETHOVEN	No. 2 in B flat for Pianoforte
	No. 3 in C minor
	No. 5 in E flat (Emperor)
	In D for Violin
BRAHMS	In D for Violin
	No. 1 in D minor for Pianoforte
	No. 2 in B flat for Pianoforte
GRIEG	In A minor
HANDEL	Concerto Grosso No. 4 in A minor
	No. 6 in G minor
	No. 12 in B minor
HINDEMITH	No. 1 for Pianoforte
HOWELL, DOROTHY	In D minor
LISZT	No. 1 in E flat for Pianoforte
MOZART	No. 23 in A major for Pianoforte
	No. 4 in E flat for Horn
	No. 3 in G for Violin
	No. 4 in D for Violin
	No. 5 in A major for Violin

OVERTURES AND PRELUDES

BEETHOVEN	Coriolan
	Egmont
	Fidelio
	King Stephen
BERLIOZ	Benvenuto Cellini
	Le Carnaval Romain
BRAHMS	Academic Festival Overture
	'Tragic' in D minor
DEBUSSY	L'Après-midi d'un Faune
DELIBES	Prelude and Mazurka
DVOŘÁK	Carnival
ELGAR	Cockaigne
HAYDN	L'Isola disabitata
HUMPERDINCK	Hänsel and Gretel
MACKENZIE	Britannia
MENDELSSOHN	Ruy Blas
MOZART	Le Nozze di Figaro
	The Magic Flute
NICOLAI	Merry Wives of Windsor
ROSSINI	William Tell
SCHUBERT	Rosamunde
SCHUMANN	Manfred
SMYTH, ETHEL	The Wreckers
SULLIVAN	Di Ballo
THOMAS, AMBROISE	Mignon
WAGNER	The Flying Dutchman
	'Faust'
	Lohengrin
	Lohengrin Act III
	The Mastersingers
	The Mastersingers Act III

WAGNER	Parsifal – Prelude
	Rienzi
	Tannhäuser – Overture
	Tristan and Isolde – Prelude and Liebestod Act III
WEBER	Euryanthe
	Der Freischütz

SYMPHONIC POEMS, SUITES

BACH	Suite No. 3 in D
CHABRIER	España
DELIUS	Dance Rhapsody No. 1 in A
ELGAR	The Wand of Youth No. 2
FALLA	Suite from Ballet 'El Amor Brujo'
GRANADOS	Three Spanish Dances
GRIEG	Peer Gynt No. 1
	No. 2
HOLST	The Planets – (a) Mercury; (b) Saturn; (c) Jupiter
HOWELLS, HERBERT	Puck's Minuet
MCEWEN, J. B.	Grey Galloway (Border Ballad No. 3)
O'NEILL, NORMAN	Four Dances – The Blue Bird
RAMEAU	Ballet Suites
RAVEL	Mother Goose (Ma Mère l'Oye)
RIMSKY-KORSAKOV	Scheherezade
SATZ, ILIA	The Blue Bird Suite
SIBELIUS	Finlandia
	En Saga
SPAIN-DUNK, SUSAN	Poem for Orchestra in C minor – Elaine
STRAUSS	Death and Transfiguration (Opus 21)
	Don Juan
TCHAIKOVSKY	Casse-Noisette
	Francesca da Rimini
	Theme and Variations from Suite No. 3 in G Major

MISCELLANEOUS ORCHESTRAL WORKS

BACH	Toccata in F, for Orchestra
BAX, ARNOLD	Symphonic Variations in E
BEETHOVEN	Rondino in E flat for Wind Instruments
BERLIOZ	Marche Hongroise
BERNERS, LORD	Fantaisie Espagnole
BOCCHERINI	Minuet in A for Strings
BORODIN	Danse Polovtsienne (Prince Igor)
BRAHMS	Two Hungarian Dances (G minor and D)
	Three Hungarian Dances (G Minor, D minor and F)
BRIDGE, FRANK	There is a Willow Grows Aslant a Brook
DAVIES, WALFORD	Solemn Melody for Organ and Strings
DOHNÁNYI	Variations on a Nursery Song
DUPRÉ, MARCEL	Cortège et Litanie
DVOŘÁK	Slavonic Dance No. 1 in C
	Humoreske (No. 7 from Opus 101)
ELGAR	Variations on an Original Theme
	Pomp and Circumstance No. 4 in G
GERMAN	Three Dances from Henry VIII

GRAINGER, PERCY	Handel in the Strand
GRIEG	Symphonic Dance No. 2 in A
HANDEL	Largo in G
HELY-HUTCHINSON, C.V.	Variations, Intermezzo, Scherzo and Finale
LALO	Norwegian Rhapsody
LISZT	Hungarian Rhapsody No. 2 in D minor and G
LISZT–BUSONI	Rhapsodie Espagnole
MASSENET	Le Cid
MOSZKOWSKI	Malaguena from the Ballet 'Boabdil'
MOZART	Andante for Strings (Cassation No. 1 in G)
MUSSORGSKY	Fantasie – Night on the Bare Mountain
PADEREWSKI	Minuet in G
PURCELL	Fantasia Upon One Note
RIMSKY-KORSAKOV	Flight of the Bumble Bee
SIBELIUS	Valse Triste
STANFORD	Irish Rhapsody No. 1 in D minor
TCHAIKOVSKY	Overture-Fantasia – Romeo and Juliet
	Danse Cosaque (Mazeppa)
	The Battle of Poltava (Mazeppa)
	Marche Slave
	Capriccio Italien
THOMAS, AMBROISE	Gavotte – Mignon
WAGNER	Götterdämmerung – Siegfried's Journey to the Rhine
	Lohengrin – Bridal Procession
	Mastersingers – Dance of the Apprentices
	Procession of the Masters
	Homage to Sachs
	Parsifal – Good Friday Music
	Klingsor's Magic Garden and Flower Maidens' Scene
	Rheingold – Entrance of the Gods into Valhalla
	Siegfried – Forest Murmurs
	Träume (Dreams)
	Die Walküre – Ride of the Valkyries
	Tannhäuser Introduction, Act III

VOCAL SOLOS

BACH	Ich ende behende (Cantata 57)
	Merke, mein Herze (Cantata 145)
	Come sweetest death (Phoebus and Pan)
	My lord, it's all the wind (Phoebus and Pan)
BEETHOVEN	An die ferne Geliebte
	The drums loud are beating (Egmont)
	Joyful and mournful (Egmont)
	Creation's Hymn
	The Erl King
	Ah, perfido!
BIZET	Micaela's Song (Carmen)
	Agnus Dei (L'Arlésienne)
GLUCK	Où suis-je? (Alceste)
GOUNOD	She alone charmeth my sadness (La Reine de Saba)
	Valse Song (Romeo and Juliet)
HANDEL	Love in her eyes (Acis and Galatea)

HANDEL	Nasce al bosco (Ezzio)
	Sound an alarm (Judas Maccabæus)
	Care selve (Atalanta)
	Lusinghe più care (Alessandro)
	Hear me! ye winds and waves (Julius Cæsar)
HAYDN	With verdure clad (Creation)
	With joy the impatient husbandman (Seasons)
RONALD, LANDON	Adonaïs
LEONCAVALLO	Pagliacci – Prologue
MOZART	Bella mia fiamma – Concert Aria No. 2
	Non più! Tutto ascoltai – Concert Aria No. 10
	Non paventar (Magic Flute)
	Infelice, sconsolata (Magic Flute)
	Dalla sua pace (Don Giovanni)
	Il mio tesoro (Don Giovanni)
	Madamina! (Don Giovanni)
	Porgi amor (Figaro)
	Deh vieni, non tardar (Figaro)
	Non più andrai (Figaro)
MUSSORGSKY	My power is absolute (Boris Godounov)
SAINT-SÄENS	O Love from thy power (Samson and Delilah)
STANFORD	Three Sea Songs
SULLIVAN	Woo, thou thy snowflake (Ivanhoe)
TCHAIKOVSKY	Tatiana's Letter Scene (Eugène Onegin)
	Lenski's Aria 'Oh where has fled' (Eugène Onegin)
VERDI	Eri tu (Ballo in Maschera)
WAGNER	The term is past (The Flying Dutchman)
	Senta's Ballad (The Flying Dutchman)
	Elizabeth's Greeting (Tannhäuser)
	Wotan's Farewell and Fire Music (Walküre)
	Gerechter Gott! (Rienzi)
	Was duftet (Mastersingers)
	Wahn! Wahn! (Mastersingers)
	Song of the Rhine Daughters (Götterdämmerung)
	Forging Songs (Siegfried)
	Siegfried Idyll
	Elsa's Dream (Lohengrin)
	Isolde's Narration to Brangäne (Tristan and Isolde)

Repertoire 1938
SYMPHONIES

BEETHOVEN	No. 1 in C
	No. 2 in D
	No. 3 in E flat (Eroica)
	No. 4 in B flat
	No. 5 in C minor
	No. 6 in F (Pastoral)
	No. 7 in A
	No. 8 in F
	No. 9 in D minor (Choral)

BRAHMS	No. 1 in C minor
	No. 2 in D
	No. 3 in F
	No. 4 in E minor
DVOŘÁK	No. 4 in G
	No. 5 in E minor (From the New World)
DYSON	in G
FRANCK	in D minor
HAYDN	No. 45 in F sharp minor (Farewell)
	No. 92 in G (Oxford)
MENDELSSOHN	No. 4 in A (Italian)
MOERAN	in G minor
MOZART	No. 38 in D (Prague) (K. 504)
	No. 39 in E flat (K. 543)
	No. 40 in G minor (K. 550)
RACHMANINOV	No. 3 in A minor
SCHUBERT	No. 8 in B minor (Unfinished)
	No. 9 in C
SIBELIUS	No. 1 in E minor
	No. 2 in D
	No. 3 in C
TCHAIKOVSKY	No. 5 in E minor
	No. 6 in B minor (Pathétique)
VAUGHAN WILLIAMS	Pastoral

OVERTURES

BANTOCK	The Frogs
BEETHOVEN	Coriolan
	Fidelio
	Leonora No. 1
	Leonora No. 2
	Leonora No. 3
	Prometheus
BENJAMIN	Overture to an Italian Comedy
BERLIOZ	Benvenuto Cellini
	Le Carnaval romain
	The Corsair
BRAHMS	Academic Festival
	Tragic
BUSONI	Comedy
DVOŘÁK	Carnival
ELGAR	Cockaigne
	In the South (Alassio)
GLAZOUNOV	Carnival
HANDEL	Messiah
	Solomon
HINDEMITH	News of the Day
HOLBROOKE	Prelude to Bronwen
MENDELSSOHN	A Midsummer Night's Dream
	Ruy Blas
MOZART	Don Giovanni
	The Magic Flute

RACHMANINOV	The Avaricious Knight (Op. 24)
ROSSINI	The Barber of Seville
	William Tell
SCHUBERT	Alfonso and Estrella
	Rosamunde
SCHUMANN	Manfred
SIBELIUS	The Tempest
SMETANA	The Bartered Bride
SMYTH	The Wreckers
TCHAIKOVSKY	1812
VAUGHAN WILLIAMS	The Wasps
WEBER	Euryanthe
	Oberon

MISCELLANEOUS

BACH	Brandenburg Concerto No. 1 in F
	No. 2 in F
	No. 3 in G
	No. 4 in G
	No. 5 in D
	No. 6 in B flat
BACH—RESPIGHI	Passacaglia and Fugue in C minor
	Sinfonia from the Easter Oratorio
	Suite No. 2 in B minor
	No. 3 in D
	No. 4 in D
BACH—KLENOVSKY	Toccata and Fugue in D minor
BACH—WOOD	Toccata in F
BAX	In the Faery Hills
	London Pageant
BERLIOZ	Danse of the Sylphs (Faust)
	Hungarian March (Faust)
	Minuet of the Will o' the Wisps (Faust)
BERNERS	Fantaisie Espagnole
BLISS	Conquest of the Air
	Introduction and Allegro
	March: Things to Come
BORODIN	Polovtsian Dances (Prince Igor)
BOYCE	Suite for Strings and Organ
BRAHMS	Two Hungarian Dances (G minor and D)
	Variations on a Theme of Haydn
BRIDGE	The Sea
BRITTEN	Variations on a Theme of Frank Bridge
BUSONI	Rondo Arlecchinesco
BUTTERWORTH	A Shropshire Lad
CHOPIN	Funeral March
DEBUSSY	La Mer
	Prélude à l'Après-midi d'un Faune
DELIUS	A Song of Summer
	Brigg Fair
	Dance Rhapsody No. 1
D'ERLANGER	Prélude Romantique

D'INDY	Istar
DOHNÁNYI	Symphonische Minuten
DUKAS	L'Apprenti Sorcier
DVOŘÁK	Slavonic Rhapsody No. 3 in A flat
	Symphonic Variations
ELGAR	Enigma Variations
	Introduction and Allegro
	Pomp and Circumstance No. 4
FRANCK	Le Chasseur Maudit
GARDINER	Shepherd Fennel's Dance
GRAINGER	Handel in the Strand
	Molly on the Shore
GRANADOS	Three Spanish Dances
HANDEL	Concerto Grosso in G minor (Op. 6, No. 6)
HANDEL – HARTY	Suite from The Water Music
HOLST	Mercury, Saturn, Jupiter (The Planets)
HONEGGER	Pacific 231
HURLSTONE	Fantasie-Variations on a Swedish Air
IRELAND	The Forgotten Rite
KODÁLY	Ballet Music
	Háry János
LAMBERT	Horoscope
LISZT	Hungarian Rhapsody No. 2 in D minor and G
MILHAUD	Suite Provençale
MOSSOLOV	Factory – Music of Machines
MOZART	Masonic Funeral Music
	Theme, Variations and Rondo, for Wind
MUSSORGSKY	Gopak (The Fair at Sorotchintsi)
POOT	Allegro Symphonique
PROKOFIEV	Scherzo and March (Love for Three Oranges)
PURCELL – WOOD	Trumpet Voluntary
RAVEL	Bolero
	Spanish Rhapsody
RIMSKY–KORSAKOV	The Flight of the Bumble Bee
	Schcherazade
ROUSSEL	Flemish Rhapsody
SCHUBERT	Military March, in D
SIBELIUS	En Saga
	Finlandia
	Tapiola
	The Return of Lemminkainen
	Valse Triste
STRAUSS	Death and Transfiguration
	Don Juan
	Ein Heldenleben
	Till Eulenspiegel
STRAVINSKY	The Firebird
SVENDSEN	Carnival in Paris
TCHAIKOVSKY	Casse-Noisette Suite
	Capriccio Italien
	Cossack Dance
	Polonaise (Eugene Onegin)

TCHAIKOVSKY	Slavonic March
	The Battle of Poltava (Mazeppa)
VAUGHAN WILLIAMS	Fantasia on a Theme of Tallis
WALTON	Façade (Second Suite)
WEBER – WEINGARTNER	Invitation to the Dance
arr. WOOD, H. J.	Fantasia on British Sea Songs

CONCERTOS

BACH	Piano – No. 2 in E
	2-Piano – No. 1 in C minor
	No. 2 in C
	3-Piano – No. 1 in D minor
	Organ – Sinfonia (Cantata No. 29)
	2-Violin – in D minor
	Violin, Flute and Piano – No. 8 in A minor
BAX	Piano – Symphonic Variations
BEETHOVEN	Piano – No. 1 in C
	No. 2 in B flat
	No. 3 in C minor
	No. 4 in G
	No. 5 in E flat (Emperor)
	Violin – in D
	Two Romances No. 1 in G
	No. 2 in F
	Piano, Violin, Cello – in C
BRAHMS	Piano – No. 1 in D minor
	No. 2 in B flat
	Violin – in D
	Violin and Cello – in A minor
BRITTEN	Piano – No. 1 in D
DELIUS	Piano
ELGAR	Violin – in B minor
	Cello – in E minor
FOGG	Bassoon – in D
FRANCK	Piano – Symphonic Variations
GOOSSENS	Oboe
GLAZOUNOV	Piano – in F minor
GRIEG	Piano – in A minor
HANDEL – LAMBERT	Piano – in B flat
	Organ – No. 9 in B flat (Hallelujah)
	No. 10 in D minor (Set 2, No. 4)
	No. 11 in G minor (Set 2, No. 5)
IRELAND	Piano
LISZT	Piano – No. 1 in E flat
MENDELSSOHN	Violin – in E minor
MOZART	Piano – No. 23 in A (K. 488)
	– in B flat (K. 450)
	Violin – No. 5 in A (K. 219)
	Clarinet – in A (K. 622)
PAGANINI – KREISLER	Violin in C
RACHMANINOV	Piano – No. 2 in C minor
	No. 3 in D minor

RACHMANINOV	Piano – Rhapsody on a Theme of Paganini
SAINT-SAËNS	Piano – No. 2, in G minor
	2-Piano – Le Carnaval des Animaux
SCHUMANN	Piano – in A minor
	Violin – in D minor
SIBELIUS	Violin – in D minor
TCHAIKOVSKY	Piano – No. 1 in B flat minor
	No. 2 in G
	Cello – Variations on a Rococo Theme
VIVALDI	4-Violin – in B minor
WALTON	Viola

VOCAL AND CHORAL

BACH	Amore traditore (Cantata 203)
	Beloved soul, thy thoughts withdraw
	Come, sweetest death
	Hence, all ye evil doers (Cantata 135)
	In faith I quietly wait
	Jauchzet Gott in allen Landen (Cantata 51)
	My heart ever faithful (Cantata 68)
	Praise God the year is nearly ended (Cantata 28)
	Slumber now, ye weary eyelids (Cantata 82)
	Stone beyond all jewels (Cantata 152)
BANTOCK	Daughter of Zeus (Sappho)
BEETHOVEN	Abscheulicher (Fidelio)
	Adelaide
	Ah! perfido
	Choral Fantasia
	Creation's Hymn
	In questa tomba
	To the beloved afar
BLOCH	Psalm No. 114
BRAHMS	Liebeslieder (Walzer)·
COLERIDGE–TAYLOR	Onaway! Awake, Beloved! (Hiawatha)
DELIUS	Idyll
DYSON	The Wife of Bath
ELGAR	King Olaf heard the cry (King Olaf)
GLUCK	Armez-vous (Iphigenia in Aulis)
GOUNOD	Vulcan's Song (Philemon and Baucis)
HANDEL	And the glory of the Lord (Messiah)
	Arm, arm, ye brave (Judas Maccabaeus)
	Fallen is the foe (Judas Maccabaeus)
	For unto us a Child is born (Messiah)
	Furibondo (Partenope)
	Hallelujah (Messiah)
	He gave them hailstones (Israel in Egypt)
	Lift up your heads, O ye gates (Messiah)
	Lusinghe più care! (Alessandro)
	O voi del Erebo (Resurrection)
	The Lord gave the word (Messiah)
	Wretched lovers (Acis and Galatea)
HAYDN	In native worth (Creation)

HAYDN	O how pleasing to the senses (The Seasons)
JACOB	Helen of Kirconnel
LAMBERT	The Rio Grande
LEWIS	Overture for Unaccompanied Chorus
MOZART	Alleluja (Motet, Exsultate Jubilate)
	Batti, Batti (Don Giovanni)
	Deh vieni alla finestra (Don Giovanni)
	Fin ch'han dal vino (Don Giovanni)
	Ma che vi fece, o stelle (K. 368)
	Non più di Fiori (La Clemenza di Tito)
PARRY	Blest pair of Sirens
PUCCINI	E lucevan le stelle (Tosca)
	Recondita armonia (Tosca)
PURCELL	My heart is inditing
RACHMANINOV	Vocalise
RONALD	Adonais
SCHUBERT	The Shepherd on the Rock
SIBELIUS	The Ferryman's Brides
STANFORD	Songs of the Sea
TCHAIKOVSKY	Don Juan's Serenade
	Song of Farewell (Joan of Arc)
VERDI	Ah, fors è lui (La Traviata)
	Caro nome (Rigoletto)
	Credo (Othello)
	Ella giammai m'amo (Don Carlos)
	Vieni! t'affretta! (Macbeth)
WEBER	Softly sighs (Der Freischütz)

WAGNER (Orchestral)

Faust	Overture
Flying Dutchman	Overture
Lohengrin	Bridal Procession
	Introduction to Act III
	Prelude
Mastersingers	Dance of the Apprentices
	Homage to Sachs
	Prelude
	Prelude (Act III)
	Procession of the Masters
Parsifal	Good Friday Music
	Klingsor's Magic Garden
	Prelude
Rhinegold	Entry of the Gods
Rienzi	Overture
Siegfried	Idyll
Siegfried	Wotan's Spear and the Sleeping Brunnhilde
	Forest Murmurs
Tannhäuser	March
	Overture
	Overture and Venusberg Music
	Venusberg Music
Tristan and Isolde	Prelude to Act III

Twilight of the Gods	Siegfried's Funeral March
The Valkyrie	Siegfried's Journey
	Song of Rhinedaughters
The Valkyrie	The Ride of the Valkyries

WAGNER (Vocal)

Flying Dutchman	The term is past
	Senta's Ballad
Lohengrin	Elsa's Dream
	Love Duet (Act III)
	Lohengrin's Farewell
	Lohengrin's Narration
Mastersingers	Hans Sachs's Monologue
	Prize Song
	Trial Songs
Parsifal	Amfortas' Prayer
	Kundry's Song
Siegfried	Forging Songs
	Love Duet, Act III, Scene 3
Tannhäuser	Elizabeth's Greeting
	Elizabeth's Prayer
	Tannhäuser's Pilgrimage
	Wolfram's Arias
Tristan and Isolde	Isolde's Narration
	Love Duet, Act II
	Prelude and Liebestod
Twilight of the Gods	Closing Scene
	Waltraute's Narration
The Valkyrie	Wotan's Farewell and Magic Fire Music

From 1947

Friday, August 22nd

The BBC Symphony Orchestra
BEETHOVEN CONCERT
Conductor
Sir Adrian Boult

Overture: Leonora No. 3 .... BEETHOVEN
Scena and Aria, Abscheulicher (Fidelio) .... BEETHOVEN
Symphony No. 1, in C .... BEETHOVEN
Pianoforte Concerto No. 4, in G .... BEETHOVEN
Symphony No. 2 .... WALTER PISTON
(First performance in England)
Comedy Overture .... BUSONI

JOAN HAMMOND
Solo pianoforte: POUISHNOFF

Saturday, August 23rd

The BBC Symphony Orchestra
Conductor
Sir Adrian Boult

Overture: Prince Igor	BORODIN
Three Sea Pictures	ELGAR
Violin Concerto in E minor	MENDELSSOHN
Prélude à L'Après-Midi d'un Faune	DEBUSSY
Till Eulenspiegel, an old Rogue's Tale in Rondo Form	STRAUSS
The Rio Grande, for Pianoforte, Chorus and Orchestra	CONSTANT LAMBERT

(Conducted by the Composer)

Suite: The Firebird	STRAVINSKY

(Conducted by Stanford Robinson)

GLADYS RIPLEY
Solo violin: ALAN LOVEDAY
Solo pianoforte: KYLA GREENBAUM
THE BBC CHORUS

Monday, August 25th

The London Philharmonic Orchestra
TCHAIKOVSKY CONCERT
Conductor
Basil Cameron

Cossack Dance (Mazeppa)	TCHAIKOVSKY
Pianoforte Concerto No. 1, in B flat minor	TCHAIKOVSKY
Symphony No. 3, in D (Polish)	TCHAIKOVSKY
Three Pictures, for Flute, Strings and Percussion	EUGENE GOOSSENS

(First performance in England)

Air de Lia (L'Enfant Prodigue)	DEBUSSY
Overture for a Masque	E. J. MOERAN

BETSY DE LA PORTE
Solo Flute: GEOFFREY GILBERT
Solo pianoforte: SHULAMITH SHAFIR

Tuesday, August 26th

The BBC Symphony Orchestra
WILLIAM WALTON CONCERT
Conductor
Sir Adrian Boult

Overture: Scapino	WILLIAM WALTON
In Honour of the City of London, for Chorus and Orchestra	WILLIAM WALTON
Sinfonia Concertante, for Orchestra and Pianoforte	WILLIAM WALTON
Belshazzar's Feast, for Baritone, Chorus and Orchestra	WILLIAM WALTON

(Conducted by the Composer)

Petite Suite	ELISABETH LUTYENS

(First Concert performance in London)

Symphonic Fragments, Daphnis and Chloé (Second Series) .... RAVEL

DENNIS NOBLE
Solo pianoforte: ERNEST LUSH
THE BBC CHORAL SOCIETY

Wednesday, August 27th

The London Philharmonic Orchestra
MOZART–BRAHMS CONCERT
Conductor
Basil Cameron

Overture: The Magic Flute .... MOZART
Aria: Ombra felice (K. 255) .... MOZART
Symphony No. 35, in D (Haffner) .... MOZART
Pianoforte Concerto No. 2, in B flat   .... BRAHMS
Alto Rhapsody .... BRAHMS
Academic Festival Overture   .... BRAHMS

KATHLEEN FERRIER
Solo pianoforte: DENIS MATTHEWS
THE BBC MEN'S CHORUS

Thursday, August 28th

The BBC Symphony Orchestra
Conductor
Sir Adrian Boult

Brandenburg Concerto No. 2, in F, for Violin, Flute, Oboe,
  Trumpet and Strings   .... BACH
Pianoforte Concerto No. 3   .... BARTÓK
Symphony No. 1, in C minor .... BRAHMS
Divertimento for Orchestra .... LENNOX BERKELEY
Symphonic Fantasy, Pohjola's Daughter   .... SIBELIUS

Solo violin: PAUL BEARD
Solo flute: LAMBERT FLACK
Solo oboe: EDWARD SELWYN
Solo trumpet: JACK MACKINTOSH
Solo pianoforte: LOUIS KENTNER

Friday, August 29th

The London Philharmonic Orchestra
BEETHOVEN CONCERT
Conductor
Basil Cameron

Overture: Prometheus .... BEETHOVEN
Pianoforte Concerto No. 1, in C .... BEETHOVEN
Symphony No. 6, in F (Pastoral)   .... BEETHOVEN
Violin Concerto   .... ARNOLD BAX
Trojan March   .... BERLIOZ

Solo violin: MARIE WILSON
Solo pianoforte: MARJORIE BLACKBURN

Saturday, August 30th

The London Philharmonic Orchestra
Conductor
Basil Cameron

Overture: Ivan the Terrible .... RIMSKY–KORSAKOV
Song with Orchestra, Mad Bess .... PURCELL
Scherzo in G minor from Octet .... MENDELSSOHN
Pianoforte Concerto in A minor .... GRIEG
Symphony No. 5, in E flat .... SIBELIUS
An American in Paris .... GERSHWIN
Dances of Galanta .... KODÁLY

MURIEL BRUNSKILL
Solo pianoforte: LANCE DOSSOR

Monday, September 1st

The BBC Symphony Orchestra
WAGNER CONCERT
Conductor
Sir Adrian Boult

Excerpts from The Mastersingers .... WAGNER
  (a) Prelude and Chorale
  (b) Hans Sachs' Monologue and Scene with Eva (Act II)
  (c) Introduction, Act III – Dialogue between Hans Sachs and David –
      Hans Sachs' Monologue
  (d) Quintet – Entry of the Guilds – Dance of the Apprentices –
      Homage to Hans Sachs
  (e) Walter's Prize Song and Finale
      (*Conductor: Stanford Robinson*)
Symphonic Suite, Scheherazade .... RIMSKY–KORSAKOV

Eva: VICTORIA SLADEN
Magdalene: JANET HOWE
Walter: FRANK TITTERTON
David: DAVID LLOYD
Hans Sachs: TOM WILLIAMS
Pogner: GEORGE JAMES
Mastersingers: THE BBC SINGERS
THE GOLDSMITHS' CHORAL UNION

Repertoire 1948

SYMPHONIES

BAX	No. 7
BEETHOVEN	No. 1, in C
	No. 2, in D
	No. 3, in E flat (Eroica)
	No. 4, in B flat
	No. 5, in C minor

BEETHOVEN	No. 6, in F (Pastoral)
	No. 7, in A
	No. 8, in F
	No. 9, in D minor (Choral)
BERLIOZ	Fantastique
BORODIN	No. 2, in B minor
BRAHMS	No. 1, in C minor
	No. 2, in D
	No. 3, in F
	No. 4, in E minor
DVOŘÁK	No. 2, in D minor
	No. 4, in G
	No. 5, in E minor (New World)
ELGAR	No. 2, in E flat
FRANCK	In D minor
HAYDN	No. 94, in G (Surprise)
HINDEMITH	Mathis der Maler
MENDELSSOHN	No. 4, in A (Italian)
MOZART	No. 29, in A (K. 201)
	No. 35, in D (K. 385) (Haffner)
	No. 38, in D (K. 504) (Prague)
	No. 40, in G minor (K. 550)
	No. 41, in C (K. 551) (Jupiter)
RACHMANINOV	No. 3, in A minor
SCHUBERT	No. 5, in B flat
	No. 8, in B minor (Unfinished)
	No. 9, in C
SIBELIUS	No. 1, in E minor
	No. 2, in D
	No. 5, in E flat
	No. 7, in C
TCHAIKOVSKY	No. 4, in F minor
	No. 5, in E minor
	No. 6, in B minor (Pathétique)
VAUGHAN WILLIAMS	London
	A Sea Symphony
	No. 6, in E minor
WALTON	No. 1

OVERTURES

AURIC	Overture
BAX	Overture to a Picaresque Comedy
BEETHOVEN	Coriolan
	Egmont
	Fidelio
	Leonora No. 1
	Leonora No. 3
	Prometheus
BERLIOZ	Benvenuto Cellini
	Le Carnaval romain
	The Corsair
BORODIN	Prince Igor

BRAHMS	Academic Festival
COOKE	Processional
DVOŘÁK	Carnival
ELGAR	Cockaigne
GLUCK	Alceste
IRELAND	A London Overture
MENDELSSOHN	Ruy Blas
MOZART	Così fan tutte
	The Marriage of Figaro
	The Seraglio
	The Magic Flute
ROSSINI	The Barber of Seville
	William Tell
SCHUBERT	In the Italian Style, in C
	Rosamunde
SMETANA	The Bartered Bride
STEVENS	Fugal
SULLIVAN	Di Ballo
TCHAIKOVSKY	1812
	Hamlet
	Romeo and Juliet
VAUGHAN WILLIAMS	The Wasps
WEBER	Der Freischütz
	Euryanthe
	Oberon

MISCELLANEOUS

BACH	Brandenburg Concerto No. 1, in F
	No. 2, in F
	No. 3, in G
	No. 4, in G
BACH—ELGAR	Fugue in C major
BACH—RESPIGHI	Passacaglia and Fugue in C minor
	Suite No. 1, in C
	No. 3, in D
BERLIOZ	Royal Hunt and Storm ⎫ (The Trojans)
	Trojan March ⎭
	Menuet des Follets ⎫ (La Damnation de Faust)
	Marche Hongroise ⎭
BLISS	Music for Strings
BORODIN	Polovtsian Dances (Prince Igor)
BRAHMS	Rondo (Serenade No. 1, in D)
	Variations on a Theme of Haydn
BRITTEN	Four Sea Interludes (Peter Grimes)
	The Young Person's Guide to the Orchestra
CHABRIER	Joyeuse Marche
DEBUSSY	La Mer
	Prélude à l'Après-midi d'un Faune
DELIUS	Brigg Fair
	Dance Rhapsody No. 1
	Nocturne, Paris
	On Hearing the First Cuckoo in Spring

DELIUS	The Walk to the Paradise Garden (A Village Romeo and Juliet)
DUKAS	L'Apprenti Sorcier
DVOŘÁK	Slavonic Dance No. 3, in A flat
	Symphonic Variations
ELGAR	Enigma Variations
	Falstaff
	Introduction and Allegro
	Pomp and Circumstance March No. 1
	Serenade for Strings
FAURÉ	Pavane
GRAINGER	Danish Folk Music Suite
GRIEG	Two Elegiac Melodies: The Wounded Heart; Springtide
HANDEL—HARTY	Water Music
HOLST	The Perfect Fool
	Mars ⎫
	Venus ⎬ (The Planets)
	Jupiter ⎭
JAUBERT	Suite Française
KODÁLY	Dances of Galanta
	Háry János
LAMBERT	Horoscope
	The Rio Grande
LISZT	Mephisto Walzer
MENDELSSOHN	Scherzo from Octet in G minor
MILHAUD	Suite Française
MOERAN	Serenade in G
MOZART	Eine Kleine Nachtmusik (K. 525)
	Divertimento No. 11, in D (K. 251)
PURCELL—WOOD	Trumpet Voluntary
RAVEL	Bolero
	Daphnis and Chloe (2nd Series)
	Mother Goose
	Rapsodie Espagnole
	La Valse
REGER	Variations and Fugue on a Theme of Mozart
RESPIGHI	The Fountains of Rome
RIMSKY–KORSAKOV	Capriccio Espagnol
SAINT-SAËNS	Le Rouet d'Omphale
SEARLE	Fugue for Orchestra
SIBELIUS	En Saga
	The Swan of Tuonela
	The Return of Lemminkainen
	Tapiola
	Valse Triste
SMETANA	Vltava
	From Bohemia's Woods and Fields
STRAUSS	Don Juan
	Don Quixote
	Till Eulenspiegel
	Death and Transfiguration
STRAUSS, J.	Waltz, The Beautiful Blue Danube
STRAVINSKY	The Firebird

TCHAIKOVSKY	Capriccio Italien
	Casse-Noisette
	Cossack Dance (Mazeppa)
	Marche Slave
	Polonaise (Eugene Onegin)
	Suite No. 3 in G
	Waltz (The Sleeping Beauty)
VAUGHAN WILLIAMS	Fantasia on a Theme of Thomas Tallis
	Partita for Double String Orchestra
WALTON	Crown Imperial
WOOD	Fantasia on British Sea-Songs

CONCERTOS

BACH	Piano – No. 1, in D minor
	No. 5, in F minor
	2-Piano – No. 1, in C minor
	No. 2, in C
	4-Piano – in A minor (Vivaldi)
	Violin – No. 2 in E
	2-Violin – in D minor
BARTÓK	Piano – No. 3
BEETHOVEN	Piano – No. 1, in C
	No. 2, in B flat
	No. 3, in C major
	No. 4, in G
	No. 5, in E flat (Emperor)
	Violin – in D
	Violin, Piano and Violoncello – in C
BERKELEY	Piano – in B flat
BRAHMS	Piano – No. 1, in D minor
	No. 2, in B flat
	Violin – in D
CHAUSSON	Violin – Poème
DELIUS	Piano
	Violin
DOHNÁNYI	Piano – Variations on a Nursery Song
DVOŘÁK	Violin – in A minor
	Violoncello – in B minor
ELGAR	Violin – in B minor
	Violoncello – in E minor
GRIEG	Piano – in A minor
HANDEL	Organ – in G minor (Op. 4, No. 1)
HANDEL – WOOD	in D minor (Op. 7, No. 4)
	in G minor (Op. 7, No. 5)
HAYDN	Piano – No. 1, in D
	Violin, Violoncello, Oboe, Bassoon – Sinfonia Concertante in B flat
HOLST	2-Violin
IRELAND	Piano – in E flat
	Legend
KABALEVSKY	Piano – No. 2, in G minor
LISZT	Piano – No. 2, in A
	Hungarian Fantasia

LISZT–BUSONI	Piano – Spanish Rhapsody
MARTINU	Piano – Concertino
MENDELSSOHN	Violin – in E minor
MOZART	Piano – No. 21, C (K. 467)
	No. 24, in C minor (K. 491)
	No. 27, in B flat (K. 595)
	2-Piano – in E flat (K. 365)
	Violin and Viola – Sinfonia Concertante in E flat (K. 364)
	Horn – No. 4, in E flat (K. 495)
	Oboe – in C
PROKOFIEV	Piano – No. 3, in C
RACHMANINOV	Piano – No. 1, in F sharp minor
	No. 2, in C minor
	No. 3, in D minor
	Rhapsody on a Theme of Paganini
RAWSTHORNE	Violin
SAINT-SAËNS	2-Piano – Le Carnaval des Animaux
SCHUBERT–LISZT	Piano – Wanderer Fantasia
SCHUMANN	Piano – in A minor
SCOTT	Oboe
SIBELIUS	Violin – in D minor
STRAVINSKY	2-Piano (without orchestra)
TCHAIKOVSKY	Piano – No. 1, in B flat minor
	No. 2, in G
	No. 3, in E flat
	Violin – in D
	Violoncello – Variations on a Rococo Theme
VAUGHAN WILLIAMS	Violin – The Lark Ascending
WALTON	Piano – Sinfonia Concertante
	Violin – in B minor

VOCAL and CHORAL

BACH	I know that my Redeemer lives (Cantata 160)
	My heart ever faithful (Cantata 68)
	Schlage doch (Cantata 53)
	Stone beyond all Jewels (Cantata 152)
BORODIN	Vladimir's Cavatina (Prince Igor)
BOUGHTON	Song of Creation ⎱ (The Immortal Hour)
	Faery Song ⎰
BRAHMS	Alto Rhapsody
DELIUS	Appalachia
DYSON	The Wife of Bath (Canterbury Pilgrims)
ELGAR	Sabbath Morning at Sea (Sea Pictures)
GRIEG	Ragnhild
	Solveig's Lullaby (Peer Gynt)
HANDEL	The Prison Scene (Theodora)
IRELAND	These Things shall be
LAMBERT	The Rio Grande
MOZART	Osmin's Aria, Hah, wie will ich triumphieren (The Seraglio)
	Aprite un po' quegl' occhi (Marriage of Figaro)
	Deh vieni alla finestra (Don Giovanni)
	Il mio tesoro (Don Giovanni)

MOZART	Madamina (Don Giovanni)
	Non mi dir (Don Giovanni)
PARRY	Blest Pair of Sirens
PROKOFIEV	Peter and the Wolf
PUCCINI	In quelle trine morbide } (Manon Lescaut)
	Sola perduta abbandonata
	Vissi d'arte (Tosca)
SAINT-SAËNS	O Love from Thy Power (Samson and Delilah)
SCHUBERT	Lieschen's Aria (The Twin Brothers)
	The Erl King
TCHAIKOVSKY	Joan of Arc's Farewell (Joan of Arc)
	Tatiana's Letter Song (Eugene Onegin)
VAUGHAN WILLIAMS	Serenade to Music
VERDI	Ma dall'arido stello (Un Ballo di Maschera)
	Pace, pace (La Forza del Destino)
	Tu che le vanità (Don Carlos)
WEBER	Softly sighs (Der Freischütz)

WAGNER (Orchestral)

Flying Dutchman	Overture
Lohengrin	Prelude
Mastersingers	Prelude (Act I)
Parsifal	Good Friday Music
Siegfried	Forest Murmurs
Tannhäuser	Overture
	Träume
Twilight of the Gods	Daydawn and Sunrise
	Siegfried's Journey to the Rhine
	Song of the Rhinedaughters
The Valkyrie	Ride of the Valkyries

WAGNER (Vocal)

Mastersingers	Hans Sachs' Monologue and Scene with Eva (Act II)
	Introduction, Act III – Dialogue between Sachs and David – Sachs' Monologue (Act III)
	Quintet – Entry of the Guilds – Dance of the Apprentices – Homage to Sachs (Act III)
	Walter's Prize Song and Finale (Act III)
Siegfried	Act I, Scene 3
Tannhäuser	Elizabeth's Greeting
Tristan and Isolde	Love Duet, Act II
Twilight of the Gods	Duet, Beloved Hero
	Closing Scene
The Valkyrie	Wotan's Farewell and Magic Fire Music

From 1957

Monday, July 22nd

The BBC Symphony Orchestra
SIBELIUS
Conductor
Sir Malcolm Sargent

Tone Poem, Finlandia	SIBELIUS
The Swan of Tuonela	SIBELIUS
Violin Concerto in D minor	SIBELIUS
Symphony No. 3, in C	SIBELIUS
Overture: Athalie	FRANK MARTIN

(First performance in Great Britain)

Symphonic Variations	DVOŘÁK

Solo violin: MAX ROSTAL

Tuesday, July 23rd

The BBC Symphony Orchestra
Conductor
Sir Malcolm Sargent

Overture, Le Carnaval romain	BERLIOZ
Rhapsody on a Theme of Paganini	RACHMANINOV
Symphony No. 2, in D	SIBELIUS
Burlesque, for Pianoforte and Orchestra	STRAUSS
Capriccio Espagnol	RIMSKY-KORSAKOV

Solo pianoforte: SHURA CHERKASSKY

Wednesday, July 24th

The BBC Symphony Orchestra
BACH
Conductor
Sir Malcolm Sargent

Sonata (Cantata No. 31, Der Himmel lacht)	BACH
Pianoforte Concerto No. 5, in F minor	BACH
Suite No. 1, in C	BACH
Brandenburg Concerto No. 5, in D for Flute, Violin, Pianoforte and Strings	BACH
Suite No. 3, in D	BACH
Litany, for Double String Orchestra	RACINE FRICKER

(First public performance in London)
(Conducted by the Composer)

Variations on a Hungarian Folk-Song (The Peacock)	KODÁLY

Solo violin: PAUL BEARD
Solo flute: DOUGLAS WHITTAKER
Solo pianoforte: DENIS MATTHEWS

Thursday, July 25th

The London Symphony Orchestra
Conductor
Basil Cameron

Overture: The Bartered Bride	SMETANA
Aria: Martern aller Arten (The Seraglio)	MOZART
Pianoforte Concerto No. 2, in A	LISZT
Symphony No. 5, in E minor	TCHAIKOVSKY
Canadian Carnival	BENJAMIN BRITTEN
Symphonic Poem, Le Chasseur Maudit	FRANCK

MIMI COERTSE
Solo pianoforte: ILONA KABOS

Friday, July 26th

The London Symphony Orchestra
BEETHOVEN
Conductor
Basil Cameron

Symphony No. 1, in C	BEETHOVEN
Pianoforte Concerto No. 2, in B flat	BEETHOVEN
Symphony No. 8, in F	BEETHOVEN
Violin Concerto	BAX
Overture: Bartholomew Fair	IAIN HAMILTON

(*First performance in England*)

Solo violin: FREDERICK GRINKE
Solo pianoforte: NATASHA LITVIN

Saturday, July 27th

The London Symphony Orchestra
Conductor
Basil Cameron   .

Overture: William Tell	ROSSINI
An English Rhapsody: Brigg Fair	DELIUS
Pianoforte Concerto No. 2, in C minor	RACHMANINOV
Suite: Casse-Noisette	TCHAIKOVSKY
Recitation with Orchestra: Peter and the Wolf	PROKOFIEV
Rhapsody: España	CHABRIER

FRANK PHILLIPS
Solo pianoforte: COR DE GROOT

From 1958

Monday, August 4th

The BBC Symphony Orchestra
Conductor
Sir Malcolm Sargent

Overture: The Barber of Seville	ROSSINI
Symphony No. 8, in B minor (Unfinished)	SCHUBERT
Pianoforte Concerto No. 2, in C minor	RACHMANINOV
Variations and Fugue on a Theme of Purcell	BENJAMIN BRITTEN
(The Young Person's Guide to the Orchestra)	
Symphonic Suite: Scheherazade	RIMSKY-KORSAKOV

JULIUS KATCHEN

Tuesday, August 5th

The BBC Symphony Orchestra
Conductor
Sir Malcolm Sargent

Prelude: Lohengrin	WAGNER
Pianoforte Concerto No. 5, in E flat (Emperor)	BEETHOVEN
Symphony No. 9	VAUGHAN WILLIAMS
Dance Scene	RACINE FRICKER
(Conducted by the Composer)	
Symphonic Variations	DVOŘÁK

HEPHZIBAH MENUHIN

Wednesday, August 6th

The BBC Symphony Orchestra
BRAHMS
Conductor
Sir Malcolm Sargent

Tragic Overture	BRAHMS
Four Serious Songs	BRAHMS—SARGENT
Violin Concerto in D	BRAHMS
Symphony No. 1, in C minor	BRAHMS

NORMA PROCTER
CAMPOLI

Thursday, August 7th

The London Symphony Orchestra
BACH–HANDEL
Conductor
Basil Cameron

Overture (Music for the Royal Fireworks)	HANDEL—HARTY
Harpsichord Concerto No. 1, in D minor	BACH
Brandenburg Concerto No. 3, in G, for Strings	BACH

Organ Concerto in D minor (Op. 7, No. 4).. HANDEL
Coronation Anthem, Zadok the Priest   .... HANDEL
Carmina Burana, for Soli, Chorus and Orchestra   .... CARL ORFF

APRIL CANTELO
ANDREW PEARMAIN
JOHN HAUXVELL
GEORGE MALCOLM
GERAINT JONES
THE BBC CHORUS
THE BBC CHORAL SOCIETY
A Section of
HIGHGATE SCHOOL CHOIR

Friday, August 8th

The London Symphony Orchestra
BEETHOVEN
Conductor
Basil Cameron

Overture: Prometheus.. BEETHOVEN
Pianoforte Concerto No. 2, in B flat   .... BEETHOVEN
Symphony No. 3, in E flat (Eroica).. BEETHOVEN
Five Orchestral Pieces (Revised version).. SCHOENBERG
The Garden of Fand   .... BAX

CYRIL PREEDY

Saturday, August 9th

The London Symphony Orchestra
TCHAIKOVSKY
Conductor
Basil Cameron

Waltz (Eugene Onegin)   .... TCHAIKOVSKY
Pianoforte Concerto No. 1, in B flat minor   .... TCHAIKOVSKY
Love Duet (Romeo and Juliet)   .... TCHAIKOVSKY
Fantasia after Dante, Francesca da Rimini   .... TCHAIKOVSKY
Serenade for Strings   .... TCHAIKOVSKY
Lenski's Aria (Eugene Onegin)   .... TCHAIKOVSKY
Capriccio Italien   .... TCHAIKOVSKY

AMY SHUARD
JANET HOWE
RICHARD LEWIS
VENTSISLAV YANKOFF

Monday, September 1st

The BBC Symphony Orchestra
Conductor
Sir Malcolm Sargent

Overture: Benvenuto Cellini   .... BERLIOZ

Aria: Zeffiretti lusinghieri (Idomeneo) .... MOZART
Violoncello Concerto .... WILLIAM WALTON
Symphony No. 7, in A .... BEETHOVEN
Music for Strings .... ARTHUR BLISS
(Conducted by the Composer)
Symphonic Poem, Till Eulenspiegel .... STRAUSS

JOSEPHINE VEASEY
ERLING BENGTSSON

Tuesday, September 2nd

The BBC Symphony Orchestra
MOZART–ELGAR
Conducted by Maurice Miles

Overture: Idomeneo .... MOZART
Symphony No. 40, in G minor (K. 550) .... MOZART
Conducted by Sir Malcolm Sargent
The Dream of Gerontius .... ELGAR

MARJORIE THOMAS
RICHARD LEWIS
JOHN CAMERON
THE CROYDON PHILHARMONIC SOCIETY
THE ROYAL CHORAL SOCIETY

Wednesday, September 3rd

The London Philharmonic Orchestra
MENDELSSOHN–BRAHMS
Conductor
Basil Cameron

Overture: Ruy Blas .... MENDELSSOHN
Symphony No. 4, in A (Italian) .... MENDELSSOHN
Pianoforte Concerto No. 2, in B flat .... BRAHMS
Symphony No. 2, in D .... BRAHMS

MARIA DONSKA

Thursday, September 4th

The London Philharmonic Orchestra
Conductor
Basil Cameron

Overture in D minor .... HANDEL–ELGAR
Royal Hunt and Storm (The Trojans) .... BERLIOZ
Pianoforte Concerto No. 4, in G minor .... RACHMANINOV
Symphony in D minor .... FRANCK
Soliloquy, for Violoncello and Orchestra .... EDMUND RUBBRA
Bolero .... RAVEL

JOAN DICKSON
LAMAR CROWSON

Friday, September 5th

The BBC Symphony Orchestra
BEETHOVEN
Conductor
Sir Malcolm Sargent

Overture: Fidelio.. BEETHOVEN
Pianoforte Concerto No. 4, in G .... BEETHOVEN
Symphony No. 6, in F (Pastoral) .... BEETHOVEN
Pianoforte Concerto, Op. 101 .... SHOSTAKOVICH
(First performance in Great Britain)
Suite: The Firebird.. STRAVINSKY

EILEEN JOYCE

Saturday, September 6th

The BBC Symphony Orchestra
TCHAIKOVSKY–STRAVINSKY
Conductor
Basil Cameron
Music from the Ballet

Waltz (The Sleeping Beauty) .... TCHAIKOVSKY
Pianoforte Concerto No. 2, in G .... TCHAIKOVSKY
Suite: Casse-Noisette .... TCHAIKOVSKY
Ballet Suite: Pulcinella (after Pergolesi) .... STRAVINSKY
Le Sacre du Printemps .... STRAVINSKY

KENDALL TAYLOR

Repertoire 1959
SYMPHONIES

ALWYN, WILLIAM	No. 4
BEETHOVEN	No. 1, in C
	No. 2, in D
	No. 3, in E flat (Eroica)
	No. 4, in B flat
	No. 5, in C minor
	No. 6, in F (Pastoral)
	No. 7, in A
	No. 8, in F
	No. 9, in D minor (Choral)
BERKELEY, LENNOX	No. 2
BERLIOZ	Fantastique
BRAHMS	No. 1, in C minor
	No. 2, in D
	No. 3, in F
	No. 4, in E minor
DVOŘÁK	No. 2, in D minor
	No. 4, in G

DVOŘÁK	No. 5, in E minor (From the New World)
FRANCK	in D minor
JONES, DANIEL	No. 5
MENDELSSOHN	No. 3, in A minor (Scottish)
	No. 4, in A (Italian)
MOZART	No. 35, in D (K. 385) (Haffner)
	No. 39, in E flat (K. 543)
	No. 40, in G minor (K. 550)
	No. 41, in C (K. 551) (Jupiter)
PROKOFIEV	Symphonie Classique, in D
SCHUBERT	No. 8, in B minor (Unfinished)
	No. 9, in C
SCHUMANN	No. 4, in D minor
SEARLE, HUMPHREY	No. 2
SHOSTAKOVICH	No. 5
SIBELIUS	No. 2, in D
	No. 3, in C
	No. 5, in E flat
	No. 7, in C
TCHAIKOVSKY	No. 4, in F minor
	No. 5, in E minor
	No. 6, in B minor (Pathétique)
VAUGHAN WILLIAMS	A London
	Pastoral
	A Sea
	Sinfonia Antartica
	No. 4, in F minor
	No. 5, in D
	No. 6, in E minor
	No. 8
	No. 9
WALTON, WILLIAM	No. 1

CONCERTOS

BACH	Piano – No. 1, in D minor
	Organ Solos – Two Chorale Preludes
	Toccata, Adagio and Fugue in C
BARTÓK	Piano – No. 1
BEETHOVEN	Piano – No. 1, in C
	No. 2, in B flat
	No. 3, in C minor
	No. 4, in G
	No. 5, in E flat (Emperor)
	Violin – in D
	Two Romances (No. 1 in G; No. 2 in F)
BERG	Violin
BOWEN, YORK	Piano – No. 4, in A minor
BRAHMS	Piano – No. 1, in D minor
	No. 2, in B flat
	Violin – in D
	Violin and Violoncello – in A minor
DOHNÁNYI	Piano – Variations on a Nursery Song

ELGAR	Violoncello – in E minor
FRANCK	Piano – Symphonic Variations
GRIEG	Piano – in A minor
HANDEL	Organ – in B flat (Op. 7, No. 1)
	in D minor (Op. 7, No. 4)
	Harp – in E flat
HAYDN	Trumpet – in E flat
	Violoncello – in D
IBERT	Oboe – Symphonie Concertante
IRELAND	Piano – in E flat
LISZT	Piano – No. 1, in E flat
	No. 2, in A
MACONCHY, ELIZABETH	Oboe and Bassoon
MARTINU	Oboe
MENDELSSOHN	Violin – in E minor
MILHAUD	Percussion
MOZART	Piano – No. 19, in F (K. 459)
	No. 20, in D minor (K. 466)
	No. 23, in A (K. 488)
	Two Pianos – in E flat (K. 365)
RACHMANINOV	Piano – No. 2, in C minor
	No. 3, in D minor
	Rhapsody on a Theme of Paganini
RAVEL	Piano – in G
RODRIGO	Harp – Concerto-Serenata
SCHUBERT–LISZT	Piano – Wanderer Fantasia
SCHUMANN	Piano – in A minor
SEIBER, MÁTYÁS	Violoncello – Tre Pezzi
SIBELIUS	Violin – in D minor
STRAVINSKY	Violin – in D
	Piano – Capriccio
TCHAIKOVSKY	Piano – No. 1, in B flat minor
	No. 2, in G
	Violin – in D
	Violoncello – Variations on a Rococo Theme
	Pezzo Capriccioso
WHETTAM, GRAHAM	Two Pianos – Dance Concertante
WILLIAMSON, MALCOLM	Piano

OVERTURES

BEETHOVEN	Coriolan
	Egmont
	Fidelio
	Leonora No. 1
	Leonora No. 2
	Leonora No. 3
	Prometheus
BERLIOZ	Benvenuto Cellini
	Le Carnaval romain
BRAHMS	Academic Festival
DVOŘÁK	Carnival
ELGAR	Cockaigne

GLINKA	Ruslan and Ludmilla
HANDEL—JACOB	Theodora
IRELAND, JOHN	A London Overture
	Satyricon
KABALEVSKY	Colas Breugnon
MENDELSSOHN	A Midsummer Night's Dream
	Ruy Blas
MOZART	Il Seraglio
NICOLAI	The Merry Wives of Windsor
RAWSTHORNE, ALAN	Street Corner
ROSSINI	The Barber of Seville
	The Journey to Rheims
	The Silken Ladder
	William Tell
SCHUBERT	Rosamunde
SMETANA	The Bartered Bride
STRAUSS, JOHANN	Die Fledermaus
SULLIVAN	Di Ballo
SUPPÉ	Pique Dame
TCHAIKOVSKY	1812
	Hamlet
	Romeo and Juliet
WAGNER	The Flying Dutchman
	Lohengrin
	The Mastersingers
	Tannhäuser
WEBER	Oberon

MISCELLANEOUS

ARNELL, RICHARD	Harlequin in April
BACH	Brandenburg Concerto, No. 3, in G
	Brandenburg Concerto, No. 5, in D
	Suite No. 3, in D
BAX	Tintagel
BERLIOZ	Dance of the Sylphs
	Hungarian March } (The Damnation of Faust)
	Minuet of the Will-o'-the-Wisps
BIZET	L'Arlésienne
BORODIN—SARGENT	Nocturne
BRAHMS	Variations of the St Anthony Choral
BRITTEN	Variations and Fugue on a Theme of Purcell
CHABRIER	Rhapsody: España
DEBUSSY	Iberia (Images No. 2)
	La Mer
	Prélude à l'Après-midi d'un Faune
DELIBES	Introduction to Act III, Sylvia
DELIUS	A Dance Rhapsody, No. 1 in A
DUKAS	L'Apprenti Sorcier
DVOŘÁK	Symphonic Variations
ELGAR	Enigma Variations
	Introduction and Allegro for Strings
	Pomp and Circumstance March No. 1, in D

FALLA	Scenes and Dances (The Three-Cornered Hat)
GRIEG	Two Elegiac Melodies
	Peer Gynt No. 1
	Symphonic Dances, Nos 2 and 4
HANDEL—HARTY	Suite from The Water Music
HINDEMITH	Symphonic Metamorphosis of Themes by Carl Maria von Weber
HOLST	The Perfect Fool
	The Planets
IRELAND	The Forgotten Rite
JANÁČEK	Sinfonietta
KODÁLY	Háry János
	Peacock Variations
LEIGHTON, KENNETH	Burlesque
MOZART	Eine kleine Nachtmusik (K. 525)
	Serenata Notturna (K. 239)
PANUFNIK, ANDRZEJ	Polonia
PROKOFIEV	Scherzo and March (The Love of the Three Oranges)
RAVEL	Bolero
	La Valse
RIMSKY-KORSAKOV	Capriccio Espagnol
	Suite from Le Coq d'Or
	Scheherazade
ROSSINI—RESPIGHI	La Boutique Fantasque
ROSSINI—BRITTEN	Soirées Musicales
SCHUBERT	Entr'acte in B flat ⎱ (Rosamunde)
	Ballet Music in G ⎰
	Marche Militaire in D
SIBELIUS	Festivo
	Finlandia
	The Swan of Tuonela
	Tapiola
	Valse Triste
SMETANA	From Bohemia's Woods and Fields
STRAUSS, OSCAR	Selection, A Waltz Dream
STRAUSS	Le Bourgeois Gentilhomme
	Don Quixote
	Ein Heldenleben
	Till Eulenspiegel
	Der Rosenkavalier
STRAUSS, JOHANN	The Blue Danube
	New Pizzicato Polka (Op. 449)
	Tales from the Vienna Woods
STRAVINSKY	The Firebird
	Three Scenes from Petrushka
TCHAIKOVSKY	Andante Cantabile, for Strings
	Capriccio Italien
	Francesca da Rimini
	Marche Slave
	Polonaise and Waltz (Eugene Onegin)
	The Sleeping Beauty
	The Swan Lake
	Theme and Variations (Suite No. 3, in G)

TIPPETT, MICHAEL	Ritual Dances (The Midsummer Marriage)
WAGNER	The Mastersingers – Prelude, Act III
	Dance of the Apprentices
	Entry of the Masters
	The Rhinegold – Entry of the Gods
	Siegfried Idyll
WALTON, WILLIAM	Façade
arr. WOOD, HENRY	Fantasia on British Sea Songs

VOCAL AND CHORAL

ARNE	Rule, Britannia
BACH	Ein' feste Burg ist unser Gott (Cantata No. 80)
	Sing ye to the Lord
BEETHOVEN	Abscheulicher (Fidelio)
	Adelaide
BORODIN	Polovtsian Dances (Prince Igor)
BRAHMS–SARGENT	Four Serious Songs
COLERIDGE–TAYLOR	Hiawatha's Wedding Feast
ELGAR	The Dream of Gerontius
	Three Sea Pictures
GLINKA	Ruslan's Aria (Ruslan and Ludmilla)
GLUCK	Che farò (Orfeo)
HANDEL	Ombra mai fù (Xerxes)
	Plague Choruses (Israel in Egypt)
	Zadok the Priest
HAYDN	The Creation
	O how pleasing to the senses (The Seasons)
HONEGGER	King David
LAMBERT	The Rio Grande
MAHLER	Lieder eines fahrenden Gesellen
MOZART	Exsultate jubilate (K. 165)
	Non paventar ⎱ (The Magic Flute)
	Infelice, sconsolata ⎰
PARRY	Jerusalem
PROKOFIEV	Peter and the Wolf
QUILTER–SARGENT	To Julia
STRAUSS	Four Last Songs
STRAVINSKY	Symphony of Psalms
TCHAIKOVSKY	Joan of Arc's Farewell (Joan of Arc)
	Lenski's Aria (Eugene Onegin)
	Love Duet (Romeo and Juliet)
	Tatiana's Letter Song (Eugene Onegin)
WAGNER	The Mastersingers – Wahn! Wahn!
	The Valkyrie – Closing Scene (Act III)

From 1963

Royal Philharmonic Orchestra
GLYNDEBOURNE FESTIVAL OPERA
Conductor
John Pritchard

L'Incoronazione di Poppea .... MONTEVERDI

Ottone: WALTER ALBERTI	*First Soldier: DENNIS BRANDT*
Second Soldier: GERALD ENGLISH	*Poppea: MAGDA LASZLO*
Nerone: RICHARD LEWIS	*Arnalta: JEAN ALLISTER*
Ottavia: FRANCES BIBLE	*Drusilla: LYDIA MARIMPIETRI*
Seneca: CARLO CAVA	*Page: DUNCAN ROBERTSON*
Pallade: ELIZABETH BAINBRIDGE	*Maid: SOO-BEE LEE*
Liberto: JOHN SHIRLEY-QUIRK	*Lucano: HUGUES CUENOD*
Amor: ANNON LEE SILVER	*A Lictor: DENNIS WICKS*

GLYNDEBOURNE FESTIVAL CHORUS

A concert performance of the stage production of the opera given in the Glyndebourne
Festival

Tuesday, July 30th

London Symphony Orchestra
Conductor
Leopold Stokowski

Passacaglia and Fugue in C minor .... BACH
Symphony No. 2 .... MAHLER

RAE WOODLAND
JANET BAKER
BBC CHORUS
BBC CHORAL SOCIETY
GOLDSMITHS' CHORAL UNION
HARROW CHORAL SOCIETY

Wednesday, July 31st

Philharmonia Orchestra
Conductor
Sir Malcolm Sargent

Overture: Ruy Blas .... MENDELSSOHN
Rhapsody on a theme of Paganini .... RACHMANINOV
Symphony No. 2, in D .... SIBELIUS
Symphony No. 12 .... SHOSTAKOVICH

PETER KATIN

Thursday, August 1st

BBC Symphony Orchestra
Conductors
Sir Malcolm Sargent　　**Meredith Davies**

Overture: The Magic Flute .... MOZART

Symphony No. 1, in B flat (Spring) .... SCHUMANN
War Requiem .... BRITTEN

HEATHER HARPER
PETER PEARS
THOMAS HEMSLEY
MELOS ENSEMBLE (Conducted by Benjamin Britten)
BBC CHORUS
BBC CHORAL SOCIETY
HIGHGATE SCHOOL CHOIR

Friday, August 2nd

BBC Symphony Orchestra
Conductor
Sir Malcolm Sargent

Brandenburg Concerto No. 3, in G .... BACH
Concert Rondo for piano and orchestra (K. 382) .... MOZART
Symphony No. 3, in E flat (Eroica) .... BEETHOVEN
(a) Ave Maria .... BRUCKNER
(b) Friede auf Erden .... SCHOENBERG
(c) Der Geist hilft unsrer Schwachheit auf .... BACH
(Conducted by John Alldis)
Organ Solo: Fantasia and Fugue in G minor .... BACH

ALASDAIR GRAHAM
ARNOLD RICHARDSON
JOHN ALLDIS CHOIR

Saturday, August 3rd

BBC Symphony Orchestra
Conductor
Sir Malcolm Sargent

Overture: Prince Igor .... BORODIN
Lisa's Aria: Act III (The Queen of Spades) .... TCHAIKOVSKY
Piano Concerto No. 2, in C minor .... RACHMANINOV
Simple Symphony for string orchestra .... BRITTEN
Ballet Music: The Perfect Fool .... HOLST
Variations on an original theme (Enigma) .... ELGAR

MARIE COLLIER
COLIN HORSLEY

From 1970

Thursday, September 3rd

Amsterdam Concertgebouw Orchestra
Conductor
Bernard Haitink

Serenata Notturna (K. 239) .... MOZART

Concerto for piano and orchestra .... KEES VAN BAAREN
(First performance in this country)
Symphony No. 9 .... MAHLER

Solo piano: THEO BRUINS

Friday, September 4th
BBC Symphony Orchestra
Conductor
Pierre Boulez

Three Nocturnes... DEBUSSY
Et exspecto resurrectionem mortuorum .... MESSIAEN
The Rite of Spring .... STRAVINSKY

BBC WOMEN'S CHORUS

Saturday, September 5th
Amsterdam Concertgebouw Orchestra
Conductor
Bernard Haitink

Overture: Coriolan .... BEETHOVEN
Violin Concerto in E minor... MENDELSSOHN
Sinfonietta .... JANÁCEK
Symphony No. 6, in B minor (Pathétique) .... TCHAIKOVSKY

Solo violin: JEAN-PIERRE WALLEZ

Sunday, September 6th
Orchestra of the Royal Opera House, Covent Garden
Conductor
Georg Solti

Das Rheingold.. WAGNER

Wotan: DAVID WARD (bass)
Donner: JOHN SHAW (baritone)
Froh: ERMANNO MAURO (tenor)
Loge: JOHN DOBSON (tenor)
Alberich: ZOLTAN KELEMEN (bass-baritone)
Mime: JOHN LANIGAN (tenor)
Fasolt: MARTTI TALVELA (bass)
Fafner: MICHAEL LANGDON (bass)
Fricka: JOSEPHINE VEASEY (mezzo-soprano)
Freia: AVA JUNE (soprano)
Erda: HELEN WATTS (contralto)
Rhinemaidens: { *ELIZABETH ROBSON (soprano)*
               ANNE HOWELLS (mezzo-soprano)
               ELIZABETH BAINBRIDGE (contralto)

Monday, September 7th

BBC Symphony Orchestra
Conductor
Colin Davis

Symphony No. 84, in E flat major .... HAYDN
Violin Concerto No. 2 .... CROSSE
The Planets .... HOLST

Solo violin: MANOUG PARIKIAN
BBC WOMEN'S CHORUS

Tuesday, September 8th

BBC Symphony Orchestra
Conductors
Colin Davis   Norman Del Mar*

Symphony No. 40, in G minor (K. 550) .... MOZART
Piano Concerto No. 4, in G major .... BEETHOVEN
Essence of our Happinesses* .... LUTYENS
(Commissioned by the BBC. First performance)
Fantasia and Fugue in C minor .... BACH

Piano: STEPHEN BISHOP
Tenor: RICHARD LEWIS
Organ: DAVID SANGER
BBC CHORUS

Wednesday, September 9th

Hurwitz Chamber Orchestra
Conductor
Charles Mackerras

St John Passion .... BACH

Soprano: SHEILA ARMSTRONG
Contralto: ALFREDA HODGSON
Tenor: ALEXANDER YOUNG
Tenor: KENNETH BOWEN
Bass: NORMAN BAILEY
Bass: STAFFORD DEAN
BBC CHORUS

Thursday, September 10th

London Symphony Orchestra
Conductor
Jascha Horenstein

London Symphony Orchestra Wind Ensemble
Conductor
Gervase de Peyer

Serenade in C minor (K. 388) .... MOZART
Symphony No. 8, in C minor .... BRUCKNER

Friday, September 11th

BBC Symphony Orchestra
Conductor
Colin Davis

Overture: Leonora No. 3	BEETHOVEN
Cantata on the death of Emperor Joseph II	BEETHOVEN
Symphony No. 9, in D minor (Choral)	BEETHOVEN

Soprano: HEATHER HARPER
Mezzo-soprano: PATRICIA KERN
Tenor: RONALD DOWD
Bass: RAIMUND HERINCX
Bass: MICHAEL LANGDON
BBC CHORUS
BBC CHORAL SOCIETY
LONDON PHILHARMONIC CHOIR

Saturday, September 12th

BBC Symphony Orchestra
Conductor
Colin Davis

Hail, all hail to the Queen (The Trojans)	BERLIOZ
Songs: Zaide }	
La Belle Voyageuse }	BERLIOZ
Piano Concerto No. 2	RAWSTHORNE
The Shire Suite	TIPPETT
March: Pomp and Circumstance No. 1, in D major	ELGAR
El Salón México	COPLAND
Fantasy for audience and orchestra	ARNOLD

(Commissioned by the BBC. First performance)

Jerusalem	PARRY orch. ELGAR
National Anthem	

Soprano: SHEILA ARMSTRONG
Piano: MALCOLM BINNS
SCHOLA CANTORUM OF OXFORD
BBC CHORAL SOCIETY

Repertoire 1972

SYMPHONIES

BEETHOVEN	No. 3, in E flat major (Eroica)
	No. 4, in B flat major
	No. 5, in C minor
	No. 6, in F major (Pastoral)
	No. 7, in A major
	No. 9, in D minor (Choral)
BLISS	A Colour Symphony
BRAHMS	No. 1, in C minor

BRAHMS	No. 2, in D major
	No. 4, in E minor
BRUCKNER	No. 3, in D minor
	No. 4, in E flat major (Romantic)
	No. 8, in C minor
DVOŘÁK	No. 7, in D minor
	No. 8, in G major
HAYDN	No. 52, in C minor
	No. 93, in D major
MAHLER	No. 2
	No. 6, in A minor
	No. 7
	No. 8, in E flat major
MENDELSSOHN	No. 4, in A major (Italian)
MOZART	No. 38, in D major (K. 504) (Prague)
	No. 40, in G minor (K. 550)
SCHOENBERG	Chamber Symphony No. 1, in E, Op. 9
SCHUBERT	No. 4, in C minor (Tragic)
	No. 9, in C major
SHOSTAKOVICH	No. 10
SIBELIUS	No. 4, in A minor
	No. 5, in E flat major
STRAVINSKY	No. 1, in E flat
TCHAIKOVSKY	No. 4, in F minor
	No. 6, in B minor (Pathétique)
TIPPETT	No. 3
VAUGHAN WILLIAMS	Pastoral Symphony
	No. 6, in E minor

CONCERTOS

BACH	Brandenburg Concertos No. 1, in F major
	No. 2, in F major
	No. 3, in G major
	No. 4, in G major
	No. 5, in D major
	No. 6, in B flat major
	Oboe and violin – in C minor
	Violin – in A minor
	Two violins – in D minor
BEETHOVEN	Piano – No. 2, in B flat major
	No. 3, in C minor
	No. 4, in G major
	No. 5, in E flat major (Emperor)
	Violin – in D major
BRAHMS	Piano – No. 1, in D minor
	No. 2, in B flat major
	Violin – in D major
CARTER	Concerto for Orchestra
CHOPIN	Piano – No. 2, in F minor
ELGAR	Cello – in E minor
	Violin – in B minor
HAYDN	Trumpet – in E flat major

MENDELSSOHN	Violin – in E minor
MOZART	Clarinet – in A major (K. 622)
	Oboe – in C major (K. 314)
	Piano – in B flat major (K. 456)
	in D major (K. 537) (Coronation)
	Sinfonia Concertante in E flat major (K. 364)
	Violin – in G major (K. 216)
	in D major (K. 218)
MIYOSHI	Concerto for Orchestra
SCHUMANN	Cello – in A minor
STEVENSON, RONALD	Piano – No. 2 (The Continents)
STRAVINSKY	Two pianos
TCHAIKOVSKY	Piano – No. 1, in B flat minor
VIVALDI	Violin – in E flat major, Op. 8, No. 5
	Two violins – in A minor, Op. 3, No. 8
	Three violins – in F major
	Four violins – in B minor, Op. 3, No. 10
WALTON	Viola

OVERTURES

BEETHOVEN	Egmont
	Prometheus
MOZART	Don Giovanni
WAGNER	Tristan and Isolde
WALTON	Scapino
WEBER	Jubel

VOCAL AND CHORAL

ARNE	Rule, Britannia
BACH	Cantata No. 67: Halt im Gedächtnis Jesum Christ
	Cantata No. 191: Gloria in excelsis Deo
	The Christmas Oratorio
BEETHOVEN	(Missa Solemnis) Mass in D major
BERLIOZ	Benvenuto Cellini
	Hail, all hail to the Queen (The Trojans)
	Te Deum
BIRTWISTLE	Nenia on the Death of Orpheus
	Down by the Greenwood Side
BOULEZ	E. E. Cummings ist der Dichter
BRITTEN	Hymn to St Cecilia
CARDEW	The Great Learning, Paragraph One
CROSSE	Celebration
GABRIELI, ANDREA	Magnificat for three choirs
GABRIELI, GIOVANNI	In ecclesiis benedicite Domino
	Jubilate Deo a 8 (1613)
GIBBONS	Hosanna to the Son of David
	The Silver Swan
	What is our life?
HANDEL	Coronation Anthem: The King shall rejoice
HAYDN	(Harmoniemesse) Mass in B flat major
	Orfeo ed Euridice, Act IV
	(Theresienmesse) Mass in B flat major

JANÁČEK	Glagolitic Mass
LEHÁR	Aria: Vilja (The Merry Widow)
MAXWELL DAVIES	Blind Man's Buff
MESSIAEN	Poèmes pour Mi
MONTE, C. DE	Plaude decus mundi
MONTEVERDI	Il ritorno d'Ulisse in patria
	Vespers of the Blessed Virgin (1610)
MOZART	Die Entführung aus dem Serail
	Requiem Mass (K. 626)
	Vesperae Solennes de Confessore (K. 339)
PARRY	Jerusalem (orchestrated by Elgar)
PURCELL	King Arthur
RAINIER	Requiem
SCARLATTI, A.	Magnificat (Vespers of St Cecilia)
SCHOENBERG	Pierrot Lunaire
SCHUBERT	Chorus of Huntsmen (Rosamunde)
	Gesang der Geister über den Wassern
	Nachthelle
	Ständchen
SCHÜTZ	Psalm 100: Jauchzet dem Herren alle Welt
	Psalm 150: Lobet den Herren
	Saul, was verfolgst du mich?
STOCKHAUSEN	Carré
STRAUSS, JOHANN	Csárdás (Die Fledermaus)
STRAVINSKY	Le Rossignol
	Symphony of Psalms
SULLIVAN	The Gondoliers
	The Grand Duke
	HMS Pinafore
	Iolanthe
	The Pirates of Penzance
	Utopia Ltd
TALLIS	O Lord, give thy holy spirit
	O sacrum convivium
TAVENER, JOHN	Celtic Requiem
WAGNER	Parsifal, Act I
	Parsifal, Acts II and III
WALTON	Belshazzar's Feast
	A Song for the Lord Mayor's Table
	Troilus and Cressida, Act II
WEBER	Aria: Leise, leise (Der Freischütz)
WEILL	Kleine Mahagonny
VERDI	Requiem Mass

MISCELLANEOUS

BACH	Prelude and Fugue in B minor (S. 544)
BARTÓK	Music for strings, percussion and celesta
	Sonata for two pianos and percussion
BEETHOVEN	Romances – No. 1, in G major, Op. 40
	No. 2, in F major, Op. 50
BRITTEN	Variations and Fugue on a theme of Purcell
CAGE, JOHN	First Construction in Metal

CAGE, JOHN	Hpschd
CRUMB, GEORGE	Echoes of Time and the River
DEBUSSY	Three Nocturnes
ELGAR	March: Pomp and Circumstance No. 1, in D major
GABRIELI, ANDREA	Ricercare a 4
GABRIELI, GIOVANNI	Canzona noni toni
	Canzona septimi
	Sonata pian' e forte
HOLLIGER	Siebengesang
HOLST	The Planets
ISHII	Kyoso
IVES	The Fourth of July
LAMBERT, JOHN	Formations and Transformations
LISZT	Hexameron, for 6 pianos and orchestra
MOZART	Masonic Funeral Music (K. 477)
	Piano Quartet in G minor (K. 478)
MESSIAEN	Seven Haikai
PURCELL	Chaconne in G minor
RACHMANINOV	Rhapsody on a theme of Paganini
RAVEL	Alborada del gracioso
RAWSTHORNE	Theme and Variations for two violins
STRAUSS, JOHANN	Csárdás (Ritter Pásmán)
	Emperor Waltz
	Galop: Banditten
	Polka: Freikugeln
	Spanish March
	Waltz: The Blue Danube
STRAUSS, JOSEPH	Feuerfest: Polka française
	Polka: Plappermäulchen
	Waltz: Mein Lebenslauf ist Lieb und Lust
STRAUSS, RICHARD	Tod und Verklärung
STRAVINSKY	Ballet: The Firebird
	Ballet: Petrushka (1911)
	Capriccio, for piano and orchestra
	Octet
	The Rite of Spring
	Symphonies of wind instruments (original version)
THOMSON	The Plough that Broke the Plains
TIPPETT	Fantasia on a theme of Handel
VAUGHAN WILLIAMS	Fantasia on a theme of Thomas Tallis
WEBER	Invitation to the Dance (arranged by Berlioz)
ZIMMERMANN	Canto di Speranza
	Music for Maximilian I

From 1974

Sunday, 21 July

BBC Symphony Orchestra
Conductor
Pierre Boulez

Gurrelieder .... SCHOENBERG

Soprano: MARITA NAPIER
Soprano: FELICITY PALMER
Tenor: JESS THOMAS
Tenor: GERALD ENGLISH
Baritone: SIEGMUND NIMSGERN
Speaker: GUNTHER REICH
BBC SINGERS
BBC CHORAL SOCIETY
GOLDSMITHS' CHORAL UNION
LONDON PHILHARMONIC CHOIR

Monday, July 29

Christ Church Cathedral Choir, Oxford
Conductor
Simon Preston

Ten Blake Songs .... VAUGHAN WILLIAMS
Mass in G minor .... VAUGHAN WILLIAMS
Six Metamorphoses after Ovid .... BRITTEN
Cantata: Rejoice in the Lamb .... BRITTEN

Oboe: JANET CRAXTON
Tenor: IAN PARTRIDGE
Organ: STEPHEN DARLINGTON

Monday, July 29th

Intermodulation

Monody for piano, with live electronic modulation .... SMALLEY
Across the Boundary .... STOCKHAUSEN
Zorna, for soprano saxophone and drums .... SOUSTER
Les Moutons de Panurge .... RZEWSKI

Piccolo clarinet: ALAN HACKER
Soprano saxophone: TONY COE
Tenor saxophone: EVAN PARKER
Trumpet: KENNY WHEELER
Trombone: PAUL RUTHERFORD
Trombone: JOHN WHITE
Double-bass: BARRY GUY
Drums: JOHN MARSHALL

Tuesday, July 30th

BBC Symphony Orchestra
Conductor
John Pritchard

Overture in the South .... ELGAR
Dance Rhapsody No. 1 .... DELIUS
The Hymn of Jesus .... HOLST
Hammarskjöld Portrait .... WILLIAMSON
(Commissioned by the BBC. First performance)
The Young Person's Guide to the Orchestra .... BRITTEN

Soprano: ELISABETH SÖDERSTRÖM
BBC SINGERS
BBC CHORAL SOCIETY

Wednesday, July 31st

BBC Symphony Orchestra
Conductor
Alexander Gibson

Symphony No. 8, in B minor (Unfinished) .... SCHUBERT
3 Harfenspieler Lieder .... WOLF
Mignon .... WOLF
Anakreons Grab .... WOLF
Schlafendes Jesuskind .... WOLF
In dem Schatten meiner Locken .... WOLF
Der Rattenfänger .... WOLF
Er ist's .... WOLF
Symphony No. 2, in D major .... BRAHMS

Soprano: ELISABETH SÖDERSTRÖM
Baritone: THOMAS HEMSLEY

Thursday, August 1st

Monteverdi Orchestra
Conductor
John Eliot Gardiner

Music for the Royal Fireworks .... HANDEL
Dixit Dominus .... HANDEL
Masque for the Queen of Sheba, Act III Solomon .... HANDEL

Soprano: FELICITY PALMER
Mezzo-soprano: MAUREEN LEHANE
Tenor: PHILIP LANGRIDGE
Baritone: THOMAS ALLEN
MONTEVERDI CHOIR

Friday, August 2nd

BBC Symphony Orchestra
Conductor
John Pritchard

Symphony No. 39, in E flat major (K. 543)	MOZART
Piano Concerto No. 4, in G major	BEETHOVEN
Symphony No. 6, in E flat minor	PROKOFIEV

Piano: PETER KATIN

Saturday, August 3rd

Black Dyke Mills Band
Grimethorpe Colliery Band
Conductor
Elgar Howarth

Severn Suite	ELGAR
Grimethorpe Aria	BIRTWISTLE
A Moorside Suite	HOLST
I'm seventeen come Sunday	GRAINGER

BBC Concert Orchestra
Conductor
Ashley Lawrence

Brigg Fair	GRAINGER
Brigg Fair: an English rhapsody	DELIUS
A Lincolnshire Posy	GRAINGER
Trial by Jury	GILBERT–SULLIVAN

Usher: BRYAN DRAKE (bass-baritone)
Defendant: ANTHONY ROLFE JOHNSON (tenor)
Learned Judge: FRANCIS EGERTON (tenor)
Counsel: STUART HARLING (baritone)
Plaintiff: SALLY LE SAGE (soprano)
Forman of the Jury: MICHAEL FOLLIS (bass)
BBC SINGERS

Repertoire 1977

ARNOLD, MALCOLM	Overture: Beckus the Dandipratt
BACH	Magnificat in D major
	Cantata No. 118: O Jesu Christ, mein's Lebens Licht
	Motet: Komm, Jesu, komm!
	Brandenburg Concerto No. 3 in G major
	No. 4 in G major for violin, two flutes and strings
BALASSA, SÁNDOR	Quartet for Percussion
BARRAQUÉ	Chant après chant
BARTÓK	Piano Concerto No. 2
	Violin Concerto No. 2

BARTÓK	Dance Suite
	Sonata for two pianos and percussion
BEETHOVEN	Piano Concerto No. 3 in C minor
	No. 4 in G major
	No. 5 in E flat major (Emperor)
	Violin, Cello and Piano Concerto in C major
	Overture: Leonora No. 2
	Symphony No. 2 in D major
	No. 3 in E flat major (Eroica)
	No. 5 in C minor
	No. 6 in F major (Pastoral)
	No. 7 in A major
	No. 9 in D minor (Choral)
BENNETT, RICHARD RODNEY	Actaeon for horn and orchestra
BERG	Concert Aria: Der Wein
BERIO	Coro
BERKELEY	Serenade for string orchestra
BERLIOZ	Te Deum
	The Damnation of Faust
	Overture: Benvenuto Cellini
BIRTWISTLE, HARRISON	Melencolia I
BLISS	Music for strings
BODY, JACK	Marvel not, Joseph
BOULEZ	Cummings ist der Dichter
	Rituel: In memoriam Maderna
BRAHMS	Piano Concerto No. 1 in D minor
	Violin Concerto in D major
	Academic Festival Overture
	Symphony No. 2 in D major
	No. 3 in F major
	No. 4 in E minor
BRITTEN	Cantata academica
	Cantata: Phaedra
	Hymn to St Cecilia
	A Hymn to the Virgin
	Les Illuminations
	The Young Person's Guide to the Orchestra
BRITTEN–BERKELEY	Mont Juic: Suite of Catalan dances
BRUCKNER	Symphony No. 4 in E flat major
	No. 9 in D minor
BULLER, JOHN	Proença
CAMPRA	Messe des Morts
MAXWELL DAVIES	The Martyrdom of St Magnus
	St Thomas Wake: Foxtrot for orchestra
DEBUSSY	Poème dansé: Jeux
DELIUS	Fantasy: In a Summer Garden
DIEPENBROCK	Entr'acte: Marsyas
DUPARC	Au pays où se fait la guerre
	L'invitation au voyage
	Le manoir de Rosemonde
	Phidylé
	La vie antérieure

DVOŘÁK	Cello Concerto in B minor
	Symphony No. 8 in G major
	Four Slavonic Dances from Op. 46
ELGAR	Cello Concerto in E minor
	Symphony No. 2 in E flat major
	March: Pomp and Circumstance No. 1 in D major
	Variations on an original theme (Enigma)
FAURÉ	Requiem
GABRIELI, G.	Buccinate in neomania
	Jubilate Deo a 8
	Sonata pian e forte
	Sonata a 8
GERHARD, ROBERTO	Concerto for orchestra
GOEHR, ALEXANDER	Pastorals
GRIFFITHS, DAVID	Salve Regina
HARRIES, DAVID	The Three Men
HAYDN	Symphony No. 44 in E minor (Trauer)
	No. 57 in D major
	No. 86 in D major
	No. 100 in G major (Military)
	No. 103 in E flat major (Drum Roll)
HENZE	The Raft of the 'Medusa'
HOLST	The Planets
JANÁČEK	Sinfonietta
KEURIS, TRISTAN	Sinfonia
LIGETI	San Francisco Polyphony
LISZT	Piano Concerto No. 1 in E flat major
	Prelude and Fugue on Bach
MAHLER	Symphony No. 1 in D major
	No. 7
MENDELSSOHN	Violin Concerto in E minor
MESSIAEN	Turangalîla Symphony
	Couleurs de la cité céleste
	Oiseaux exotiques
MEWS, DOUGLAS	The May Magnificat
MONTEVERDI	Vespers of the Blessed Virgin (1610)
MOZART	Don Giovanni
	Concert Aria: Ch'io mi scordi di te (K. 505)
	Clarinet Concerto in A major (K. 622)
	Piano Concerto No. 9 in E flat major (K. 271)
	No. 12 in A major (K. 414)
	No. 23 in A major (K. 488)
	No. 27 in B flat major (K. 595)
	Concerto for Two Pianos in E flat major (K. 365)
	Overture: The Marriage of Figaro
	Symphony No. 31 in D major (Paris) (K. 297)
	No. 39 in E flat major (K. 543)
	No. 40 in G minor (K. 550)
	Divertimento in D major (K. 136)
	Serenade in D major (Serenata Notturna) (K. 239)
	Serenade No. 11 in E flat major (K. 375)
MUSGRAVE	Rorate coeli

PALESTRINA	Missa Assumpta est Maria
PARRY orch. ELGAR	Jerusalem
PARSONS, ROBERT	Ave Maria
JOSQUIN DES PRÉS	Tulerunt Dominum
PROKOFIEV	Piano Concerto No. 1 in D flat major
	Symphony No. 3 in C minor
PURCELL	Hail, bright Cecilia: a song for St Cecilia's Day, 1692
RACHMANINOV	Three Symphonic Dances
RAVEL	Ballet: Daphnis et Chloé
	Rapsodie Espagnole
	La Valse: poème chorégraphique
	Valses nobles et sentimentales
REUBKE	Sonata on the 94th Psalm
ROXBURGH, EDWIN	Montage
SCHOENBERG	Chamber Symphony No. 1
	Transfigured Night
	Song of the Wood Dove (Gurrelieder)
SCHUBERT	Mass in E flat major
	Gesang der Geister über den Wassern
	Overture in C minor
	Symphony No. 3 in D major
	No. 8 in B minor (Unfinished)
	No. 9 in C major
	Quintet in A major (The Trout)
SCHUMANN	Four Songs, Op. 141
	Piano Concerto in A minor
SCHÜTZ	Es erhub sich ein Streit im Himmel
	Ich beschwöre euch; Veni Sancte Spiritus
	Wie lieblich sind deine Wohnungen
SHOSTAKOVICH	Symphony No. 4
	No. 5 in D minor
SIBELIUS	Symphony No. 7 in C major
	Tone Poem: The Oceanides
STANFORD	Magnificat for double choir
STOCKHAUSEN	Adieu
JOHANN STRAUSS II	Czárdás (Die Fledermaus)
	Overture: Die Fledermaus
	March: The Gypsy Baron
	Waltz: The Blue Danube
JOHANN II – JOSEF STRAUSS	Pizzicato Polka
JOSEF STRAUSS	Polka: Plappermäulchen
	Polka: Eingesendet
STRAUSS	Concerto for oboe and small orchestra
	Symphonic Poem: Death and Transfiguration
	Till Eulenspiegel
	Serenade in E flat major for thirteen wind instruments
	Songs: Zueignung
	Ruhe, meine Seele
	Waldseligkeit
	Wiegenlied
	Meinem Kinde
	Befreit

STRAVINSKY	Symphony of Psalms
	Concerto for piano and wind
	Ballet: The Firebird
	Pulcinella: Ballet in one act with solo voices
	Ballet: The Rite of Spring
	Divertimento: The Fairy's Kiss
	Orpheus
SULLIVAN	Overture di Ballo
SULLIVAN arr.	Suite from the Ballet: Pineapple Poll
MACKERRAS	
TCHAIKOVSKY	Symphony No. 5 in E minor
	Violin Concerto in D major
	Fantasia after Dante: Francesca da Rimini
	Overture-fantasy: Hamlet
TIPPETT	The Midsummer Marriage
	Concerto for Double String Orchestra
VAUGHAN WILLIAMS	Job: a masque for dancing
	Serenade to Music
WAGNER	Prelude and Liebestod (Tristan und Isolde)
WALTON	Belshazzar's Feast
	Violin Concerto in B minor
WILLIAMSON, MALCOLM	Organ Concerto
arr. HENRY WOOD	Fantasia on British Sea Songs
XENAKIS	Phlegra

From 1979

Saturday, August 18th

BBC Northern Symphony Orchestra
Conductor
Janos Fürst

Symphony No. 8, in F major	BEETHOVEN
Piano Concerto No. 21, in C major (K. 467)	MOZART
Overture: Light Cavalry	SUPPÉ
Waltz: Artist's Life	JOHANN STRAUSS II
Csárdás from Die Fledermaus	JOHANN STRAUSS II
Waltz: Roses from the South	JOHANN STRAUSS II
Radetsky March	JOHANN STRAUSS I

Soprano: TERESA CAHILL
Piano: BERNARD ROBERTS

Monday, August 20th

Royal Philharmonic Orchestra
Philip Jones Brass Ensemble
Conductor
Elgar Howarth

Pre-Prom talk
Harrison Birtwistle

La Mer: three symphonic sketches .... DEBUSSY
The Triumph of Time .... BIRTWISTLE
Pictures from an Exhibition .... MUSSORGSKY
(arr. for brass ensemble by Elgar Howarth)

Tuesday, August 21st

Welsh National Opera
Welsh Philharmonia Orchestra
Conductor
Richard Armstrong

Billy Budd Act I .... BRITTEN

Tenor: NEVILLE ACKERMAN
Tenor: ARTHUR DAVIES
Tenor: NIGEL DOUGLAS
Tenor: STUART KALE
Tenor: CHARLES LEWIS
Baritone: THOMAS ALLEN
Baritone: NICHOLAS FOLWELL
Baritone: JULIAN MOYLE
Baritone: HENRY NEWMAN
Baritone: GARETH RHYS DAVIES
Baritone: GORDON WHYTE
Bass: RICHARD VAN ALLAN
Bass: RALPH HAMER
Bass: PETER MASSOCCHI
Bass: GEOFFREY MOSES
Bass: FRANK OLEGARIO
Bass: FORBES ROBINSON
Men's voices: WELSH NATIONAL OPERA CHORALE

Wednesday, August 22nd

Philharmonia Orchestra
Conductor
Norman Del Mar

Symphony No. 35, in D major (Haffner) (K. 385) .... MOZART
Piano Concerto No. 22 in E flat major (K. 482) .... MOZART
Variations on a recitative, Op. 40 .... SCHOENBERG
Symphonic poem: Also sprach Zarathustra.. STRAUSS

Piano: IMOGEN COOPER
Organ: TIMOTHY BOND

Thursday, August 23rd

BBC Symphony Orchestra
Conductor
Gennadi Rozhdestvensky

Symphony No. 14 .... SHOSTAKOVICH
Symphony No. 1, in D minor .... RACHMANINOV

Soprano: FELICITY PALMER
Bass: NICOLA GHIUSELEV

Friday, August 24th

London Sinfonietta
Conductor
Simon Rattle
Sasono Mulio Gamelan of Surakarta

A Mirror of Whitening Light .... MAXWELL DAVIES
Piano Concerto in G major .... RAVEL
Gamelan Music with dancers
Trois petites liturgies de la Présence Divine .... MESSIAEN

Piano: PAUL CROSSLEY
Ondes-martenot: JEANNE LORIOD
Women's voices: BBC SINGERS

Saturday, August 25th

BBC Symphony Orchestra
Conductor
Gennadi Rozhdestvensky

Pre-Prom talk
Hugh Wood

Five Klee Pictures .... MAXWELL DAVIES
Scenes from Comus... HUGH WOOD
Symphony No. 1, in A flat major .... ELGAR

Soprano: YVONNE KENNY
Tenor: BRIAN BURROWS

APPENDIX D
Ticket prices 1895-1979

QUEEN'S HALL

Year	Promenade *(unreserved)*	Balcony *(numbered and reserved)*	Grand Circle *(numbered and reserved)*	Season ticket (Prom) *(transferable)*
1895–1914	1/–	2/–	3/– (front row 5/–)	one guinea (21/–)
1915	1/–	2/–	3/–, 5/–	no season tickets advertised between 1915 and 1929
1916–17	1/2 (with entertainment tax)	2/2	3/3, 5/3	......
1918	1/6	2/8	3/6, 5/9	......
1919	2/–	3/–	4/–, 6/6	......
1920–9	2/–	3/–	5/–, 7/6	......
1930–1	2/–	3/–	5/–, 7/6	35/–
1932	2/–	3/–	5/–, 6/–, 7/6	35/–
1933–40	2/–	3/–	5/–, 6/–, 7/6	37/6 (winter seasons 10/–)

ROYAL ALBERT HALL

Year	Promenade	Balcony	Amphitheatre, stalls and boxes	Season ticket (Prom)
1941–2	2/–	3/–	7/6, 6/–, 5/– (3/– unreserved)	28/– (1941) 37/6 (1942)
1943–4	2/–	3/–	7/6, 6/–, 5/–, 4/–	42/–
1945	2/–	3/–	7/6, 6/–, 5/–, 4/–	37/6
1946	2/– (prom in gallery as well as arena from 1946 on)	3/–	7/6, 6/–, 5/–	37/6 (winter 12/–)
1947–50	2/–	3/6 *(now numbered and reserved)*	7/6, 6/–, 5/–	37/6
1951	2/–	3/6	7/6, 6/–	36/6 (excl. last concert)
1952	2/–	4/–	8/6, 6/–	45/– (incl. last concert)
1953–5	2/6	5/–, 3/6	8/6, 7/6, 5/–	50/–
1956–8	2/6	6/–, 4/–	8/6, 6/–	50/–
1959	3/–	6/6, 4/6	8/6, 6/6	60/–
1960–1	3/–	6/–	9/–, 6/–	60/–

Year	Promenade	Balcony	Amphitheatre, stalls and boxes	Season ticket (Prom)
1962	3/6	7/6, 6/–	10/6, 7/6	65/–
1963–4	3/6	10/6, 7/6	12/6, 10/6	65/–
1965–7	5/–	11/–, 8/–	15/–, 11/–	125/–

From the early 1960s onwards it has been customary to have a number of 'special events' at the RAH and at other venues. Different prices are charged for these. The figures given refer to the normal concerts at the RAH.

Year	Promenade	Balcony	Amphitheatre, stalls and boxes	Season ticket (Prom)
1968	5/–	12/6, 8/–	20/–, 12/6	125/–
1969	6/–	12/6, 9/–	20/–, 12/6	150/–
1970	6/–	14/–, 10/–	22/–, 14/–	150/–
1971	35p	80p, 45p	£1.25, 80p	£8
1972	40p	£1.00, 80p	£1.50, £1.00	£9
1973	45p	£1.00, 70p	£1.70, £1.00	£10
1974	50p	£1.20, 80p	£2.00, £1.20	£12
1975	50p	£1.30, 90p	£2.20	£13
1976	60p (gallery 50p)	£1.50, £1.00	£2.50	£13
1977	70p (gallery 60p)	£1.50	£3.00	£18
1978	75p (gallery 60p)	£1.75, £1.25	£3.50	£20
1979	75p (gallery 60p)	£1.75, £1.25	£4.00	£20

Bibliography

BBC Written Archives, Caversham (correspondence, memoranda, press cuttings)

Programmes and prospectuses, Promenade Concerts 1895–1979

Aprahamian, Felix; Grindea, Miron; Russell, Thomas (editors): *Homage to Sir Henry Wood – a world symposium* (London, 1944)

Arditi, Luigi: *My Reminiscences* (London, 1896)

Ayre, Leslie: *The Proms* (London, 1968)

Blyth, Alan: *Colin Davis* (London, 1972)

Boult, Adrian C.: *My Own Trumpet* (London, 1973)

Carse, Adam: *The Life of Jullien* (Cambridge, 1951)

Chancellor, E. Beresford: *Life in Regency and Early Victorian times* (London, 1926)

Clark, Ronald: *The Royal Albert Hall* (London, 1958)

Elkin, Robert: *Queen's Hall, 1893–1941* (London, 1944)
 Royal Philharmonic (London, 1947)
 The Old Concert Rooms of London (London, 1955)

Foss, Hubert and Goodwin, Noël: *London Symphony – Portrait of an Orchestra* (London, 1954)

Gazzetta Musicale di Milano (Milan, 1876–)

Glock, William: *The BBC's Music Policy* (BBC lecture, London, 1963)

Goossens, Eugene: *Overture and Beginners* (London, 1951)

Hill, Ralph and Rees, C. B.: *Sir Henry Wood – Fifty years of the Proms* (London, 1944)

Langley, Hubert: *Dr Arne* (Cambridge, 1938)

Newmarch, Rosa: *A Quarter of a Century of Promenade Concerts at Queen's Hall* (London, 1920)
 Henry J. Wood (London, 1904)
 Numerous articles and programme notes for the Proms

Orga, Ates: *The Proms* (London, 1974)

Pound, Reginald: *Sir Henry Wood* (London, 1969)

Reid, Charles: *Sir Malcolm Sargent* (London, 1968)

Rivière, Jules P.: *My Musical Life and Recollections* (London, 1893)

Russell, Thomas: *The Proms* (London, 1949)
 Philharmonic Decade (London, 1945)
 Philharmonic Project (London, 1952)

Sands, Mollie: *Invitation to Ranelagh, 1742–1803* (London, 1946)

Scholes, Percy A.: *The Mirror of Music*, 2 vols (London, 1947)

Scott, W. S.: *Green Retreats – the story of Vauxhall Gardens* (London, 1955)

Shore, Bernard: *The Orchestra speaks* (London, 1938)

Wood, Henry J.: *My Life of Music* (London, 1938)
 About Conducting (London, 1945)

Wood, Jessie: *The Last Years of Henry J. Wood* (London, 1954)

Wyndham, H. S.: *August Manns and the Saturday Concerts* (London, 1909)

Young, Patricia, and others: *The Story of the Proms* (London, 1955)

Index

of the main text and of significant premières

Abbado, Claudio, 238
Accademia Monteverdiana, 214–15
Adler, Larry, 172
Albéniz, I., 71
Albert Hall, see Royal Albert Hall
Alexandra, Queen, 43
Alexandrov, A. V., 136
Alldis, John, 222
Allen, Thomas, 236
Allin, Norman, 69, 71, 98
Alwyn, William, 101, 179 (première), 206 (première), 209 (première), 273, 280, 283, 287
Amoyal, Pierre, 248
Annan Committee, 244
Ansermet, Ernest, 201
ApIvor, Denis, 280 (première)
Aprahamian, Felix, 105
Aranyi, Jelly d', 73, 75, 80
Arditi, Luigi, 17–18
Arensky, A., 58
Arne, Dr Thomas, 12, 51, 102
Arnell, Richard, 179
Arnold, Malcolm, 175 (première), 190, 194 (première), 216 (première), 281, 292, 293, 295
Arnold, Matthew, 214
Arts Council of Great Britain, 120, 133, 161
Arup Associates, 133
Ashkenazy, V., 197
Askew, Reginald, 122
Asquith, A., 64
Atherton, David, 222, 250
Auden, W. H., 178
Auric, G., 167
Austin, Frederic, 44, 59, 81; premières, 263, 265, 272
Austral, Florence, 80
Ayrton, Michael, 152

Bach, C. P. E., 220
Bach, J. C., 12
Bach, J. S., 18, 38, 43, 53, 58, 61, 70, 76, 77, 79, 80, 101, 102, 104, 107, 136, 137, 143, 149, 151,

167, 173, 175, 187, 188, 196, 207, 210, 211, 212, 214, 216, 218, 219, 221, 224,
Bachauer, Gina, 176
Backhaus, W., 48
Bagenal, Hope, 120
Bagrinovsky, M., 70
Baillie, Isobel (Bella), 78–9, 98
Bainbridge, Simon, 301 (première)
Bainton, Edgar, 44, 49 (première), 62, 261
Bairstow, Edward C., 79
Baker, George, 71
Baker, Janet (Dame), 212, 221, 231, 237, 250
Balakirev, M., 41
Balfour, Margaret, 98
Banks, Don, 214 (première), 236, 292
Bantock, Granville, 44, 58, 59, 77, 107 (première), 137 (première), 146, 153; premières; 263, 275, 278
Barber, Samuel, 134, 137
Barbirolli, Sir John, 143, 146, 154, 157, 161, 165, 172, 173, 178, 179, 210, 212, 218 (death), 238
Barenboim, Daniel, 221, 224, 231
Barnard, John, 228
Bartók, Béla, 69–70, 77, 80, 168, 169, 179, 220, 222, 224, 228, 240, 253
Bate, Stanley, 281 (première)
Bath, Hubert, 70, 264 (première)
Bax, Arnold, 48, 61, 75 (première), 76, 77, 94, 101, 102 (première), 105, 108, 152, 167, 169; premières; 265, 266, 269, 270, 273
Bazelaire, Paul, 41
BBC Choral Society, 98, 222
BBC Chorus, 98, 197, 211, 235
BBC Concert Orchestra, 178, 212, 216, 222, 236, 238, 248
BBC Northern Singers, 240

BBC Northern Symphony Orchestra, 225, 236, 248
BBC Opera Orchestra, 170
BBC Scottish Symphony Orchestra, 232, 248
BBC Singers, 147, 152, 235, 240
BBC Symphony Orchestra, 91 (début at Proms, 1930), 94, 98, 99, 103, 111–12, 119, 123, 124, 130, 140, 145–7, 151, 156–7, 159, 165–6, 172–3, 176, 185, 190–2, 199, 201, 203, 215, 220, 235, 236, 238, 240, 242, 246, 248, 250, 252
BBC Theatre Orchestra, 147, 170
BBC Welsh Symphony Orchestra, 220, 236, 248
BBC World Service (previously General Overseas Service), 136, 253
Beard, Paul, 94, 124, 130, 160
Beaux Arts Trio, 218
Beckett, John, 253
Bedford, David, 222, 238 (première); 301
Bedford, Steuart, 237
Beecham, Sir Thomas, 27, 67, 68; conducts a Prom (1915); 70; 94, 116, 123, 161, 173
Beethoven, L. van, 13, 18, 20, 26, 34, 35, 36, 38, 47, 49, 53, 58, 59 (symphonies and concertos), 61, 69, 73, 75, 76, 80, 101, 104, 106, 107, 109, 132, 134, 135, 143, 146, 151, 155, 167, 173, 175, 185, 187–8, 199, 204, 206–7, 210, 212, 218 (bicentenary), 219, 221 (Missa solemnis), 222, 224, 226, 228, 240, 241, 242
Benedict, Sir J., 20
Benjamin, Arthur, 176; premières, 273, 280
Bennett, R. R., 209 (première), 244, 245, 287, 305
Bennich, Tosta de, 93, 97
Berg, Alban, 103, 105, 175, 179, 184, 201, 206, 214, 215, 248

Berio, L., 197, 204, 216, 219, 225, 240

Berkeley, Lennox (Sir), 102, 135 (première), 167 (première), 168, 176, 207 (première), 208 (première), 225 (70th birthday – Sym. No. 3 and commission), 248 (Sym. No. 4); premières 276, 277, 279, 280, 285–6, 299

Berlin Philharmonic Orchestra, 222

Berlioz, H., 18, 20, 38, 87, 137, 149, 186, 196, 197, 204, 209, 212, 216 (centenary), 220, 222 (*Damnation of Faust*)

Berners, Lord, 75, 102, 103; première 269

Bertini, Gary, 190

Black, Leo, 200

Binns, Malcolm, 208

Birtwistle, Harrison, 214 (première), 222, 236; 292

Bishop, Sir Henry, 12, 13

Bizet, G., 238

Blacher, Boris, 215

Black Dyke Mills Band, 236, 238

Blackman, P. J., 232

Blake, David, 244 (première); 304

Blake, Ernest, 48, 260 (première)

Bliss, Arthur (Sir), 77, 78, 81, 101, 103, 108, 124, 129, 134, 152, 170, 171, 175, 190, 209, 211, 219 (80th birthday); premières 270, 272, 280

Bloch, Ernest, 77, 152, 163, 168, 171

Blockx, J., 41

Blom, Eric, 45, 87, 171

Boosey, William, 65–6, 83, 84, 86

Borodin, A., 45, 76, 149

Borwick, Leonard, 75

Bosc, A., 15

Boston Symphony Orchestra, 67

Boswell, James, 12

Boughton, Rutland, 44, 49, 81; premières, 261, 267

Boulez, Pierre, 161, 190, 199, 201, 203, 207, 211, 212, 215, 219, 220 (wide range of styles), 221, 222, 225, 236, 237, 238, 240, 242, 248, 253

Boult, Sir Adrian, 90, 94, 108, 111, 119; shares Prom conducting with Wood and Cameron, 123–4; 129, 130, 132, 133, 136, 137; conducts Jubilee Concert, 138; 140; wishes to withdraw from Proms, 142 ff.; 154; attitude to Schoenberg's music, 156; 157–8, 164, 166, 167–9, 172–3, 175, 179, 194, 196, 218 (in his 81st year), 219–20, 222, 231, 236

Bournemouth Symphony Orchestra, 175, 248

Bowen, York, 50, 59 (première), 71, 76; premières, 261, 264, 270

Boyce, William, 12

Bracken, Brendan, 129

Brahms, J., 20, 38, 47, 49, 50, 53, 61, 72, 76, 80, 90, 101, 103, 104, 124, 134, 136, 143, 151, 154, 155, 167, 172, 173, 187, 199, 203, 218, 220, 236, 241

Brailowsky, A., 76

Brain, Aubrey, 80

Brain, Dennis, 169

Brendel, Alfred, 220, 231

Brian, Havergal, 59, 63 (première), 190, 211; premières, 263, 266

Bridge, Frank, 59, 62 (première), 70, 73, 76, 77, 79, 101 (première), 103, 104; premières, 263, 266, 267, 268, 271, 273

Brindle, Reginald Smith, 209 (première), 288

British Broadcasting Company, 83–4, 86

British Broadcasting Corporation: involvement, 82 ff.; 'The BBC and the Proms', 100, 101; BBC Symphony Orchestra not available after outbreak of war, 110; connection with BBC severed 1940–1, 111 ff.; sponsorship of BBC re-established for 1942 season, 122 ff.; Promenade Jubilee and the BBC, 127 ff.; Wood offers the BBC the right to use the title 'The Henry Wood Promenade Concerts', 127–8; 21st anniversary of BBC taking over Proms (1948), 158; BBC policy regarding Proms, 106, 112, 139–40, 149, 163; Diamond Jubilee of Proms (1954), 173; 'Broadcasting in the Seventies', 197; planning the Proms, 232 ff.

British National Opera Company, 86

Britten, Benjamin (later Lord), 94, 134 (première), 137, 140, 151, 171, 172, 173, 179, 188, 207, 208, 209, 211, 212, 215, 216, 220 (conducting Purcell's *Fairy Queen*), 224 (60th birthday), 228, 238, 242 (*War Requiem*), 244, 248, 252; première 276

Broadcasting in the Seventies, 197, 234

Brompton Oratory, 225

Brosa, Antonio, 108

Brott, Alexander, 175

Browning, Robert, 153

Bruch, Max, 58

Bruckner, A., 44 (Sym. No. 7), 179 (Sym. No. 4), 207, 211,

220 (Sym. No. 2 and No. 5), 221, 236, 242, 248 (Sym. No. 8)

Brunskill, Muriel, 98, 107

Buller, John, 245 (première); 305

Bunting, Christopher, 178

Burgess, Russell, 216

Burney, Dr Charles, 12

Burns, Robert, 175

Burt, Francis, 208 (première), 287

Busch, William, 136 (première), 277

Bush, Alan, 103, 135 (première), 152 (première), 168 (première), 171, 176, 216 (première); premières, 277, 278, 279, 294

Busscher, Henri de, 61

Butterworth, George, 71, 77; premières, 269, 270

Byrd, William, 211, 214, 215, 240

Cage, John, 199, 221, 235

Cambridge University Madrigal Society, 173

Camden, Archie, 103, 154, 181

Cameron, Basil, 116; Wood's first 'associate' conductor of Proms, 122; career and character 122–3; 124, 130, 133, 135, 137, 140, 142, 143, 146–7; opened first Prom after war (1945), 151; 154; in and out of favour with BBC, 157–8; 163, 167 ff., 185, 187, 194, 196, 207, 208–9 (80th birthday concert and last season, 1964)

Campoli, Alfredo, 171

Canning, Vera, 171

Cannon, Philip, 281 (première)

Cantores in Ecclesia, 220

Čapek, Karel, 81

Carewe, John, 207

Carnegie Collection of British Music, 87

Carnegie Hall, New York, 44

Carpenter, John Alden, 71, 77

Carte, D'Oyly, 147

Carter, Elliott, 200, 211, 221, 240, 244

Casals, Pau, 56, 72, 171

Casella, Alfredo, 75, 107

Castelnuovo-Tedesco, M., 163, 280

Cathcart, Dr George, 26–7 (French pitch), 44, 55, 82

Catterall, Arthur, 55, 58, 104, 135

Cavalli, P. F., 197, 214, 220

Central Hall, Westminster, 84

Chabrier, E., 71, 142, 149, 186

Chagrin, Francis, 279 (première)

Chamberlain, Neville, 109

Chappell and Co., 43, 65–7, 71, 82 ff, 111 ff.

Chapple, Brian, 244 (première), 304

Charpentier, M. A., 215
Chávez, Carlos, 186
Chelsea Opera Group, 192
Chicago Symphony Orchestra, 246
Chopin, F., 59, 74, 210
Christoff, Boris, 199, 224
Churchill, Winston, 56
City of Birmingham Symphony Orchestra, 94, 124
Clark, Edward, 93–4
Cleveland Orchestra, 240
Clutsam, G. H., 34, 256 (première)
Coates, Eric, 62 (première), 63 (première), 75 (première), 77; premières, 265, 266, 268, 269, 272
Cohen, Harriet, 75, 76, 80, 107, 169, 173
Cole, Maurice, 135
Coleridge-Taylor, S., 38, 48, 50, 62
Colonne, Edouard, 54
Concertgebouw of Amsterdam, 196, 212
Connolly, Justin, 246
Cooke, Arnold, 207 (première), 238 (première); premières, 286, 294, 302
Cooke, Deryck, 209 (Mahler No. 10)
Copland, Aaron, 136, 176, 179, 244
Covent Garden Opera, 175, 188, 199, 203, 208, 211, 212, 215, 219 (first stereo broadcast), 224, 237, 238, 242
Covent Garden Theatre, 15–18, 23, 26, 87
Cowen, F. H., 20, 23, 48, 70; premières, 267–8
Cowie, Edward, 238 (première), 246; première, 302
Cox, Garnet Wolseley, 59
Craxton, Harold, 77
Craxton, Janet, 225
Creston, Paul, 152
Crosse, Gordon, 194 (première), 212 (première); 290, 298
Crossley, Paul, 238
Crown and Anchor Tavern, 13
Croydon Philharmonic Society, 176
Crumb, George, 200, 244, 252
Crystal Palace, 19, 25, 45, 56
Cui, C., 41
Cundell, Edric, 77
Cunningham, G. D., 79
Curzon, Clifford, 79, 80, 105, 137, 197
Czech Army Choir, 136
Czech Philharmonic Orchestra, 196, 216

Daily Express, The, 102, 160
Daily Telegraph, The, 83, 114, 130, 132, 168, 187, 216
Dalby, Martin, 237 (première), 300
Dale, Benjamin, 62, 266 (première)
Danks, Harry, 94, 96
Darke, Harold, 79
Davies, H. Walford, 61, 69 (première), 71, 78, 87 (as broadcaster), 117; premières, 263, 267, 271
Davies, Meredith, 208
Davies, Peter Maxwell, 207 (première), 216 (première), 221 (Fires of London), 228, 244, 248, 252, 286, 294
Davis, Andrew, 238, 248
Davis, Colin: takes over from Sargent at 1967 Proms, 191; career and acceptance as Prom conductor, 192 ff.; 199, 203; success with Oedipus Rex, 204, 206; 207, 212 (The Trojans), 216, 218, 219, 221, 224 (Covent Garden Fidelio), 237, 238, 240, 242, 250
Dawson, Peter, 80
Debussy, Claude, 50 (L'Après-midi), 54, 56, 61, 62, 63, 70, 103, 105, 107, 186, 201, 204, 209, 214, 220, 225, 242 (Pelléas et Mélisande), 252, 253
Delibes, L., 135
Delius, F., 59, 76, 103, 104, 105, 106, 137, 152, 212, 236, 274–5 (premières)
Del Mar, Norman, 194, 207, 209, 211, 250
Demuth, Norman, 136 (première)
Desmond, Astra, 78–9, 98
Devant, David (Animated Photographs), 30
Diaghilev, S., 147
Dieren, Bernard van, 77, 270 (première)
Disney, Walt, 253
Dods, Marcus, 212
Dohnányi, E. von, 63, 78, 81
Donne, John, 219
Dorati, Antal, 212
Douglas, Clive, 169
Douglas, Keith, 115 ff., 135
Dowd, Ronald, 206, 212, 218
Dreyfus, Louis, 114
Drinkwater, John, 90
Drucker, Nina, 232
Dryden, John, 153
Dufay, G., 197, 241
Dukas, Paul, 59
Dunhill, Thomas, premières 267, 269
Dunstable, J., 197, 215

Dupré, Marcel, 101, 103
Dushkin, Samuel, 104
Dustin, Judy, 228
Dvořák, A., 36 (première), 38, 41, 44, 61, 76, 211, 215, 221, 257
Dyson, George, 79, 272 (première)

Early Music Consort, 220, 242
Easton, Robert, 98
Edward VII, King, 43
Edwards, Bill, 196
Elgar, Edward (Sir), 38, 39, 41, 44, 48 (Pomp and Circumstance No. 1), 49, 61, 62, 70, 71, 73, 76, 77, 87, 102, 103, 104, 105, 106, 107, 117, 123, 135, 137, 151, 153, 155, 165, 172, 176 (centenary), 191, 192, 210, 212, 218, 222, 224, 236, 244; premières 264, 266, 267, 274
Eliason, Edward, 13
Elizabeth II, Queen, 224, 244 (Silver Jubilee)
Elwes, Gervase, 58, 69, 71, 76, 104
Enesco, Georges, 61, 62
English Chamber Orchestra, 214, 221
English National Opera, 238, 244
English Opera Group, 237
English Singers, The, 79
Ensemble InterContemporain, 253
Erlih, Devy, 153
Evans, Edwin, 89
Evans, Geraint (Sir), 207
Evelyn, John, 11

Falkner, Keith, 79
Falla, Manuel de, 80, 81
Fantasia on British Sea-Songs (arr. Wood) 51–3, 61, 73–4, 194
Farjeon, Harry, 136 (première)
Fauré, G., 35, 49, 63, 76
Ferguson, Howard, 173
Ferrier, Kathleen, 154
Février, Jacques, 104
Fires of London, 221, 244
Flagstad, Kirsten, 178
Fogg, Eric, 76, 79, 103; 274 (première)
Forbes, Sebastian, 219 (première); 295
Forster, E. M., 23
Forsyth, Cecil, 58 (première)
Foss, Hubert, 157
Foster, Lawrence, 248
Fox, George, 47 (première)
Franck, César, 49 (Symphonic Variations), 75
Fransella, Albert, 55
Frewin, T. H., 34, 40 (première), 256–7 (premières)
Fricker, P. Racine, 156, 163, 171,

172, 173, 176, 179, 208
(première); 287
Fulton, Norman, 173

Gabrieli, Andrea, 214–15
Gamelan Music, see Sasono
  Mulio
Gardiner, Balfour, 59 (première),
  70 (première), 262, 264, 267,
  269
Gardiner, John Eliot, 214, 216,
  225, 240, 246
Gardner, John, 281 (première)
Gazzetta musicale di Milano, 17
George V, King, 55, 66, 73
George VI, King, 108, 129
Gerhard, Roberto, 179, 186, 190,
  208, 212, 219, 222
Gerhardt, Elena, 105
German, Edward, 36, 48
Gershwin, George, 244
Gertler, André, 175
Gibbons, Orlando, 79
Gibbs, Armstrong, 76, 271
  (première)
Gibson, Alexander (Sir), 220,
  242
Gielen, Michael, 248
Giester, Hans, 211
Gieseking, Walter, 79
Gilbert, Donald, 117
Gilels, Emil, 250
Gipps, Ruth, 277 (première)
Giulini, Carlo-Maria, 188
Glazunov, A., 35, 41, 102
Glière, R., 59
Glinka, M., 41, 224
Glock, William (Sir), 52, 94, 135,
  142, 152, 155; appointed
  Controller of Music, BBC,
  182 ff.; 190 ff., 200 ff., 204 ff.,
  228, 233–5, 237 (pianist) 250,
  253
Glossop, Peter, 248
Gluck, C. W. von, 38, 250
Glyndebourne Opera Company,
  188, 207, 208, 210, 211, 212,
  214, 215, 216, 219, 221, 224,
  237, 238, 242, 248, 252
Goehr, Alexander, 200, 206
  (première); 284
Goehr, Clare, 232
Goldmark, C., 228
Goldsack, Jessie (later Lady
  Jessie Wood), 48, 93, 111, 116,
  119, 122, 124, 126, 132–3, 159
Goldschmidt, Berthold, 209
Goldsmith, Oliver, 12
Gomez, Jill, 221
Goodwin, Noël, 171
Goossens, Eugene, 63 (première),
  69 (première), 76 (première),
  103, 137, 143, 179, 206;
  premières, 267, 269, 270, 274,
  279

Goossens, Léon, 78, 103, 152,
  167, 179
Goossens, Marie, 79, 179
Goossens, Sidonie, 108, 179
Gounod, Ch., 18, 34, 35, 38, 72
Graham, Colin, 222
Grainger, Percy, 50, 61, 62, 63
  (premières), 103, 236, 267, 268
Gramophone Company, The, 133
Granados, E., 75
Greater London Council, 133
Greatrex, Muriel Ellen (Lady
  Wood), 55, 92
Greenbaum, Kyla, 151, 175
Greene, Plunket, 69
Greenwood, John, 281 (première)
Grieg, E., 29, 38, 50, 58, 59, 61,
  74, 137, 176, 178, 250
Grimethorpe Colliery Band, 236,
  238
Grinke, Frederick, 108
Grinke Trio, 105
Gromadsky, Vitaly, 211
Grove, Freda, 196, 237
Grove, George (Sir), 19, 45
Groves, Charles (Sir), 175, 208,
  218, 250
Grumiaux, A., 153
Guy, Barry, 304 (première)

Hacker, Alan, 236
Hadley, Patrick, 146 (première),
  153 (première), 278
Haitink, Bernard, 190, 196, 212,
  215, 216, 220, 222, 224, 231,
  238, 240, 242, 248
Haley, W. J. (Sir), 127–9, 137,
  149, 157
Halifax Madrigal Society, 79
Hall, Marie, 58, 77
Hall, Marshall, 59
Hallé, Sir Charles, 178
Hallé Concert Society, 86, 178
Hallé Orchestra, 19, 143, 161,
  172, 173, 178, 210, 211, 212,
  238, 248
Halsey, Louis, 210
Hambourg, Mark, 48
Hamilton, Iain, 176, 179; 289
Handel, G. F., 12, 18, 26, 61, 78,
  80, 105, 146, 151, 153, 172, 188,
  191, 206, 209, 210, 211, 214,
  215, 219 (Messiah), 224, 240
Harper, Edward, 246
Harper, Heather, 208
Harris, W. H., 135 (première),
  136 (première), 276–7
Harrison, Beatrice, 75, 78, 103,
  135, 137
Harrison, Jane, 231
Harrison, Julius, 266 (première)
Harrison, May, 75, 103
Harty, Hamilton (Sir), 59
  (première), 61, 70, 264–5
  (premières)

Harvard Glee Club, 176
Harvey, Trevor, 169–70, 172
Haselböck, Hans, 236
Haydn, J., 59, 79, 101, 171, 173,
  179, 199, 206, 208, 210, 211, 215
  (complete concert), 224, 252 (La
  Fedeltà premiata)
Hely-Hutchinson, V., 101, 102,
  140, 142 ff., 154, 155
Hemsley, Thomas, 208
Henderson, Roy, 98, 134, 137
Henry Wood Hall, 133
Henry Wood Proms Circle, 231
Henschel, G., 18
Henze, Hans Werner, 178, 190,
  210, 240; 302 (première)
Her Majesty's Theatre, 16
Herbage, Julian, 93–4, 102, 119,
  140, 142–3, 153, 157–9, 176, 183
Herbert, William, 176
Herincx, Raimund, 206, 212
Hervé (Florimond Ronger), 16
Hess, Myra (Dame), 61, 75, 80,
  101, 103, 119, 137, 173
Hibberd, Stuart, 132
Hindemith, P., 81, 101, 102,
  103, 104, 140, 152, 163, 171
Hirschhorn, Philip, 197
Hislop, Joseph, 80
Hitler, Adolf, 109, 130, 134
Hoban, John, 225
Hoddinott, Alan, 176
Holbrooke, J., 44, 47 (première),
  49; premières, 259, 263, 267
Holden, Jules, 228
Holliger, Heinz, 221
Hollingsworth, John, 169–70,
  172, 175, 178, 209
Holloway, Robin, 222, 237
  (première), 246 (première); 300,
  307
Holmboe, Vagn, 250
Holmes, Edmund, 55
Holst, Gustav, 75, 76, 77, 78, 79,
  80, 103, 104, 105, 167, 191, 224,
  236, 237 (centenary), 252
Holst, Henry, 175
Holt, Harold, 119
Honegger, A., 79, 81, 87, 102,
  103, 168, 169, 181, 253
Hook, James, 12
Hooton, Florence, 136
Horder, Lord, 129, 132
Horenstein, Jascha, 190, 209, 216,
  220
Horrocks, Amy, 41 (première),
  258
Horsley, Colin, 167
Howard, Michael, 220
Howarth, Elgar, 236
Howell, Dorothy, 77; premières
  269–70, 273
Howells, Herbert, 76 (première),
  102, 168; premières 270, 271,
  280

Howgill, R. J. F., 114, 163–5, 168, 182
Huband, Paul, 186
Huber, Hans, 48
Hunter, Rita, 248
Hyde, Elizabeth, 229

Ibert, Jacques, 79, 107, 178, 181
Incorporated Society of Musicians, 115
Indy, Vincent d', 38, 59, 80
Intermodulation, 219
International Society for Contemporary Music (ISCM), 94, 214
International Youth Orchestra, 238
Ippolitov-Ivanov, M., 41
Ireland, John, 71, 94, 103 (Piano Concerto), 123, 136 (BBC commission), 152, 163, 173, 228, 253 (Piano Concerto revived); premières, 269, 274, 276–8
Isaacs, Leonard, 156
Israel Philharmonic Orchestra, 231, 253
Iturbi, José, 79
Ives, Charles, 206, 211, 218, 219, 236, 237, 240, 244

Jacob, Gordon, 81, 102, 154, 168, 169, 190; premières, 273, 279, 280, 281
Jacob, Sir Ian, 166
Jacobs, Arthur, 160
Jacques, Edgar E., 28, 45
Janáček, I.., 103, 173, 237 (Katya Kabanova), 248 (anniversary)
Järnefelt, A., 77
Jarred, Mary, 98, 137
Jeunesses Musicales World Orchestra, 248
Joachim, J., 58, 59, 72, 74
John Alldis Choir, 221
Johnson, Patricia, 206
Johnson, Dr Samuel, 12
Johnstone, Maurice, 108, 163–5, 183, 192, 233
Jones, Daniel, 163, 170 (première), 280
Jones, Parry, 98, 106
Jongen, J., 173
Josquin des Prés, 215, 219
Joyce, Eileen, 137, 167
Jullien, Louis, 16
Jullien, L. A., 13–15, 16, 32, 35, 58

Kabalevsky, D., 136, 167
Kalisch, Alfred, 45
Karajan, Herbert von, 222
Kars, Jean-Rodolph, 197, 199
Keller, Hans, 200–1
Kempe, Rudolf, 209, 221, 242 (death)

Kennedy, Daisy, 90
Kennedy, Joseph P., 135
Kent Opera, 238
Kentner, Louis, 134, 137
Kenyon, Nicholas, 91n.
Kern, Patricia, 222
Kersey, Eda, 137
Kétèlbey, Albert W., 13
Khachaturian, A., 136, 137
Khan, Imrat, 199, 248
Kiddle, Frederick, 59, 78, 88
King's Singers, 199, 220
Klemperer, O., 192
Klenovsky, Paul (Henry Wood), 102, 136, 209
Kletzki, P., 165
Knightley, T. E., 22–3
Knussen, Oliver, 252 (première); 308
Kodály, Zoltán, 101 (Háry János), 103, 105, 107, 176
Kohler, Irene, 137
Kontarsky, Aloys, 207, 215, 225
Krenek, Ernst, 103
Krenz, Jan, 196, 212
Kubelik, Rafael, 165

Lacombe, L. T., 15
Lacomblé, Corinne, 168
Lago, S., 25
Laine, Cleo, 199, 220
Lambert, Constant, 102, 103, 134, 140, 142–3, 146–7, 152, 153, 169, 170
Lambert, John, 222 (première); 298
Lamond, F., 75, 103
Larsson, Lars-Erik, 105
Lasso, O. di (Lassus, Orlandus), 215
Lawrence, Ashley, 236
Leclair, J. M., 215
Ledger, Philip, 222
LeFanu, Nicola, 225 (première); 299
Leningrad Philharmonic Orchestra, 220
Leppard, Raymond, 214, 220, 221, 225
Lewis, Anthony, 276, 279 (premières)
Lewis, Richard, 207, 219, 221
Liadov, A., 41, 59
Ligeti, G., 220
Liszt, F., 18, 20, 29, 34, 35, 36, 38, 45, 48, 61, 70, 104, 105, 137, 142, 152, 167, 222, 246
Litolff, H. C., 15
London Bach Orchestra, 220
London Philharmonic Orchestra, 94, 98, 112, 117, 123, 124, 130, 133, 140, 147, 161, 172, 173
London Sinfonietta, 201, 222, 250
London Symphony Orchestra,

18, 98, 111, 112, 115, 130, 133, 135, 140, 147, 151, 157, 172–3, 209, 221, 225
London Wireless Orchestra, 91
Los Angeles Philharmonic Orchestra, 236, 237
Loughran, James, 231, 238, 250
Loveridge, Iris, 154
Lucas, Leighton, 136 (première), 176, 277
Lucas, Mary Anderson, 136 (première)
Lumsdaine, David, 242
Lutoslawski, W., 212, 228, 248, 250
Lutyens, Elisabeth, 94, 135 (première), 154, 169 (première), 184, 206 (première), 219 (première), 244; premieres, 276, 280, 285, 295, 299
Lyceum Theatre, 11

Maazel, Lorin, 216, 222, 240
McCarthy, Patrick, 237
McCunn, Hamish, 48
MacDowell, E., 48
MacEwan, Desirée, 77
McEwan, J. B., 271 (première)
Macfarren, Sir G. A., 98
Mackenzie, A. C., 20, 34, 36, 47, 48, 51
McNaught, William, 157
Macpherson, Stewart, 262 (première)
Machaut, G. de, 197
Mackerras, Charles (Sir), 209, 211, 214, 216, 218, 236, 237, 238, 244
Maconchy, Elizabeth, 103 (première), 107, 181, 225; premières, 274, 277, 281, 289
Mahler, Gustav, 44 (Sym. No 1), 61, 149, 188, 208, 209 (Sym. No 10), 210 (Sym. No 6), 211, 215, 216, 219, (Sym. No 8), 299 (Sym. No 9), 221, 222, 238, 240, 242, 248 (Sym. No 2), 253; 288
Malcolm, George, 175, 207, 221
Malcuzynski, W., 153
Malipiero, G. F., 71, 80, 108, 173
Manén, Joan, 104
Manning, Jane, 220
Manns, August, 19, 45
Marchant, Dr Stanley, 74, 75
Maréchal, Maurice, 103
Martin, Easthope, 265 (première)
Martin, Frank, 173, 175
Martin, Nick, 232
Martinu, B., 167, 181
Mase, Owen, 115
Masefield, John, 129–30, 152
Mason, Berkeley, 87–8
Massenet, J., 34, 38, 59
Matheson, James, 248
Maw, Nicholas, 207 (première), 252 (première); 286, 308

Mayer, Sir Robert, 147, 248
Mays, Edgar, 96, 159, 172, 187, 196
Meale, Richard, 242
Medtner, N., 87
Mehta, Zubin, 231, 236, 253
Meister Glee Singers, 41
Mellers, Wilfrid, 216 (première); 294
Melliard, Lesley, 231
Mellon, Alfred, 16
Mendelssohn, F., 20, 23, 29, 30, 35, 36, 38, 47, 48, 104, 171, 215, 221, 240
Menges, Isolde, 75, 78
Menuhin, Yehudi, 153, 248
Messager, A., 212
Messiaen, O., 197, 207, 210, 215, 216, 220, 221, 248 (anniversary), 252
Mewton-Wood, Noel, 137, 170
Meyer, Marcelle, 104
Miaskovsky, N., 78
Miles, Maurice, 173
Milhaud, D., 152, 156, 167, 176, 181, 206
Milner, Anthony, 206 (première), 285
Milton, John, 61
Moeran, E. J., 135 (première), 167 (première), 171, 277, 279
Moiseiwitsch, B., 69, 70, 71, 80, 119, 134, 137, 178
Monteux, Pierre, 186, 209
Monteverdi, C., 77, 188, 197, 208, 214, 215, 216, 218, 220, 221, 224, 238
Monteverdi Orchestra, 240
Moore, Gerald, 116
Morrison, Angus, 102, 103, 134
Moscow Chamber Opera, 248
Moscow Radio Orchestra, 190, 196, 215
Mottl, Felix, 26
Mozart, W. A., 12, 13, 38, 47, 59, 61, 76, 79, 80, 101, 104, 124, 146, 151, 167, 176, 182, 186, 188, 190, 201, 204, 206, 207 (operas), 208, 210, 212, 215, 216, 218, 220, 221, 222, 224, 234, 236, 237, 248
Munich Philharmonic Orchestra, 221
Munrow, David, 220, 242 (death)
Murdoch, William, 70, 71
Murrill, Herbert, 158–9, 163, 170–2
Musard, Philippe, 11, 13
Musgrave, Thea, 206 (première), 207 (première), 214, 225 (première); 284, 286, 300
Musical Times, The, 19, 35, 55, 68, 83, 182, 204
Musicians' Benevolent Fund, The, 133

Musicians' Union, 83–4
Mussorgsky, M., 48, 59, 61, 70, 75, 199, 208, 224
Muti, Riccardo, 250

Nash, Heddle, 98, 106
National Youth Orchestra of Great Britain, 175, 178, 179, 220, 236, 238, 250
Naylor, Bernard, 209 (première), 210, 220 (première); 288, 297
Nelsova, Zara, 218
Neumann, Vaclav, 216
New Irish Chamber Orchestra, The, 253
New Symphony Orchestra, 54
Newman, Ernest, 89
Newman, Robert, 9; early career, 23, 25; appoints Wood conductor of Proms, 25–7; 29–30, 32, 35, 36, 42, 43, 44, 45, 53, 54, 55; women in orchestra, 56–7; 61; against boycotting of German music, 64–5; death (1926), 74, 80–2; 88, 110, 158, 178
Newmarch, Rosa (Mrs), 45, 59, 63, 87, 89, 93; death of, 136
Newson, George, 219, 220 (première); 297
New York Philharmonic Orchestra, 238, 240
NHK Symphony Orchestra of Japan, 221
Nicholls, Agnes (Lady Harty), 9
Nicolls, B. E. (Sir Basil), 111 ff., 119, 123, 133, 143, 149
Nielsen, Carl, 210, 250
Nono, Luigi, 208
Norrington, Roger, 220, 238
Northern Sinfonia, 221, 248
Nottingham Symphony Orchestra, 44

Observer, The, 82, 168, 171, 182, 192, 212, 218, 225
Offenbach, J., 13
Ogdon, John, 210, 211
Ogilvie, F. W., 120
Oistrakh, D., 197, 215
Olympic Theatre, 25
Opéra Comique (London), 30
Ord, Boris, 173
Orff, Carl, 179, 236 (Carmina Burana)
Orloff, Nicholas, 80
Otterloo, Willem van, 236
Ouroussoff, Princess Olga (Mrs Henry Wood), 41, 43, 44, 55, 58, 92

Paderewski, I. J., 35, 61, 72
Palestrina, G. P. da, 210, 240
Palm, Siegfried, 215
Palmer, Felicity, 221

Palmgren, S., 76, 135
Panufnik, A., 175, 181
Park Sisters, 35
Parker, Fry, 27
Parry, Sir C. H. H., 20, 87, 191
Pärt, Arvo, 252
Partridge, Sir Bernard, 84
Payne, Anthony, 252 (première); 308
Payne, Arthur, 27, 44, 54
Pears, Peter (Sir), 151, 208, 221, 242
Penderecki, K., 190, 210, 212, 250
People's Palace, 87
Pepys, Samuel, 11
Performing Right Society, 133
Perkin, Helen, 103
Petrassi, G., 156, 163, 171, 178
Petri, Egon, 50, 80
Peyer, Gervase de, 219
Philharmonia Orchestra, 248, 250
Philharmonic Choir, 98
Philip Jones Brass Ensemble, 199
Phillips, Montague, 137
Piatigorsky, G., 105
Pick-Mangiagalli, R., 78
Piston, Walter, 136, 172
Pitt, Percy (Sir), 30, 34, 36, 41, 45, 47, 91, 94; premières, 256–8, 260, 265, 267
Pizzey, George, 138
Plaistow, Stephen, 200
Play of Daniel, The, 241–2
Poldowski, 62, 266 (première)
Polish Army Choir, 136
Polish Radio Orchestra, 196, 212
Ponsonby, Robert, 203, 227, 233 ff.
Poole, John, 238, 240
Porter, Andrew, 178
Post, Joseph, 169
Postnikova, Victoria, 248
Pouishnoff, L., 76, 119, 137, 167
Poulenc, Francis, 103, 104
Pound, Reginald, 93
Powell, Allan, 129
Prausnitz, Frederik, 211, 219
Pré, Jacqueline du, 224
Previn, André, 221, 225, 236
Primrose, William, 169
Prince Albert, 36, 119, 215 (anniversary); 294
Prince Charles, 168, 241
Pritchard, John, 207–8, 212, 215, 219, 220, 224, 237
Prokofiev, S., 71, 76, 137, 152 (Sym. No 5), 154, 175, 211, 236, 252; 268 (première)
Puccini, G., 178 (centenary)
Punch, 84
Purcell, Henry, 172, 188, 190, 210, 214, 215, 220 (Fairy Queen), 221 (King Arthur), 244

Queen's Hall: 9, 11; building and
description, 22–3; 25–7, 30;
destruction of, 117, 119; 126,
135, 158–9, 227
Queen's Hall Orchestra, 19, 26,
28, 32, 42–3, 44, 45, 54, 56, 57,
58, 64–5; became New Q.H.
Orchestra, 66; 74, 84; became
'Sir Henry Wood and his
Symphony Orchestra', 88
Quilter, Roger, 59, 62, 75
(première), 87; premières, 264,
266, 270

Rachmaninov, S., 47, 56, 70, 98,
134, 155, 167, 211, 225
(centenary), 241, 242, 252
Radio Times, 114, 182
Raff, J., 38, 228
Raimondi, Ruggiero, 216
Rainier, Priaulx, 209 (première),
225 (première), 248; 288, 300
Rameau, J. P., 218, 240, 246
Ranelagh Gardens, 11, 12
Rascher, Sigurd, 107
Rattle, Simon, 248
Ravel, M., 59, 61, 62, 63, 70, 104,
105, 142, 170, 219, 220, 238
(centenary), 252
Rawsthorne, Alan, 136, 140, 152,
154, 168, 178, 190, 207
(première), 210, 214 (première);
premières, 278, 282, 286, 293
Reed, W. H., 38, 41, 44
Reed, W. L., 136
Rees, C. B., 146, 159, 167
Reger, M., 56
Reith, John (Sir, later Lord), 82, 84
Remedios, Alberto, 206
Renard, G., 55
Reynolds, Howard, 41
Richter, Karl, 214
Riddle, Frederick, 238
Riefling, Robert, 178
Riley, Terry, 218
Rimbaud, A., 151
Rimsky-Korsakov, N., 18, 34, 35,
71
Ripley, Gladys, 103
Rivière, Jules, 15–16
Robbins, Tessa, 186
Robert, Pierre, 215
Robinson, Stanford, 147, 157,
167 ff., 222
Rodrigo, J., 181
Ronald, Landon, 47 (première),
68, 76, 259
Rossi, Mario, 215, 216
Rossini, G. A., 13, 18, 36, 38, 138
Rostal, Max, 168
Rostropovich, M., 197, 215
Rothwell, Evelyn (Lady
Barbirolli), 154, 181
Round House, 199, 219, 220, 224,
235, 238, 240, 250, 252, 253

Roussel, A., 77
Rowlandson, Thomas, 12
Rowley, Alec, 136 (première)
Roxburgh, Edwin, 244
(première); 306
Royal Academy of Music, 25, 36,
74, 117, 119, 126
Royal Albert Hall, 11, 68, 98,
decision to hold Proms in, 119;
description, 119; acoustics, 120;
129, 130, 160, 227
Royal Choral Society, 18, 98, 117,
154, 176
Royal College of Art, 236
Royal College of Music, 236
Royal Philharmonic Orchestra,
161, 172–3
Royal Philharmonic Society, 18,
22, 65, 72, 114 ff.
Roze, Marie, 48
Rozhdestvensky, G., 190, 211,
246, 248, 252
Rubbra, Edmund, 94, 108, 135
(première), 152, 168, 175, 211;
premières, 276, 277
Rubinstein, Anton, 38, 61
Ruggles, Charles, 219
Russell, Thomas, 145

Sabata, Victor de, 77
Sadler's Wells Opera Company,
151, 169, 192, 206, 224
St Augustine's Church, Kilburn,
235, 238, 250
St James's Hall, 18
St Sepulchre's Church, Holborn,
152
Saint-Saëns, C., 35, 41, 48, 61,
77, 78 (*Carnival of the Animals*),
105 (centenary concert), 178,
186
Sammons, Albert, 69, 70, 76, 102,
106, 134, 135
Samuel, Harold, 75
Samuelson, Christopher, 196
Santoliquido, F., 77
Sarasate, P. de, 74
Sargent, Malcolm (Sir): at Proms
first as composer, 72; 76, 79,
117, 133; career and first Prom
season as conductor, 147; 154;
success at Proms, his musical
character, 155–7; 'Last Night'
control, 159–60; relations with
BBC, 163 ff.; 167 ff., 183;
principal Prom conductor under
Glock, 185 ff.; last season, 190;
illness and death, 190–2; 194,
196–7, 206, 208, 209, 211, 228,
231, 250
Sasono Mulio Gamelan of
Surakarta, 228, 252
Satie, Erik, 103, 206
Scharrer, Irene, 71, 80
Schelling, Ernest, 69

Schidlof, Peter, 192
Schmidt-Isserstedt, Hans, 215
Schmitt, Florent, 75
Schnabel, A., 182
Schoenberg, Arnold, 56, 62 (*Five
Orchestral Pieces*), 140, 151,
156–7, 178, 184, 185, 190
(*Moses and Aaron*), 199, 200,
204, 206–7, 209 (*Erwartung*),
210, 215, 218, 220, 221 (*Pierrot
Lunaire*), 222, 225 (*Gurrelieder*),
235, 237 (centenary), 238, 248
(*Die Glückliche Hand*), 253
Scholes, Percy A., 82, 87
Schreker, F., 79
Schubert, F., 20, 29, 34, 35, 36,
38, 49, 61, 79, 87, 104, 105,
165, 167, 186, 210, 218, 236,
248 (anniversary)
Schuman, William, 136, 154
Schumann, Elisabeth, 105, 153
Schumann, R., 20, 35, 38, 61,
104, 135, 220, 225
Schütz, H., 219, 220
Schwabacher, Siegfried, 55
Schwarz, Rudolf, 166, 183
Schytte, Ludwig, 48
Score, The, 182
Scott, Cyril, 44, 49 (première),
59, 70, 77, 103, 167 (première),
228; premières, 261, 264, 267
Scottish National Orchestra, 203,
235, 248
Scottish Opera, 220, 242
Scriabin, A., 56, 71, 76, 211
Seaman, Christopher, 232, 236,
238, 250
Searle, Humphrey, 94, 156,
167 (première), 168, 176, 181,
214 (première); 279, 292
Seiber, Mátyás, 175, 181
Sellick, Phyllis, 216
Sessions, Roger, 220, 244
Shaw, Bernard, 26, 34
Shelley, Percy B., 178
Shield, William, 12
Shirley-Quirk, John, 221
Shore, Bernard, 103
Shostakovich, D., 105 (Sym. No
1), 137 (Sym. No 8), 152 (Sym.
No 9), 179, 211, 228, 248 (Sym.
No 4), 252
Shuard, Amy, 218
Sibelius, J., 43, 44 (Sym. No 1),
48, 58, 59 (Violin Concerto), 101
(*Tapiola*), 104, 105 (Sym. No 7),
107, 123, 130, 143, 152, 155,
171, 172, 173, 179 (memorial
concert), 250
Sidwell, Martindale, 214, 220
Simpson, Robert, 212
Singcircle, 248
Slobodskaya, Oda, 96, 106, 137
Smalley, R., 219 (première); 297
Smetana, B., 20

Smith, Cyril, 135, 216
Smyth, Ethel (Dame), 49, 70, 77, 79, 81, 103, 104; premières, 272, 275
Soft Machine, The, 197, 199
Solomon, 69, 70, 104, 119, 134
Solti, Georg (Sir), 188, 208, 211–12, 219, 246
Souster, Tim, 199, 219 (première); 296, 301
Sowerby, Leo, 169
Spain-Dunk, Susan, 79, 81, 101 (première); 272–3
Speyer, Sir Edgar, 42–3, 54, 55, 61, 64–6, 82, 88
Spivakovsky, J., 76
Spohr, L., 20
Squire, Isobel, 228
Squire, W. H., 38
Stalman, Roger, 206
Stanford, Sir C. V., 20, 30, 34, 48, 55; premières 256, 265
Stanley, John, 12
Starokadomsky, Mikhail, 154
Steggall, Reginald, 48 (première), 260
Stern, Isaac, 197
Stevens, Bernard, 167 (première), 279
Stevens, Denis, 214
Stevens, Nigel, 232
Stevenson, Ronald, 222 (première); 298
Stiles-Allen, 98
Stockhausen, K., 197, 199, 214 (Gruppen), 215, 219, 225, 240, 242, 248 (anniversary)
Stokowski, Leopold, 70, 102, 186, 188, 208, 209
Stosch, Leonora von (Lady Speyer), 42–3
Strauss, Johann II, 238
Strauss, Richard, 34, 38, 49, 56, 62, 63, 104, 107, 152, 167, 169, 221, 224, 253
Stravinsky, I., 63, 77, 104, 107, 152, 153, 161, 179, 185, 197, 201, 204, 206, 207 (80th birthday concert), 210, 214, 215, 216, 218, 219, 220, 222, 225, 238, 248, 252, 253
Strube, 102
Stuart, Charles, 147
Suddaby, Elsie, 98, 103, 104
Sullivan, Arthur (Sir), 15, 20, 35, 38; letter to Wood 38–9; 41; Gilbert and Sullivan, 147, 212, 222, 234, 236, 238; 244 (Patience)
Susskind, Walter, 179, 209
Sutherland, Joan, 173
Svetlanov, Evgeny, 215
Swingle Singers, 216
Sydney Symphony Orchestra, 236

Szánto, Theodor, 59
Szigeti, J., 104, 153
Szymanowski, K., 210 (Stabat Mater), 250

Tailleferre, Germaine, 80, 105, 108
Tallis, Thomas, 240
Tansman, A., 156
Tauber, Richard, 134
Tausky, Vilem, 178
Tavener, John, 214 (première), 216, 222, 240; 293
Taverner, John, 240
Taylor, Deems, 105
Tchaikovsky, P. I., 18, 25, 29, 34, 35, 36, 38, 41, 44, 45, 47, 48, 49, 50, 51, 58, 61, 69, 76, 77, 101, 104, 137, 143, 151, 155, 167, 172, 173, 178, 179, 185, 186, 209, 210, 211, 219 (Eugene Onegin), 222, 228, 236, 241, 246, 253
Telemann, G. P., 210
Telmanyi, Emil, 153
Tertis, Lionel, 103
Teyte, Maggie, 77, 137
Thalben-Ball, G., 132, 138
Theatre Royal, Drury Lane, 13
Thomas, Mary, 221
Thompson, Randall, 176
Thompson, W. W. ('Tommy'), 74, 86, 88, 93, 94, 119, 122, 140, 142, 158–60
Thomson, Virgil, 190, 210
Thrale, Mrs., 12
Three Choirs Festival, 169
Thurston, Frederick, 171
Ticciati, F., 75, 77, 271
Tillett, John, 115
Time and Tide, 89
Times, The, 19, 83, 90, 102, 113, 114, 123, 135, 149, 168–9, 175, 192, 225
Timyn, William, 192
Tippett, Michael (Sir), 94, 168, 170, 171, 179, 181, 190, 210, 219, 224, 228, 238 (70th birthday), 246
Titterton, Frank, 98, 105
Toch, Ernst, 105 (première)
Toscanini, A., 99, 145
Toushmalov, S., 70
Tovey, Donald Francis, 50
Treacher, Graham, 206
Tribe, Joan, 135
Turina, Joaquín, 71
Turner, Eva, 98, 104, 137
Tyers, Jonathan, 11

USSR State Orchestra, 196, 215

Valentino, Henri, 13
Van Wyk, Arnold, 277 (première)

Varèse, Edgar, 211, 215
Varga, Tibor, 206
Varviso, Silvio, 188
Vaughan Williams, R., 59 (première), 61, 63, 79, 81, 94, 98, 101, 103, 107, 123, 134, 143, 152, 155, 161, 167, 169, 172, 173, 179, 192, 209, 212, 224, 244; premières, 263, 275, 277
Vauxhall Gardens, 11–13
Veal, John, 175
Verbrugghen, Henri, 44, 58, 59
Verdi, G., 18, 176, 190, 208 (Otello), 210, 215, 216, 242 (Falstaff), 248 (Requiem; Macbeth, original version)
Vickers, John, 238
Victoria, Queen, 22, 32, 36, 43, 52, 109, 119
Villa-Lobos, H., 103
Vishnevskaya, Galina, 242
Vivaldi, A., 43

Wagner, R., 18, 20, 22, 28, 29, 32, 34, 35, 36, 38, 47, 49, 51, 53, 58, 61, 65, 70, 73, 75, 76, 79, 80, 101, 103, 104, 105, 122, 132, 134, 138, 146, 151, 153, 168, 176, 178, 203, 208 (150th anniversary), 211, 218, 219, 220, 221, 225, 226, 236, 242
Wallace, William, 76, 107, 263 (première)
Walsworth, Ivor, 103
Walton, William (Sir), 94, 101 (première), 103, 107, 108, 113, 135, 136, 152, 155, 165, 167, 168, 170, 172, 175, 176, 178, 179, 188, 190, 192, 210, 215 (complete concert), 221 (70th birthday), 244; première, 274
Wandsworth Boys' Choir, 216
Warlock, Peter, 102
Washington State Symphony Orchestra, 244
Weber, C. M. von, 13, 34, 38, 48, 175, 210
Webern, Anton (von), 103, 184, 201, 204, 220, 235
Weill, Kurt, 218, 222
Weingartner, Felix, 48
Weischell, Mrs, 12
Wellington, Lindsay, 185
Welsh National Opera, 252
Wenzinger, August, 219
Westminster Cathedral, 199, 219, 222, 225, 235, 238, 250
Whyte, Ian, 107, 278 (première)
Widdop, Walter, 98
Widor, C. M., 75
Wilde, David, 222
Wilde, Oscar, 79
Wilkinson, Stephen, 240
Willaert, A., 215
Williams, Harold, 98, 104

Williams, R. Vaughan – *see*
Vaughan Williams
Williamson, Malcolm, 194
(première), 237 (première);
premières, 285, 290, 297, 301
Wilson, H. Lane, 27
Wilson, Marie, 91, 94
Wilson, Steuart (Sir), 79, 154,
155, 157–8, 168
Wilson, Thomas, 214 (première);
292
Wireless Military Band, 86
Wireless Singers, 147
Wittgenstein, Paul, 104, 248
Wolkov, N. de, 41
Wolseley, Sir Garnet, 16
Wood, Henry (Sir), 9, 15, 18, 19,
20, 23; early career, 25;
appointed musical director of
Proms, 26–7; first Prom season,
27–9; composition at Prom, 35;
his marriage to Princess Olga
Ouroussoff, 41; breakdown in
health, 43–4; a month in
America, 44–5; Strauss and
Wood, 49–50; 'Deputy' system,

53–4; death of Olga, 55;
knighthood, 55; marriage to
Muriel Greatrex, 56; allowing
women players in orchestras,
56–7; wooed by Boston, 67;
Gold Medal of RPS, 72; Royal
visit (1924) to Proms, 72–4;
students' orchestra (RAM), 74;
failure of his second marriage,
92–3; Golden Jubilee as
conductor, 98–9; 'Klenovsky',
102; unhappy relations with
BBC after outbreak of war,
109 ff.; Royal Philharmonic
Society and the Proms 1940–1,
114 ff.; return to BBC
sponsorship, 122 ff.;
correspondence with BBC
Director-General, 127–9; Proms
Jubilee and death, 130–1; 137,
151–2, 154, 155, 158–60, 164–5,
171–2, 178, 184, 187, 190, 192,
194, 196, 204, 209,
216 (centenary), 226, 241, 246,
250, 253

Wood, Mrs Henry (Olga) – *see*
Ouroussoff
Wood, Hugh, 218, 222; premières,
290, 295
Wood, Lady Jessie – *see*
Goldsack
Woodgate, Leslie, 152, 165
Woodhouse, Charles, 72, 78, 88,
91
Woodward, Roger, 224
Wooldridge, David, 308
Wordsworth, William, 173
Wormser, André, 73
Wright, Kenneth, 140, 155
Wyss, Sophie, 151

Yeats, W. B., 168
Yorke, Simon, 229
Young, Filson, 90
Young, Alexander, 222
Young, Patricia, 158
Ysaÿe, E., 72

Zabaleta, Nicanor, 176, 181

Acknowledgements

Photographs are reproduced by kind permission of the following: Erich Auerbach, pages 95 bottom, 180 bottom, 223 bottom, 251; British Broadcasting Corporation, 24 top, 95 top, 118, 125, 131, 144, 148, 162, 180 top, 189, 202, 230, 247 top; BBC Hulton Picture Library, 10 bottom, 60, 98, 121 bottom; Camera Press Ltd, 121 top, 141, 198 bottom; G. MacDomnic, 174, 177, 193, 195, 213, 217 bottom, 239, 243, 249, 255; Mansell Collection, 10, 14 top; Chris Samuelson, 198 top, 205, 217 top, 223 top; *The Times*, 247 bottom. Picture research by Diana Souhami.